Haiti Fights Back

Critical Caribbean Studies

Series Editors: Yolanda Martínez-San Miguel, Carter Mathes, and Kathleen López

Focused particularly in the twentieth and twenty-first centuries, although attentive to the context of earlier eras, this series encourages interdisciplinary approaches and methods and is open to scholarship in a variety of areas, including anthropology, cultural studies, diaspora and transnational studies, environmental studies, gender and sexuality studies, history, and sociology. The series pays particular attention to the four main research clusters of Critical Caribbean Studies at Rutgers University, where the coeditors serve as members of the executive board: Caribbean Critical Studies Theory and the Disciplines; Archipelagic Studies and Creolization; Caribbean Aesthetics, Poetics, and Politics; and Caribbean Colonialities.

For a list of all the titles in the series, please see the last page of the book.

Haiti Fights Back

The Life and Legacy of Charlemagne Péralte

YVELINE ALEXIS

Rutgers University Press
New Brunswick, Camden, and Newark, New Jersey, and London

Library of Congress Cataloging-in-Publication Data

Names: Alexis, Yveline, author.
Title: Haiti fights back : the life and legacy of Charlemagne Péralte / Yveline Alexis.
Description: New Brunswick : Rutgers University Press, [2021] | Series: Critical Caribbean
    studies | Includes bibliographical references and index.
Identifiers: LCCN 2020040320 | ISBN 9781978815407 (paperback) |
    ISBN 9781978815414 (hardcover) | ISBN 9781978815421 (epub) | ISBN 9781978815438 (mobi) |
    ISBN 9781978815445 (pdf)
Subjects: LCSH: Péralte, Charlemagne, 1885–1919. | Haiti—History—American occupation,
    1915–1934. | Haiti—History—1844–1915. | Péralte, Charlemagne, 1885–1919—Influence. |
    Revolutionaries—Haiti—Biography.
Classification: LCC F1927.P43 A44 2021 | DDC 972.94/04092 [B]—dc23
LC record available at https://lccn.loc.gov/2020040320

A British Cataloging-in-Publication record for this book is available from the British Library.

♾ The paper used in this publication meets the requirements of the American National
Standard for Information Sciences—Permanence of Paper for Printed Library Materials,
ANSI Z39.48-1992.

www.rutgersuniversitypress.org

Manufactured in the United States of America

For my Poto Mitans,
gran-gran Charmante Rinvil, maman Marie Agathe Nicolas,
matante Marie Alexis, and my sys Marie Guerda Nicolas
Onè ak respè for Ayiti and all of her people

Contents

List of Illustrations (Ilistrasyon) — ix

Introduction: Haiti Fights (Ayiti Goumen) — 1

1 Liberty, Equality, and Fraternity/Humanity (Libète, Egalité, ak Fratènite/Imanite) — 22

2 U.S. Invasion (Envazyon Etazini) — 35

3 Haitians—Rise and Defend! (Ayisien(ne)—Leve epi defann!) — 54

4 Péralte Leads (Péralte kòm Lidè) — 80

5 Violence (Vyolans) — 109

6 We're Still Fighting (Nou Toujou ap Goumen) — 129

7 Second Revolution (Dezyèm Revolisyon) — 148

8 Péralte Resurrected (Péralte Resisite) — 157

9 Liberation with Péralte (Liberasyon ak Péralte) — 182

10 Péralte Will Never Die; He Remains Alive in Popular Memory (Péralte p'ap janm mouri; li rete vivan nan memwa popilè) — 189

Acknowledgments — 197
Notes — 201
Bibliography — 231
Index — 241

Illustrations

1. Jean-Jacques Dessalines and Charlemagne Péralte, mural, Haiti, ca. 2006–2008   2

2. Haitians listed in the archives as "A Few of The Country's 'Bad Men,'" Port-au-Prince, Haiti, 1915   56

3. *Cacos* chiefs, or generals, Haiti, about October 1915   59

4. Colonel Littleton W. T. Waller, USMC, Commander of Marine Expeditionary Forces in Haiti, negotiating with Haitian *cacos* leaders, including Charlemagne Péralte, October 1915   64

5. Haitian *cacos* revolutionary leader, General M. Codio, March 1916   68

6. Map of Haiti, 1923   100

7. Femme *cacos*   121

8. "Haiti Says Good-bye: Natives gather at Cape Haïtien to bid farewell to the U.S. Marines," August 6, 1934   146

9. Philomé Obin, The Crucifixion of Charlemagne Péralte for Freedom [Crucifixion de Charlemagne Péralte pour la Liberté], 1970   166

10. Flag of the Charlemagne Péralte National Liberation Front   179

11. Tug of war mural, Haiti, ca. 2006–2008   191

12. Charlemagne Péralte Boys' School, Hinche, Haiti, 2008   193

Haiti Fights Back

Introduction

• •

Haiti Fights (Ayiti Goumen)

On a busy street in Port-au-Prince, Haiti's capital, a bright picture reminds you of the nation's 1804 past and its 2004 realities (Figure 1). The mural features two men known for their dedication to freedom: Jean-Jacques Dessalines, iconic hero of the Haitian Revolution and Charlemagne Péralte, twentieth-century freedom fighter defending his country's independence during the United States' invasion. On one side of the mural, Dessalines wears his revolutionary uniform with his face pointed to the left and Péralte dressed in his black suit and red bowtie, stares out front, reminding passersby of a long, intergenerational story of struggle.

After the (in)voluntary departure of President Jean-Bertrand Aristide in 2004, during the nation's 200th independence celebrations, the United Nations Stabilization Mission in Haiti (MINUSTAH) occupied Haiti in what might be described as only one of multiple, ongoing attacks on Haitian sovereignty, this time led by a multinational coalition of troops.[1] Sovereignty means the right to rule oneself without foreign interference. It struck an all-too-familiar chord with many Haitians. In murals, art, conferences, and on the radio, some asked if 2004 was simply a repeat of 1915, when U.S. troops, steeped in the culture of the Jim Crow era, took over their country. Haitians wondered if a new 1804 was necessary. They questioned whether MINUSTAH, so heavily directed by the most powerful nations in the world, was simply a reconstituted arm of U.S. imperial control.

In 2004, as the nation celebrated the bicentennial of independence from French colonial rule, Haiti struggled again politically. The MINUSTAH soldiers arrived, as they initially put it, to "secure and stabilize the capital."[2] Haitians

FIG. 1 Unknown artist, Jean-Jacques Dessalines and Charlemagne Péralte picture,
Haiti, ca. 2006–2008

recognized the similarity between these moments in their political history. The
Dessalines-Péralte image makes this connection between centuries obvious and
demonstrates that Haitians knew they would need to defend their sovereignty
once again.

Activism and art came together in protest in the neighborhoods where
MINUSTAH set up stations. Haitians fought foreign troops head on, firing bullets at both soldiers and infrastructure such as MINUSTAH stations (where
they kept their munitions) and trucks. Others communicated with fellow Haitians about the urgent mobilization required in the face of this foreign danger.
Across Cité Soleil, a neighborhood in Port-au-Prince, other murals with historical
reminders and political messages appeared. Observers of Haiti's public history
were amazed by the murals' colors, their patriotism, their historical accuracy, and
their critical stance. The muralists' actions echoed what Péralte declared during
his fight against the U.S. military: "It is not the work of 1804, of Dessalines,
Pétion, etc., and so many other brave souls, their auxiliaries, that we must smash
or cause to be smashed. . . . To be sure, we shall not permit the insulting strangers to step on us like they are our masters, especially in our hills and our immense
savannas, on the mortal and scattered remains of those who, black and mulatto,
marched heroically to their death to leave us this nation."[3] The muralists, Haitian citizens, like the *cacos* fighters of Péralte, confronted the foreign soldiers. This
underestimation of Haitian commitment, power, and ability is not new. In 1915,

the U.S. military had not anticipated that the *cacos* had such intellectual skills or military prowess. Foreign media sources often label Cité Soleil a slum, criticize its residences as "volatile" and as supportive of the government MINUSTAH came to overthrow. The Cité Soleil murals, however, contradict this portrayal, exemplifying how the so-called economically disadvantaged, the politically dispossessed, and the frustrated subaltern speak and act.

These activist murals illuminate both the purpose and theoretical frame of *Haiti Fights Back*. Like the murals, this study recovers Péralte historically, retelling his story from a Haitian perspective. It identifies and discusses Péralte as the *nasyonalis* martyr Haitians have memorialized since his death in 1919. The English term "nationalist" is not the same as the Haitian Kreyòl term *nasyonalis*. Lexico defines the former as "a person who strongly identifies with their own nation and vigorously supports its interests, especially to the exclusion or detriment of the interests of other nations."[4] In the Haitian context *nasyonalis* means one who loves and defends Haiti. When Haitians refer to Péralte as a *nasyonalis*, they mean he is pro-nation. *Haiti Fights Back* also brings to light rare archival sources that situate the important intervention and legacy of Péralte and the *cacos* fighters in relationship to the U.S. empire, the Caribbean, and their native Haiti.

Recovering Péralte Historically and Understanding Haitian *Nasyonalisme*

There are competing narratives about Charlemagne Péralte. By always starting his story with his use of his gun rather than his pen and the image of his cadaver rather than his political portraiture, the U.S. invaders argued that Péralte was a lawless bandit. My work, which relies on U.S. military archival sources, other primary documents, oral interviews in Haiti, and artistic representations, presents a different narrative. I intervene in the story about Péralte by beginning the story in his homeland with his birth, rather than at the moment when the U.S. military encountered him in 1915. By analyzing his theories and actions, I present Péralte as a multidimensional individual who acted for Haitians and for their nation. He was both an intellectual and a guerrilla fighter, despite the U.S. military attempts to ignore and dismiss these important attributes.

The U.S. military created a narrative for political gain and to suppress Haitian opposition. They assassinated the resistance leader on October 31, 1919. On November 1 they displayed his body in a public square and photographed it. U.S. soldiers then boarded planes and dropped photographs bearing the image of his corpse. It became a triumphant narrative for the U.S. military. They had hunted the *cacos* and successfully murdered their leader. The U.S. soldiers' gruesome exhibit of their kill was reminiscent of the Jim and Jane Crow culture of their homeland. Through Péralte's body, the U.S. military inscribed their dominance and attempted to scare Haitians into submission. These brutal actions, including the subsequent medal ceremony for the soldiers, were all violent, public enunciations of power. These demonstrations of white masculine and racialist rhetoric and actions sought to literally and physically dominate Péralte *and* his historiography.

Péralte's fighting for his nation's autonomy, however, of course did not justify U.S. action. He was taking up a long tradition of freedom fighting, inspired by all those who came before. Born in 1885, he became a staunch defender of the world's first black republic in his short thirty-four years. He made innumerable contributions to Haitian society as an agriculturalist, statesman, and *cacos* leader.

Péralte endangered the U.S. invasion of his country. According to the *cacos*, the United States invaded their nation state in 1915. Yet, President Woodrow Wilson claimed it was an intervention for democracy and peace in the broader Americas. Wilson's neutral phrasing denied the violence of his country's actions. The United States took over Haiti and her citizens and called it "an intervention." The word stripped the very act of its power and its violence.

Péralte and most Haitians interpreted the takeover differently. A learned intellectual, Péralte called Haitian citizens to remember the glorious revolution of 1791, culminating in Haitian independence in 1804. The Haitian Revolutionary era (1791–1804) left a strong legacy that inspired resistance fighters of the U.S. invasion.

Péralte's *nasyonalisme* drew from Haitians' popular memory of their nation's forebears, the 1804 Acte de l'Indépendance (the Haitian Declaration of Independence), and the nation's 1805 constitution.[5] In the popular history about the revolution's end, Dessalines heroically led Saint-Domingue's (colonial Haiti) last battle, the Bataille de Vertières in November 1803 and later declared Haitian independence on January 1, 1804, with L'Acte de l'Indépendance. In this document Dessalines addressed his audience as citizens and the "people of Haiti," in contrast to the colonizers' racist references to this population.[6] The then commander-in-chief criticized the French as "barbarians who have bloodied our land for two centuries" and united the "Natives of Haiti" under the banner of defending the nation. Of the three words encapsulating Haiti's revolutionary slogan—"Liberté, Egalité, et Fraternité"—Dessalines repeatedly called on Haitians to protect, defend, and fight for the first. The document read:

Citizens:

We must, with one last act of national authority, forever ensure liberty's reign in the country of our birth; we must take any hope of re-enslaving us away from the inhumane government that for so long kept us in the most humiliating stagnation. In the end we must live independent or die.

Independence or death . . . let these sacred words unite us and be the signal of battle and of our reunion. . . .

Let us frighten all those who would dare try to take it from us again; let us begin with the French.[7]

Dessalines's final paragraphs asked Haitians to pledge their allegiance to what he predicts will be an ongoing fight for independence:

Let us vow to ourselves, to prosperity, to the entire universe, to forever renounce France, and to die rather than live under its domination; to fight until our last breath for the independence of our country. . . .

Therefore, vow before me to live free and independent and to prefer death to anything that will try to place you back in chains. Swear, finally, to pursue forever the traitors and enemies of your independence.[8]

Dessalines laid the two-part foundations of Haitian *nasyonalisme* that Péralte would draw from—the acknowledgment and memory of their revolutionary fight *and* the duty to protect their independence at all costs. By 1805 Dessalines was emperor of Haiti and the writers of his 1805 constitution reinforced his aspiration for the protection of national and personal freedoms in three clauses. Article 1 stated: "By this document the people living on the island formerly called Saint-Domingue agree to form a free and sovereign state, independent of all the other powers of the universe, under the name of the Haitian Empire."[9] In Article 2 the authors declared: "Slavery is abolished forever."[10] Article 12 expressed that "No white man, regardless of his nationality, may set foot in this territory as a master or landowner, nor will he ever be able to acquire any property."[11] The national documents conveyed the idea that being Haitian meant that both the nation and individual were free and that defending against foreign encroachment was fundamental in maintaining Haitian independence.

Over a century later in 1915 when the United States undermined Haitian independence, Péralte followed the instructions of Dessalines and his forebears. Between 1915 and 1919, the *cacos* leader reminded Haitians about their ancestors' revolution, specifically naming Dessalines and declaring it their duty to protect Haiti's independence. Péralte mobilized the *cacos* and other Haitians with historical memory in this excerpt:

Haitians, a day like the first of January 1804 will soon rise. For four years, the Occupation has insulted us in every way: every morning brings us a new sadness. . . . Haitians, let us be firm. . . . For it is not a vain thought that was written on the grave of the great Dessalines: "Upon the first shot, the towns disappear, and the nation rises."

Do not fear! We have arms! Let us chase those ravenous people whose ravenousness is represented in the person of their President. . . . Hurrah for independence! Hurrah for Union! Hurrah for legitimate war! Down with the Americans![12]

Though Péralte was free and a century removed from slavery, the history of bondage inspired and animated his fight for national autonomy. Despite Haitians' declaration of freedom and independence, Whites continued to justify their colonial and, later, imperial political and economic violence on Black republics and on Black bodies. French colonialists reasoned that they were "civilizing" people of African descent during the period of enslavement and U.S. imperialists argued that they were doing the same for Haitians during the invasion. Lying about Haitians' supposed inferiority justified the violent rhetoric and actions of Whites, both colonists and imperialists, for generations. Abuses during the U.S. imperialist period mirrored the French Code Noir's repressive tone and practice during the colonial era. The Code Noir, a seventeenth-century legal decree defining the conditions of slavery in the French empire, was an early blueprint for stamping out Black lives and culture. It attacked Africans' religion and their rights to matrimony, food, education, and clothing before Haitians abolished slavery.[13]

The U.S. military, patronizingly, considered themselves a kind of "big brother" to Haiti and the broader Caribbean. The United States, a nation that has always struggled to accept the very citizens (indigenous, African Americans, Asian Americans, and Latinx) that built its own country, hypocritically justified its invasion of Haiti as a way to "stabilize" the nation.[14] Furthermore, France, in the nineteenth and twentieth centuries, was anything but politically stable. And yet, despite France's political fragility and instability, the U.S. could not occupy nor intervene on this European state. The U.S. excuse of Haiti's political mayhem was just a pretext to invade.

Péralte was cognizant of these historical fictions of Haiti and the outside world. He and other Haitians experienced the contradictions of the United States attempting to "stabilize" Haiti. Brenda Gayle Plummer's *Haiti and the Great Powers, 1902–1915* proves that foreign powers like the United States and Haiti's elite (Haitians and non-Haitians) undermined the nation's sovereignty through economic manipulations and by fomenting political chaos. Once the United States had invaded, its military's methods of managing the mayhem it helped to create included martial law, restrictions on freedom of speech and religion, imprisonment, and other abuse. The U.S. military forced many Haitians into unpaid *corvée* work to "build" the nation's infrastructure. When some of these *corvée* workers attempted to escape, they were tortured or murdered. Thus, twentieth-century Haitians likened their abuse under the U.S. invasion and the *corvée* specifically to slavery and colonialism's historical traumas. The politician and *cacos* leader appealed to history and *nasyonalisme* in how he recruited Haitians. For Péralte, his enslaved ancestors had succeeded; therefore, twentieth-century citizens had a responsibility to continue this fight and defend Haiti.

His *nasyonalis* strategy worked. Péralte commanded thousands of *cacos*, all of whom pledged their lives to fight the U.S. invasion. In some Haitians' efforts to help the guerrilla fighters, they placed themselves in danger to advance Péralte and the *cacos'* pro-Haiti mission. For example, in chapter 5, I examine how a woman, not identified as a *caco* protected the group. She used silence to resist. These unnamed figures served another, undercover, and useful purpose. They fed and harbored the *cacos* and promoted their agenda. Péralte also inspired other Haitians to participate in nonviolent protests. Haitians marched, formed political groups, participated in strikes, organized rallies, formed women's groups, and wrote literature and news pieces, all protesting the U.S. presence in their country. I see this resistance activity as "patriotic kinship," what Péralte used as political strategy to inspire the wider Haitian community from 1915 to 1934 to defend Haiti by any means necessary. The idea of patriotic kinship has continued as Haitians have recalled Péralte since the U.S. invasion in their desire to protect Haiti's sovereignty. More specifically, during the U.S. invasion, Péralte used patriotic kinship to mobilize the *cacos* as guerrilla fighters. He also motivated Haitians to participate in noncombat struggles against the invaders. These patriotic kin, while not engaged in military battles, fought for the invasion's end in different ways. Some protected and harbored the *cacos* while others supported the fight for Haiti's independence through writing and spoken testimonies about the invasion. Post U.S. invasion, some Haitians continued Péralte's call for patriotic kinship. They explicitly recalled the *caco* leader in their defense of Haiti's sovereignty.

Because of the danger he posed, the U.S. military eliminated Péralte. Yet they failed to tarnish his image and his legacy. *Haiti Fights Back* develops a different narrative about Péralte's purpose and his impact. Despite the U.S. military's efforts to portray him as anything but a politician and revolutionary, Haitians gazed at the *cacos* chief's body—both in person and through circulated images— with patriotic awe.

Péralte as *Nasyonalis* Martyr

Haiti Fights Back also explores the ongoing Haitian memorialization of Péralte. His status as national martyr began at the moment of his unjust death and the gruesome exhibiting of his body. Haitians immediately revised the dominant colonialist or imperialist narrative of dispossession and banditry. They formulated their own historiography of the *cacos* leader that recognized the exceptional nature of his moral leadership. Péralte was their hero, patriot, and revolutionary fighter. Péralte became known to Haitians as a quintessential citizen, a model of what dedication to national sovereignty can be. My book identifies and connects the ways that Haitians have deployed the memory of Péralte from 1919 to 2008. The *cacos* leader offers a useful commentary and example of anti-U.S. imperialist ideology and action. He also offers a critique of Haitians who are not mobilized for nation.

A historical nationalism that signals its resistance through Péralte's legacy manifests itself in a cyclical fashion. Theoretically, Haitians formulated a Péralte-inspired resistance, which defined the leader's legacy. This style of resistance does not mention nor encompass the *cacos*, but rather is specific to the man and the leader. Indeed, despite his predecessors and his successor, Benoît Batraville, it is Péralte who remains fixed in the people's imagination. Haitians project their desires of sovereignty on Péralte. He remains the most recent, palpable image of a hero and a revolutionary *nasyonalis* in the twentieth and twenty-first centuries. The injustice of his untimely end—and the way that it inspired generations to come—is not new to Haiti. Toussaint L'Ouverture, a formerly enslaved leader of the Haitian Revolution, was imprisoned and left to die in the Jura Mountains of France. L'Ouverture never knew of Haiti's independence just like Péralte did not witness the end of the invasion that he fought against so diligently. Haitians, and other Caribbean citizens, often feel called to continue the work of leaders whose struggles remain unfinished, whose unjust and untimely deaths left their project for sovereignty unrealized. Through the end of the invasion in 1934, Haitians used their memory of Péralte to fuel their ongoing resistance.

My research also uncovers and traces the linking of Péralte to Haitian independence and the repeated resurrection of him as a *nasyonalis* martyr across seven decades, in Haiti and elsewhere. Though the U.S. military withdrew from Haiti in 1934, U.S. economic and political control of the nation or its leaders remained through the twenty-first century. In the twentieth and early twenty-first centuries, the memory and meaning of Péralte loomed large in Haitian society, as well as in the U.S. diaspora. The book offers a new approach to understanding people who acted against U.S. imperialism. Haitians attached Péralte's rhetoric and actions to various projects in different political moments: *désoccupation* (which marked the invasion's end) and the immediate postoccupation years (1930–1944), populism (1946–1948), an authoritarian dynasty (1957–1986), a fleeting democracy (1986–1991), and then back to foreign intervention in Haiti (2004 to present).

Documenting and analyzing these seemingly disparate moments reveal that some Haitians used Péralte's legacy to fight for sovereignty over time. Some Haitians protested against the consistent, even if hidden, presence of U.S. domination and/or against the Haitian elites. Others used Péralte's legacy for their own benefit. In 1934, for President Sténio Vincent it meant that a man of his time resisted the United States. By honoring Péralte with a mock funeral, Vincent reminded Haitians that he too had protested against the United States before rising to become head of state. Yet, while in power, Vincent proved less of an antagonist in his alliance with the United States. In 1944 and 1970, Haitian artist Philomé Obin painted artworks about the invasion period and the *cacos* leader. Obin artistically protested against the United States' continued involvement in Haiti's political and economic affairs during Vincent's administration and François Duvalier's brutal dictatorship. Obin's paintings reminded Haitians to mobilize and act like Péralte. In 1986, the political party the Charlemagne Péralte National Liberation Front (CPNLF) was founded. Members used Péralte's memory as a political, socialist statement against the Duvaliers' authoritarian regime, Haitian elites, and the United States, who militarily and financially supported this dictator. When priest and presidential candidate Jean-Bertrand Aristide used Péralte's memory to ascend to political power from 1986 to 1991, he criticized U.S. intrusion and Haitian elites. Further, as Haitians migrated and established institutions in the United States, they "imported" Péralte. He became the face of an organization serving Haitian immigrants in Brooklyn, New York, and he also had a park named after him in Montreal, Canada, during the late twentieth century. The twenty-first-century mural in Port-au-Prince depicting Dessalines and Péralte is just one of many examples of how Haitians have used the *cacos* leader as a weapon. Thus, in any given decade, Péralte meant resistance, which could be launched against the Haitian state, against its citizens, and against the United States.

My work explores the various ways the memory of the *cacos* leader has functioned posthumously. Since his death in 1919 and continuing to the present, Haitians used Péralte's memory and narrative in paradoxical ways. *Haiti Fights Back* examines the dynamics and political aspects of this nostalgia.

Archival Interventions: Articulating Péralte's Resistance

By examining the utility of this nostalgia, my book intervenes in the archival historiography and traces how Haitians have documented historical acts. They have worked as lay historians to revive Péralte's memory. Haitians preserve his words and actions for a free Haiti in the popular, global archive (beyond Haiti, including all of the Americas). Despite Péralte's similarity to figures of anti-U.S. imperialism, this Haitian leader is comparatively understudied. From the beginning, the United States downplayed his influence. On close reading, the U.S. military records on Péralte and the *cacos* depict a man without a movement. The invaders divorced the *cacos*' anti-invasion stance from the guerrilla fighters' military actions, and this narrative became more common and more powerful thanks to U.S. travelogues and news reports during the invasion.

The silencing of his story has been intentional. Two issues are at work here. First, the *cacos* struggle as a political movement was unfathomable to Americans. As Haitian anthropologist Michel-Rolph Trouillot argues in *Silencing the Past: Power and the Production of History*, slaveowners did not view people of African descent as thinkers or resisters.[15] Even during the Haitian Revolution, a successful twelve-year struggle for abolition and independence, most Europeans found the notion of active slave resistance unthinkable. The French, shocked and embarrassed by the blow to their colonial empire, downplayed its significance. For two centuries, even scholars did not question the dominant European narrative. Scholars also contributed to the silencing of Haiti's role during the Age of Revolutions.

Silence, even though it might be a technical absence, is an active strategy to maintain power. It first manifests at the moment of fact creation, and this has a lasting impact on scholarly attention to the topic. Scholars have discussed Haiti's absence from the Age of Revolutions in a robust historiography.[16] The act of omitting Haiti and its historical contributions is literally and intentionally a part of the historicization of this African Revolution in the Americas. Consider as examples the erroneous classification of the revolution as an "insurrection" or a "negro revolt."[17] These descriptions efface and erase enslaved Africans' repeated and successful fight for abolition, emancipation, and self-rule.

In addition to denying attention to the Haitian Revolution, silence works by removing attention to the initial injustice of slavery. The historiography on Saint-Domingue has a telling obsession with the bloody and violent methods of the 1791–1803 period. The fixation on the bloodiness of the revolution obscures the humane reason for the revolt: freedom and slave abolition. These reflections do not dwell on the brutality of slavery for centuries across the Americas and, specifically, the blood extracted from enslaved Africans during French rule of Saint-Domingue. Rather, this type of reflection documents White slave owners' harm and their deaths. It is an inversion and a bias. Its continual occurrence prompts the question: What revolution is not violent? Certainly, all nations that emerged from the Age of Revolution (United States, France, and Haiti) evolved from intellectual and political pontifications *and* bloody, violent struggles. However, Haiti's heroic tale remains frozen in dominant narratives and contemporary discourse as a bloodbath against slave-owning Whites. It does not read as a successful revolution for human rights, global emancipation, nor as the purest example of Western Civilization.

A century later, the denial of Haitians' humanity continued to color colonial narratives about Haiti. The silencing of the Haitian Revolution's greatness was an active one—and became worse throughout the nineteenth century. Biological determinism certainly did not help. And the growing backlash against formerly enslaved people in the southern United States certainly influenced those going into Haiti as invaders from a segregated army in 1915 through the end of the Second World War. During the invasion of Haiti, many in the U.S. military could not conceive of Haitian people as thinkers. The files of the soldiers' claims to White superiority and beliefs in black inferiority are voluminous. Often, soldiers expressed apprehension about Black people's ability to rule themselves without White, male supervision. Thus, the *cacos*, despite leaving manifestos on city walls and writing letters to President Wilson, and despite their military battles against U.S. soldiers, still were not considered political thinkers. Even as U.S. military figures acknowledged the *cacos*' political purpose, they silenced it with disparaging, broad, and public diatribes against the guerrilla fighters. They published and distributed this analysis in the country's newspapers and proclamations, and recruited Haitians in opposition to this *cacos*' movement, namely the U.S.-Haitian gendarmes. Silence plays a paradoxical role here.

The U.S. military acknowledged the *cacos* and understood their role, but they sought to shape, and contain the narrative of the fighters. They silenced them by labeling the *cacos* as bandits. While bandits exist in historiography as political actors, the U.S. military framed Haitian bandits as negative, unscrupulous beings. They were, according to their invaders, wild, without an agenda, thieves, Satanic worshippers who preyed on their fellow Haitians. Such description of the *cacos*, and not as fighters and politicians, worked to silence the *cacos'* patriotic actions. The *cacos*, according to the U.S. soldiers, were not active citizens of an independent nation.

In public discourse—newspapers, broadsides, proclamations, and the like—the U.S. military engaged in doublespeak throughout the invasion. They fixated on controlling Haitian resistance *and* they tried to act as though Haitian resistance was nonexistent. They also promoted the invasion as a peacekeeping effort even as their documents declared otherwise. The U.S. military's doublespeak always had the word "but" attached. For example, they held Haitian presidential elections in 1915 but acknowledged they controlled the Haitian government; they promoted the *corvée* as good but admitted to the atrocities committed against the workers, and they dismissed Péralte's resistance as political but listed his political tactics. Doublespeak appears as mere lies, but the particular way the military masked these fallacies repeatedly is noteworthy. Doublespeak became the invaders' strategy of justifying, excusing, and explaining their undemocratic behavior. Proverbially in Kreyòl, Haitians refer to this doublespeak method as *Kouto 2 bò* (a double-edged knife) and as *Voye wòch, kache men*, meaning one who throws rocks and hides their hands.[18]

Though occurring in different eras, the negative, dehumanizing portrayal of both moments (the Haitian Revolution and the *cacos* resistance) made Haitian actors invisible, nonrevolutionary, and doomed to failure. Such a characterization invites the question: Were Péralte and the *cacos* movement successful? Leading Haitian scholars like Kethly Millet, Roger Gaillard, and Suzy Castor, and U.S. scholars like Hans Schmidt, have examined this question. Though each summarize the movement as a loss, I take a different view. Although the invasion persisted after Péralte death, and neoimperialism ensued in Haiti, following the invasion, Péralte and the *cacos* could boast of different types of victories. These triumphs included the mobilization of Haitians and engagement with U.S. presidents and the military in an ideological, political, and public battle about the rights of nations and citizens. The achievements of Péralte, the *cacos*, and other Haitian agitators allow us to expand the definitions and framing of win and loss, of success and failure, beyond the trope of military and physical dominance. Péralte galvanized various individuals and his success shocked the U.S. soldiers. They could not imagine instances where Haitian newspapermen would plot with Haitian peasants or collaborate with Dominican guerrilla fighters. Ironically, as I show, the U.S. soldiers' refusal to accept the *cacos'* movement as a diverse political struggle worked to the advantage of the guerrilla fighters.

Silencing also works through repression, although repression acknowledges the power of those who resist. The U.S. military tried to limit the impact of the *cacos* fighters. Their assassination of Péralte is a clear example. The clandestine operation against Péralte—from the U.S. surveillance of him to their infiltrating his camp—contradict their supposed belief in his inabilities. Why launch such an extensive military operation against a "bandit"?

Haitians have added a different dimension to this public historiography, despite U.S. military attempts to circulate a derogatory narrative about Péralte and the *cacos*. They have picked up Péralte's story and have not only intervened in the dominant historiography, they preserved it their own way. This intervention finds its way onto Haiti's walls, currency, and on a monument. They publicly displayed him in a heroic, patriotic manner, and in the process, brought the public into a conversation about urgency and vigilance. Muralists, scholars, and others framed a new public narrative of Péralte.[19] Their public interventions confront the military's public violation of Péralte, used posthumously as an example of Haitian defeat and U.S. military victory. For Haitians, the image of Péralte as alive, and not as the victim of an assassination, is intentional. They continue to rupture the dominant pictorial narrative of Péralte as slain, deceased, and fallen. Rather, they recall him as a respectable politician and one who fights for Haiti still. Roger Gaillard's 1986 book *Charlemagne Péralte: Le Caco* engages in the same practice. The book's front cover showcases Péralte with his bowtie and suit, a portraiture of Black respectability. The image bears similarities to the women and men on the U.S. Black Heritage stamps and early images of Black history figures well-dressed, well-coiffed, and poised. In 2006, Péralte appeared similarly in the mural as a living political figure. In Gaillard's book, it is not until the back cover that the historian portrays Péralte's death. These pictorial interventions awaken us to new narratives and reimaginings of Péralte and his legacy.[20] Furthermore, these interventions occur in the public domain as art, scholarship, and murals. The very public assassination is reflected in very public forms of remembrance.

Thus, despite Péralte's absence from or distortions in dominant U.S. and Latin American historiography, he remains alive in Haitian historiography. From Péralte's time to the present, Haitians have rescued his story from the margins and footnotes of history. For them, his story of resistance is a primary narrative.

Research Methods

The pioneering work of scholars of the invasion like Roger Gaillard, Suzy Castor, Kethly Millet, Brenda Gayle Plummer, Hans Schmidt, and Mary Renda, as well as the key scholarship about Haitian history by Patrick Bellegarde-Smith, Alex Dupuy, Robert Fatton, and François Pierre-Louis Jr., helped inspire *Haiti Fights Back*.[21] The works of scholars like Chantalle Verna, Millery Polyné, and Matthew Smith have richly added to our understanding of the postinvasion periods as well as interactions between Haiti and the United States.[22] Collectively, their works critically examine Haitian society, the Haitian diaspora, and U.S. diplomacy before, during, and after the invasion. I build on their foundation by focusing on the topic of resistance.

Since Haitians have revived Péralte in diverse and ingenious ways, *Haiti Fights Back* is an interdisciplinary text. While history is the disciplinary foundation of my examination of the *cacos* leader, my methods also draw from Africana and Caribbean Studies. My research locates Péralte's story in Haiti's archives and libraries as well as in historical materials in the United States. I also "found" Péralte in the monuments of his hometown of Hinche, on the city walls in Port-au-Prince, and on a Haitian stamp. I observed how Haitians honored Péralte and collected material that commemorated him (namely the coin and photographs). I read about Péralte in Jacques Stephen Alexis's and Edwidge Danticat's fictional writings. Alexis upheld the figure in his 1930s creative works about the deleterious effects of the U.S. invasion on Haitian women.[23] Decades later, in her work of the 1990s, *Breath, Eyes, and Memory*, Danticat named the protagonist Sophie Caco. The fictional protagonist Sophie Caco bears the name of the guerrilla fighters, and Danticat elaborates on the strength of the group when she describes Sophie as "a true Caco woman; she is very strong . . . strong as mountains."[24] Sophie's grandfather is called Charlemagne le Grand Caco, a name certainly inspired by Péralte.[25] Popular renditions of Péralte tell his story in diverse ways. I "saw" Péralte at barbershops, mechanic shops, and community centers in neighborhoods across Haiti and the U.S. diaspora. I documented the memory of Péralte in interviews with his living kin and with the many Haitians who remember his story. For them, the "past is not the past."[26] For them and for this moment, since the international invasion in 2004, Péralte is very much alive.

What follows is the first scholarly attempt to use these diverse sources about Péralte to create a full picture of the man and his memory. When the *cacos* leader is studied, there are select moments that people often recite—his arrest, death, and public display. This book includes the entire story of Péralte, from birth in 1885 to Haitians' resurrection of him in the twenty-first century. I examine how he is presented, reproduced, and reconstructed in Haiti. I intentionally place primary materials, stories, and memories of Péralte from Haiti and the U.S. in conversation with each other. This interdisciplinary endeavor captures the varying, creative ways that his story has persisted. By assembling Péralte's writings from 1918 and his granddaughter's memory of him in 2006, I demonstrate how Haitians have narrated his story across time and space. These uses of Péralte send a double message about the U.S. stronghold in Haiti and the place of Haitian resistance.

Research in Haiti was crucial to the creation of my narrative. One cannot adequately research Haiti and its citizens from U.S. and French archives alone. Using Haitian sources avoids what Nigerian novelist Chimamanda Ngozi Adichie calls the "danger of a single story."[27] My fieldwork in Haiti provided enriching counternarratives to the U.S. invasion of Haiti. As Gina A. Ulysse argues in *Why Haiti Needs New Narratives*, the desire to praise Haiti for its revolution and berate it for its subsequent history needs to cease.[28] Further, the use of Haiti as a symbol and its people as a site to study from abroad does not disturb colonialist narratives. My sources in Haiti included interviews with Haitians who shared their knowledge, which enhanced my understanding of Haitian and U.S. diplomacy. *Haiti Fights Back* prioritizes Haitian sources in its research of the U.S. invasion of the Americas. My sources from U.S. archives largely depicted Haitians as a group acted upon—rather than as agents in this story. Furthermore, U.S. historical sources are in English, while the nation's citizens are multilingual. Judging from some of their awkward or inaccurate translations of documents from French to English, the foreign soldiers could not communicate with the majority of the population in Haiti who spoke Kreyòl. Sources in Haitian Kreyòl and French were fundamental to my narrative. By incorporating multilingual sources from both nations, my book presents a thicker examination of Péralte's story as well as Haitian and Caribbean history more generally.

The use of oral history was critical to incorporating Haitian perspectives. It was essential to include how Haitian people remembered Péralte and the *cacos*. I interviewed three of Péralte's family members, both in his hometown of Hinche and in Port-au-Prince. Five other Haitians—including one in the United States—also offered their reflections on the *cacos* leader. My sample of Haitians was diverse in age, class, and profession. Despite my search for more female informants, only one woman in Haiti—Péralte's granddaughter—agreed to be interviewed.[29]

Living among Péralte's relatives provided me with a unique perspective as historian-observer and community member. His family members encouraged my academic pursuits and eagerly stated their knowledge of historical events. Visiting Hinche also showed me how Péralte remained alive in the popular memory. The town's institutions of learning, recreation, and even the automobile shop all bear his name. Perhaps the crowning public memorial was the Charlemagne Péralte Park. This site is the center of Hinche, a place where residents convene for political forums, religious revivals, and recreational activities. This park gives residents the opportunity to commemorate Péralte while continuing with their normal activities. In a tangible and visceral way, the monument functions as a nod to Péralte as Hinche residents use it for everyday activities. I found this practical use of the *cacos* embedded in the Haitian diaspora as well. In Brooklyn a barbershop changed its name to the Charlemagne Péralte barbershop. Each of these instances records Haitians' nostalgia for and use of Péralte for their specific, varying agenda.

The Haitians whom I interviewed are living archives. These people operate outside of and alongside the traditional repositories and historical collections (like libraries, national archives, and museums). Their knowledge gave me fresh insights into Péralte's story. Their input was invaluable. My interactions with them illustrate the need for multilingual publications of scholarly texts. Translating their reflections from Kreyòl to English was often a challenge. When one interviewee commented that the Haitian gendarmes wore blue jeans, he meant that the U.S. gave these Haitian men a tiny piece of power. They distinguished themselves from the dispossessed peasant with U.S. military attire on their Black, Haitian bodies. Further, how does an interviewer translate participants' hand gestures and the sounds that affirm their sentiments? One of my interviewees would say "ou la" after every point he made. The literal translation of "you're here?" would not convey his meaning of "you understand, right? I can move on with the narrative, right?" "Ou la" also symbolizes the call-and-response tradition of griot (storytellers) at events where the listener (audience) participates in the history that the griot shares. These encounters demonstrate the urgent need for multilingual scholarly fieldwork, research, and writing in our larger academy. These phatic expressions are speech acts that I interpret from a polylingual lens.[30]

My use of multiple Haitian voices (including interviews and art) allows for diverse retelling and remembering of this subject. Through my analysis of public spaces, historical records from both countries, humans as living archives, and how silence operates in the crevice of a text, my work is a new and innovative analysis of Haitian history and Haitian-U.S. diplomacy. In addition, my book offers a unique perspective on the larger transnational history of the Americas. Haiti was not the first nation that the U.S. military invaded. And the United States' actions, legislation, and interpretation of that history are not unique. Indeed, from 1898 to 1934—to use the verbiage of another *cacos* fighter—the United States spread its eagle wings over Cuba, Puerto Rico, Guam, Philippines, Haiti, the Dominican Republic, Panama, Nicaragua, and Mexico. *Haiti Fights Back* fills a gap in the historiography about Haitian resistance against foreign aggression. It adds a new element to global historiography: how invaded people speak and act.

Haiti Fights Back presents Péralte's story and the story of Haitians who have defended their revolution since 1804 from ideological and military angles. Only by delving into Haiti's past and Péralte's story can we understand the reconciliations sought by the muralists in 2006. They remind observers that history repeats. They also proclaim that when the lions (meaning the U.S. military) narrate history, their prey (Haitians, those invaded) is silenced. By recovering Péralte with an intellectual lens, the work intervenes in the lacunae and biases about his story. This is a Haitian story, but it also makes contributions to the study of the wider Americas and larger Caribbean Studies.[31] It also engages studies of power. U.S. military policy grew out of its nineteen-year invasion of Haiti.[32] Thus, this also becomes a story of U.S. military history. By recovering Péralte's story, subverting the U.S. military bias, using Haitians as narrators, and pointing to the enduring political project that Péralte remains, *Haiti Fights Back* changes how we see the Haitian people. They become actors in, collectors of, and griots of their past.

I incorporate their methods of historical documentation and collection. Documenting Caribbean history traditionally involves neat practices with archival visits and data collection. It also necessitates literally and figuratively moving through the landscapes of that particular Caribbean nation, in addition to drawing on its historiography, and employing its data collection methods. The Citadel is a public archive that is accessible to all. In fact, the unofficial tour guides that climb the 270-foot structure with you are local residents who circulate the entrance key among themselves. They saturate you with their knowledge of the site and of Henri Christophe as you climb the structure, breathless and drenched in sweat. Once you reach the top, the key/gate keeper permits you to roam the site, touch the memorabilia from the nineteenth century, photograph the cannons, enter the crevices of the fort, and talk about Christophe's burial site. Yet, how does a historian cite their Citadel public history tour in their bibliography? The experience is multisensory, encompassing sight, smell, touch, hearing, your sixth sense, and more. To avoid the beating of Cap's bright sun, your voyage to the site of the Citadel typically happens before sunrise. After a minimum two-hour climb, the public site greets you with a deceptive fog. Your eyes and gut become how you order your steps. There are no hand railings for those with different abilities, or places to rest. You are left with the steep climb, with no more than rocks for a rough rest stop, and fog. The physical experience of history is itself an archive to be studied.

In another example, during 2015, for the centennial of the invasion, I traveled to most of the *cacos* battle sites in a car from Port-au-Prince to Cap-Haïtien. Along the way, we passed through Las Caobas, Leogane, Hinche, Acayé, and Le Trou. Upon hearing of my project, the mayor of Cap invited me to a reenactment of the August 21, 1791, *Bwa Kayiman* ceremony. It was at that moment that I noted that history erupts in Haiti everywhere. It is in the crevices of landmarks, on monuments, in how people retell the past, and in moments when a whole department (the equivalent of a state in the United States) reenacts before the public what has passed down for centuries about the night of *Bwa Kayiman*. This becomes another example of this historian's question: How do you document the sights, smells, and sounds of the globally acclaimed Haitian band Boukman Eksperyans playing tunes, the Haitian assuming the role of Cécile Fatiman, and the dancers who artistically demonstrate what is said to have happened that night? Not one of us was alive in 1791, but the story captured what elders have passed on for generations about what was said to have occurred that night of August 21. The twenty-first-century artists slaughtered the black pig, shared the blood, and spoke in different tongues. It was a breathtaking experience to document. History functions in Haiti as a living, tangible, accessible, material good. When scholars of the Americas use the archival tools and preservation methods (forms of memorializing) of those we study, we practice respect for our subject's research theories and methods. That practice acknowledges research as a site of exchange and reciprocity, and not a one-sided professional relationship where we study and then report.

Finally, in Haiti, a conversation about Péralte often makes reference to 1804 and 2004 in the same breath. Truly, I found it amusing that in a thirty-minute exchange, an interviewee would jump several centuries in succinct and clear ways. Further, their sounds, dramatic retellings, and physical reenactment played a role in their recounting. In documenting these oral histories, a type of performance of history emerges. The microphone was turned on and Haitians testified. They claimed their space, got comfortable, and regaled me with tales of Péralte, the *cacos*, and different eras of Haitian history. They educated and schooled me during this fieldwork. Naively, I expected that data collection would be orderly, meaning that participants would respond to my questions directly. Rather, it was beautifully chaotic. Proverbs and anecdotes accompanied their theoretical formulations. Further, there was a type of positioning on their part. I collected these oral histories in intimate spaces (private homes, backyards) and in public (at hostels, parks, and libraries). In each instance, the interviewee made themselves comfortable and extended the invitation. Thus, what I thought would be an hour of introduction and interview routinely became four hours. They wanted to have a meal first or go to a café or give me a tour of where we were. I did not realize that in these encounters I functioned as observer, participant, document collector, and subject as well. By the last, I mean that my fellow Haitians inquired: Why was I interested in Péralte? Why did I speak Kreyòl? Why was my Kreyòl *lou* (heavy, diaspora-ish)? And personally: What was my family's name and their ongoing connection to Haiti? I enjoyed how they turned the tables and sized up me and my qualifications for this study. Scholars like Sibylle Fischer, Joan (Colin) Dayan, and, more recently Toni Pressley-Sanon have discussed how these assemblages, fragments, and intentional silences on the part of a subject are part of how we gather, listen to, and contribute to Haitian and Caribbean historiography.[33]

As Leanne Martin assesses in her work on Maroons, "history [functions] *as* identity."[34] I am a witness to this experience in Haiti over and over, whether it was the *Bwa Kayiman* ceremony in 2015 or the personal reflections about Péralte from my oral history participants in 2006–2008. For them, the *cacos* story was part of their identity as radical or rebellious Haitians who defended Haiti.

Kote Famn Yo? (Where Are the Women?) Say Their Names

Haiti Fights Back also contains some silences.[35] Women *cacos* leaders and fighters are not named in the archives. Despite their military participation, *Ayisienne* (Haitian women) often appear as nameless and voiceless. Notations mark their presence as "caco spy" and broadly as "market women." They are boxed into these two, nondescript, general categories. They also exist in the repositories in explicitly gendered ways (as the girlfriends and wives of *cacos* leaders and as [caco] camp women). The homogenization of *Ayisienne* is important to reflect on as another example of silencing. It screams that they exist but only within this man-made boundary. It limits a full examination of their actions as spies (military intelligence), as mothers who offer guerrilla strategies, as overall full participants (thinkers and fighters) in this twentieth-century struggle. In one chapter I present a woman who was suspected of being a spy who was in fact a *caco*. Another image is preserved in the archives with the notation as a "fighting *caco* woman." Both of their names and voices are otherwise absent. I found records that spoke for these female guerrilla fighters' experiences—rather than their being able to narrate their own stories—during the invasion. I analyze these tensions in several chapters.

I have sought to fill this gap by listening to these women in different epistemological ways. When we hear from *Ayisienne*, the invasion is often harming them. The U.S. military wielded its power and privilege in how it preserved these records. Mary Renda references John Houston Craige's cavalier statement about rape in Haiti is preserved in the archives and his memoir. Renda cites another soldier who reportedly fathered 246 children in Haiti in his efforts to whiten the race.[36] While we know of these men and their wrongdoings, we do not know the names of the Haitian women they abused. It is challenging to re-present these predominantly male-narrated incidents because it reproduces a type of "archival violence" against *Ayisienne*.[37] The U.S. Senate Inquiry in Haiti is an example of that type of archival violence, documenting soldiers' tremendous abuse of Haitians, including sexual and physical harassment of these women. Nevertheless, it is important to list *and* reinterpret these experiences from the women's perspective. It is one of the few sources where *Ayisienne* voice their experiences. Nadève Ménard captures the voices of Haitian women during the invasion period, through a historical-comparative literature lens.[38] She shines light on the literary works of *Ayisienne* like Cléante Desgraves (also known as Virgile Valcin) and Annie Desroy, whose works appeared in 1934. Their creative works, published during the final year of an invasion that limited freedom of the press, contribute to the invasion archives through a feminist, female lens.[39] Thus, while I could not locate a named female version of Charlemagne Péralte, I do address how *Ayisienne* are talked about.

Acknowledging Haitian women—by both listing their names and naming otherwise unnamed *Ayisienne*—is another intervention. The pedagogical tools of Haitian feminist like Madeleine Sylvain-Bouchereau and Haitian scholar Myriam J. A. Chancy shaped this decision. In 1957, Sylvain-Bouchereau noted: "The history of Haiti has been entirely written by men and for men, so there is little trace of women, [their] moral, social and economic influence."[40] Her dissertation, *Haïti et ses femmes: Une étude d'évolution culturelle*, proceeds to name women, from those of Hispaniola's indigenous period like Anacaona to the *Ayisienne* involved in the mid-twentieth-century suffrage movement. The feminist sociologist added Haitian women's names and their contributions to the archives. Forty years later, in 1997, Chancy offered a similar critique, writing: "Since a codified history of Haitian women has yet to be written, the project of recovering the roots of Haitian women's self-definition is made possible only through the evaluation of narrative forms."[41] In her efforts to unsilence Haitian women, Chancy also lists the name of Geneviève Affiba (Toussaint L'Ouverture's sister) and centers the voices of Haitian female literary writers.[42] Influenced by these women's scholarship, I have decided to name the nameless women I "encounter" in the invasion's archives. With honor and respect, I give them names, rather than the typical generic archival references to Haitian women like: *cacos* spy, market woman, and *Madan* Sara.

Further, it is important to list the names of Haitian women who figuratively shaped the twentieth-century *cacos*' struggle. Péralte and his fellow fighters often referenced the 1791–1804 male revolutionaries. The *cacos* leaders adopted a male-gendered narrative, even as *Ayisienne* drove their movement forward. Péralte and other male *cacos* included L'Ouverture, Dessalines, and Pétion and excluded *Ayisienne* fighters from that same period, like Cécile Fatiman, Marie-Jeanne Lamartinière, (Suzanne) Sanité Bélair, Claire Heureuse, Henriette St. Marc, Madame Magdelon, Madame Guittone, and Catherine Flon.[43] Despite *Ayisienne*'s fight for nation, emancipation, and human rights during the colonial era, Haiti silenced Haitian women in constitutional records. The nation's first constitution features women as wives and maternal figures, as if they had not fought in the revolution through battles, infanticide, and the like.[44] The 1805 constitution also removed citizenship from *Ayisienne* if they married foreigners, while protecting the rights of Haitian men who did the same. The sexist tenets accentuated a tone set by the colonial period. This tone spilled over into how the nation functioned with women as visible actors of their nation-state but made invisible due to lack of citizenship. *Ayisienne* could uphold a nation and keep it functioning, yet that very state erased or omitted their roles in dominant narratives and limited their basic rights (suffrage and citizenship). The 1805 blueprint set the tone for delayed civil and political rights for *Ayisienne* who earned suffrage over a century later, in 1950 and 1957.[45] It is from this perspective that I name the *Ayisienne* who came before Péralte. As the *cacos* leader relied on historical nationalism, I posit that Haitian women, like Louise Nicolas of the *piquets* cause, and the *Ayisienne* who defended President Salnave in 1867, shaped the *cacos* movement.[46] Saying these women's names is important to how we study and document *Ayisienne*'s legacies.[47] Fortunately, Grace (Louise) Sanders Johnson's pioneering work on the Haitian feminist movement is enhancing the historiography about Haitian women.[48] Finally, beyond the invasion period, I document *Ayisienne*'s role in their state as much as possible.

The Book's Structure

The book proceeds chronologically, examining Péralte's life and his legacy. Chapter 1 focuses on Haiti and U.S. relations prior to 1915 and Haitians' defense of their nation. Chapter 2 analyzes the structure of U.S. empire in Haiti from

1915 to 1917 and examines how Haitians immediately protested against the seizure of their state. In chapter 3, I position the *cacos* wars against the U.S. military as one continuous political movement during the invasion years, and I examine how the guerrilla fighters framed their struggle as Haiti's second revolution. The chapter also offers an in-depth analysis of these battles from 1915–1917. Chapter 4 examines Péralte's leadership of the *cacos* from 1918 to 1919, his assassination, and the U.S. military's exposition of his body. Chapter 5 explores the U.S. military's excessive violence against Haitians from 1919 to 1921, as well as the *cacos'* and patriotic kin's response to these aggressions. Chapter 6 looks at the final years of the invasion from 1921 to 1934, exploring how Haitians sought to dismantle U.S. empire through fiction writing, strikes, and fleeing to the Dominican Republic and Cuba. Chapter 7 looks at how citizens used the *cacos* leader from the *désoccupation* period through the 1946 populist revolt. Chapter 8 documents the apotheosis of Péralte during the authoritarian period from 1957 to 1986. Chapter 9 explores Aristide's use and disuse of the *cacos* leader during his political rise. Finally, chapter 10 looks at Péralte's significance to Haitians during the MINUSTAH "supervision" of their nation in the twenty-first century.

The United States constructed an empire in the larger Americas. It illegally invaded various nations between 1898 and 1934, and later, Trinidad and Tobago. Documents such as the Platt and Teller amendments, treaties, and the rewriting of these nations' constitutions eventually made these U.S. acts legal. My research for *Haiti Fights Back* analyzes how President Woodrow Wilson acknowledged the U.S. intrusion in Haiti's affairs in 1915 and how he proceeded with the invasion anyway. I often chose to replace the terms "U.S. occupation" and "U.S. intervention" with "U.S. invasion."[49] The documents in the U.S. archives fail to analyze the horrors that transpired in Haiti for nineteen years—not to mention the atrocities in other nations in the Americas. They neglect to reflect on these instances of race, power, and male dominance. The U.S. military wielded its power and privilege in how it preserves these records.

The Book's Title

Haiti Fights Back is a historical Africana Studies book about the Caribbean and the larger Americas. While the text offers a microhistory of U.S. military and economic power in Haiti, its central focus is how Haitians who came before and after Péralte, in addition to the *cacos* leader's movement, have worked to dismantle the U.S. empire. The title and text position them as fighters and agents in their complex, contradictory, and multilayered struggles for freedom. *Haiti Fights Back* uses Haitians to tell this long history, including Jean-Jacques Dessalines, Charlemagne Péralte, Madeleine Sylvain-Bouchereau, and Jean-Bertrand Aristide. Using a rich array of sources and interdisciplinary methodology, the work showcases how Haitians speak through silence, legislation, opinion pieces, music, art, novels, murals, organizations, political parties, parks, public spaces, and oral histories. This is their story. It documents how Haitians engage memory, particularly the collective remembrance of their revolution and the *cacos'* defense of 1791–1804, to launch radical, political, and physical protest across time. I hope that the book and its use of traditional and alternative archives cast light on underexplored moments, movements, and figures in Caribbean history.

1

Liberty, Equality and Fraternity/Humanity (Libète, Egalité, ak Fratènite/Imanite)

● ●

Introduction

The formal U.S. seizure of Haiti was not a spontaneous event. Rather, the invasion in 1915 by an all-white U.S. Navy- and Marine-led force was the culmination of the United States' multidimensional surveillance of its Black neighbor for more than a century. By surveillance, I mean the United States kept a close watch on the Caribbean region in an effort to ensure its own economic and political gains in the hemisphere. A U.S. soldier's report confirms the country's long fascination with Haiti: "And so from 1804 to 1914, during which period every ruler of the Republic of Haiti, with but few exceptions, met misfortune of some character, the United States has kept a careful observation over the incidents occurring in that country."[1] During the Age of Revolution, both nations freed themselves from their respective colonial powers, France and Great Britain. Yet, over a century after their respective national independence, the first postcolonial nation in the Western Hemisphere, built on the institution of slavery, invaded the first antislavery postcolonial nation in the Western Hemisphere.

The U.S. obsession with Haiti centered on slavery, abolition, and race. As Haiti established itself as the first independent Black republic, the United States and France, whose national stories celebrated the egalitarian ideals of their revolutions, did not allow Haiti to share in the history of victory and progress that became the official narrative of the Age of Revolution. The intricate relationship between colonialism and slavery, which the United States did not disturb, allowed for an erasure of the profundity of Haiti's national independence. When Haiti banned slavery in 1805 and invited those fleeing the institution to its shores, the colonial world, including the United States, read that diplomatic, humane move as a declaration of war. Haiti had challenged the very system that the world relied on for its wealth and growth—a system that the United States did not challenge.

For the United States, France, Portugal, Britain, Spain, and the Netherlands, Haiti's early abolitionist example and stance was much too early and akin to blasphemy. U.S. relations with Haiti revolved around this tension as the United States continued, well into the twentieth century, to deny equal status to its enslaved and formerly enslaved, and their descendants. At the time of its invasion of Haiti, the United States also limited Haiti's influence in the Western Hemisphere through economic and military might. Haitians, through legal language, intellectual prose, and in their use of their land, rejected this abuse. The nation and its citizens stood up against the United States. Haiti's example of abolition and its call for others to emulate this practice glaringly exposed to the world who was civilized and who was not. Further, its success in establishing Black self-rule undermined many of the justifications for slavery that Whites had used. In effect, Haiti's establishment proved that Blacks were capable of independence, as well as theorists and practitioners of civilization. Haitians were a danger to slave capitalism and those who practiced democracy in slave societies.

Haiti and the United States, 1804–1915

Jean-Jacques Dessalines famously declared in 1804, after Haitian independence, that he had "avenged America."[2] His work had been in response to the mistreatment of enslaved Africans and their descendants—an injustice that formed the foundation of the European takeover in the Americas. Those in power in the United States, however, never understood the fundamental injustice of the institution of slavery, the raison d'être of Haitian independence.

The United States enacted racist policies toward its neighbor for generations before its invasion of Haiti. White U.S. politicians, preachers, and journalists incited racial fear to dehumanize and erase the injustice of slavery. The U.S. media created a negative image of the Haitian Revolution based on fear: a fear of rebellious Africans in general, the revolution's influence on slave societies, and the war's economic impact on slavery. This ideology of "fear" became an excuse to limit, shape, and contain the existence and behavior of Africans and their descendants. This persistent narrative of fear shifted discussions about slavery—and its ongoing unjust legacy—from white violence to white vulnerability. It erased the justice of Haiti's declaration of independence and focused on the way that their abolitionism aimed at the heart of colonial power structures. For example,

Dessalines's strategy of *koupé tet boulé kay* (cut heads, burn homes) is an oft-cited moment of the revolution, yet rarely do scholars discuss the scars left on Dessalines's back from slave owner's assaults.

Despite the nations' shared visions of liberty, the United States still relied on slavery, the racist economic institution that Haitians overthrew. The United States therefore attempted to contain Haiti's influence in the nineteenth century. In 1805, President Thomas Jefferson used the revolt to argue against abolition. Some newspapers banned articles on Haiti altogether, while other journals decried the rebellious slaves as "cannibals." Legislators from the U.S. Congress declared in 1826: "Our policy in Hayti is plain. We can never acknowledge her independence." They further emphasized: "Let our government direct all our ministers in South America and Mexico to protest against the independence of Hayti."[3] In an especially egregious move, the United States waited to extend diplomatic recognition to Haiti until June 5, 1862, several decades after the revolution.[4] While President Abraham Lincoln acknowledged the Black republic, he brazenly donated money to relocate African Americans to the nation. The United States' racially charged sentiments toward its African American citizens, and toward Haiti, shaped its diplomatic policies.

At the same time, U.S. officials appointed Frederick Douglass, an escaped slave and prominent African American, to the position of minister resident and consul general of Haiti. They dispatched him to the nation in October 1889, with orders to negotiate access to the Môle (Pier) Saint-Nicolas. U.S. officials desired the Môle because of its prime location on the northern tip of Haiti. The Môle faced the Atlantic, and the U.S. Navy wanted this property both as a refueling station and a place for surveillance on the wider Caribbean. Douglass hesitated. As an abolitionist, he was proud of the "only self-made Black Republic of the world."[5] As a U.S. American, Douglass had viewed the annexation of Hispaniola as a whole, as spreading "the progressive values of U.S. society."[6] But Haitian officials adamantly objected to parting with the Môle. Douglass mused about his negotiations for the property:

> This harbor is properly styled the Gibraltar of that country. It commands the Windward Passage, the natural gateway through which the commerce of the world will pass when the Nicaragua Canal shall be completed. The nation, which can get it and hold it, will be master of the land and sea in its neighborhood. It is not strange that our nation should want it nor is it strange that the statesmen of Haiti should not want to part with it.[7]

When Haitian president Florvil Hyppolite refused Douglass's diplomatic appeal for the Môle, U.S. president Benjamin Harrison sent Bancroft Gherardi, rear admiral of the navy, with an implicit threat of military action. President Hyppolite and his minister of finance, commerce, and foreign relations, Anténor

Table 1
US Ships and Landing Years

Landing Year	Name of US ship
1876	*Plymouth* and *Vandalia*
1888	*Galena*
1889	Several unnamed ships present in Port-au-Prince
1891	Seven ships arrived at Haiti
1892	*Kearsarge*
1893	*Atlantic*
1902	*San Francisco* and USS *Cincinnati*
1903	*Hartford*
1904	*Bancroft, Denver, Newark,* and *Newport*
1905	*Denver, Topeka,* and *Castine*
1906	*Marietta*
1907	*Padoush*
1908	*Eagle, Des Moines, Dubuque, Dolphin, Marietta,* and *Tacoma*
1909	*Tacoma*
1910	*Birmingham*
1911	*Birmingham, Chester, Marietta, Salem, Des Moines,* and *Petrel*
1912	*Nashville* and *Washington*
1913	*Nashville, Dolphin,* and *Petrel*
1914	*South Carolina,* USS *Hancock,* USS *Kansas,* USS *Montana,* USS *Eagle,* and USS *Tacoma*[a]

[a]Russell Papers, Manuscript Box 2 Haiti, Folder 1, Background on Occupation of Haiti, undated typescript: "Draft of a letter in Regard to Relations Between the United States and the Republic of Haiti from 1914 to Ratification to be signed by Mr. Robert Lansing."

Firmin, refused Gherardi's more forceful request. Seven U.S. ships surrounded Haiti during Gherardi's visit in June 1891.

Haitians disapproved of their neighbor's ongoing aggression. In *Modernity Disavowed*, Sybille Fischer reasons that "Haiti was both at an infinite distance and dangerously close."[8] Some Haitians felt the same about the United States. For some, their neighbor was a shadow-like figure that trailed the nation's every move. Prior to this 1891 display, navy ships had landed in Haiti on several occasions in the nineteenth century, and they continued to do so.[9] The U.S. Navy patrolled Haiti like a colony. Table 1 lists some of its landings from 1876 to 1914. In various reports, U.S. officials justified their patrol of Haiti each year: they sought "to protect American interests," "to investigate conditions," and "to observe conditions."[10] Yet, this annual patrol—especially during the years with multiple naval landings—amounted to an ongoing, aggressive surveillance. This was an informal, undeclared invasion. They policed Haiti and the nation's example as an abolitionist state. Through different, continuous measures the United States sought to undermine the Black republic's credibility as a republic and undercut its progress.

In addition to this military presence, the United States also asserted gross economic authority over Haiti during the early 1900s.[11] The United States competed with France and Germany for complete control over the country. France still treated Haiti as a colonial possession. The nation and the losses it incurred from Haiti's successful revolt occupied its mind. In 1825, the French mandated a reparations agreement for their lost property and lands from Haitians in exchange for diplomacy and trade.[12] The agreement economically crippled Haiti, forcing it to pay many times over for its freedom. The financial payments for "lost property" including the humans that French colonists had enslaved. Subsequent to this bold and unreasonable request, France became Haiti's main source of credit and its primary export market. For their part, the Germans used matrimonial alliances with Haitians to their economic advantage since their arrival in Haiti in 1860. The Germans had also established schools and a bank (Berliner Handelsgesellschaft), and by the 1900s, they controlled most Haitian commerce.[13] The Banque Nationale d'Haïti and Haiti's other foreign industries became an economic battleground for Germany, France, and the United States. Each country sought to limit the others' influence on the nation. The Banque Nationale's very structure revealed Haiti's lack of control of its own economic affairs. France owned the bank, and its headquarters were in Paris; France, Germany, and the United States all held interests.[14] As Lester Langley asserts, the foreign bank influenced Haitian politics.[15] By 1913, U.S. American Roger L. Farnham served as the vice president of the bank. Historian Hans Schmidt aptly details the "financial strangulation" of Haiti. He explains how between 1914 and 1915, the United States caused Haiti to default on its loan repayments and forced the country into a customs receivership.[16]

Along with the United States asserting control over Haiti's economic affairs, in 1910, the Haitian president Antoine Simon acquiesced to the plan by U.S. entrepreneur J. P. MacDonald (sometimes listed in records as McDonald) to build railway lines from Port-au-Prince in the central area to the northern sections of Cap-Haïtien and Hinche, a vast amount of territory. MacDonald also successfully negotiated for banana cultivation.[17] Because of these collective incidents, Haitian citizens felt unprotected by their state. Many counterprotested some of these changes.

Haitian Complicity and Resistance

Haiti was created in revolution and that struggle has never ceased. Creating a new nation was made more arduous by the hostility of foreign powers. People struggled for political control, equity, and agricultural access. Haitians, immediately after the revolution, launched protests against each other, against the state, and against foreigners. Domestically, Haitians had to figure out how to equitably govern diverse citizens who once were free, had been freed, *and* those who were still enslaved. Its citizens launched efforts to protect the republic and themselves. Further, the Haitian state instigated universal abolition, a radical position. Haiti also needed to defend itself externally, against global powers that benefitted from slavery as a world economic system. The period featured competing claims for sovereignty or for alliances with foreigners, namely France and the United States. These realities shine light on a nation caught between *participating* in the Age of Revolutions and *defending* its revolutionary victory.[18] For a time Haitians understood what the revolution meant, and also its distributions of freedom, equality, and fraternity to their diverse populace. In the midst of this fight for these rights was the unaddressed subject of agricultural egalitarianism. During the revolution, French colonials and Toussaint L'Ouverture believed that the formerly enslaved should still produce for Saint-Domingue. Providing this class with access to land as owners was rarely discussed.[19] Thus, former enslaved woman like Madame Guittone and others engaged in labor strikes.[20] Their protest shed light on the larger issues of Saint-Domingue's laboring class: freedom, equality, access, and the economy. Given the few landowners and the large numbers of Haitians who for centuries were without land or even access to it, the practice of agricultural egalitarianism has yet to be achieved by any Haitian government.

Considering the large number of narratives that Haiti and her predominantly African citizens were somehow not ready for self-rule, it is prudent to reflect on how the nation's chance of survival was limited from its inception.[21] Global powers punished Haiti for its revolutionary victory and its bold act against slavery. This international reprimand came in the denial of diplomatic recognition and the refusal to trade with the young republic. Literally, Haitians could not trade without global permission. Yet the United States kept an active trade with the nation despite its refusal to accept Haiti's existence internationally. The 1825 indemnity agreement with France highlights how important Haiti found international trade; even if the agreement hurt its citizens, what other choice did it have?[22] The "agreement" stipulated that Haitians owed France compensation for their liberty. France demanded 150 million francs for their loss of property, including humans. Other nations in the Caribbean and the larger Americas were not yet sovereign for Haiti to trade with regionally. Moreover, the United States' delayed formal recognition of Haiti *and* its directive to others to avoid contact made trade difficult for the young nation. World powers established a situation that limited Haiti's existence and the potential reverberations of its abolitionism. They intentionally sought to limit Haiti's influence on Blacks because of the example it set for manumission.

Yet, this period also invites reflections on Haiti's internal state in the nineteenth century. The rulers during this era envisioned Haiti as a monarchy, republic, nation, or as a territory reunited as Hispaniola or as part of the United States. As a young nation, nineteenth-century Haiti wrestled with how to define itself politically and how to rule over a diverse citizenry, which included a mix of classes, colors, and personhoods (free, freed, and enslaved). Defending Haiti's revolutionary ideals against hostile foreign powers made the country's domestic challenges even more complex. Some welcomed foreign allies and investments and others viewed one or the other as a threat to Haitian sovereignty. Less than a year into the leadership of Emperor Jean-Jacques Dessalines, in 1806, opponents of his policies assassinated him. Joan (Colin) Dayan argues that the leader's effort to distribute land equitably signed his death warrant. The subsequent heads of state split the nation into two entities.[23] Alexandre Pétion ruled the south and west while Henri Christophe governed the north.[24] Haiti became both a republic and a monarchy from 1806 to 1820. Some Haitian presidents ruled for decades, like Jean-Pierre Boyer, from 1820 to 1843. He desired a reunification of Hispaniola when he took control over colonial Santo Domingo (modern-day Dominican Republic). The colonial Treaty of Ryswick signed in 1697 had unevenly carved Haiti and the Dominican Republic into colonial entities. Despite the Taino-Arawak name for Española/Hispaniola, they named one third of the island French Saint-Domingue and the remaining two thirds Spanish Santo Domingo. Boyer ruling the relatively new nation of Haiti and Santo Domingo, which in 1820 was not free of Spanish rule nor enslavement, proved problematic. Citizens in Haiti revolted, and collaborated with people in Santo Domingo to oversee Boyer's downfall. Others, like Sylvain Salnave and Florvil Hyppolite, sought alliances with France and the United States for strategic, trade, and self-serving purposes. After Salnave's victory, he went as far as to offer Haiti as a protectorate of the United States.[25] Luckily, certain U.S. politicians knew this would generate criticism internally and internationally, so they dropped the matter.

Defending against foreign encroachment was fundamental to maintaining Haitian sovereignty in the nineteenth century. Two leaders, Emperor Dessalines and Anténor Firmin, at different moments in the century, took action to limit the influence of foreign governments.[26] Dessalines, as mentioned in the introduction, used parts of the 1805 constitution to protect the republic and its citizens. As slavery grew in importance around the world, formerly enslaved Haitians overthrew their oppressors and publicly banned them from the nation beginning in 1804. Through their 1805 constitution, Haitians at once addressed the issues of race and color, slave capitalism, and diplomacy.[27] This defense of Haiti's lands and territories carried over into the invasion. In fact, in 1918, through a U.S.-authored constitution, then assistant secretary of the navy, Franklin Delano Roosevelt, would rescind Article 12 in which Dessalines and others had declared: "No white person, of whatever nationality, shall set foot on this territory with the title of master or proprietor nor, in the future, acquire property here." The fact that FDR homed in on and undermined Dessalines's clause demonstrates the United States' long surveillance of Haiti and its politics of abolition and self-rule. Over a century later, FDR removed the very protection of Haiti that Dessalines had declared in 1805. The move to undo this specific law illustrates U.S. obsession with Haiti and its intrusion in the nation's affairs.

At the same time as he was drawing up a constitution, Emperor Dessalines ordered the military to construct a series of forts around Haiti to protect the nation against potential foreign attacks, a pattern continued by one of his successors, Henri Christophe (1806–1820).[28] The Citadel, an imposing structure build between 1805 and 1820, is a physical testament to Haiti's lack of diplomatic recognition by France and the United States.[29] The Citadel was one of Haiti's defense measures. Allegedly built by coerced Haitian laborers, this wonder of the world demonstrated that Haitian leaders failed to protect and respect their early citizens. The Citadel's construction was offensive to Haitian citizens, who were traumatized and healing from slavery.

Early leaders oscillated between policies that focused on restrictive rule and those that offered land and opportunity to citizens. King Christophe's rural code "imposed a harsh labor regime that guaranteed the continuation of the export-oriented plantation economy," complete with mandatory morning prayers.[30] This state-mandated discipline reflected the tenets of Haiti's founding documents from 1801, 1804, and 1805. Collectively, these legal blueprints defined a good Haitian as religious, male, and one who would serve the state in his profession as a military and agricultural man. Women existed in these documents as an empress or wives and mothers. Yet Pétion, on the other hand, sought a practice of agricultural egalitarianism originally started by Moïse, Toussaint L'Ouverture's adopted nephew. Pétion's policies also drew from Emperor Dessalines. It differed from the "agrarian militarism" of Christophe. Pétion's distribution of land to Haitian peasants earned him the nickname, *Papa bon kè* (Father with a good heart). If citizenship is a political relationship between a state and its people, early Haitians were likely confused as to how to relate to their government. A Haitian was either a citizen of a republic or the subject of a monarchy, receiving land or forced to till this land for his state. A situation of changing rulers, differing policy, and intense foreign interference characterized Haiti in its first postindependence decades.

Haitian citizens engaged in active resistance in order to address many of the issues with their government. For example, in the 1840s a southern peasant movement mobilized as L'Armée de Soufrrant (the army of sufferers). Because of their 8-foot pike weapons, L'Armée has been referred to as the *piquets*. Their 1843–1844 movement promoted some citizens' calls for Haiti's interests above those of foreigners and for ending the 1825 French indemnity agreement. The bulk of the *piquets'* demands advocated for internal changes, including upholding the 1843 constitution, access to public education, and land reform. The appearance and actions of the *piquets* record how Haitians used their military talents, ordained by the constitutions of 1801–1805, to right a wrong. While it did not meet its objectives, the *piquets'* movement demonstrated Haitian resistance and a common desire for justice among the citizenry. Its leadership by peasants underscores this idea that while the nation became independent in

1804, the spoils of the revolutionary war reinforced class power dynamics. Agricultural egalitarianism was an illusion, an afterthought of the revolution focused on emancipation, fraternity, and equality.

Haitian peasants from the nineteenth through the early twentieth centuries lived in a nation where they were in the majority but whose "political and cultural leadership class" was a tiny group of native Haitians *and* non-Haitians, like Germans and Syrians.[31] Brenda Gayle Plummer's *Haiti and the Great Powers, 1902–1915* deftly analyzes the interplay between Haiti's elite and foreign powers (Britain, Germany, France, and the United States) in limiting the nation's independence. The group protected its interests above ordinary Haitians by inciting and financing political warfare, manipulating the nation's economy, using foreign capital, and offering Haiti as a protectorate to the United States.

By the end of the nineteenth century, global powers had shifted such that the abolition of slavery became increasingly common. With the rise of biological racism, however, the original racialized categories, ones that Europeans had invented to justify the existence of slavery, not only remained, they became even more powerful. Haitian leader Anténor Firmin's classic work of 1885, *De l'égalité des races humaines (The Equality of the Human Races)*, manifested itself as ideological protest and positioned Haiti as, once again, central to the intellectual movement for racial equality that had motivated its independence in 1804. Firmin engaged anthropology in a transnational dialogue about race and resistance. His text was an intellectual, scientific rebuttal to a founding text of biological racism, Count Arthur de Gobineau's racist, four-volume work *L'inegalité des races humaines (The Inequality of Human Races)*, which proclaimed White superiority and Black inferiority. Firmin's chapter "Intellectual Evolution of the Black Race in Haiti" positioned his nation as a prime example of Black people's equality with Whites: "I believe indeed that the small Haitian Republic, a shining buoy in the Antilles archipelago, will provide sufficient evidence in support of the idea of the equality of the races in all its ramifications."[32] To counter the circulated dogma of racial inequality, Firmin presented examples of scholars and artists from Haiti. Both the dedication of his text to Haiti's well-known revolutionary Toussaint L'Ouverture and his use of Haitians as models of Black success, demonstrate Firmin's ideological commitment to his race and nation-state. This method of proving that Blacks were equal to the Whites who created these myths of superiority and inferiority became commonplace across the Americas. It was a common way that nations like Haiti, later the Dominican Republic, and across Latin America proved that they were just as good, as democratic, as their former colonizers and the United States. Firmin's seminal text remains important.

Like many Haitian intellectuals, Firmin also served in the government, so his defense of Haiti and her people was also political. In the late 1800s, during foreign attempts to control Môle Saint-Nicolas, Firmin served as the minister of finance, commerce, and foreign relations. He declined Gherardi's aggressive demands for the pier in 1893.[33] Despite his praise of the United States as an example of equality, despite its struggle with racial inequalities, the Firmin we encounter in the late 1800s appears ready to defend Haiti against the world's stereotypes of the nation, and her Black citizens.[34] Firmin deploys a brilliant text against the limits that his field and the world imposed on Haiti. He defended Haiti and Blacks by presenting their achievements and positing them as equal citizens.

Dessalines's and Firmin's examples show that Haitian protest against the 1915 U.S. invasion was not a spontaneous response. Rather, resistance against foreign aggression began in Haiti's moment of decolonization and took shape as legal, architectural, and intellectual acts against U.S. (and other foreign) invasions. Haiti, new to the idea of independence and freedom from slavery, grappled with figuring out what that meant internally for its citizens and with defending itself from global powers like the United States and France who sought to reenslave, reconquer, and delegitimize Haiti and its example. Haitians in the nineteenth century declared, insisted, and reminded the world that it was an independent republic. They articulated this independence, abolition, and Black equality over and over. The Citadel remains an architectural marvel that served this defensive position. The fort articulated what the likes of Dessalines and Firmin, through their legal document and scholarship, argued about Haiti and its citizens' independence. Foreigners however, declared a war on Haiti without calling it so. Essentially, they sought to limit its example and contain the symbolism of 1804. Péralte's fight in the twentieth century was the continuation of over a century of struggle of defending the 1804 revolution.

Charlemagne Péralte's Early Years, 1885–1915

The conditions of François Borgia Charlemagne Péralte's birth foreshadowed his revolutionary disposition. He was born in the century of Haiti's founding, near the north central part of the nation, a place celebrated for its *mawonage* communities.[35] His great grandparents struggled for freedom, equality, and liberty, the exact causes he would champion in the twentieth century.

Popularly referred to as Charlemagne Péralte, he was the child of Rémi Masséna Péralte and Anne-Marie Claire Emmanuel. Péralte's mother enters the historical records as Marie-Claire and, after her husband's death, Masséna Péralte. Both parents were from the Central Plateau. Rémi was born in Lascahobas to Saint Yague Péralte and Mademoiselle Antoine Nicolas. Marie-Claire was born in Hinche to Emmanuel Louis and Marie Louise Malary. By the time Rémi and Marie-Claire wed, he was serving as an army general and she was working as a seamstress in Hinche. Rémi Péralte was in his forties, twice the age of his second wife, and he had already fathered four boys. Rémi had a son, Saül, by a woman named Hébé Mompoint. His first wife, Marie Claire Novembre, gave birth to his other male offspring, Saint-Rémy, Nestor, and Aurèle. When he and

Marie-Claire exchanged their vows on September 28, 1884, Marie-Claire accepted all her husband's children as her legitimate kin. A year later, on October 10, 1885, Marie-Claire gave birth to Charlemagne in Hinche.[36] As his mother's only biological child, Péralte was close to Marie-Claire. In interviews, Péralte's living family maintained that she was a loving mother.

Historian Roger Gaillard listed the Péraltes as members of the rural bourgeoisie, and one of my interviewees also described Rémi Péralte as middle class. As a son of a general, Péralte enjoyed some economic privileges. When he was an adolescent, his parents enrolled him at the prestigious Saint-Louis Gonzague school in the nation's capital of Port-au-Prince from 1900 to 1904. One interviewee recalled: "His father sacrificed [financially] to educate his children."[37] The interviewee probably meant the sacrifice of sending Péralte to a private school and housing him in the nation's capital, far away from his hometown of Hinche. An interviewee said that Rémi Péralte's death placed a significant economic strain on the family, which explains Péralte's relatively short stint at the all-boys school. In 1904, at age nineteen, Péralte returned to Hinche to manage his family's property. While knowledge of his early familial life is scarce, my interviewees situated the family as members of the political haves. Rémi's military post facilitated political access, power, and influence. One interviewee described the Péraltes as a family of *nasyonalis* who "understood the independence of their country."[38] Three brothers in particular—Saül, Saint-Rémy, and Charlemagne—agitated against the U.S. presence.

Between 1908 and 1915, Péralte emerged as a politician. Throughout his twenties, he held various administrative and military posts in Haiti and the Dominican Republic. He began his political career as the vice-consul of Haiti in the town of Elias Piña in the Dominican Republic.[39] Part of the Péralte family had lived in the Dominican Republic since the mid-1800s during Jean-Pierre Boyer's unification of the island between 1822 and 1843. On the predominantly Spanish-speaking side of the island, the Péraltes were known as the Péraltas. In 1910, Péralte became mayor of Hinche. Then he served as a justice of the peace in Mirebalais.

Part of Péralte's political ascendancy unfolded against a backdrop of wars and a military-backed, political patronage system.[40] Because of these occurrences and as an officer in the Haitian army, Péralte became acquainted with several Haitian presidents from across the political spectrum, including Cincinnatus Leconte, Oreste Zamor, and Vilbrun Guillaume Sam. In fact, his two more notable posts in Port-de-Paix in 1914 and Léogâne in 1915 resulted from fights between Davilmar Théodore, Zamor, and Sam. Péralte and his brother Saül participated in and benefited from this system. For example, both brothers participated in the fight between followers of General Davilmar Théodore and the allies of Zamor in 1914.[41] After Zamor's victory, he rewarded his supporters. During President Oreste Zamor's short administration from February to October 1914, he appointed Péralte as the commander of the Port-de-Paix administrative district.[42] The position was a powerful one. The district comprised a collection of Haitian towns of which Péralte administered the political and military affairs. With President Zamor's subsequent overthrow by Théodore at the end of 1914, Péralte lost his post in Port-de-Paix. Yet, this was only a temporary political loss for Péralte. He joined Vilbrun Guillaume Sam's fight against President Théodore, whose term was from November 1914 to February 1915. As Gayle Plummer explains, Sam had been "one of Théodore's most powerful lieutenants."[43] When Sam became president, he appointed Saül Péralte as commander of Saint-Marc. Further, Charlemagne served for several months in 1915 as district commander of Léogâne, another town in the Central Plateau, which also included the southern districts of Grand Goave and Petit Goave. Along with his political experience, Péralte's military service allowed him to familiarize himself with Haiti's terrain. One interviewee shared: "he traveled all of Haiti; when I say that, I mean he passed through the major areas. Charlemagne Péralte passed through Grand Goave, Léogâne, he passed through Okape, and Okape knows Charlemagne Péralte better than Hinche, in terms of his value. Thus, Charlemagne Péralte was promoted and became responsible for Léogâne."[44] Grand Goave is a department in the south, Léogâne in the central region, and Okape is part of north-central Haiti. His knowledge of these areas and its citizens served him well as a politician and as a *cacos* who would move through Haiti with ease and familiarity. It helped with his recruitment efforts for the guerrilla fighters too.

This political period in Haiti's history was wracked with conflicts and fleeting alliances. Péralte's mix of affiliations helped in his fight against the U.S. military. It prepared him to unify Haitians, not through political affiliation but rather through a *nasyonalis* vision. In July 1915, Péralte and his brothers greeted the U.S. invaders. They would continue the tradition of Haitian resistance.

Conclusion

From 1804 to 1915, Haiti and the United States were locked in an ongoing relationship fueled by one nation's desire for power justified by its supposed racial superiority and another nation's ardent defense of its equality and freedom. The use of military might and economic restrictions became the foreign order of the day. Nations that still relied on slavery fixated on limiting Haiti's existence and challenging its stance on emancipation. While Haitians could not survive in complete isolation from ever-present hostile foreign powers, their engagement with them often came at a high cost—Haiti's indemnity payments to France are a prime example. National sovereignty, bound to Haitians' freedom and equality, was also central to the mission of Haitian leaders because it was always at a risk.

Whether banning slave-owning Whites from Haiti, building the Citadel, or challenging the myth of White superiority, Haitians defended their home. Péralte, born at the end of a tumultuous century, continued an ongoing fight for equality. His political experience continued this tradition of resistance against the foreign military and financial control of Haiti. During the invasion, Péralte explicitly recalled the sacrifices of those who came before him, including Dessalines. He understood clearly that the U.S. invasion was part of a longstanding assault on Haitian sovereignty. As Péralte exhorted his *cacos*: "the blood of our illustrious ancestors boils in your veins, uphold the honor of our flag by rousing your population for the noble and beautiful revolutionary movements of the Haitian people."[45]

2

U.S. Invasion
(Envazyon Etazini)

• •

On July 28, 1915, 330 U.S. Navy and Marine troops arrived in Haiti. Within a week, U.S. Rear Admiral William Caperton formally controlled the republic.[1] Personnel from two ships, USS *Washington* and USS *Jason* from Guantanamo Bay, Cuba, disembarked at the two largest cities, Port-au-Prince and Cap-Haïtien. It was a strategic political and military act: their presence secured the illegal seizure of another Caribbean nation. On August 9, Caperton addressed the Haitian people in *Le Matin*:

> I am directed by the United States government to assure the Haitian people that the US has no object in view except to insure, establish, and help to maintain Haitian independence and the establishing of a stable and firm government by the Haitian people. Every assistance will be given to the Haitian people in their attempt to secure these ends. It is the intention to retain US forces in Haiti only so long as will be necessary for this purpose.[2]

Caperton, a native of Tennessee, commanded the naval troops and the Marines, then an auxiliary arm of the navy. Because of a segregated U.S. military, it was a white, male, and predominately Southern force. President Wilson relied on Caperton's extensive naval experience, and he became the face of the United States during the early years of the invasion. In this public note, Caperton attempted to appease Haitians as he and violent troops invaded Haiti. His message concealed the private and true goals of the United States in Haiti.

Influenced by its long history of monitoring Haitians and delegitimizing Haiti's existence while simultaneously seeking to control the nation, the U.S. government seized this opportunity to invade its neighbor. The State Department had charged Caperton with a three-pronged mission: to dominate Haiti's politics, to control the country's economic sphere, and to extinguish bands of resistance. The 1915 Haitian presidential election and Haitian-American Treaty, and later the 1918 Haitian Constitution all rendered Haiti an imperial entity.

According to Caperton's reports to Haitians in *Le Matin*, the U.S. military had established a "stable and firm [U.S.] government" in Haiti.[3] Yet, of course, this foreign-led government did not concern itself with the thoughts, ideas, and actions of the Haitian people. The United States orchestrated all political events. The invaders attempted to use Haitian news publications as a mouthpiece for their faux democracy. Along with Caperton's public note, articles with titles like "Notice for the Protection of the Haitian Government and People and for Better Safeguarding Their Interests under the Direction of the Government of the USA," became commonplace.[4] These publications promoted the takeover as a benevolent mission whereby the United States would restore stability. Their justifications for the invasion mirror slave owners' illogic about slavery being a civilizing, Christian, and/or whitening mission.

This method was not new. The United States notoriously presented its invasive actions as altruistic. By the time of its 1915 invasion of Haiti, the United States had invaded Cuba on several occasions in 1898, 1902, 1906, and 1912. Cuban schools used English textbooks, a colonialist cultural takeover that the United States described as an act to "better" Cuba and its citizens. In Haiti, decades later, the U.S. military promoted the idea of importing democracy to "inferior" nations. Democracy, however, is never effectuated through invasion. In correspondence, Secretary of State Robert Lansing and President Wilson admitted this and grappled with the invasion's threat to democracy. Lansing once reflected: "I confess that this method of negotiation, with our marines policing the Haytian capital, is high-handed. It does not meet my sense of a nation's sovereign rights and is more or less an exercise of force and an invasion of Haitian independence."[5] Lansing's private musing admitted his guilt as well as his nation's culpability in seizing Haiti. But he and Wilson willingly and illegally proceeded their takeover regardless. This was of many examples of the United States' doublespeak. This recognition of its attack on Haitian independence, however, is overshadowed by a larger belief in its own racial superiority—one that justified its military actions.

In response to the political events in Haiti, Lansing asserted that his view of the country "shows that the African race are devoid of any capacity for political organization and [have] no genius for government."[6] In his telegrams to President Wilson, Lansing often labeled some people as the "better element of the Haytien people," and "the intelligent Haitians," implicitly distinguishing them from those he considered inferior.[7] The racist attitude that led U.S. government decisions in Haiti was certainly not reserved for only Haitians. This period was the apex of lynching in the United States, a backlash against the freedom and equality of the formerly enslaved in the country that had been building in intensity for generations. Moreover, leaders of a segregated military were often from U.S. regions where the descendants of the enslaved faced the most unjust conditions. The bloody assassinations of black bodies demonstrate how the U.S. empire affected citizens of color, not only in the United States, but also in Cuba, Haiti, and Puerto Rico, among others. Indeed, for many U.S. officials in high office, the mission in Haiti was justified by their racist ideology.

Missions One and Two: To Control Haiti's Economy and Politics

The State Department instructed Caperton in August 1915 to first ensure a financial takeover:

> If we seek permanent peace in Haiti, it is my belief that the first steps should be to place an American collector in charge of the principal customhouses of Haiti. For years the Department of State has been of the opinion that a control over the income and expenditure of Haiti would remove from the reach of Haitian politicians the prize in money for which all wage war.... Meanwhile, I think that Admiral Caperton should be authorized to perform administrative acts in the territory under this direct control.[8]

Caperton achieved this goal within a month.[9] The *New York Times* noted that many of Haiti's custom houses were under the possession of "American naval forces."[10] Politically the United States was explicit about its objectives for Haiti. Judging from Rear Admiral Caperton's correspondence with the State Department, the presidential election was actually a selection. Per a memorandum, Caperton received orders to: "Under no circumstances [should you] hand over the government to any Haitian authorities."[11] Another notice directed the invaders to elect a "presidential successor that Washington deemed appropriate."[12]

During their selection process, Caperton and staff initially approached several prominent Haitian politicians, including Solon Ménos, Jacques Nicolas (J. N.) Léger, and François Denis (F. D.) Légitime, who all declined.[13] Léger, aware that the position would be a puppet presidency, declared: "I am for Haiti, not for the United States and I propose to keep myself in a position where I will be able to defend Haiti's interests."[14] Caperton's next choice was Philippe Sudré Dartiguenave, president of the Haitian Senate. He was willing to acquiesce to the United States' financial control of his nation. Yet, Caperton faced an issue as Dr. Rosalvo Bobo, former Secretary of State of Interior Senate, also desired the presidency.[15] The invaders sought to limit Bobo's chances for several reasons. The State Department knew of his history of opposing U.S. deals in the nation, including the J. P. MacDonald's railway plan in 1910–1911. The invaders also accused Bobo of ending Sam's presidency. They noted that on July 2, days before Sam's death, Dr. Bobo had gathered a revolutionary force of 500 men and occupied the city of Cap-Haïtien. They joked that Bobo transformed from medical doctor to jungle general. Because of the threat Bobo posed, Caperton allowed his candidacy, even though he and his staff favored Dartiguenave. Bobo's actions at the onset of the invasion document early forms of Haitian protest. These protests included the Revolutionary Committee, in which Péralte participated.

The Revolutionary Committee and its ensuing actions were a classic case of Haitians mobilizing with their patriotic kin against U.S. imperialism. Its methods would parallel the *cacos'* strategies of duplicity and covert operations. When one interprets the sources about the Revolutionary Committee from the Marine Archives in the United States, its members appear as passive beings whom the U.S. military led for its control of Haiti. Yet, as you dive deeper into these primary materials and cull sources from Haiti, another view of the committee appears. It is of the Revolutionary Committee infiltrating the U.S. military, offering its services, and fighting the military along the way. At the heart of the Revolutionary Committee's goals were the maintenance of Haitian independence and the selection of a Haitian president whom they elected. The ensuing section will unfold in the manner in which I found documents, along with my analysis. It is important to keep in mind, though, that the Revolutionary Committee was a group of all-male Haitian politicians who were or who would later become *cacos*. The Revolutionary Committee resisted the U.S. invaders peacefully and militarily.

A Revolution of Sorts

Two days after the marines disembarked, a group of Haitian men styling themselves as the Revolutionary Committee publicly demanded that liberty and order be restored to Haiti. The committee incited readers of the Haitian journals *Le Matin* and *Le Nouvelliste* to "Vive la liberté! Vive l'ordre! et Vive le progrès!"[16] Rosalvo Bobo was the founding member of the committee, which included prominent Haitian figures who served in a military and/or civic capacity: Charles Delvas, Edmond Polynice, Eribert St. Vil Noël, Emmanuel Robin, Samson Mampoint, Charles Zamor, and Charlemagne Péralte. Charles Zamor was the brother of former president Oreste Zamor, the man whom President Sam had assassinated in 1915; Charles Zamor was also part of the *cacos* movement and was an intermediary between the guerrilla fighters and U.S. soldiers.[17] In correspondence about the committee, invaders indicated that they initially thought these Haitian men were cooperative in their presence, yet they soon reported otherwise: "The activities of the Revolutionary Committee, which had been established at Port-au-Prince for the purpose of assisting Rear Admiral Caperton in maintaining order, were of such a nature, that it was necessary to direct them to resign and to assist all good forces in Haiti to restore peace and order."[18]

Though perceived as supportive, the Revolutionary Committee advocated for Haiti's sovereignty above U.S. rule by supporting Bobo. On July 30, *Le Nouvelliste* reported: "The Revolution started in the North Department under the direction of an eminent citizen, Rosalvo Bobo—support him. *Vive la liberté! Vive l'ordre! Vive le progrès! Vive Rosalvo Bobo!*"[19] With President Sam's demise, Bobo considered himself next in line as head of state. Guerrilla fighters in the north as well as politicians in the Revolutionary Committee backed him. One of Caperton's notes about the committee indicates that he was not yet cognizant that both groups collaborated: "On July 30, the Revolutionary Committee agreed to disarm all Haitian soldiers in the city by sunset of July 31. . . . During the evening of July 31, it became evident that the Haitians were openly violating the agreement."[20] From that note, it is clear that Caperton did not connect that some in the Revolutionary Committee were these *cacos* soldiers and vice versa. Bobo orchestrated events that would lead to his governance of the nation—and, at least at first, the U.S. invaders seemed unaware of the Haitian plan.

Péralte's role in this committee shows his early radicalism against the United States. Unfortunately, his service to the Revolutionary Committee is not highlighted in the dominant historical record, nor does it feature in popular memory. Péralte's Revolutionary Committee activities illustrate that he not only revolted militarily against the United States as a future *cacos* leader, but that he also stood as an intellectual who challenged the invasion with public nationalist sentiments. On August 2, as a committee member, Péralte reprimanded the foreign troops: "If you do not leave with God, we will remove your military invasion."[21] With this warning, Péralte expressed his assertive and aggressive approach to the invading soldiers. Writing from Léogâne on behalf of the committee, Péralte continued: "[I r]emain absolutely to your orders, . . . and await your instructions. In the meantime, please tell me if Jacmel is favorable or not."[22] Péralte's concern for the town in the southern locale indicates that protest against the foreigners went beyond the northern and central areas of Haiti. On August 4, Caperton reported on bandit "outbreaks" in "Petegoave, Miragoave, Jacmel, Haiti, and Petite Rivière de Nippe."[23] The pending presidential election was a major concern for both Haitians and the invaders.

The U.S. military's desire to appoint a president who would agree to its rule meant that Bobo and his supporters soon became clear adversaries. Bobo and the Revolutionary Committee's actions in support of Haitian rule guaranteed that the U.S. troops would not select him. As part of their refusal to acquiesce to U.S. domination, the Revolutionary Committee kept Haitians apprised of the locations of marine stations.[24] They also documented and reported on U.S. soldiers' abuse of Haitians. For example, committee members in Port-au-Prince notified the Haitian public of an "unjustified assault [by soldiers] of two women" and that "peaceful citizens have been gravely hurt."[25] These soldiers likely raped these women. On August 5, Caperton wrote: "Bobo wants control of city; has about two thousand soldiers in vicinity. Soldiers in city have hidden arms.

Nashville outposts allowed Bobo soldiers to enter city after disarming."[26] The rear admiral's statement points out the formidable threat that the *cacos* presented. These fighters were also Revolutionary Committee members. Unbeknown to the foreign troops, they worked in concert with one another. Further, Bobo delivered speeches throughout the country, urging Haitians to assert their sovereignty. On August 7, he received a warm ovation for a speech in which he accused the United States of spreading its eagle wings over independent republics. He asked Haitians to consider: "what's going on in this hemisphere and in our country?"[27] For the Revolutionary Committee, Haiti's cause was the cause of the larger Americas. Their tactical use of the image of the U.S. eagle as imperial offered a counternarrative to the rhetoric of democracy.

On that same day, August 7, Solon Ménos sent a cable dispatch to the Haitian minister in Washington, DC. He decried the invasion, especially the presence of naval forces. Ménos predicted that "it would be impossible to restore quiet to the interior of the country until control of civil affairs in the coast towns was restored to Haytians."[28] His warning proved accurate. All this resistance happened quickly after the United States seized banks.

Bobo led troops to the capital and other *cacos* also battled U.S. soldiers across Haiti. On August 9, they fought against marines and bluejackets (naval men) deployed by the invaders from the capital to Saint-Marc, Pétionville, and Aux Croix des Bouquets. In Cap-Haïtien, Caperton announced that he would not permit the revolutionary leaders to interrupt commerce among Cap residents and in its environs. In Saint-Marc, U.S. soldiers reported an uprising of two hundred troops, led by *caco* general Auguste, which ultimately resulted in his death.

Haitians outwitted the U.S. military as protests grew from different venues simultaneously. Péralte and other committee members sent a letter to the National Assembly in support of Bobo on August 9. Recognizing that the U.S. military pressured the Haitian National Assembly to elect Dartiguenave, they argued at length.

> With a heart filled with sadness, we have just respectfully requested your high authority to fill the vacancy of the Executive Power with a wise man of the state, by election to the presidential seat as soon as possible, one loyal and of whom the public spirit has already approved. In the presence of this great danger, which menaces and threatens to crush our black and yellow Republic, of which all Haitians are rightly proud, a movement of love and sentiment for the nation and for our cherished ancestors operates and affords us a definitive understanding among all our classes and political parties.[29]

In the opening paragraph, they invoked sympathy for Haiti's political state and also declared the U.S. presence a menace. Additionally, Péralte asserted his vision for a unified Haiti that would include its diverse citizens:

No!—It is not the work of 1804, of Dessalines, Pétion, etc., and so many other brave souls, their auxiliaries, that we must smash, or cause to be smashed. For too long a time we have worked, alas, to have this terrible catastrophe fall upon us. It is again the time. There are some men, some well-meaning souls capable of defending the soil of our ancestors. To be sure, we shall not permit the insulting strangers to step on us like they are our masters, especially in our hills and our immense savannas, on the mortal and scattered remains of those who, black and mulatto, marched heroically to their death to leave us this nation. It is rather the divisions, the political parties without a legitimate base that we have to crush. A unanimous call, a patriotic cry from all our breasts which is the voice of our elderly mothers, great-grandmothers and alas![30]

Péralte appealed to Haitian sensibilities through history. He deliberately used the historical figures of Dessalines and Pétion. Through these ancestors, Péralte articulated a new vision and narrative for Haiti. Haitian popular memory conceives of Dessalines as a militant Black *nasyonalis* who overcame slave owners.[31] Comparatively, Alexander Pétion, of mixed race and free, is remembered for his bravery during the revolution, along with his contributions, after their victory, in the agricultural and educational sectors.[32] Péralte's pairing of these seemingly divergent—although comparable—political actors, who together represented Haiti's "black and yellow republic," was a diplomatic move. In the 1805 constitution Dessalines had declared that all Haitians will henceforth be known as *noir*, bringing together people of different ancestry. Péralte also appealed to Haitians from all backgrounds in defense of their nation.

Péralte and other writers recalled the nation's indigenous past and the Taino-Arawak's name for Haiti, *Ayiti*, and Santo Domingo, *Quisqueya*. The letter repeats the call for unity over and over: "These men, these patriots who made the face of Haiti so brilliant, want us to see them today. A great task calls us to unity." The writers' explicit use of the words "free," "independent," and "patriots," also furthered their strategy. These are words that U.S. Americans touted repeatedly even as they seized parts of the Caribbean. Perhaps Péralte and others thought they could appeal to the U.S. military's sense of patriotism. They were reclaiming those words for their own project.

We know for certain that America does not seek glory, as a moral person, to measure herself by us—we accept, nevertheless, that, to our shame, she has come to help us to maintain order and peace among ourselves, without having been invited. This should cause us to reflect at some length.[33]

Péralte appears to appease the invaders in his acknowledgment of their help. Yet he quickly reminded Haitians that the invaders' presence was an intrusion. The phrase "we march in harmony" conveys both military formation and Haitian patriotic kinship in action.

The Revolutionary Committee was deployed the day before the election; its members, with no formal legal standing, ordered the dissolution of the Haitian Congress. The Revolutionary Committee also attempted to seal the Chamber of Deputies doors on August 11. The U.S. military threatened them through written message and placed two additional ships in Port-au-Prince. Finally, the foreigners seized control of the telegraph office. The U.S. military anticipated violence and attempted to shut down any possibility of Bobo assuming the presidency.

Despite Haitian protests against U.S. rule and for Bobo's election, the United States succeeded in its political objective.[34] On August 12, the Haitian Congress elected Dartiguenave.[35] U.S. administrators boasted of it as a democratic exemplar:

> Election Day passed without disorder. Under the protections of the United States Marines, Haiti had her first absolutely free election. Thirty-Nine Haitian senators and one hundred and two deputies met in the legislature and by an overwhelming majority elected Sudre Dartiguenave the President of Haiti. President Dartiguenave in a moving speech promised full and complete cooperation with the United States in her efforts to bring Haiti out of bloodshed and chaos into her rightful place in the world.[36]

The report's claim that this was Haiti's "first absolutely free election" is part of an ongoing U.S. practice of promoting its invasion as a benevolent political enterprise. Caperton remarked, "The Haitians themselves, without outside influence had made [Dartiguenave] their president." By insinuating that Haitians somehow had failed to rule themselves, the United States asserted itself as a protector rather than an invader—further promoting the false notion of its own racial superiority, an ideology that had guided its political approach to Haiti for generations. As part of its doublespeak though, Secretary of State Lansing admitted to President Wilson: "I do not see why it would not be as easy to control a government with a president as it is to control the Haitian Congress and administrative officers."[37] U.S. government correspondence confirms that the goal was always to assert foreign control. Despite the illusion of fairness, various reports surfaced that the election had been compromised.[38] The U.S. invaders equated Dartiguenave's selection with their complete control of Haiti. They remarked: "The election of Dartiguenave is preferred by the US. . . . That the Haitian government will grant no territorial concessions to any foreign Governments will be insisted upon by the US. The question of the cession of Mole St. Nicolas will be taken up later by the US government."[39] In short, the United States finally took by force a country that it had attempted to ignore, manage, and control for over a century.

Dartiguenave served as a front man for the puppet government from 1915 to 1922. Yet, despite his selection by U.S. officials, Dartiguenave often objected to

U.S. policies that adversely affected Haiti and its populace.[40] At one point, he complained to U.S. officials about soldiers harassing the Haitian people. Caperton's successor, Colonel Littleton W. T. Waller, rebuked the president. He reminded Dartiguenave, "You are president because we Americans are in Haiti. If you continue to denounce me, I'll have my government recall its troops for twenty-four hours and by the time we pass by Gonaives, you'll be chased out of the Presidential Palace."[41] Even slight attempts to support the Haitian people against U.S. military overreach resulted in a threat to Dartiguenave's position.

U.S. troops reacted to the Revolutionary Committee by using Haitian journals as a medium against them. The foreign soldiers published pro-U.S. articles. Moreover, the invaders made sure that the journals would not publish voices opposing or critiquing these articles. Captain Alexander S. Williams, the U.S. provost marshal, restricted the freedom of speech. He declared:

> The freedom of the press will not be interfered with, but license will not be tolerated. The publishing of false or incendiary propaganda of Haiti, or the publishing of any false indecent or obscene propaganda, letters signed or unsigned, or matter which tends to disturb the public peace will be dealt with by the Military Courts. The writers of such articles and the publishers thereof will be held responsible for such utterances and will be subject to fine or imprisonment, or both, as may be determined.[42]

Williams's order attests to the Revolutionary Committee's impact. Haitians resisted early and the United States sought to dismantle this right. Despite their own country's constitutional dedication to free speech, soldiers like Williams disapproved of Haitians criticizing the U.S. empire freely and democratically.

By year's end, it appeared that the Revolutionary Committee had disintegrated. Caperton reported to President Wilson that he had "dissolved the revolutionary committee and informed them that they have no further authority in Port-au-Prince and would be considered public enemies of the United States if they attempted to give any further orders or to menace U.S. policies."[43] Caperton's premature conclusion reveals his blindness about the situation at hand. Haitians resisted covertly and overtly as individuals and as part of a collective. In fact, committee members had increased other kinds of service to the *cacos* and protested against the invasion in other ways.

The Revolutionary Committee's ongoing influence was often under the radar of U.S. troops. While records on the Revolutionary Committee are sparse, the available pieces of information are enlightening. For example, Haitian radicals, politicians, and intellectuals strategized against the intrusion into their country's liberty.[44] These men plotted a revolt to regain their nation and elect a candidate of their choice. Not only did they organize guerrilla fighters, they appealed to the U.S. military's patriotic consciousness. Calling on the U.S.'s own dedication to the cause of democracy in the First World War, the committee used the ideal of democracy and the U.S. image of itself as an eagle to discredit it and call for an end to the invasion. Haitian resistance ebbed, flowed, and spanned intellectual and physical battle lines. In fact, the *cacos* as guerrilla fighters did not simply pick up arms, they also articulated their disapproval of the invasion despite censorship. The intellectuals resisting the U.S. military not only publicly denounced the soldiers, they also fought them in battles. Resisters in political positions and those who were market women and laborers desired one goal: to topple the U.S. regime in Haiti. As Péralte's respectful and stern note to the invaders illustrated, members of the resistance invoked images of liberty, justice, and God to reason with the marines. And yet, members from this very "respectable" committee also served as *cacos*, a group that the U.S. soldiers routinely defamed as bandits. Instead of a haphazard group of peasants, however, the resisters were, in fact, working cooperatively from above and below.

Péralte Encounters U.S. Troops

The U.S. military removed Péralte from his Léogâne commander post because of his actions with the Revolutionary Committee and his refusal to acquiesce to U.S. demands. In the five months that he served his residents, Péralte treated them with sincerity and respect. For example, he expressed his condolences to residents affected by President Vilbrun Guillaume Sam's massacre of prisoners on July 27, 1915. He shared their grief, as his relative Gaspard Péralte was among the 167 murdered. In *Le Nouvelliste*, he wrote: "To the weeping families of my relatives and friends, who have had the misfortune of being the victims of the general massacre of the prisoners, and together with all the people of Léogâne, I extend my sympathies and condolences. Peace to the martyrs of destiny."[45] From his various correspondences, we can also see that Péralte used his post in public office to engage the U.S. military. In one telegram to the Revolutionary Committee, dated one day after the U.S. troops had landed, Péralte reported: "I am eager to respond to your dispatch Number 3 of today, the contents of which have received my immediate attention. . . . Agreeing entirely with your orders and waiting for your instructions."[46] Péralte was poised for a fight. In another missive to the Revolutionary Committee, Péralte penned: "Order and peace reign in the area of my command. Exerting myself without slacking, in order to maintain this happy situation."[47]

Péralte's correspondence also sheds light on why individuals in his political position became Revolutionary Committee men. Their posts gave them both the access and the power to recruit constituents to fight against the invasion. One letter highlights Péralte's recruitment tactics. On August 2, 1915, he addressed the "gallant people of Léogâne" in a telegram:

The new social strata that I greet here should bow before itself. Your beautiful patriotic gestures gives you an incontestable right to posterity's homage. . . .

Also, this is why you have understood me so well; is this why I feel happy and proud of being again at your head.... Glory to you, people of Grand Goave, Petit Goave, and all of Léogâne ... like your ancestors who knew only hard toil and who are demanded by the authorities to maintain order, peace, and secure conditions, without which no well-being is possible.[48]

Péralte's rhetoric works to inspire his readers. He brings them in by commenting on their common understanding. He compliments the people for their shared dedication to a noble mission. Then he links that mission to a longstanding one of their common ancestors. His rhetoric is meant to be motivation for the resistance.

His mother expressed both pride and consternation over Péralte's politics. Madame Masséna wrote, "I am more than pleased to hear that the people of Léogâne are charmed with you. And try to conduct yourself always to do good rather than harm to the rich as well as the poor. I pray [to] the Immaculate One night and day for you. If you can remain quiet and peaceable, God and the people of Léogâne will save you in all circumstances, because you have acted well towards the people. If you see that things are quiet, remain quiet also. Mind well the situation of our country."[49] Her short missive reads as a warm inquiry into her son's overall health. We can also read the letters exchanged between the two of them as intelligence gathering. She behaves as a mother with concerns and as one who could offer her support through her intelligence tactics. Despite his mother's hopes, the people of Léogâne could not save Péralte.

Five days after the presidential election, U.S. troops encountered Péralte face to face. When they disembarked in Léogâne on August 17, 1915, Péralte refused to grant them entry. In a cheeky manner, Péralte explained that these orders should come from the Haitian president.[50] The event remains vivid in memory today. During my research in 2006, one interviewee detailed the moment:

They [the invaders] try to characterize him as a bandit for this.... Charlemagne Péralte was the one responsible for the community. When the sentinel came, he said, he does not have the power to lodge them and he does not want the marines' boots in Léogâne.

That is the courage of a *nasyonalis* it was normal for him to defend [his country]. When the sentinel returned, one of the chiefs said it was the president who gave him [access to Léogâne]. Charlemagne Péralte said, well, if the president gave you authorization, the president also gave me the power to be in charge of this area, so he knows the formalities, and thus would need to go through the formalities with me.[51]

The interviewee's detailed accounts are part of a long tradition of oral history. This story of resistance was important enough for it to be noted, shared, and passed down. Someone passed it down to him and he had committed this knowledge to memory and recounted it proudly in interviews in 2006, over ninety years after the fact. He emphasized that Péralte was first and foremost *nasyonalis*. The interviewee reasoned:

> He was a very disciplined man, and he knew what steps the president needed to take. He made them [the invaders] understand that the president needed to defend Haiti as a nation, like Haitians needed to defend the nation. If the president did not do it, that does not mean he should not. [Péralte] resisted the demands of the Chief Marines to allow them to remain in the area. It is here that Péralte would be considered a symbol. [The invaders] would come to understand that they needed to do away with Péralte.

The story of this encounter is one of the dominant portrayals of Péralte as a brave, selfless citizen. While U.S. records archive it as an example of Péralte's recalcitrant behavior, for Haitians, it has become a legendary act of Péralte defending Haiti and, by extension, protecting them. A tall, lanky Haitian man alone faced off with the foreign military in support of his beloved Haiti. For this act, Haitians remember him as a hero.

That same month, the U.S. soldiers, strengthened by the authority of their client, the Haitian government, fired Péralte for this infraction. To this day, Haitians recall the loss of his post as an example of President Dartiguenave's complicity with the foreigners. Additionally, they paint the Haitian head of state as a weak puppet and the foreigners as imperialists. A key detail of this narrative of Péralte as a legend was the transparency from which he operated in this instance. In his farewell to his district residents, Péralte said,

> My dear compatriots, I would be lacking in high moral duty if I were to remain cold and insensitive to your sobbing hearts, to so many tears that you have shed over my removal, and so I say, that I testify loudly and publicly as to my gratitude before so much sympathy and the many acts of kindness that you have displayed towards me under these remarkable circumstances. My gratitude goes to all of you, people of Léogâne, Petite-Goave and Grand-Goave, all you men, women, and children, who have not ceased for a minute to honor me with your solicitude and your moving respect.[52]

Péralte, though respected and admired by his fellow citizens, was a threat in the eyes of the invaders. The U.S. military could not send him into exile and silence him—that might make protests worse. Rather, they imprisoned him in 1917–1918. An interviewee reflected on the reasons for Péralte's ousting and subsequent jailing. His animated account underscores how this moment lives on in Haitians' popular imagination as a courageous act.

It is normal for them to uncover that he was a *nasyonalis*. If you want or not, when a stranger is burning your soil, the first person they're going to attack is a *nasyonalis*. It's true that wood [Péralte] cannot fight with iron you're here? So, [the U.S. military] would always attempt to bring [Péralte] down. Now even if wood cannot fight with iron, the wood also has its strength. Thus, [Péralte] came and reclaimed his power. History shows us that the fashion that the Marines, the American troops operated: it was oppression.[53]

The interviewee asserts that the U.S. military imprisoned Péralte for being proindependence. His story focuses on Péralte as a brave Haitian *nasyonalis*. This is the popular tale that formed the apotheosis of Péralte as a martyr. For many contemporary Haitians, Péralte could do no wrong.

After leaving Léogâne in 1915, Péralte mostly retreated to a life of farming in Hinche, but he and his brother Saül remained active against the invasion. Though Saül never led the *cacos*, he was committed to their politics.[54] As an interviewee said: "They speak more about Charlemagne but his older brother [Saül] was even more militant than he."[55] The U.S. takeover of his homeland through documents like the 1915 treaty heightened Péralte's radicalism against the U.S. military.

The Haitian-American Treaty

The Haitian-American Treaty highlighted the lack of U.S. democratic ideals in its foreign affairs. The treaty's provisions rendered Haiti an imperial entity and granted the United States far-reaching fiscal and political rights. The treaty featured sixteen articles in French and English, signed by Robert Beale Davis Jr., the chargé d'affaires (account manager) of the United States, and Louis Borno, the Haitian secretary of state for foreign affairs and public instruction. The treaty made the illegal invasion "legal." In several of the articles, the following clause appears: "The President of Haiti shall appoint, upon nomination by the President of the United States. . . ."[56] This neutral wording downplays the powers that the United States asserts with the treaty's provisions. Six articles elucidate the United States' actual intentions to control Haiti. Article 8 states: "The Republic of Haiti shall not increase its public debt except by previous agreement with the President of the U.S." Article 9 continues: "The Republic of Haiti will not without a previous agreement with the President of the United States, modify the customs duties in a manner to reduce the revenues therefrom." Both articles sanctioned U.S. control of the sovereign nation's economic affairs. The United States positioned itself as something of an older sibling—patronizing and condescending, but, thanks to a longstanding racist portrayal of Haiti, justified in its "assistance" to the country. The enactment of this treaty was a threat to Haiti's sovereignty. A free nation does not require the permission of another to legislate, engage in trade, nor protect its people.

The United States employed neutral language to mask its control of its neighbor state. In Article 10, the United States mandated that Haiti cultivate a peaceful atmosphere, and police itself with the aid of U.S. soldiers. It states:

> The Haitian government obligates itself, for the preservation of domestic peace, the security of individual rights and full observance of the provisions of this treaty, to create without delay an efficient constabulary, urban and rural, composed of native Haitians. This constabulary shall be organized and officered by Americans appointed by the President of Haiti, upon nomination by the President of the United States.[57]

While the first half of the article indicated that Haitians would comprise this force, the remaining section illustrates that the United States would actually control law and order. Both Articles 11 and 14 stripped Haiti of its sovereignty. Article 11 says:

> The Government of Haiti agrees not to surrender any of the territory of the Republic of Haiti by sale, lease, or otherwise, or jurisdiction over such territory, to any foreign government or power, nor to enter into any treaty or contract with any foreign power or powers that will impair or tend to impair, the independence of Haiti.[58]

By prohibiting Haiti from engaging in free trade, the United States guaranteed its supremacy in Haiti's diplomatic affairs. Article 14 further stipulates:

> The high contracting parties shall have authority to take such steps as may be necessary to insure the complete attainment of any of the objects comprehended in this treaty; and, should the necessary occur, the United States will lend an efficient aid for the preservation of Haitian independence and the maintenance of a government adequate for the protection of life, liberty, and the protection of property and individual liberty.[59]

Again, despite the condescending phrasing—"lend an efficient aid"—this article gave the United States an excuse to intervene in Haiti's affairs at any time. Articles 11 and 14 were reminiscent of earlier laws imposed by the United States on another nation that it had invaded. In 1901, the Platt Amendment had imposed similar restrictions on Cubans. One article declared that the "U.S. reserves and retains the right of intervention for the preservation of Cuban independence and the maintenance of a stable government adequately protecting life, property, [and] individual liberty." Another article dictated: "No government shall be deemed to have authority to enter into any treaty or engagement with any foreign power which may tend to impair or interfere with the independence of Cuba."[60] The similarities between the 1901 Platt Amendment and the 1915 Haitian American Treaty demonstrate the continuation of an empire-building project by the United States in the Caribbean.[61] In claiming to protect independence in both countries, the United States was claiming its authority to enter into treaties and otherwise act on their behalf—exactly the opposite of independence.

Finally, the treaty's concluding article, Article 16, shows the United States' desire to have Haiti as a protectorate. Despite Admiral Caperton's previous statement to Haitians that the invasion would be short-term, Article 16 showed the true motives of the United States. It stipulated:

> The present Treaty shall remain in full force and virtue for the term of ten years, to be counted from the day exchange of ratifications, and further for another term of ten years if, for specific reasons presented by either of the high contracting parties, the purpose of this treaty has not been fully accomplished.[62]

This article stipulated that the United States would remain in Haiti for ten years and threatened that it might stay as long as twenty. Furthermore, the length of the invasion would depend on how well Haitians behaved. When a nation is in revolt in the manner that Haiti was against the U.S. military, no one "behaves," save for the good of the nation.

The Haitian-American Treaty did not sit well with Haitians, who recognized it as an affront to their independence. Due to protests, there was a gap between the time it was signed and when it was ratified. The two countries' representatives, Borno and Davis Jr., signed the document in Port-au-Prince on September 16, 1915. Yet, before its ratification, U.S. officials took steps to assert their authority on the nation. Then on October 6, the Haitian Chamber of Deputies ratified it, with the Haitian Senate following months later in February 1916.[63] President Dartiguenave approved it in March and on May 3, it became official in Washington, DC. This was when the two countries finally proclaimed the Haitian-American Treaty.

Judging from the extensive presence of U.S. soldiers across the northern, eastern, and southern parts of Haiti, Haitian resistance was in full force across the nation during the treaty's deliberations.[64] Even though the treaty's provisions had not yet been fully ratified, the U.S. Marines sent troops everywhere to assert their authority. They wrote: "The acceptance of the Treaty being practically certain, conditions in the coast cities and towns of Haiti, were assured by sending marine detachments to Jacmel, Aux Cayes, Jeremie, Miragoane, Petit Goave, Gonaïves, and Port-de Paix. Thus, the ten largest seacoast towns all came under the jurisdiction of the American forces."[65] Another indicator of the strength of Haitian resistance was the United States' implementation of Article 10: "the American forces took immediate steps to provide the constabulary mentioned therein, the preservation of order and the protection of individual rights being the most urgent need at the time."[66] The constabulary became the military and police force in Haiti known as the Gendarmerie d'Haïti, or simply the gendarmes.[67]

The quick formation of the gendarmes—including the compiling and issuing of the group's protocol by August 24, 1916—is also another example of how the United States quickly implemented measures to control Haiti and to subdue any resistance. In Article 10, the invaders defined the various responsibilities of the gendarmes, which included establishing and administering a coast guard. The United States carefully outlined the administrative components of the force, including uniforms, transportation, and wages. Even though the gendarmes were technically a Haitian military force, Article 10 established a hierarchy between the U.S. soldiers and any potential Haitian officers. Only when U.S. gendarmes deemed Haitians fit—a designation which including passing an exam—could they serve. Furthermore, despite the gendarmes being one unit, U.S. Americans and Haitians were subject to the different laws of their respective nation states. The commandant of the gendarmerie, the U.S. American Alexander S. Williams, held discretion over disciplining Haitian and U.S. gendarme officers for any infractions.[68] The loopholes and biases in this disciplinary structure became evident with their revival of the *corvée*, or forced labor in lieu of taxes.

In the past, Haitian presidents had alternately introduced and revoked this controversial work requirement. Haitian laborers protested against the system's brutal abuses and its sole benefit to the state. This antiquated 1864 legislation had instituted a class bias.[69] The revival of the *corvée* during the U.S. invasion raised swift objections. Despite the archaic nature of the labor system, invading officials touted the *corvée* as a means of modernizing the nation. The soldiers explained:

> The Gendarmerie, on approval of the President of the Republic, undertook to perform road construction and repair work under authority of Article 54 of the Rural Code of the Republic of Haiti; which reads that "public highways and communications will be maintained and repaired by the inhabitants, in rotation, in each section through which these roads pass and each time repairs are necessary. . . . The enforcement of this law being in the hands of the police, the Gendarmerie took the necessary steps to recruit laborers. Working parties obtained under this law, similar in effect to the road tax laws in the United States whereby citizens are either required to pay a certain road tax, or work in lieu thereof a certain period on the public highways, were called "*corvées*."[70]

The U.S. justifications for the *corvée* included its being a former Haitian law and similar to former U.S. labor laws. This skewed reasoning shows that U.S. officials recognized the *corvée*'s problematic structure from the onset. Still, the system was put in place. The gendarmes kept Haitian workers at *corvée* camps.

The term "*corvée* camps" illuminates the coerciveness of the system: the gendarmes claimed that "these workmen were housed and [we] furnished them [with] food, drink, and entertainment," rather than wages or freedom.[71] The gendarmes downplayed their use of forced labor by boasting of their accomplishments with the *corvée*, including the building of a 112-mile road from Port-au-Prince to Gonaïves and Haitian president Dartiguenave's being able to ride through the towns in his automobiles.[72]

Nonetheless, the use of citizen laborers to build hospitals, roads, and schools was inhumane in several ways. Although the *corvée* was mandatory, monied Haitians could purchase their way out of this mandate. Thus, the majority of people who composed the *corvée*'s pool of laborers were poor. Essentially, U.S. administrators forced poor Haitians to labor. The U.S. Americans attempted to excuse their keeping of more than 4,000 *corvée* laborers by claiming these poor Haitians were "attracted by free food and lodging and the constant contact with their fellows."[73] Their dismissive tone concealed the fact that they were orchestrating and supervising an inhumane labor practice. In October 1917, the brigade commander dismissed reports of Haitians who escaped *corvée* work by migrating to the Dominican Republic. He commented: "Received a report yesterday concerning emigration from Haiti to Santo Domingo particularly from the section of the Plain of the Cul de Sac; my informant stated that this was due to the application of the *corvée* system. . . . But in my opinion the reports are much exaggerated, and I doubt whether the *corvée* system has much to do with it."[74] When reports of the *corvée* camps and abuses surfaced, U.S. troops initially deflected blame to local Haitian mayors.

> The weak point in the application of the *corvée* had been the connection of Haitian civil officials with it. . . . Persons who did not wish to work and could pay a sum of money, whether or not the sum prescribed to exempt inhabitants from work, paid the various mayors and did not have to work. If a person had no money, he was put on *corvée* and when each period of work was completed, his name placed on the working list, and again forced to work. . . . The Gendarmes, although proven dependable if directly under the command of an American officer, saw their chance to make money on the *corvée* and many of them failed to remain true to their trust.[75]

According to the invaders' logic, Haitians would commit *corvée* abuse unless U.S. Americans supervised them. Still, news surfaced of the harsh recruitment methods and brutality of the practice. As one observer noted: "The occupant seized men anywhere, within their family, on their small farms or on the roads, day or night and forced them to run into the remote rural areas. Those who dared to resist, or even protest, were beaten . . . their families often had no news about their whereabouts."[76] When the U.S. Americans finally acknowledged their culpability, they discussed it as a rare occurrence, rather than the norm. As an excuse, they claimed: "In some rare cases, too zealous American officers held laborers more time than they were required to labor and even transferred them out of the immediate neighborhood of their homes to work in other sections, a procedure not permitted by law."[77] Yet, the U.S. troops knew that the nature of the *corvée* work and the various abuses resulted in what the marines themselves labeled as "*corvée* killings."[78]

Partly due to the escalating reports of the *corvée*'s atrocities, the U.S. troops begrudgingly discontinued the *corvée*. U.S. officials further distanced themselves from the *corvée* by appointing the Department of Public Works to supervise the new paid labor. Although they admitted that the *corvée* "was doing more harm than good," and ceased its practice on October 1, 1918, it was not until a year later that the practice was fully abolished.[79] Resistance by Haitians against the *corvée* contributed to its end. The troops reported on incidents where Haitians attacked gendarmes who delivered *corvée* cards and once killed a gendarme in Jacmel. In a disturbing coincidence, U.S. troops found funds to hire paid laborers in June 1919. Why did they not have that money beforehand to pay Haitians for road construction and repair? John H. Russell notified Haitians of the *corvée*'s end on October 16, 1919, in *Le Nouvelliste*:

> Citizens you are all aware by this time that the *corvée* system has been definitely abolished. Such work was by your government at one time considered necessary in order to open up for you parts of your country, which were almost inaccessible but over a year ago, it was decided that the necessity for such work no longer existed and consequently the corvée was abolished and will never be again enforced in Haiti. . . . The occupation intends to establish permanent peace for you in your land to permit you to engage in agricultural and other pursuits to gain an honest living thereby. . . . The occupation is determined that the laws of Haiti shall not be violated and that all good and peaceful citizens shall be fully protected while the lawless element will be run down.[80]

The use of the term *abolish* is significant. Why not use *terminate* or *end* to describe U.S. actions to bring this practice to a close? The explicit use of the word abolish connotes an acknowledgment that conditions were reminiscent of slavery, the colonial, forced-labor practice whose abolition drove the desire for Haitian independence. Though technically abolished in the United States, culturally forced labor of prisoners was not unusual for U.S. Americans. Further, the implication of the Haitian government in this U.S. coercion stands out, too. President Dartiguenave is rightly to blame, and the existence of the *corvée* law is part of how the nation did not protect its citizens. However, the United States did not acknowledge that Dartiguenave did not govern Haiti. Rather, the United States administered, implemented, and abused the *corvée*.

The proposal of "good and peaceful citizens," or those who behave, strikes a chord. The U.S. military definition of a "good and peaceful" citizen was a person who supported its invasion. Therefore, Dartiguenave was good and Péralte was bad. The myth of the invasion as a benevolent enterprise for Haiti partly originates from this forced practice. Rather than honestly state, *we forced Haitians to labor over these national projects*, the discourse became, *Haitians under U.S. supervision opened Haiti*. To create accessibility, they built and shored up roads, highways, hospitals, and the like—grueling work in tough terrain. In the same way that some discussed slavery without its horrific violence for centuries, the U.S. military touted the *corvée*'s successes, sans its horrors. With the U.S. soldiers' doublespeak, the "progress" of these projects became the focus, rather than the inhumane treatments and death of Haitian laborers. For these Haitian laborers, the harsh conditions, lack of compensation, and other basic employee rights, made the foreign Whites equivalent to slave owners and the forced work to slavery. Péralte, in his rhetoric of historic nationalism, was one who often likened the *corvée* to slavery.[81] Many Haitians were harmed and killed in these projects between 1915 and 1919.[82] The omission of the abuse involved is deafening. Even today, the myth of Haiti prospering because of the U.S. invasion uses these core projects as evidence, obscuring the reality of the period.

Péralte and other Haitians were outraged by the invasion's persistent use of the *corvée* and the U.S. soldiers' reckless abuse of their people. Millet has argued that *corvée* abuse alienated people to the extent that they decided to fight the invasion and thus increased the numbers of *cacos* soldiers.[83] Not only were the battles between the U.S. troops and the *cacos* incessant and bloody affairs, but the U.S. soldiers also shot at Haitians, whether or not these individuals were anti-invasion agitators. On August 7, 1915, *Le Nouvelliste* reported that the U.S. troops had killed two people who had not provoked them.[84] The U.S. soldiers' violence toward Haitians remains part of the collective psyche a century later.

3

Haitians—Rise and Defend! (Ayisien(ne)— Leve epi defann!)

•••••••••••••••••••••

The 1915–1922 *cacos* were continuing a tradition initiated by their ancestors. The *cacos* existed as a group in Haiti between 1802 and 1922, increasing and decreasing in the intensity of their actions. Despite their longstanding presence, though, a full historiography of the group is lacking. The works of several scholars, including Kethly Millet, Roger Gaillard, André-Georges Adam, Alex Dupuy, and David Nicholls, provide details about different periods of the *cacos*. Tracing their history and involvement in Haitian political life demonstrates how important national involvement was in rural areas. The earliest *cacos*, those involved in Haiti's revolution and independence, influenced the *cacos* of the invasion. These seemingly marginal citizens in fact contributed to the formation of the Haitian state in significant economic and political ways.

The name *cacos* itself has two origins. The less common idea is that the name derives from a garment that peasants wore, *caraco*. The most widely cited belief, however, is that the name derives from the Haitian national bird known as Tacco Hispaniola. The 1802 use of the term *tacco* relates to the maroon and guerrilla fighters who fought against French soldiers like Victor-Emmanuel Leclerc, Donatien de Rochambeau, and thousands of troops sent by Napoleon Bonaparte to reinstate slavery and reconquer Saint-Domingue. The Tacco bird feasts on *zandolites* (large lizards). When the *cacos* attacked, proverbially it meant that the *zandolites* were their enemies, oppressors, and victims. *Zandolites* could be internal threats (government forces) and/or external ones (foreigners, including corporations and the U.S. military). Just like the two ideas about the group's name, there are different accounts of their origin and their objectives. In both the historical record and in some Haitians' memory, the *cacos* were freedom fighters, peasants, bandits, *mawons*, and guerrilla fighters.

The *cacos*' ancestors, known as the *taccos*, were the heart of the abolitionist movement during the final years of the revolution.[1] They were an active rural or agricultural population who learned that neither the leaders of the revolution nor the French were interested in their freedom. This sense of political activism and duty to political activism is a fundamental part of Haitian society. In 1867 the *cacos* were defending their state against domestic wrongs and foreign intrusion made possibly by President Sylvain Salnave's cowering to the United States.[2] These 1867 *cacos* defended Dessalines's 1805 constitutional declaration that precluded foreigners from owning Haiti's lands. The 1867 *cacos* also shielded Haiti from relinquishing its hard-won and long-fought-for independence. There is a strong connection between national independence and freedom that motivates so much of Haitian politics.

While scholars emphasize the lack of economic and political power they had, others blame political instability on the *cacos*. However, this type of grassroots political action in Haiti had always been about ensuring national independence. Therefore, Haitian political activism was always more complex and sophisticated than has previously been understood. Foreigners, especially racist invaders, did not get this. In reading about, examining, and talking to people about the *cacos*' historiography, I have found that the actions of this group were not uncharacteristic of a larger struggle for sovereignty. During the U.S. invasion years, the *cacos*' battles were not against internal discord, but rather the foreign threat that descended upon Haiti.

The 1915 *cacos*, like their 1802 ancestors, were freedom fighters who often used *mawon*-like strategies against the U.S. soldiers. *Cacos* in both periods battled with their feet. They fled, returned to engage in battles with their oppressors, and helped their peers. The earlier *cacos* destroyed slave-owner tools from plantations that brutalized their bodies and, generations later, their descendants in the early twentieth century destroyed imperialist tools to build railway tracks that economically and physically trapped "free" Haitians. Similar to their 1867 forerunners, these *cacos* protested against foreign intrusion. They upended Salnave with his policies that failed to protect his citizens, and they fought against imperialists who selected a puppet president and created a version of the Haitian army (gendarmes) designed to brutalize them for defending the state. Like their 1905–1915 counterparts, the guerrilla fighters sought to end the invasion. The Marines' archives tell the story of their actions as if they were lawless, yet the *cacos* were far from it. The aim of their political actions was to create a governmental structure to protect and enhance their way of life and wellbeing. The invaders' doublespeak permeates their descriptions of the *cacos* and their extensive battles.

FIG. 2 Haitians listed in the archives as "A Few of The Country's 'Bad Men,'" Port-au-Prince, Haiti, 1915 (Reference Collection, Marine Corps History Division, Quantico, VA)

U.S. troops helped to create and buttress erroneous depictions of the guerrilla fighters. In one of their definitions of the *cacos*, U.S. soldiers offered this description of the situation:

> Here lived, in the rugged chains of the north and east near the Dominican border, according to the best estimates, some twenty-five to fifty thousand cacos. The word caco is a Creole word, meaning eagle or bird of prey. These gentry were free soldiers of fortune, who lived on the country as bandits in normal times … descending from their mountains during revolutions to form a part of one or other of the armies of the candidates for the Presidency. On these happy occasions, they would plunder a few towns; burn a few houses; cut a few throats; and then go back to their native mountains with their pockets full of plunder. The American Occupation naturally put an end to these activities, much to the discontent of the cacos.[3]

This reference describes the *cacos* as citizens who senselessly misbehaved (Figure 2). Rather than contextualize the group's existence at that time, the note makes broad accusations. Further, it falsely records the stories of the U.S. troops' encounters with the guerrilla fighters. In later years, Major General John H. Russell accused the *cacos* of forcefully recruiting poor Haitians. He claimed: "For the poor class, revolutions were a diversion into which they were frequently forced against their wills. Thousands were taken from the field, tied together with ropes and sent to the nearest headquarters of the revolutionists. Whether they liked it or not, they went as 'recruits.' The message one officer sent to his headquarters was typical: 'Here are fifty volunteers, please send back the rope.'"[4] This reference actually describes how some of the U.S. troops obtained *corvée* workers in forceful ways. This was how U.S. troops corralled rural Haitians and kidnapped these people.

U.S. military records of them as "savage" foes, "lawless negroes," and "professional bandits," dismiss the *cacos* as apolitical agents.[5] For the marines, these fighters had to be renegades, vagabonds, peasants, nonelite, noneducated, and followers of a dynamic leader. To revert to the slave period, these willful myths are what slave owners and antiabolitionists used against Blacks: savage, barbarians, apolitical. Péralte could not be an orator *and* a revolutionary fighter. In these foreign military descriptions and defamations of the *cacos*, there are both truth and lies. Some *cacos* did come from the peasantry—those who fought for economic and political justice. Others were formally educated, such as Zamor and the Péralte brothers, or elite newspaper editors. They *were* renegades—against the invaders. Many of their leaders *were* dynamic, Benoît Batraville was a schoolteacher and an *houngan* (Vodou male priest). During the invasion, the *cacos* both behaved and misbehaved. Some, like Péralte, acted for Haiti's good. Others accepted deals with the invaders for employment and compensation. Some protected their fellow citizens, others terrorized their brothers and sisters—sometimes because they allied with the invaders.[6]

The longstanding misinterpretation of the *cacos'* importance stems from an unsurprising U.S. refusal to accord them agency. A pattern of dehumanizing Haitians who were asserting their right to freedom characterizes all colonial or imperialist narrative about them. Like their depictions of the Zapatistas, Sandinos, *gavilleros*, and Cuban insurgents, the U.S. images of these guerrilla fighters could never be revolutionary. For the marines, these "bandits" acted against democracy. Yet in fighting for their nation's sovereignty in Mexico, Nicaragua, Haiti, Cuba, and the Dominican Republic, these "bandits" spread democracy.

Some Haitians understand clearly that the foreign portrayal of the *cacos* got them wrong. For them, the *cacos* were not savages but freedom fighters who resisted political and economic wrongs. Péralte was not a bandit but a patriot. Batraville was not a vagabond but a Vodou practitioner. Rosalvo Bobo was a medical doctor who challenged the invasion, not a renegade. The positioning of the *cacos* as freedom fighters and those who worked for the good of their fellow citizen remains strong in Haitians' popular imagination in the twenty-first century. During my fieldwork, Haitians described Péralte and the *cacos* in laudatory terms. Their Péralte could do no wrong. His sacrifice in 1919 was one they fondly remembered during the nation's bicentennial in 2004 and onward. These perceptions of the *cacos* during the invasion era as political revolutionaries stand in direct contrast to the U.S. military's negative stereotypes of the guerrilla fighters.

My examination of the *cacos* during the invasion, and particularly during Péralte's leadership of the group, demonstrates that a colonial perspective often hinders a more accurate understanding of history. The guerrilla fighters' battles against the U.S. military was their symbolic defense of the Haitian Revolution. They defended what the 1802 *taccos* fought for during the wars for independence. Their *nasyonalis* agenda for a sovereign Haiti and their fight contradict the views of them as simply mercenaries and bandits. The *cacos* strategy of unifying Haitians from across classes in this fight posed a danger to the U.S. military. Under Péralte's leadership, a *caco* could derive from an elite family like his and their leaders could be of a type of "peasant stock" like the market women. During this revolt, Péralte involved peasant leaders like Adhémar Francismar and d'Estravil (or Estraville)[7] He also mobilized newspapermen, *cacos* spywomen, gendarmes, prison guards, and entrepreneurs like Turenne St. Juste and Louis Poux.

What Péralte's story and the people who joined his movement show is that the *cacos* during the invasion period were pro-Haiti and anti-imperialism. Though some argue that the *cacos* fought in a moment, I argue that the guerrilla fighters fought during the invasion *with hopes of an enduring change*. It was not their own limited vision or power that prevented revolutionary shifts. Rather the U.S. military's brutal assassinations and imprisonment of the *cacos* prevented the fighters' implementation of long-term plans. Thanks to their birth at a time of nation building for freedom, the *cacos* initiated a specifically Haitian cultural tradition. These fighters appear and reappear when needed, and then blend back into the state as ordinary citizens. This type of strategic engagement involves choice, planning, and vision. The fight of the *cacos* versus the U.S. military was visionary. These guerrilla fighters boldly formed armies with several camps and revolted against a global power from 1915 to 1922. They fought the foreigners without uniform, with bare feet, with munitions made of bamboo, and they sacrificed their bodies to defend what their predecessors had fought for generations before. The *cacos* were both laborers for and defenders of Haiti (Figure 3).

1915: Invasion and Immediate Resistance

Within the first months of the 1915 invasion, the U.S. military learned of the *cacos*' leader Pierre Benoît (P. B.) Rameaux. In the tradition of these guerrilla fighters, Rameaux incited his fellow Haitian males by invoking their revolution. He, like all the *cacos* leaders, not only viewed the invasion as a threat to their nation but also linked the *corvée* and the foreigners' presence to slavery. This linkage of their present reality with U.S. troops to their ancestors' history of bondage became a rallying cry and raison d'être for the revolt. While the chronology obviously differed, Péralte and Rameaux saw a continuation of justice between slavery and invasion. Rameaux lamented:

FIG. 3 *Cacos* chiefs, or generals, Haiti, about October 1915 (Reference Collection, Marine Corps History Division, Quantico, VA)

This is a solemn hour! The country of Toussaint L'Ouverture, of Dessalines, of Capoix, and all the others who sacrificed themselves to give us liberty is menaced. Mr. Dartiguenave possessed with ambition for power has assented to the Americans treading our soil as Masters—Fellow Citizens, under this insult given to the Nation, under the shame, which is brought to each one of us, are we to remain insensible? Have you forgotten the motto of 1804? Are you going to relinquish voluntarily this country, which was bequeathed to you at the price of such great sacrifice? No! Gentlemen before this slavery which menaces us as in the times of the Colony, the entire Nation, as one man, must arise to reclaim their outraged liberty, their violated independence.[8]

He positions the *cacos* as defenders of 1804, a direct comparison of the invasion to slavery. With the phrase "one man," he makes the invasion story into the story of men like himself, Péralte, and Batraville. Rameaux continues, now exhorting his listeners to act and instructing them how to do so:

Now away with parties, political opinions, hate, and rancor, lose no time. Forward. It is a common cause since it concerns the land of our birth. Let the Government, which seeks to establish itself on Haitien soil against the law of arbitration. Might makes right. Gentlemen each Haitien ought to feel the shame of seeing his cities occupied by Americans, soon it will be the entire country, that is to say slavery, which is worse than death. In the face of this situation all Haitiens loving their country, truly loving their liberty and their families ought to unite for the country, go directly to God, it is a most enviable fate. Young and old arm yourselves and fight to the last breath, thus you will die content and free, your sons will enjoy tomorrow the "liberty" which you would have acquired at the price of your blood the same as our ancestors.

Rameaux operated in this text as a general with his commands of "Forward, fight, and die content and free." For these *cacos*, their fight manifested as both a defense of 1804 and an offense against 1915. Their reminders to their fellow citizens baited Haitians with that recollection and thus unified them:

Then you will have accomplished the grandest of duties for it is the duty above all others: With these sentiments, dear fellow citizens let us all shout, Long Live Independence, Long Live Liberty, Long Live the Union of the Haitian Family.

Rameaux's instructions were typical of *cacos'* rhetorical strategy. He appealed to their conscience about Haiti's founding. He then bestowed Haitians with the duty of guarding this feat. To be a *caco*, one pledged to sacrifice one's life for the good of nation. The *cacos* reasoned that, just as Rameaux's and Péralte's generation inherited the victory of 1804, their offspring would benefit from the freedoms won through this revolution against the invasion. Additionally, for the *cacos*, unity was prudent. This is what Dessalines once envisioned. Haitians had to unite under their flag, irrespective of political opinions. Rameaux's commands convey an imagery of Haitians in military formation poised for battle.

And the *cacos* literally did develop a military plan based on the strategies of Haiti's earlier revolutionaries. Disturbance was one of their major tactics. Just as their forebears disrupted plantation production, the *cacos* interrupted commerce, trade, and railway construction. These guerrilla fighters saw that each of these areas cemented the U.S. forces' economic grip on Haiti. By disrupting these sites, they hastened the end of the invasion. Ironically, the *cacos'* disturbances of American wealth contributed to the U.S. idea of them as vagabonds and bandits. And yet, this vandalism articulated the *cacos'* political vision. Further, their attacks against U.S. forces were unrelenting. *Cacos'* battles were sometimes spread days apart or featured multiple battles in one day. The guerrilla fighters appointed generals and chiefs for each *cacos* unit. The soldiers developed a system of espionage that infiltrated the gendarmerie, the *corvée* system, and prisons. *Cacos* recruited men and women in these specific areas to advance their revolt. The strategy of joining the gendarmes would serve them well. It provided intelligence about the U.S. troops' cognizance of *cacos'* activities.

These protests tell the *cacos'* story, even if it was not articulated in a manifesto. The guerrilla fighters reasoned that railways benefited U.S. Americans while dispossessing Haitian peasants of their lands. Thus, in addition to fighting U.S. forces physically, the *cacos* deployed familiar approaches of the *mawons* and slaves—arson, destruction, and appeals. U.S. forces often reported that *cacos* engaged them around railway tracks. On September 21, 1915, for example, Caperton sent the following observations to the secretary of the navy: "When *Cacos* learned of preparations for opening railroad, they started firing and began destroying railroad tracks one-half to one and one-half miles outside of Gonaives."[9] Arson also became their modus operandi against the machinations of empire. This is precisely what revolutionary participants had employed from 1791 to 1803 against plantation and slave owners. The strategies of 1791–1803 became the *cacos*' weapons. They opened fire by battling the U.S. troops and they used literal fire to upend these foreign corporations. Also, just as L'Ouverture decried bondage and others promoted the ideals of freedom and equality in their pamphlets and travels abroad, *cacos* leaders like Péralte appealed to British and French ambassadors for the invasion's end. He wrote letters to U.S. president Wilson, and Haitian masons did the same, appealing for a free Haiti. The *cacos* unleashed overlapping and intersecting attacks on U.S. forces. Their tactics echoed their ancestors' earlier strategies.

Even the sites of early *cacos*' protests, mostly in the towns of Gonaïves, Hinche, and Cap-Haïtien, recalled the 1804 revolution. The mountainous central and northern areas—where the border between the Dominican Republic and Haiti was more porous—provided the *cacos* with an advantage over foreigners.[10] In August 1915, U.S. troops headed north to deal with the guerrilla fighters. *Le Nouvelliste* commented on the brewing *cacos* activity and reported: "We confirmed that two American boats left yesterday headed to the north with troops to proceed to disarm the northern region."[11] Rear Admiral Caperton once labeled the north as "*Cacos* country," specifically identifying the following areas: "Cape Haitien, Dondon, San Raphael, Pignon, Carice, Mont Organise, Ouanaminthe, and mouth of Massacre River."[12] In missives to the secretary of the navy, Rear Admiral Caperton commented on the size and locations of the guerrilla fighters. In one letter, he recorded "about 400 *Cacos* near Gonaives stopping trade from entering that town."[13] By fanning out across the north, the guerrilla fighters paid practical homage to their ancestors and it worked.

The year 1915 was difficult for the invaders and their daily reports demonstrated their preoccupation with the *cacos*. At first, the marines were optimistic. The Naval Landing Force Headquarters noted on August 10, 1915: "The attention of all officers and men is called to the necessity of treating the natives with the utmost kindness and consideration. It is most imperative that our men and officers create a good impression in the minds of the natives of this country.... A cheerful word, a friendly pat on the man's back or the horses' rump, goes far to vitiate the sting of humiliation and will do much to change the natural feeling of resentment to one of respect and friendship."[14] Haitians were aware of the United States' seizure of their state.

In fact, less than two months into the invasion, the commanding forces enacted martial law first in Port-au-Prince and Gonaïves.[15] The Haitian journal *La Plume* printed an appeal by Haitians who requested permission to work within the confines of this law. A Haitian doctor pleaded that medical professionals be allowed to respond to emergencies at night: "We know that circulation is permitted up to nine; ... For instance, might it not be agreed upon that doctors and midwives, and such persons of necessity who might be sent for during the night, could be allowed to pass unchallenged by carrying a lantern? We are perfectly sure that the American would not wish anyone to suffer or to die for want of medical attendance."[16] The doctor's request was an example that the *cacos* already posed a formidable threat, since they marked every Haitian as hostile. In 1915, the invaders declared that a "hostile" Haitian, that is, "any Negro or any dark person out of doors after 9 o'clock, whose behavior makes him seem like a sympathizer with *Caco* rebels, is to be shot on sight by the patrol if he does not surrender."[17] This broad description defined almost every Haitian as a threat. Because of this definition, many Haitians mistakenly died at the hands of U.S. troops. The next chapter addresses some of the crimes U.S. forces were charged with and acquitted of during this period. Already, U.S. troops recognized that *cacos* existed and "*cacos* sympathizers" were also present. Both those who fought and those who protected the guerrilla fighters are examples of Haitian resistance.

Despite their assertions that attempt to dismiss and diminish Haitian resistance, the U.S. forces employed several strategies for handling the *cacos*. They obsessively documented their interactions with the *cacos* and the guerrilla fighters' actions. On September 7, 1915, Rear Admiral Caperton reported on Rameaux's move: "Gonaives was reported 'uneasy,' and much excitement existing among the natives. Two hundred *Cacos* under Chief Rameau[x] were close to the town, and a detachment was landed from the *Castine* to reinforce the Seventh Company of Marines."[18] They used additional troops in select areas. On September 18, the U.S. soldiers noted, "a working party engaged in repairing a water main at Varigoa, near Cape Haitien, was fired on by the *Cacos*. Their fire was returned, and one *Caco* was killed and another severely wounded. The *Castine* landed men to support the marines."[19] The same day, shots were exchanged between the marines and the *cacos* near Gonaïves.[20] Read uncritically, these reports appear as mere notes. Yet these brief and persistent notations are rich with archival detail on how *cacos* protested. We see that these battles were a unified struggle for sovereignty. They were not isolated incidents but coordinated. The *cacos*' success forced the U.S. to unleash fiercer efforts to stop the fighters. The invaders negotiated with the *cacos* to surrender. One of the troops wrote:

> In northern Haiti the *Cacos* situation is becoming critical. Because of their leaders, who are endeavoring to obtain exorbitant bribes, these *cacos* will not come within our lines and surrender arms and will not be disbanded. ...

Liberal offer of fifteen gourdes per soldier and one hundred gourdes per chief have been made to pay for their rifles and to give them sufficient money to return to their homes; but the offers were not accepted. In Cape Haitien, these *Cacos* have again begun infesting Cape Haitien and are preventing market people and foodstuffs entering. As recommended in my radiogram 16029, I believe that furnishing work on railroad construction in the vicinity of Cape Haitien might induce many men desert their chiefs and go to work.... Unless prompt measures are taken I shall be forced to consider very soon offensive operations against these *cacos*.[21]

His dehumanizing language when describing the *cacos* as an infestation also informs us about the guerrilla fighters' spread and force in numbers across several departments in the nation. Additionally, the military's discussions about employment communicates its conceptions and misconceptions of the *cacos* as being only from the underemployed class.

By September 20, the escalating resistance forced Caperton to almost triple his offer for the *cacos*' capitulation: fifty thousand gourdes to each one thousand *cacos* "who would proceed to Cape Haitien, or other ports, and surrender 1,000 service rifles and ammunition to the American forces within a given period."[22] On September 29, in a meeting at Cap, Colonel L.W.T. Waller, representing the U.S. and the Haitian governments, signed a two-part agreement with two *cacos* chiefs, General Antoine Morency and General Jean Baptiste Pétion (Figure 4).[23]

The two-part treaty suggests that the foreigners viewed the *cacos* as a political group. They would not engage in treaty discussion with "mere bandits." In part one, the *cacos*' chiefs promised to disarm, and if they were found with arms, they would be "treated as bandits." The second stipulation named the threats the *cacos* posed to various industries in Haiti. It reads: "*Caco* Chiefs and men to go to their homes, not to oppose in arms the present Government of Hayti, not to interfere with the railroads, commerce, agriculture, and industries of the county."[24] In another proviso, the governmental representatives granted the *cacos* chiefs access to Haitian politics. It states: "*Caco* Chiefs agree to send delegation to Port au Prince to consult and confer with the Dartiguenave Government concerning participation in the Civil Government of Hayti and to abide by such terms as may be agreed upon."[25] That specific provision records the U.S. soldiers' early cognizance and acceptance that the *cacos* would remain a force.

In part two, Waller agreed to grant amnesty to *cacos* who relinquished their weapons. Part two concluded with the following: "That when practicable *Cacos* who have observed Part One, may have representation in such Constabulary or Police as may or be organized in Hayti."[26] Given the number of *cacos* who already worked as gendarmes and prison guards, it is probable that the guerrilla fighters used this particular provision to further their anti-invasion movement.

FIG. 4 Colonel Littleton W. T. Waller, USMC, Commander of Marine Expeditionary Forces in Haiti, negotiating with Haitian *cacos* leaders, including Charlemagne Péralte, October 1915 (Reference Collection, Marine Corps History Division, Quantico, VA)

A prime example was Charles Zamor, who witnessed the signing of this peace accord. Zamor was a Revolutionary Committee member and *caco*, and he served as a liaison between U.S. troops and the Haitian resisters. At one time, Caperton hinted in a letter to Captain E. H. Durell that he had suspicions about Zamor. Explaining that the marines had given Zamor a letter that granted him permission to travel throughout Haiti and that also advised Caperton to supervise his whereabouts, Caperton wrote to Durrell: "His activity in Haitian politics you are probably well aware of. He is a strong force in the north, and if he will use his influence for peace and order, he will be of valuable aid. I desire that he be given the necessary protection within the limits of your command. I suggest you keep a good watch on him and see if he carries out his assurances."[27] The invaders were right. Zamor used his position as an intermediary for the *cacos'* good.

The treaty negotiations between the *cacos* leaders and U.S. military also demonstrate the diversity of the *cacos'* ideas and strategies. As part of a *nasyonalis* movement, the leaders and fighters engaged in multiple strategies against imperialism. Some fought until their deaths while others, as in this treaty, negotiated with the invaders. These instances allow room for us to expand our thinking about who comprised the *cacos* and how they fought through military and other means. Both fight and flight were complex protest acts that go beyond a simple framework of passive versus aggressive. The acts were both assertive and aggressive in dealing with a combative and racially tense United States invasion. In a similar vein, we can see some *cacos*' apparent complicity with the U.S. military as simply *a* strategy among many *cacos*' plans. Some, weary of incessant battles, opted to surrender. The *cacos* who surrendered chose to no longer battle on their own terms with this treaty. That complicity when reframed as a *choice* is an act of resistance.

Despite this agreement between the U.S. government and the *cacos*, the following months of October and November were replete with *cacos* attacks.[28] In Grande Rivière, they fired on U.S. soldiers in the Thirteenth Company on October 20. Four days later, hundreds of *cacos* attacked U.S. soldiers stationed in the Bahon area. Major Smedley Butler described this event to Colonel Cole:

> Arrived at Le Valliere 11 a.m. [October] 26. After dark, evening of 24, while command was crossing river in deep ravine, suddenly fired upon by about 400 *Cacos* in bushes 100 yards from fort; one horse killed. Fought our way forward to good position and remain there for night surrounded by *Cacos*, who kept up continuous but poorly aimed fire. We returned fire only when necessary to repel their actual advances toward us. Owing to our good position, no men or horses injured during night. At daybreak three squads in charge of Capt. Upshur, Lieut. Ostermann, and Sergt. Daly, which had been covering our position during the night, advanced in three different directions. Eight *Cacos* killed, and 10 wounded; this number verified. Many more reported; Pvt. Fredericks slight flesh wound left arm. Upshur and Ostermann advancing from two directions captured Dipotie, with a total of 13 Marines, putting garrison to flight. Demolished and burned fort; all three squads burned all houses from which fire had been coming.[29]

From this letter, we learn that the *cacos*' resistance erupted in everyday life. They used the cover of darkness and the nation's forts to their favor. Both shielded them from the military to the point where this particular battle lasted all evening and resulted in the soldiers' destruction of these forts. If the *cacos* were "poorly armed," why did U.S. soldiers not advance toward the fighters with ease? Also, Butler's observation that the fighters' gunshots came from homes attests to the *cacos*' wide distribution. They and their fellow citizens hid in plain sight. Rather than arrest those suspected of endangering their lives, the U.S. troops burned these homes. For this battle, U.S. troops—like Captain William P. Upshur—later received commendations for their "conspicuous gallantry."[30] The United States made legal its illegal seizure of a Caribbean nation while the First World War operated in the background. Further, they elevated themselves as defenders and made bandits Haitians who defended their state. The U.S. military strategy of managing anti-imperialist resistance in Puerto Rico, Cuba,

Guam, the Philippines, Dominican Republic, Nicaragua, and Haiti offers a blue-print of absolution and self-righteousness. The U.S. military excused its behavior, killed resistors, and then rewarded itself for both of these crimes.

Moreover, the U.S. forces kept heavy surveillance on the *cacos*. For instance, they noted on October 23: "Our Marines in Hayti have been busy this past week in responding vigorously to attacks from rebels, and quite a number of the latter have been killed."[31] In the same report, we learn there were other attacks on October 25 and 28. In another note, U.S. forces wrote: "All reports show gathering of *Cacos* at Capois and neighborhood" on October 29.[32] The next day Caperton directed Waller to treat these "Cacos as bandits . . . to take active measures to suppress them," and keep this plan secret to prevent the *cacos'* escape into the mountains.[33] *Cacos* armies continued their relentless attack on the U.S. soldiers with assaults on November 2, 4, and 5.

The United States advertised minimal loss on its end and heavy casualties and deaths of the *cacos*. Its descriptions attempt to dismiss the results of the battles as one-sided when they were not. One of my interviewees assessed this discrepancy: "history in itself is true, but those writing history can flounder. They do not give truly how many Marines died, they always show you the other, and a way to psychologically hold the population to show the force was strong. If ten Marines died, they would say one, or that there were injuries."[34]

The U.S. forces responded aggressively. Oftentimes the death of one U.S. soldier escalated the U.S. military's brutal tactics against all Haitians. U.S. patrols attacked several *cacos* in Forts Selon and Berthol, and near Capois. On November 9, Colonel Waller communicated with Rear Admiral Caperton that: "All houses in *Caco* country now displaying white flags, and people say they have had enough; no ammunition and leaders have fled."[35] Were these houses of *cacos* fighters or those who protected them? Either way, the image and, more importantly, the idea of *cacos* neighborhoods supports the idea that the guerrilla fighters were organized, widespread, and effective.

Despite reports of this alleged surrender, fights between *cacos* and U.S. forces occurred daily, from November 10 through November 12. Another notable battle ensued on November 17. Colonel Cole wrote to Colonel Waller, narrating the U.S. soldiers' capture of Fort Rivière.

> Capture of Fort Rivière affected by four columns. . . . All companies were in their position at time specified and Butler and Low's company made the assault supported by five other companies. . . . Twenty-nine killed there and 22 jumped parapets, but all were killed by fire from the automatics, all avenues of escape being blocked. Forty-seven rifles and considerable ammunition found in fort after capture. . . . The fact that this fort was taken without a single casualty on our side speaks worlds for the ability and good judgment of all officers concerned. Have sent to the cape for dynamite to destroy fort, as its complete destruction by blowing up will have great moral effect.[36]

The forts built in the 1800s to defend Haiti's independence became sites of Haitians' fight against imperialism. Dessalines and Christophe ordered them built precisely because of this encounter with hostile global powers. The *cacos* used their ancestors' forts with practicality and intention. They harbored their camps and fought foreigners. The invaders blew them up in order to do away with *cacos* resistance, even as they promoted themselves as helping to build Haiti.

Public displays of power became another U.S. strategy. For their actions during this specific attack, several soldiers—including Lieutenant Colonel Smedley Butler, First Sergeant Ross L. Iams, and Corporal Samuel Gross—received awards for their "conspicuous coolness and bravery in entering Fort Rivière at the head of the attacking force, when such action on his part seemed almost certain to result in his being killed or wounded."[37] Colonel Cole's decision to blow up forts and the public commendations they received for these acts, were all part of this violent spectacle of U.S. control. These methods of grandeur contradicted the U.S. military's depiction of the guerrilla fighters as not effective. U.S. forces deluded themselves about the *cacos* and their attempts to dismiss the guerrilla fighters.

The *cacos* continued their attacks on the invaders during the final month of 1915. Battles erupted on December 4, 6, 12, and 21. In one note to the State Department, Caperton acknowledged that his forces had not subdued Haitian resistance. He advised maintaining troop levels: "In view of present unsettled relations between United States and Haiti and necessity of maintaining present military control of situation until appointments under modus vivendi are made . . . I recommend that marine force now ashore in Haiti be not reduced at this time beyond detachment of Twelfth Company."[38] As of December 31, 1915, the U.S. soldiers totaled ninety officers and 1,846 enlisted marine corpsmen. The *cacos* battled the foreign troops through year's end.

1916: *Cacos* Continue

In 1915, Caperton hoped for the *cacos*' end in 1916. In a report dated January 3, he concluded that the United States had already achieved it: "Colonel Waller, during the operations of October and November in north Haiti, with the expeditionary force of Marines and the seamen from the squadron, effectively crushed all armed resistance to the American invasion and the Haitian Government, and has maintained peace and order in all parts of the country."[39] Given the *cacos*' activities during December, Caperton's report was erroneous and hasty. In fact, U.S. forces greeted their second year in Haiti by uncovering a plot. They later reported in the *Army and Navy Journal*:

> Disturbance Wednesday morning, Jan. 6, at Port-au-Prince was part of well-organized plot covering Port-au-Prince, Les Cayes, and Southern Hayti in general. Those engaged belonged to black party as distinguished from mulatto.

FIG. 5 Haitian *cacos* revolutionary leader, General M. Codio. Archives record that he "asks to be shot," March 1916. (Reference Collection, Marine Corps History Division, Quantico, VA)

Leaders in Port-au-Prince were Pierre Paul, Misaelcodio, Pradel, Annabel Hilaire, and Philogene. Latter three have been captured with several other minor leaders and have been confined. Pierre Paul and Misaelcodio escaped. It appears that this movement was made in favor of former Senator Paulin or Bourand for President. Plot contemplated assassination of President. Northern Haiti entirely quiet and does not seem to be concerned in this affair. No cause for alarm. Situation well in hand.[40]

The guerilla fighters were growing in strength given their activities in southern and central Haiti. Also, the *cacos'* leadership spread out. The presence of *cacos* chiefs in these new regions sounded an alarm for U.S. forces accustomed to the battles up north. On January 6, *cacos* led by Missal Dodio (sometimes listed as Misael Codio or Misaelcodio) and others attacked local authorities in Port-au-Prince.[41]

U.S. forces responded swiftly. This time they enacted a new strategy for eliminating the *cacos* problem—prison. On March 21, the U.S. provost court sentenced Missal Dodio to fifteen years' hard labor for "conspiracy against the Republic of Haiti and the United States forces" (Figure 5).[42] They sentenced Exileu Codio, another *cacos* leader, to three years for conspiring with Dodio, aiding in his escape, and conspiracy.[43] They charged Jean Benoît with conspiracy and collecting weapons, and they sentenced him to six years of hard labor. The use of prisons to punish Haitian agitators would prove to be a double-edged sword for the U.S. forces. Haitians often used them as another hub of organization against the United States.

The year 1916 was one of escalating *cacos* battles. On March 6, 1916, the *cacos* spread their wings wide. Rather than just one battle, the *cacos* now engaged the

U.S. forces at least twice a day *and* in different locations. On March 9, for example, *cacos* fired at troops in Le Trou, Limonade, and Acul Samedi. On March 11, two *cacos* camps repeated this attack pattern at Ranquitte and St. Michale. On that same day, the secretary of the navy radioed Caperton, instructing him to "relinquish no part of military control which you are now exercising in Haiti, nor without receipt of further instructions, put [an] end to martial law as now in force."[44] The instruction to the soldiers to not relinquish control of Haiti to either the *cacos* or other Haitians shows the guerrilla fighters' success. They were a formidable threat.

The means of U.S. control of Haiti was the antithesis of free will and free governance. In one example, in a message dated March 13, Caperton stated: "the total shore forces in Haiti amounted to not more than 1,700 enlisted men and stated that it was not considered practicable to maintain military control of the country with a smaller force, and that the strength could not be reduced by a single unit without greatly prejudicing the control and prestige of the United States in Haiti."[45] Caperton's concern rested with the image of his troops and ultimately his nation. Very few of the troops' records during this time discussed the United States' remaining in Haiti for the betterment of Haitians. The troops' behavior certainly contrasted sharply with the stated ideals for the invasion. In *Taking Haiti*, Mary Renda has researched well and argued against the culture and practice of toxic White masculinity. She writes that these soldiers used their privilege as foreigners and white men to intimidate Haitians.

But the *cacos* did not care and pledged their lives for their nation's and citizens' freedoms. They remained relentless during March. On March 16, they attacked Caracol. Eight days later, U.S. forces reported the escape of seventeen prisoners from a prison at Fort Liberté. A brutal *cacos* attack ensued on March 28 at Cerca-la-Source. The guerrilla fighters ambushed the area and they killed the Haitian gendarme Private Ducas Colbert. They brandished machetes and left their fellow Haitian in pieces. The same *cacos* army attacked gendarmes at Castellieur. The *cacos*' targeting of the gendarmes was no surprise. The gendarmerie was the institution charged with managing Haitian resistance. The presence of Haitians who worked for the invaders infuriated the *cacos*. They conceived of the Haitians in the gendarmerie as traitors and enemies of the state. The mutilation of Ducas was the most violent of the *cacos*' warnings to the Haitians who had allied with U.S. officials. *Cacos* armies ended that month's actions on March 29, when they *simultaneously* attacked La Mielle, Cerca-la-Source, and Acul Samedi.[46]

On May 30, 1916, over 500 prisoners escaped the National Penitentiary in Port-au-Prince. The U.S. military blamed *cacos* leader Antoine Pierre-Paul who was not present at the prison for this bold, collective act. Some had fled to the mountains in the back of the capital while others sought refuge in sewers. The image and example of 500 Haitians escaping prison and engaging all the *cacos* tools (flight, hiding in plain sight, and crossing the border into the Dominican Republic) were glaring. The U.S. military shot, killed, rounded up, and reimprisoned those whom they found. Furthermore, they court-martialed the Haitian gendarmes who had failed at their prison guard duties. They called these men cowards and analyzed their weakness as a "lamentable lack of courage."[47] The 1916 prison break embarrassed the U.S. military. It was an example of their lack of control over Haitian resistance. A *caco* not imprisoned directed a successful prison break. They questioned whether the gendarmes were in cahoots with these *cacos*. The guerrilla fighters were sophisticated and working together.

The prison break helps explain why the U.S. military established a secret service. These men (it is not known if they were Haitians, U.S. Americans, or both) spied on Haitian citizens, especially politicians and the police. In their report during the formative period of the invasion from 1915 to 1920, they disclosed that this secret service "reported on plots and if necessary, fomented plots to report." U.S. government and banking officials had done this before in the years leading up to the invasion. Their secret service fits with the whole illegal and disorderly seizure of Haiti. It is almost expected that they would have an intelligence wing. This move acknowledged the power of the *cacos*. Back home they spied on the National Association for the Advancement of Colored People (NAACP), the Universal Negro Improvement Association (UNIA), other civil rights groups, and nonpolitical citizens. Thus, it is not a surprise that they enacted this method under their empire in the Caribbean. However, the report does not disclose the result of this unit. Of note, the ambiguous "foment plots" absolves them of blame while also making them culpable.

Continuing during the month of May, Haitian protests erupted in various forms. On May 6, *Le Nouvelliste* editors asked pointedly whether the invasion was Haiti's humiliation, rhetorically inviting readers to reflect on the invasion's purpose.[48] As they raised the question during the month when Haitians celebrate Flag Day, one has to wonder if this was also the editors' act of protest. Were they inciting Haitians to revolt to force the invasion's end? Given the U.S. surveillance of Haitian newspapers, their question was necessarily subtle and deliberate. It communicated their frustrations with their reality *and* invited proud Haitians to respond. The following day, some Haitians lit fires, and the gendarmes threatened to arrest them and banned arson. Similarly, during the revolution (from 1791 to 1803), slave owners had banned the use of fire, perceiving arson as a threat to their economic profits (humans, plantations, and commodities like coffee). That same month, the gendarmes reported they had completed the road from Les Cayes to Port-au-Prince. While they did not mention the work of Haitian laborers, it was they who worked arduously. Despite its previous bans, the *corvée* remained in effect. The *corvee*'s persistence was itself violent, part of the humiliation that the *Le Nouvelliste* editors inquired about. Their people were dying and imprisoned under imperialism.

Toward the midpoint of 1916, U.S. forces reported on another escalating problem: prisoners who fled. Colonel Waller communicated with the secretary of the navy that their soldiers were constantly pursuing political prisoners who escaped. The *cacos* had devised a system to free themselves from prison. In some cases, they escaped on their own. In other instances—such as Péralte—they partnered with *cacos* masquerading as gendarmes and prison guards, fleeing with their assistance.

Both in and out of prison, the *cacos* were a thorn in the side of U.S. soldiers. On June 3, an expedition of two sets of U.S. troops landed in Croix-des-Bouquets and Port-au-Prince to deal with the battling guerrilla fighters. Haitian resistance had reached a boiling point. Now the French minister offered to send another French ship to the capital to aid the United States, joining its cruiser *Descartes* already stationed there. Colonel Waller declined the French offer, but Haitians were cornered by a former colonizer and an imperial power. Haitians' range of protests, including fight and flight was sensible.

Gendarmes vs. *Cacos*

A year into the invasion, U.S. troops cemented their military status in Haiti. They prohibited the press and the carrying of weapons. The United States designated the gendarmerie as head of operations against the *cacos*, with Major Smedley Butler in command. Butler proved all too eager to "hunt the *cacos* down."[49] After one battle, he boasted that the *cacos* were "baying like bloodhounds all through the bushes."[50] These casual comments reveal the racist attitudes of these troops. Despite their physical control of the nation, however, they could not control Haitians, especially the guerrilla fighters.

The soldiers held many conceptions of the *cacos*. In 1915, for example, Caperton acknowledged the revolutionary component of the guerrilla fighters. In a message to the secretary of the navy, Caperton declared: "This last movement of *Cacos* appears to have been of a revolutionary nature against the present government and the American occupation as well as brigandage. While petty brigandage will continue from time to time, yet it is hoped, that no more such organized brigandage or revolutionary activities will occur."[51] Yet, Caperton also conceptualized the fighters as "bandits purely and simply, owning no allegiance to the Government or any political faction, but organized under petty chiefs for the sole purpose of stirring up strife against the Government and robbing, pillaging, and murdering innocent people."[52] In 1916, Colonel Waller presented what had become the dominant perception of the group. He stated: "It must be explained that the *Cacos* have been the controlling element in all revolutions. They were purchased by first one candidate and then another. Finishing a contract with one man, they, having put him in power, would immediately sell their services to the next aspirant to unseat the first."[53] Early in the invasion, we see the contrasting conceptions of the *cacos* as either bandit or a revolutionary element. For the foreigners, both were bad.

The U.S. troops' disavowal of the *cacos*' political agency was not without precedent. The United States later harbored similar misconceptions about the *gavilleros* in the Dominican Republic, the Zapatistas in Mexico, and the Sandinistas in Nicaragua. U.S. soldiers' musings—especially during the latter half of the U.S. presence in Haiti—illustrate how U.S. forces denied the ideas and actions of Bobo, Zamor, Batraville, and the Revolutionary Committee. Despite the *cacos'* printed critiques about the invasion and battles with the foreigners, U.S. administrators failed to connect the *cacos'* resistance to the U.S. invasion, Dartiguenave's election, the 1915 treaty, the *corvée* system, the 1918 constitution, prison construction, and restrictive legislation.

The word "banditry" is loaded. It can be political in that it describes political agitation from the ground upward. And yet, the term is depoliticized in that it is framed as reckless strife and it includes the people causing the said conflict. Some have falsely distinguished between banditry and revolutionary action based on who constitutes the movement and how it begins. They assess whether it derives from people in power at the top or if the protest swells from the bottom. Yet a political movement, whether originating from the top down or the bottom up, is still a movement. When soldiers outfitted with uniforms and in orderly regiments are seen as civilized soldiers while those armed with pikes and machetes are not, there is a problem, as it dictates who can be a revolutionary. For example, let us compare Péralte's actions with those of Theodore Roosevelt. Both were learned men who fought for their nation and for their conception of liberty. The U.S. military defamed Péralte as a bandit and praised Roosevelt as a hero. The latter acted as a bandit and seized Cuba in 1898. Péralte donned his suit and civilian clothing, and yet the U.S. military classified him as a bandit and photographed him nearly nude at the time of his death. The image of Roosevelt on the other hand, with his Brooks Brothers uniform and his Rough Rider regimentals as he invaded Cuba, was seen as an orderly image of democracy.

The term "bandit" is pejorative. It strips meaning from the *cacos* movement. These Haitian guerrilla fighters fought against one of the most powerful global powers at the time. The *cacos* were political actors who dared to articulate a vision of unity and acted for their freedom. During this war, the *cacos* wrote their protest, blew up railway tracks, and assassinated foreigners and their allies. They behaved as revolutionary fighters. The continuous disavowal and defamation of them as vagabonds and bandits, in the pejorative sense, is erroneous. These revolutionaries fought the troops from beginning to end.

Most scholars erroneously date the *cacos'* struggles as 1915–1920, or from the beginning of the invasion to Péralte's and Batraville's deaths. Yet the fight continued despite their assassinations through 1922. References to the *cacos* in later years allows us to consider how the fighters shaped Haitian resistance throughout the invasion. As late as 1930, the U.S. misconception and disavowal about the *cacos* continued. In *Haiti Under American Control, 1915–1930*, Arthur C. Millspaugh, an adviser from the State Department's Office of Foreign Trade, characterized the *cacos* as "peasants . . . stimulated by race hatred and by propaganda against the Government and Americans," engaging in a "recrudescence of lawless violence."[54] Similar depictions of the *cacos* litter the earlier U.S. historiography on the invasion. The U.S. military's description of the guerrilla fighters also correlates with the depictions of enslaved Africans fighting for freedom in 1791–1803. Despite the slaves' success in establishing a movement toward abolition and national independence, European and U.S. discourse turned to the bloodbath that occurred. It was not about the recrudescence of slave owners' violence on slaves but on oppressed beings revolting against Whites. The same shift occurs during the invasion. It becomes about White death rather than the violent act of invading a Black nation. However, the *cacos*' battles from 1915 to 1922 kept this issue at the forefront. As long as the marines were present, *cacos* were as well.

As the head of the gendarmes, Butler embarked on a campaign to end the guerrilla fighters. Although the invaders described it as a pacification initiative, their violent interactions unfolded as what Dantès Bellegarde noted, was "a campaign of terror and massacre."[55] In September 1916, Butler organized one hundred gendarmes to penetrate the northern *cacos*' area. He set out on a three-week trek through northern Haiti and the Dominican borderlands, where the gendarmes fought the guerrilla fighters. Both sides suffered casualties, and both sides celebrated victories. *Cacos* killed marines, and when the gendarmes captured these fighters, they either killed or imprisoned them.[56] This trek marked the end of what some label the First Cacos War. Despite this notation though, the reality is that the *cacos*' fight continued passed 1916, especially across the border in the Dominican Republic.

Dominican Republic and Transnational Alliances

The Dominican Republic was influenced by these conflicts. U.S. troops invaded Haiti's neighbor from 1916 to 1924. While the United States governed Haiti through a chosen government, in the Dominican Republic command was explicitly in the hands of the marines. Like the Haitian resistance, Dominican protest also included physical and intellectual dimensions. The *gavilleros*, the guerrilla fighters in the Dominican Republic, waged a similar liberation struggle. Given the proximity of Haiti to the Dominican Republic, their similar experiences under the invasion, and the existence of guerrilla groups on both sides, it is not surprising that the *cacos* and the *gavilleros* united.[57] Further, the *gavilleros* have also been defamed as mere peasants and bandits.

Historian Bruce Calder has commented on the presence of Haitians among the *gavilleros*.[58] Additionally, in their reports on Haiti, U.S. troops often commented on transports of arms and rebels along the Dominican and Haitian border. In 1915, for example, U.S. troops kept surveillance on Pierre Pinede (who used the alias Pedro Pineda). Pinede was a resident of the Haitian city Cerca-la-Source and held command of Vallières.[59] He became suspicious to Captain Hooker when they found him with "70 rifles belonging to a Dominican hidden near Cerca La."[60] Pinede's multiple surnames and his collaboration with Dominicans reveal a transnational alliance against the United States. Moreover, U.S. Marines' telegrams from 1918 also noted *cacos* who traveled to and from the Dominican border. In 1919, the U.S. Marines documented the capture of *cacos* in the Dominican town of Elías Pina.[61]

This coalition is important to emphasize especially given the contentious Dominican and Haitian relations that ensued after the invasion. In 1937, when Dominican president Rafael Trujillo ordered Haitians and darker-skinned Dominicans assassinated, people recalled that during the invasion the U.S. military trained him as part of their National Guard to extinguish the *gavilleros*. At the time, U.S. troops partnered with the Dominican Guardia Nacional, whose members crossed the border to assist marines in their assassinations of Haitian "bandits" in 1919.[62] When Trujillo seized power, his racist, sexist, and violent reign affected his citizens and Haitians.

It is important to trace the Haitian and Dominican collaboration that had existed since the colonial Spanish and French carving up of Hispaniola in 1697. Both nationalities allied during this colonial period and continue these alliances today, even in the face of volatile racial moments. The invasion of both nations highlights one of the epochs when citizens of both countries collaborated against the U.S. empire.

Given Péralte's previous political post in the Dominican Republic, it is possible that he collaborated with the *gavilleros* when he led the *cacos*. Jan Lundius and Mats Lundhal contend that Péralte had a Dominican mistress and that one of his devoted followers was from the Dominican Republic.[63] Péralte's stepson, in an interview, also confirmed that this person warned him against Jean-Baptiste Conzé, the man who betrayed Péralte and the *cacos*. His stepson recalled:

> In that era, Charlemagne Péralte ... Jean Conzé sent a letter to him, and he asked for Charlemagne Péralte to meet him at Grande Rivière. . . .
> Do you know the name of the Spanish person? I forgot. The memory is going.
> Was he born in the Dominican Republic? Yes, in Santo Domingo.[64]

His words further corroborate the marines' records about the Dominican and Haitian alliance against U.S. soldiers. In 1921, marines reported that bandit leaders had migrated to the Dominican Republic. In 1922, the provost marshal of the marines in the Dominican Republic arrested 100 guerrillas and reported that "fourteen had French names, and later that year, four more 'Haitian-French' fighters surrendered in the Dominican Republic."[65]

Despite reports that the First Cacos War had ended Haitian resistance, the guerrilla fighters remained active. In November 1915, a soldier told his colleague, General McLean, that he had concerns about the tension raised by the *cacos*. He stated: "Don't think I am a hudu, voodu, scary baby or have cold feet . . . but I do not want our officers to fall down on their job, nor do I want any good American blood to be shed."[66] His note reveals the fear that *cacos* aroused among some U.S. soldiers. Another note, by Captain Henry S. Knapp, issued a proclamation that forbade the carrying of concealed weapons or printed matter that expressed views of a "violent or inflammatory nature or that will tend to encourage the hostility or resistance to the Military Government."[67] Knapp's proclamations elucidate the ongoing Haitian resistance that still persisted.

1917: *Cacos* Remain

Two years into the invasion, the battles with the *cacos* remained incessant. U.S. soldier Faustin Wirkus explained their persistent presence: "The more I have learned about the *Cacos*, the less I have found that they deserved to be called bandits, or habitual criminals. They have always seemed to me to be foraging revolutionaries rather than brigands; men who would rather steal than starve, but rather work honestly for wages than steal. . . . The battle of the opposition against the established government is to them a battle of right against wrong. The red badge is in itself a declaration of a holy war against oppression."[68] Although his points acknowledge that *cacos* might have a genuine cause for revolution, Wirkus's musings fit with the idea that the guerrilla fighter was a peasant and needed employment. This type of rationale was common among the U.S. soldiers. Unfortunately, it did not allow for them to account for the diversity within the *cacos* fighters, nor does it account for the multiplicity of reasons they fought for economic and political sovereignty.

His comment about the red badge suggests that the *cacos* outfitted themselves with red. I have not found a mention of military attire among the group. Also, given that red is associated with the Vodou *lwa* (spirit force) of Legba, this hints at their religious practice of this African Caribbean religion.[69] In many drumming circles in Haiti today and in conversations among clergy, it is reported that Péralte and Batraville were Voduizan. Perhaps Péralte used his religion to appeal to fellow fighters and perhaps they used the red badge as a symbol of Legba. During Haiti's revolution, Vodou played a key role. It would not be surprising if elements of the religion may have been included in Haitians' fight against imperialists.[70] Also, the red could be because the Tacco bird was a red-plumed trogon.

There were common themes in U.S. soldiers' reports to the State Department. On one hand, some claimed that they were in full control. Yet these telegrams exposed this deception. In April 1917, the brigade commander Eli K. Cole asked the State Department for additional reinforcements: "In regard to the military situation, as you know, we have not enough American soldiers available to do more than put up a good bluff, but the smallness of the force is an invitation to propaganda, and while I do not anticipate any trouble, the Haitian is so unstable, one can never tell what he may try to do under the influence of disaffected persons. . . . I am glad to get the one or two extra companies at this time, for it will show the people here that we are increasing the force."[71] If U.S. forces were indeed keeping Haitian resisters at bay, there would be no need to put on a "good bluff" nor for additional marines. On May 25, 1917, the *cacos* and U.S. forces fought at Grosse Roche. Two days later, Brigadier General Cole reiterated that "the number of white troops at present in this country is entirely inadequate in case anything goes wrong. And while I hope everything will go well, it is neither advisable nor safe to reduce our forces as has been done."[72] His note about White troops distinguished them from Haitian gendarmes. Despite the fact that they created the gendarmes, and trained and supervised the officers, the U.S. military distrusted them. The mistrust was perhaps valid given the number of gendarmes who were *cacos* or who defected to that cause. During this time, the British chargé d'affaires also revealed to Cole his angst about anti-U.S. propaganda coming from Haitians.[73] And yet the troops promoted themselves as managing the resistance well.

Another example of this ambivalent message of being "in control" can be found in a letter to Admiral Knapp on July 19, 1917. He reported on a plot to overthrow the invasion, but then he reassured Knapp that his forces managed resistance:

> Had a report today to the effect that there was an attempt being made to arrange a plot throughout Haiti, to be directed against the Occupation and the Gendarmerie: this report was made by a secret service agent who is employed from Naval funds, and my own opinion is that it is not well founded, being similar to reports that have been received off and on for the last two years. . . . He has given the names of quite a number of people and as some of them were supposed to be quite strong American sympathizers, it will cause us to exercise a certain amount of surveillance of the people not heretofore suspected. My own opinion is, and it is confirmed from practically all parts of the country, that our influence throughout the country and among the vast majority of the people is decidedly paramount, and that the American Officers of the Occupation and of the Gendarmerie have gained, and are continuing to gain, the strongest sort of a hold over the people.[74]

The U.S. military deployed various tactics, including spying in their battles against the *cacos*. This surveillance soon extended to everyone. The United States kept a chart on Haitian citizens in the north, south, and central areas, including Jacmel, Léogâne, Lascahobas, and Trou. In these charts, U.S. forces noted if a Haitian was "not opposed to Occupation; absolutely with the Occupation; not opposed to Gendarmerie; or absolutely with Gendarmerie."[75]

Captain McLean knew that with the *cacos*, more troubled times loomed ahead. Indeed, as Wirkus had mused, the *cacos* struggle was a holy war. It certainly was that for Charlemagne and his brothers who pledged their lives to the anti-invasion struggle.

Madame Masséna Péralte and her son

Charlemagne's mother knew that her only son and other children were steeped in the *cacos* movement. She surely knew that U.S. forces intercepted and monitored her correspondence with them. In her missives, she appeared merely to discuss everyday life in Hinche. Yet, in her motherly advice to Péralte, Madame Masséna counseled her son to act bravely. While this letter was undated, details indicate that he still held his post in Léogâne at the time of her writing. His *maman* advised:

> You weigh things to see what you should do. You are a politician. It is not for me to tell you facts upon facts. You see the situation. Only it is for you to know what you should do in order not to be arrested (*et pour n'etes pas sur la main*) like President Oreste. Take care of yourself. Keep always ready. Be on the lookout for whatever may turn up to know the road you should follow for that particular situation. I do not know if it is true if their gentleman has left. I do not know if it is propaganda. It is not official news. If you hear that all the North is in movement, you know what to do, and if you hear nothing you will remain peaceably in your place. God alone, who knows. But lay low (*placez vous*) and get information from all the country.[76]

Her words offer caution and wisdom. She trusts Charlemagne and supports his decision to fight or be still, either way. And yet Madame Masséna also reports on local activities. She keeps him apprised of the movement and requests that he make an informed choice with her comment "get information from all the country." Her letters are a rare find and a rich source. As I lament the lack of women's voices in this invasion story, here we have a record of the mother of the most celebrated *caco*. While the marines' translations of her letter are imperfect, its preservation is remarkable! Madame Masséna speaks as her son acts for Haiti.

In a subsequent, undated missive, she informed Charlemagne that she knew that the Péralte brothers were *cacos* fighters. Madame Masséna wrote:

> You are more "*au courrant*" than I and are nearer the town. You can see how things are going (marching, advancing). You have intelligence (reports, news) to know what you should do post (inform) yourself well to see how the things are going (advancing, marching). I have heard that all these big men (*grans messieurs*) of Port-au-Prince have left, investigate (inform) yourself well to see if this true (real). We have no communication with the North. Everyone here has doubts, and Saint-Remy has already left. You keep out (*vous mettez votre personne a L'ecart*). Do not hurry to enter into anything, because we do not know the mind of the North, and everyone is bursting out (*deborder*) against the whites. No one accepts this condition. They are saying they would rather rebel than be under the white orders (*ils diraient qu'ils preferent d'envahir au*

lieu qu'ils sont sur les ordres blanc). You see the intentions of the people of Leogane, how it is if you cannot remain out of it yourself, because I believe that this is not good for the people of Haiti. And also, do not let anyone arrest (put their hand on) you. Rather you are in the woods than under arrest. Make sure to see if it is true that the gentlemen have left, to see how the things are. You who are there can see how they go (march) here. You will guard yourself well if you decide to remain at peace (*soit vous resterez en paix*). You are intelligent. You will wait. You will be careful of yourself while waiting. People are keeping things to themselves. You will not put yourself into it too quickly. Listen well before you will do anything. You will also see the overseer of your command (*l'intendant de votre commandement*) and the actions of the people towards you. You have more intelligence than I. I did not know about the situation of our country.[77]

Rather than discourage her sons from engaging in the anti-invasion struggle, she supported their activities. She decried the invasion and encouraged the Péralte men to work for its end. Her instructions "you will (wait and listen, etc.)" was her directing him and the movement.

Her missives provide another lens from how women participated in this movement as mothers and loved ones. Madame Masséna was hidden in plain sight, monitored by the United States and yet communicating with her *cacos* son in *cacos*-like terms. This particular letter stands out as she is orchestrating and informing Péralte's moves at the same time. Madame Masséna reports on Saint-Rémy, advises Charlemagne to wait, and expresses consternation about the Whites' control of Haiti. She knew her sons were beholden to this movement for a free Haiti and she encouraged them to participate in revolution.

In 1917, Madame Masséna's worst fears about Charlemagne came true: U.S. forces accused the three brothers Saül, Saint-Rémy, and Charlemagne of having connections to the "revolutionary movements." Gendarme Lieutenant Sieger arrested the siblings in Hinche on October 17. They were charged with illegal possession of arms and with participating in the *cacos*' attack on gendarme Captain John L. Doxey's home at 3 a.m. on October 11, 1917.

The provost court in Ouanaminthe oversaw their trials. In the case of Saint-Rémy Péralte, the court released him due to lack of evidence. For Saül Péralte, the prosecutors reported that he "was an intimate friend" of Charles Zamor and the *cacos*' leaders Antoine Morency and Jean-Baptiste (Pétion). Furthermore, they recorded that he hid ammunition near Hinche and lent General Pinede arms for the *cacos* attack on Hinche in October. They convicted Saül of "concealing information relative to the attack on Hinche."[78] On January 4, 1918, Captain R. S. Hooker found Charlemagne guilty of both charges and sentenced him to five years' hard labor.

The U.S. troops had succeeded in their attack against Charlemagne through imprisonment. As a member of the Revolutionary Committee, a man who published anti-U.S. invasion articles in Haiti's newspapers, and someone who openly contributed to the *cacos'* struggle, Charlemagne Péralte was a vociferous threat. This was the man who at one point reminded U.S. forces of Haiti's rebellious origins and warned them: "Noble your feelings! Study your example! This is the final criticism."[79] His recalcitrant acts for Haiti's independence profiled Charlemagne as a rebel. On January 26, 1918, Charlemagne Péralte became a prisoner at the civil prison in Cap-Haïtien.

4

Péralte Leads
(Péralte kòm Lidè)

● ●

Fueled by a false belief in its own racial superiority, the United States wanted to assert its control while also maintaining that its domination was already an accepted fact. This fallacy and doublespeak are the reasons why so many historical accounts are inaccurate. To portray the true power of Haitian resistance would be to reveal the injustice and dishonesty of the U.S. invasion. From the 1918 constitution to the development of spy tactics against the *cacos* and the heinous murder of Péralte, the U.S. invaders demonstrated that they would stop at nothing to uphold the false idea of their own superiority.

1918 Constitution

The 1918 constitution was yet another affront to Haitian sovereignty. Washington officials, specifically the assistant secretary of the navy, Franklin Delano Roosevelt, authored the nation's body of law.[1] The new constitution reversed a key clause in Haiti's 1805 body of law that forbade foreigners control of the nation. Article 5 granted U.S. Americans constitutional rights to acquire territory on the nation for residential, agricultural, and commercial enterprises.[2] The wide reach given to U.S. Americans, from building agricultural to educational industries, achieved a longstanding goal of the United States: to seize control of Haiti's territories. Well beyond the limited examples of the Môle Saint-Nicolas and the Banque Nationale, individual institutions that the United States sought to control in the nineteenth century, the 1918 constitution gave the United States all the political authority it needed to govern Haiti as it deemed fit.

The signing of the 1918 constitution frustrated many Haitians. In protest, they took to the press, to the streets, and to the battlefields. The writing and adoption of the constitution undermined Haitian law and exposed U.S. tyranny in Haiti. The United States denied Haitians access to vote on this new constitution and blatantly mocked citizens, using racist and xenophobic comments. Furthermore, the U.S. military were outraged that Haitians would protest this blatant lack of democracy. For example, one report indicated that Haitians used newspapers to launch attacks against U.S. officials. It read: "About this time the newspapers were publishing articles of a scandalous nature, attacking American officials. . . . The press construed freedom of the press to mean that the press was unbridled—it could say anything it pleased. . . . Officers on duty in Haiti not of their own will, were personally attacked, their families attacked, by these unlicensed, unbridled press."[3] In fact, one U.S. administrator's description about the adoption of the 1918 constitution demonstrates U.S. knowledge about the confusion it caused.

> In June 1918, the Constitution was placed before the people, and every effort made to make them understand it. Instructing the counselors of Agriculture and the chiefs of sections in the various sections did this and communes and having them tell the people. Of course, for an illiterate people to vote on a modern constitution understandingly, it is impossible. The word "constitution" alone means nothing to them. At one of the voting booths in Port-au-Prince when questioned, one man said he thought he was voting for a new Pope.[4]

U.S. military personnel purposefully neither provided translation in Kreyòl nor made any efforts to instruct the people whom they were there to serve. The report continued:

> Every effort was made not to exert force or in any way influence the vote. Members of the Garde were not allowed armed within thirty feet of officials at the voting booth, unless called upon to preserve order by the officials at that booth. . . . The majority in favor of the adoption [was] unanimous. Those opposed to it, if there were such, evidently did not vote.

The suggestion that an armed Garde at the onset could arouse a voter's fear demonstrated Haitians' conceptualization of the Garde as guardians of imperialism.[5] Although this report mentioned it casually, U.S. forces were conscious of the intimidating role the Garde played; they had constructed this empire unit. Finally, in the last sentence, U.S. forces admitted that this vote was tainted.

Another U.S. report admitted: "Opposition to the constitution exists. When this takes the form of public expression, and the public expression tends to incite distrust or more in the minds of the people, the persons guilty will be treated as disturbers of the peace. . . . From the receipt of this order, all officers must be particularly on the alert and be prepared to meet and handle this opposition whatever form it may take. All troops will be kept well on hand, officers will remain close to their stations and every energy devoted to the holding of a legal, quiet, and above all, peaceful, voting day."[6] Furthermore, U.S. forces distributed circulars about the constitution in Port-au-Prince on May 20, 1918, just weeks before this election. They attempted to limit the time for Haitian opposition. Using the Garde both to handle the opposition and to keep the peace was a contradictory formulation. The U.S. Americans tolerated no dissent, democratic or otherwise. The 1918 constitution was another violent display of U.S. imperialism.

The very month that Haitians voted on the constitution, U.S. forces announced another *corvée* end. They declared: "All *corvée* work will cease on Saturday night, June 8, and after being paid off, a fete with refreshments will be given the *corvée* workers. No *corvée* will be called for the week beginning June 9."[7] U.S. administrators used agriculture counselors to instruct Haitian workers on the voting process as they worked as *corvée* laborers. This third iteration of the *corvée*'s end was disturbing, since the *corvée* had been previously banned twice. To suggest that "refreshments" would be served to workers who had been abused and unpaid further demonstrates a consistent U.S. attempt to deny the horrific nature of its actions. These *corvée* administrators somehow disconnected the abuse from the person. Their actions, the *corvée*'s third ban, and now the offer to ameliorate these conditions by feeding workers demonstrate how easy it was for U.S. invaders to devalue and dehumanize Black people. The ideology behind their actions is, of course, not surprising, given the chilling nature of their hostility to Black and Brown U.S. citizens. Racist U.S. Americans behaved similarly in Haiti; it was a norm that they did not depart from during their nineteen years in the nation.

By June 18, U.S. forces tallied the questionable votes for the constitution. In one chart they listed the voting stations and the affirmative and negative votes. In a survey of ninety-three voting stations—including Hinche, Les Cayes, Marigot, Jacmel, Dame Marie—225 citizens voted "oui" for the constitution, and 768 voted "non."[8] In the districts where U.S. forces had noted heightened *cacos* activity and Haitian agitation, such as Hinche, Cap-Haïtien, and Grande Rivière, the votes were skewed. In Péralte's hometown of Hinche, voters purportedly came out 980 in favor of the constitution. In Cap-Haïtien, where the use of *corvée* laborers was excessive and the deaths of Haitians who fled this practice ran high, residents allegedly voted 601 in favor and 13 against. Similarly, in Grande Rivière, all of the 767 residents voted yes.[9] As the troops themselves noted, it was unclear how many residents were cognizant of what they were actually voting for in this election.

Péralte and the *Cacos*, 1918

Though imprisoned at the time, Péralte was aware of the constitution and its impact. A 1918 telegram reveals that a *caco* purposefully got arrested in order to relay a message to a *cacos* chief who had been sentenced to death. The new "prisoner," Anselma, informed the older one, St. Hilbert, that General Theophil at Cap-Haïtien had disguised himself as a market woman and conducted a complete tour of the north to determine the number of gendarmes posted at the various stations. General Theophil wanted this information relayed to Zamor, who was, along with Bobo, part of the movement. The span and reach of the *cacos'* strategies were impressive and remained puzzling for the United States. Dressing as a market woman in order to do reconnaissance indicates how sophisticated and well planned Haitian resistance efforts were. It also illustrates how and why the U.S. forces were in the dark about the *cacos'* vision and use of prison as a counterstrategy. The telegram stated, "Dr. Bobo and Appolon (the murderer of Lieut. McNabb) he said were in Santo Domingo and were prepared to come to Haiti as soon as the arrangements were completed."[10] From this short directive, one learns that both Zamor and Bobo were continuing their resistance. The message highlights the *cacos'* chain of command and their officers, as indicated by the use of titles such as "chiefs" and "generals." Although the marines imprisoned these guerrilla fighters and separated the leaders, the followers conspired among themselves. Jails served as resistance breeding grounds and places to recruit new converts to their movement. The 1918 constitution both mobilized Haitians to join the *cacos* and heightened the fight for those already involved.

Despite his five-year sentence, Péralte served barely eight months. In a common account of his jail time, there is a description of an insult visited upon the former politician by a gendarme. A U.S. Marine described Péralte and the incident that occurred with the gendarme as follows: "He was haughty and proud, and the imprisonment he regarded more as dishonor and shame than punishment. Then a Haitian prison guard made a bad mistake. Thinking he would break down Péralte, he gave him a task of shoveling dung. Péralte flew into a rage. The guard very calmly shoved Péralte into the whole stinking mess."[11] Various iterations of this tale remain in popular memory in Haiti. Sometimes the story goes that Péralte is cleaning Cap-Haïtien's streets. No matter the version of events, the record or the interviewee always emphasized that Péralte's chore was beneath his status as a former politician. The U.S. account indicates that asserting physical and psychological dominance over Péralte was of primary importance to the invaders.

When Péralte escaped, it was because there were prison guards who were also guerilla fighters. Gendarme Lucsama Luc, a *caco*, aided Péralte with his successful jailbreak on September 3, 1918. Péralte immediately fled to the Central Plateau. This was where and when his militant leadership of the *cacos* truly began.

When Péralte directed the *cacos*, he proclaimed, "For God feeds the little birds."[12] His figurative characterization of *cacos* as a small people fit the Haitians' dismal political and economic circumstances. The description of them as little birds feeding off the land demonstrates that the *cacos* conceived of themselves as the underdogs in a fight for their nation. Péralte's former political posts had brought him into contact with a diverse range of people. These jobs had also familiarized him with Haiti and the Dominican Republic's mountainous terrain, a knowledge that benefited him during this struggle. One marine characterized Péralte's escape as the reckoning of 1918. Péralte first concentrated his work in central Haiti and Ouanaminthe. In these locales, he recruited and structured *cacos* divisions. One marine recorded Péralte's organization:

> This section was divided up into districts, each district had its armed force, with a general in command, all being under command of the supreme bandit chief, Charlemagne Péralte, who could and did concentrate his forces for special work, such as the attack on the towns of Grand Rivière and Le Trou, in October 1919, when over three thousand *cacos* were engaged. Charlemagne surrounded himself with certain officials whom he called Minister of War, Minister of Finance, and he issued proclamations and attempted to set up a government of his own in Haiti.[13]

Péralte's activities continued to center on north and central Haiti. Péralte rejoined his fellow partisans from the attack that had landed him in jail. He created a cabinet and appointed generals who included his brothers, Batraville, and "d'Estraville, Oliver, Ectraville, Papillion, and Adhémar Francismar, etc."[14] While it is unclear who occupied the posts of minister of war and finance, Péralte selected Batraville as his chief lieutenant of the Central Plateau.[15] Batraville's work there as a teacher made this a practical move. He already knew the people and the area. Under Péralte the *cacos* became an effective military guerrilla unit. His use of ministers ensured that the *cacos* could be in Hinche and Jacmel simultaneously. Furthermore, he planned for the *cacos* to function without him, in the event of his death or the death of one of his ministers. By spreading the guerrilla fighters across Haiti, Péralte also ensured that recruits for this war and its beneficiaries would be free of imperialism. The U.S. military's assumption that Péralte was setting up a new government was perhaps true. During this war he set up ministers and spread them across the nation. He also affixed his missives with the heading of Haiti's 1791–1804 causes: *liberté, égalité, fraternité*. Péralte imagined a successful end to the invasion and that he would be alive to see God feed the "little birds."

After Péralte escaped from prison, U.S. forces accused him of disrupting the peace of 1918. Yet, it is clear from their own accounts of the constitutional vote that the "peace" they described was forced rather than chosen and that a significant and consistent resistance continued. In each step, the U.S. military lied about its reasons for seizing Haiti and its stifling of Haitian resistance. As Trouillot has noted about the Haitian Revolution, it was an unthinkable history for slave owners.[16] They called it a Negro insurrection, a slave riot—anything but a revolution. And yet, the colonizers had to also acknowledge that a successful African movement against them had occurred. Trouillot's description of unthinkable history also applies to U.S. forces in Haiti during the early twentieth century. Even as the *cacos* planned and executed battles, U.S. forces denounced it as banditry. In spite of their knowledge of the *cacos'* structure with ministers and lieutenants, they failed to acknowledge it was an organized movement. As was consistent with their doublespeak rhetoric, though, U.S. forces both dismissed Péralte's resistance and acknowledged its power. In the document below, they actually recognize Péralte's successful political tactics:

Charlemagne showed talent as an organizer and formed his own government with himself as chief and his most prominent followers as cabinet ministers. . . . Batraville was Charlemagne's principal assistant and commanded cacos in the central area while Charlemagne operated in the North. . . . The forces were scattered, there being many minor chiefs in charge of groups of men in different areas, who held rank in accordance with the importance of the areas they commanded.[17]

U.S. officials wrote about Péralte's military reach in different parts of Haiti and outlined the guerrilla fighters' access to ammunition for their fight:

The cacos' arms consisted of antiquated rifles and revolvers in poor condition which had originally been manufactured in various countries of Europe and in the United States. There being insufficient arms for all, the remainder of the bandits were armed with machetes and sharpened bamboo sticks. Most of the attacks on the Gendarmerie units in small localities were with the hope of obtaining serviceable arms and ammunition, the latter in many cases being adapted for the larger caliber of the cacos' arms by wrapping goat skin around the cartridge to make it fit the breech. It was impossible to engage the bandits in large bodies. They knew the country and were accustomed to make long marches over the difficult and mountainous trails and consequently kept out of the way of most of the troops set against them.[18]

Again, U.S. invaders note the skills and efficacy of resistance leaders even while working to dismiss the threat. These documents underscore the intelligence and sophistication of Haitian resistance fighters, demonstrating that they used tools and tactics similar to those of their *mawon* ancestors. The cover of darkness was key. Fights between the two units happened regularly during the evening. In addition to killing U.S. soldiers, *cacos* neutralized and destroyed the economic tools of empire by attacking railways, sugar factories, and the waterways that serviced these institutions. For example, the U.S. military noted that the *cacos*: "burned the Gendarmerie barracks, many houses in the towns and/or Departments of Maissade, destroyed the telephone, broke into the city hall and stole $760.00."[19] The *cacos* practiced clever politics with their feet that included harming people and belongings. Additionally, their knowledge of their nation and in particular the areas inaccessible to the U.S. military became a key advantage.

Less than a month after his escape on October 14, Péralte defended his *nasyonalis* position by battling U.S. forces. The frequency of reports to the State Department indicate that the *cacos* gave the forces no time to regroup or rest. One report explains that they had identified Péralte as the head of the guerilla fighters. The same report insisted that they had affairs under control.

> A small band of bandits had come down from the mountains at night and fired on the town on Hinche. The Gendarmes stationed at Hinche immediately engaged with them and killed thirty-five. Two Gendarmes were killed. This affair conclusively proved to my mind the efficiency of the Gendarmerie and the security of the country in their control. For years of course, it may be expected that bandits who live up on the mountains, east of Cerca la Sucre will come down into the plains for occasional raids. In this case the leader was said to be an escaped convict, Charlemagne Péralte. The Gendarmerie is trying to round up any who may have been engaged in this affair and who have escaped.[20]

This report offers a striking image of *cacos* fighters descending from the mountains to defend their nation's sovereignty against the invaders. While noting the death of some thirty-five people and acknowledging that more assaults are expected, the United States forces also try to emphasize that the situation is under their control. That they name Péralte indicates that his forces were known to them and perhaps even expected.

The U.S. troops commented on Péralte's evolution as a leader and his recruitment methods:

> His conviction as a bandit and the action of the Gendarmerie commanded by American marines in forcing him to serve his sentence at hard labor sweeping the streets of Cape Haitian engendered in Charlemagne a hate of the American Occupation that was to end only with his death. With the avowed intention of driving "the invaders into the sea and freeing Haiti," Charlemagne was soon joined by a number of those who had participated in the attack on Hinche and in a short time came to be known as the most able bandit leader operating against the marines and the Gendarmerie. Resentment against the *corvée* added many recruits to his ranks, and forced recruiting soon swelled his force to about 5,000 men in the field and a carefully estimated 15,000 more who could be counted on to join his forces for a short time when Charlemagne's

forces operated in the civility of their homes. These part-time bandits and their wives, who as market women freely circulated everywhere, were Charlemagne's intelligence unit and an efficient one.[21]

The United States acknowledges here the intricate sophisticated tactics of the *cacos*. It is a network demonstrating and motivated by patriotic kinship. While some did not fight battles against the U.S. military, they contributed to the *cacos*' intelligence unit, especially women who had some freedom of movement. The reports make plain how the *cacos* circulated their correspondence and perhaps their ideology through these market women. While they are unnamed, these *cacos* women operated in plain sight. Narratives about market women often discuss them as the backbone of Haiti's economy and argue that they have no formal political voice. Their role in this anti-imperialist fight offers a new reading of them as economic contributors and political actors. These market women, while selling goods, communicated with fellow *cacos* about the whereabouts of the invaders and other strategic plans. At the very best, these market women were *cacos* or the patriotic kin who drove their movement forward to rid Haiti of racist, imperialists. Citizens from multiple backgrounds, from politicians to vendors, participated in Haiti's defense. Moreover, the U.S. military's own sexism, just like its racism, proved to be a hindrance to its strategy. It assumed women would not be involved, so therefore did not suspect these *Ayisienne*.

One of the marines' daily reports to Port-au-Prince, dated October 19, 1918, shows the officers continued a willful misunderstanding of the *cacos*' objectives. They wrote: "Further information was received concerning the operation of some bandits at Hinche, which was reported under the date of October 17. It appears that about twelve armed bandits came down from the mountains on the Haitien-Dominican border. . . . As previously reported, this affair has no political or military significance whatsoever, and repetition of such raids by bandits hidden away in the hills on the frontier may be expected for some time to come."[22] Their acknowledgment that the *cacos*' battles would continue was correct. Throughout 1918, *cacos* activities spread across the Central Plateau, Hinche, Ranquitte, Lascahobas, Marmelade, Saint-Michel, and Mirebalais. Their military style was simple: attack, retreat, and disappear. These *mawon*-like strategies invite a comparison with Haiti's first defenders of freedom generations earlier. Spread across the towns and battling frequently, the *cacos* fighters sparked a kind of nostalgia, fueling *nasyonalisme*.

By 1918, Péralte was traumatized and infuriated by U.S. imperialism. Between 1915 and 1918, he had seen his independent republic dismantled by U.S.-sponsored legal documents; the installation of a puppet Haitian President; the killing of innocent Haitians; and the imprisonment, exile, and assassination of Haitian resistance fighters. Soon after his own escape and his reunion with family, the U.S. military assassinated Péralte's beloved kin. On October 26, 1918, Garde members captured his older brother, Saül, and while he was attempting to escape, they fatally shot him. Charlemagne channeled his rage into amassing an army that would give the *cacos* their most effective year fighting the U.S. military. In 1919, U.S. reports estimated that Péralte commanded an army of between six and fifteen thousand *cacos*. The large disparity in numbers accounted for what the U.S. labeled his "part timers." These part-time people were people who worked other jobs and contributed to the *cacos* cause as well. As part-timers, they blended in, operating in plain sight of the invaders. The actual number of *cacos* reflected Charlemagne's tactics that initially eluded U.S. forces. Indeed, the number of participants in resistance movements is difficult to calculate. Exaggerating one's numbers is, of course, an advantage. Additionally, resistance comes in all forms, so more people are a part of the movement than just those seen in combat. Conversely, the U.S. military might likely miscalculate, given both their racist inability to respect the power of resistance fighters and their desire to deny that they might not have complete control. Precise calculations are tricky in any historical period and, for the *cacos*' battles this is especially true. Suffice it to say, the *cacos* threat, strategy, effectiveness, and network were all significant and the U.S. military both feared and denied this reality.

Péralte regularly recruited members to the *cacos* movement and communicated with his chiefs through letters, which provides historians crucial details about his resistance. On March 27, 1919, Péralte addressed a letter to Benoît and Petite Longe Toussaint from Camp Gal. Like his 1804 revolutionary predecessors, the *cacos* chief affixed the heading "liberté, égalité, fraternité" and "République d'Haïti" to the missive. Péralte projected his desires for the *cacos*' revolt being a moment of *nasyonalis* unity and Haiti's independence. Péralte recalled that his 1791–1804 revolutionary ancestors used these objectives against the slave colonial French power and now in the twentieth century the *cacos* had to do the same against the U.S. empire. Péralte's heading and the content of his letter detail his call for patriotic kinship. He desired that all Haitians would aid in this fight against empire and emphasized that their unity was key. In this missive, Péralte expressed satisfaction with the *cacos*' work. He listed the different divisions of *cacos* headed by Papillion and others, stationed at Grande Rivière, Petite Rivière, and Saint-Michel. Péralte said he would visit them soon and wished them great success. He also asked them to represent themselves well. On April 2 Péralte followed up with Toussaint about his approaching visit. In another missive from April 7, Péralte addressed himself as "Minister of the Movement," and he provided details for *cacos*' actions in Lascahobas. He also reminded the *cacos* that communication was vital to making their revolution work.

On April 18, Péralte sought to incite another Haitian to join their cause. He wrote: "I am astounded to see the degree which you find the revolution. You have remained inactive. You should know my dear Ripkin that we are in an international war, that is to say we are against a foreign nation. In this case, all good citizens are required to defend their country and their flag in this circumstance.

My dear general, employ all your activity of service to the take the armies in the arrondissement of Lascahobas, and I will give you cooperation immediately."[23] Péralte viewed the *cacos'* struggle as an international conflict. It explains why Péralte reached out to British and French ambassadors. For many Haitians, the presence of the United States in the First World War juxtaposed negatively with the presence of the U.S. military in the Dominican Republic, Cuba, Puerto Rico, Guam, and the Philippines. Péralte thus called it an international war. He placed Haiti on the world's radar, reminding people that it was one of only three nations from the Age of Revolutions. While the *cacos* leader's remembrance of 1804 served to recruit Haitians, it also defended the guerrilla fighters' position to the world. Péralte positioned the *cacos'* war as a defensive one. He articulated, in word and through action, that Haitians were fighting for the cherished ideals of sovereignty and democracy. The dual purpose that Péralte's 1804 recollection served fit with the *guerre du jour*, the First World War. Péralte's reasoning to his recruits and *cacos* fighters that this was mandatory service was also reminiscent of articles in Haiti's 1805 constitution. The nation's first legal blueprint made military service synonymous with citizenry. Péralte felt that his patriotic kin had a duty to protect Haiti.

Péralte's letters to Haitian resisters and to his acquaintances demonstrate that the *cacos* leader's influence was far-ranging. Most Haitians, whom U.S. forces believed to be in favor of the invasion, were either part of the *cacos* or patriotic kin who aided the guerrilla fighters' efforts. In one example, the Garde arrested two Haitians whom they had previously considered in favor of the invasion. Turenne St. Juste and Louis Poux were residents of Port-de-Paix. The former had a coffee business, less than a quarter of a mile from the gendarmes bureau in that town. According to the U.S. file on St. Juste, merchants in Port-de-Paix recommended him as an honest and hard-working man. Though he initially aroused no suspicion, he was a general of Charlemagne, whom U.S. forces arrested on April 17. Similarly, Louis Poux was the registration director of Port-de-Paix, and he also owned a bakery shop. Poux was another general of Charlemagne. Unrecognized by the U.S. forces, who saw many fighters as solely armed peasants, the *cacos'* class diversity worked in their favor. In this case, a former politician and escaped prisoner collaborated with innocent-seeming entrepreneurs. The location of St. Juste's business near the gendarmes office allowed him to witness their comings and goings and spy on their tactics. Similarly, Poux's role as an administrator gave him inside access to the government that the *cacos* were in the process of dismantling. They all behaved like patriotic kin.

U.S. forces developed a system of espionage against the *cacos*, just as the fighters had developed one against the foreigners. They often intercepted and confiscated letters. It is unclear if Aspelly Joseph, a *cacos* general who died in battle, received this letter from Péralte dated March 22. The missive may have been confiscated beforehand. The *cacos* chief penned the following to his comrade:

> I am happy to be able to write you these lines, because it has already been six months since I have been fighting with the Americans to obtain a new independence and liberty for the poor Haitien people. God is with us. He sees our feebleness and our innocence. He will know how to aid and protect us; our cause is one of justice. I began the revolution with six men on the heights of Pinquois, but actually we have sixty-six divisions of Cacos operating at Grand Bois, at Marchand, Thomonde, Hinche, Cerca la Source, Maissade, Pillon, Mobin Crochu, Vallier, Lamielle, and in the plains of Ouanaminthe. We have more than fifteen thousand men on foot.[24]

In this short letter, Péralte reminds the *cacos* that this fight is God-ordained because it is for Haiti and her citizens' freedom. He repeats key words like "justice," "liberty," and "revolution" that enunciate that this cause is just. The mention of these words also highlights that he knew the United States was enmeshed in a world war about these principles. The *cacos* leader also records the order and strength of his unit by writing about the numbers of *cacos* divisions, their spread, and defining them as a unit. The spread of their doctrine across Haiti shows the zeal with which they organized for the invasion's end.

Péralte explicitly mentions how the movement began with six men and grew exponentially. It is unclear if the six men included his brothers, cousin Batraville, Bobo, and/or Zamor. Péralte probably exaggerated the number of *cacos* under his command because he was conscious of the U.S. forces' spy tactics. His letter continues:

> To confirm this statement, send a man you can trust, and you can assure yourself of the strength of the revolution on his return. In case the blood of our illustrious ancestors boils in your veins, uphold the honor of our flag by rousing your population for the noble and beautiful revolutionary movements of the Haitian people. You can communicate with General Turene St. Juste of Port de Paix, who is another exactly like me, as well as to General Louis Poux. They will themselves strike in this district. I count upon your devotion to your dear Haitien Fatherland for a good success, because to die in the defense of one's country is an honorable death. GOD, COUNTRY, AND FAMILY.

Péralte repeats his call for *nasyonalisme* and bravery in this call for additional resistance members. Their cause is a cause for justice, one that is supported by a higher power, one that is justified through the moral superiority of the Haitian people. For Péralte this war was a struggle for patriotic kin and nation—the entity that would ensure the freedom of his people. In his caution to Aspelly, he recognizes U.S. surveillance and infiltration, but does not back down in his assertion of the importance of his cause.

Péralte's letters offer an important insight into his strategy, but he did not communicate only in this way. He also posted proclamations to Haitians and the U.S. forces in public squares. On March 14, one such proclamation appeared in the nation's capital:

> Haitians, a day like the first of January 1804 will soon rise. For four years, the Occupation has insulted us in every way: every morning brings us a new sadness. The people are poor, and the Occupation is weighing them down with taxes: it is spreading fires and preventing people from rebuilding with wood under the false pretense of a desire to beautify the town. Haitians, let us be firm: let us follow the example of Belgium. No matter if our towns are burned. For it is not a vain thought that was written on the grave of the great Dessalines: "Upon the first shot, the towns disappear and the nation rises."[25]

Péralte uses Dessalines's words to inspire his fellow Haitians and he makes present-day comparisons to other U.S. conflicts in order to assert Haiti's need to act. His words remind Haitians that the U.S. ideology behind its invasion is not an innocent one of promoting democracy. In prior years, Péralte called on the legacies of multiple Haitian forefathers, like Pétion and Dessalines. Here, however, Péralte is channeling Dessalines's rage with the protracted revolution from 1791 to 1803. The proclamation continues to declare an outright war and to threaten the U.S. president. Péralte makes it clear that his mission is a war in defense of his nation's sovereignty.

> The Holy Cause, which is spreading in the north, has chiefs, men of good sense. The South is waiting for only one man to follow this sublime example. Do not fear! We have arms! Let us chase those ravenous people whose ravenousness is represented in the person of their President. Wilson, traitor, vagabond, rioter . . . thief, you will die with your country. Hurrah for independence! Hurrah for Union! Hurrah for legitimate war! Down with the Americans!

Péralte turns the tables on U.S. Americans by asserting that it is, in fact, their president who is a "traitor, vagabond, rioter, and thief." He reminds his audience that the U.S. forces were not peaceful beings but instead, agents of empire. Péralte exposed their doublespeak.

Péralte also addressed a letter to the bureau of the gendarmes in Saint-Marc that provided the names of eighteen gendarme chiefs whom the *cacos* refused to pardon. He followed the list with a stern reprimand and gave the marines his subsequent plans of action: "General Williams wait for me no later than July 19. Captain Brown do your business well in order that you may not be reproached. The *cacos* are asking for the heads of all the Chiefs of Gendarme of St. Marc."[26] Péralte asserts in these documents that collaborating with the United States would not be tolerated. The U.S. invaders were enemies of the state and no pardon for those who aided them would be considered.

In 1919, U.S. forces actively spied on the *cacos*, reported on their actions, and devised plots to bring them down—and they were especially determined to rein in Péralte. In telegrams sent to the Navy Department on March 18 and March 21, marines reported that a "placard intended to incite people to revolution against the US occupation and people of US" circulated. Haitians and *cacos* probably used *Le Nouvelliste* as a platform to protest. The marines responded by suspending the journal's circulation.[27]

By April, U.S. officials recorded the names and locations of eighty-four active "bandits."[28] The list included men who also served as gendarmes, folks listed as "old-time *cacos*," and new leaders, such as Benoît, Saint-Rémy, Thermide Pierce (son of Saint-Rémy Péralte), and Charlemagne Péralte. In the case of Thermide Pierce, the Péralte's family generational protest had moved from the brothers to a nephew. The U.S. surveillance never mentioned whether Péralte was married or had progeny. In interviews with me, his stepson, son, and granddaughter shared how he was a genuine family man who loved and provided for them. Péralte could have lived a duplicitous life that eluded the U.S. military surveillance of his wife and his children's mothers. The mention of his nephew Thermide and not his own descendants suggests that he might have protected his closest relatives. In the historical account of Péralte's life, there is often little information shared about his romantic partners and the women with whom he had children. He is often solely immortalized as politician, revolutionary, and martyr. There is note of his mother and brothers, but no other family information recorded extensively. His friendships appeared to be between family and his closest *cacos*, like Batraville. The U.S. military's list also contained a chart that documented the number of those reported dead, wounded, and imprisoned. The marines' daily diary reports fixated on Péralte in particular. Their notations include:

April 7, 1919: Marine patrols are out scouring the country from Maissade, Hinche, Thomasique, Thomonde, Las Cahobas, and Mirebalais. The band, which was scattered near Mirebalais on April 4, is reported to have joined band under Charlemagne Péralte, not confirmed.[29]

April 16, 1919: Péralte is reported as being ill and about ready to quit. Several letters from Charlemagne to Haitians have been turned in by the persons addressed; these letters asked the persons addressed to join him in the hills. There are no Haitians of any prominence connected with the bandits as far as is known.[30]

April 21, 1919: Marine patrol surprised bandit chief named Benoît at daylight. While it failed to capture him, it captured his horse and all his correspondence including several letters from Charlemagne implicating several natives, among them the priest at Grand Bois. Have sent patrol to bring priest in and to arrest the persons implicated.[31]

Despite the marines' hopes that Haitians of prominence did not interact with the likes of Péralte and Batraville, cross-class collaboration existed. Péralte's invitation for patriotic kin to join him in the hills recalls *mawons'* strategies of congregating in spaces inaccessible to oppressors. The U.S. surveillance of Péralte provides useful information about the extent of the *caco's* reach. The positions that these guerrilla fighters held as market women, priests, editors, politicians, and schoolteachers were all occupations that had access to recruiting additional *cacos* and influencing patriotic kin for the anti-imperialist cause. The regularity of the U.S. military's communication about Péralte documents their obsession with the *cacos* leader and exposes their lies about having the bandit problem and Haitians under control.

Silence and Feigned Ignorance as War Tactics

In 1919 Colonel Richard S. Hooker issued a proclamation with the title "Proclamation to the Haitian People in the Districts Where There Are Bandits."[32] Hooker was a lieutenant colonel in the U.S. Marines and served as assistant chief of the gendarmerie d'Haïti in Port-au-Prince that year. Prior to 1919, Colonel Hooker had served in Haiti from August 1915 to March 1918 and again in 1918 from November 24 to December 9. With his return on January 15, 1919, Colonel Hooker found the *cacos* still active.[33] The presence of Péralte and the *cacos* infuriated Hooker, who had fought for three years against the guerrilla fighters. For this new leg of the *cacos'* war, U.S. administrators stationed the colonel in Cap-Haïtien from January 20 to July 20, 1919. There, his duties were as regimental commander of the Second Regiment and district commander of northern Haiti. Judging from the extend of the *cacos'* national network, Haitians in the cities of Hinche, Mirebalais, Lascahobas, Cap-Haïtien, Léogâne, Gonaïves, and Port-au-Prince probably received his notice. Colonel Hooker's tone was one of reprimand and sheer annoyance at Haitian assistance to the *cacos*. As his proclamation reveals, this aid took the form of feigning ignorance and maintaining silence. He began:

> The Forces of the American Occupation are here to reestablish peace in this country. The forces at present here are only a small part of available forces. If reinforcements are needed, they can be called in from Port-au-Prince and from Cape Haitian [*sic*], in addition to which we have at this moment enough troops in the United States to fill this country as one would fill a box of sardines. Then they would be more numerous than the entire population of Haiti including all men, women and children. I have told you several times to return to your homes and remain quiet. I have told you that I would accord protection to all those who are honest citizens, but what have you done for me? Nothing! I cannot give protection to anyone if you will not furnish me with necessary information: information as to where the bandits are and what their plans are.

I already know that you are all aware of the bandit's movements. I also know, even though I am a foreigner, several things of which you say you know nothing "*PAS CONNAIT*" (Author's note [Hooker]: This is a Creole expression frequently used by Haitians, but it is correctly spelled *pas conné*, it is always the same answer. Have you the right to deny things in such a situation?)[34]

Hooker appears unnerved. His threat to saturate Haiti with additional reinforcement seems to indicate that the number of troops was insufficient for the United States' anti-*cacos* operation. Hooker's mention of the term *pas connait* demonstrated that the expression had become common—and his inability to spell it correctly in French (*pas connaît*) and his English invention of a Kreyòl spelling (*pas conné*) indicates his lack of knowledge of Haitian language and culture. The proclamation reveals that the number of Haitians who feigned a lack of knowledge about the *cacos'* whereabouts and their activities was such that it warranted Hooker's order to cease. Haitians' nonviolent participation in the *cacos* struggle was remarkable. Their silence worked in tandem with the *cacos'* violent battles against U.S. troops. The proclamation continued:

Finally, who are the people who are persecuting you? Charlemagne, a mad man, a man who is sick in the head, a coward, who is never present in the line of fire, and finally a man who has offered to surrender six times on condition that his life be spared. In short, he wishes to surrender leaving the little bandits: Norde, Santilma Joseph (known as Pichotte), Papillon, and their followers in the mountains to be killed like birds. Is there a single name among these names, whether he be minister, division commander, or brigade commander, which is the name of an honest Haitian citizen? Is there, among them, the name of one intelligent man? Read their history: all of their lives are those of thieves, murders, killers of women and children. They march at night because they are afraid of the light of the sun. I am asking you, good and brave citizens, not for myself but for yourselves, to assist me in putting an end to this banditry.

Colonel Hooker's appeal to Haitians reads as a desperate ploy. He aimed to tarnish the image of Péralte. These efforts were consistent with the propaganda campaign that the U.S. military launched against the *cacos* in 1915, routinely defaming them as criminals, trying to get all Haitians to side with the foreign invaders and lying about the motivations, intelligence, and sophistication of the *cacos'* tactics. Hooker's accusation that the *cacos* were murderers of innocents was his attempt to turn the tables on the guerrilla fighters. Indeed, many marines and members of the gendarmerie had recently been reprimanded for killing innocent people, including harming women and children. Despite this, U.S. troops were rarely court martialed. Notations of troop conduct between 1918 and 1919 included: "AWOL, breaking into native house," "Having cocaine in his possession," "assaulting a native," and in two entries, "Attempting to rape native girl."[35]

Hooker's attempt to divert the negative attention away from the Garde and charge the *cacos* with these violent behaviors is a strategy consistent with the dominant U.S. narrative about the invasion.

Hooker, for example, was called as a witness in the Inquiry into Haitian Matters in 1920, also known as the Mayo Court of Inquiry. The U.S. government placed Rear Admiral Henry Mayo in charge of the navy's court of inquiry in Port-au-Prince during November 1920. Several factors prompted this investigation, including ongoing Haitian resistance, reports of U.S. military abuse, and the coverage in the U.S. press about soldiers' murder of Haitians. In his role, Rear Admiral Mayo collected testimonies about the abuses of the invasion and later, and hastily concluded that these crimes were isolated, not routine incidents. During Hooker's testimony, he shared news of reports that U.S. soldiers and gendarmes "bumped off" (killed) bandits.[36] When he arrived in Cap-Haïtien and Hinche, Hooker noted several disturbing trends. He found the abolished *corveé* labor still in operation. There were a number of rumors and reports about the mistreatment of Haitians. Also, his colleague Lieutenant Williams admitted to "having executed three or four and later to five or six."[37] In sum, Hooker routinely lied about U.S. crimes and sought to accuse the Haitians of the crimes instead. As with slave owners who never understood the original violence of slavery as the motivation for revolt, he never understood the illegal invasion of Haitian territory as the inspiration for the *cacos'* sophisticated resistance.

Furthermore, Hooker dismissed valuable war tactics that the *cacos* were using, such as moving under cover of darkness, as somehow negative. In fact, these were successful strategies that their *mawon* ancestors had used and that the *cacos* were using as well. The proclamation continued:

> I am a soldier, and my government gives me money to fight and kill, but planting season has come, and if your fields are not cultivated immediately, where will you find food on which to exist in two or three months. The fields are not planted but those fields which are planted by the bandits for their food. The huts are there to shelter these people, the cattle are there to nourish them. In view of your negligence in failing to denounce these people, I have found it necessary to take very stern measures. What are these measures? It is becoming necessary to burn huts in order that the bandits are unable to find protection from the rain. It is becoming necessary to kill cattle so that the bandits will not be able to find meat to eat. It is becoming necessary to destroy life-sustaining supplies of every kind so that the bandits will not have beans, sugar cane, bananas, etc., to eat. These measures hit the bandits, the innocent, and the good citizens equally; I do not wish to be forced to take such action, but it may be necessary.[38]

This paragraph further elucidates the fundamental violence of the U.S. forces. Moreover, it continues the longstanding narrative, this doublespeak that somehow the invaders are the good guys and the victims are the bad guys. U.S. forces threated to intentionally burn homes—what they called "huts"—in order to stifle the *cacos*. Yet again the proclamation absolves U.S. forces of guilt. Hooker blames Haitians, whom he alleges to have abetted the guerrilla fighters.

Hooker's list of how the *cacos* managed their survival reads as a colonial document like the seventeenth-century Code Noir, which demonstrated French attempts to stamp out African culture, spirituality, and any resistance. Enslaved people had to convert to Catholicism and could not beat drums or congregate. The code prohibited some of the early foundations of Black family life.[39] The text also served as an instruction manual for slave owners. The monarchy instructed owners when to clothe and feed their human "commodities" and when to punish them for wrongs such as seeking freedom. Other colonizers had used similar measures against *mawons* who resisted in slave societies across the Americas. Hooker's list invites related questions: Were Haitians harboring the *cacos* in their homes and feeding the resisters? Or were the *cacos* feeding off the land they sought to protect and liberate? Haitians' silence indicated the former was at play in several departments across the nation and that a network of patriotic kin was helping the *cacos* live off the land they sought to protect. Hooker's statement concluded:

> When peace is restored, we will leave. We have no desire to stay in Haiti, far from our families who are in the United States, but each time that we have been on the point of leaving Haiti, another mad man and his stupidities have surfaced. Now I ask all intelligent citizens and patriots, all men of good will, to join together despite their differences and to find a way to put an end to banditry and re-establish peace. Form a public safety committee whose object will be to glean correct information from honest people that you know and who will tell you where the bandits are, where their cantonments are, where their leaders are hiding, and what they plan to do in the future. This information which is easy for you to get because all the inhabitants know you already, and you will always find someone who knows something. My friends[,] think seriously about what I have said. It is your country's last chance. I can tell you frankly that it is necessary for you and for your country that banditry is brought to an end. Haiti is for Haitians, but these bandits will change all that in a way prejudicial to all.[40]

The idea that the *cacos* kept the U.S. military in Haiti was false: the treaty of 1915 had granted the United States the right to remain in the nation for twenty years. The *cacos* objected to these terms, and this conflict motivated their launch of this guerrilla war.

In an additional misrepresentation of the situation, Hooker and his colleagues desired a public safety committee to legitimize their spy tactics. The name corroborated the U.S. military's characterization of Charlemagne and the *cacos* as a menace. It framed as enemies of the state the guerrilla fighters, rather than the foreign troops who seized an independent nation.

Finally, the U.S. military actively sought to depoliticize the *cacos* in public opinion. They labeled these men and women as illiterate nonintellectuals. Hooker's suggestion that "intelligent Haitians" should help the U.S. military restore order demonstrated the refusal to accept the *cacos* as clever freedom fighters and assumed that somehow there was a large population of people who accepted the invaders. The tainted 1915 election and 1918 constitutional vote expose this as a lie. Hooker even played with terms that the *cacos* routinely used in their appeals. Péralte often referred to Haitians as patriots in the *cacos'* quest to restore "Haiti for Haitians."

From Hooker's two-page proclamation, it is clear that the *cacos'* struggle was in full force and succeeding. In addition to prompting the other U.S. military initiatives to end the *cacos*, the guerrilla fighters forced Hooker to issue a proclamation. Moreover, Haitians who did not pick up arms like the *cacos* wielded silence and feigned ignorance as weapons. Their closed mouths were effective. Their silence is the hidden transcript of resistance. Haitians' silence was at once a calculated move and a subtle act. They exhibited power by remaining quiet. They protected their patriotic kin, namely the *cacos* who sacrificed their bodies in the armed struggle. Haitians' silent mouths, a form of active resistance, actively moved the *cacos'* liberation struggle along.

It became clear that Haitians had intentionally protested against U.S. troops like Colonel Hooker by refusing to cooperate with demands for information. When the colonel departed from Haiti, one citizen—Mr. Jolibois Fils, editor of the *Courier Haitien*—bid him a sarcastic farewell:

> We of the "Courier Haitien," rejoice at the departure of this infamous Colonel Hooker, the greatest detractor of the Haitian people, the American officer who has done the most harm morally and materially. . . . Colonel Hooker, we wish you good travels. As to the money you have drained from Haiti, as to the fortune you have accumulated in the country while violating our poor peasants, the brave *cacos*, you will never enjoy it. And your children will pay, up until the fourth generation, for all the evil you did to a good and peaceful people. . . . Col Hooker the curses of the widows and orphans, the grieving fiancées of your numerous victims go with you![41]

The United States gave Hooker a medaille militaire for "conspicuous conduct in the field."[42] Yet, this farewell demonstrates that Haitians were not fooled by such pomp and lies. The curse upon the invader's life and family further demonstrates the association that *cacos* leaders made between the justice of their cause and a higher power. They held the moral high ground—and for that, God was on their side.

Many Haitians like Jolibois did not obey Hooker's proclamation. They knew U.S. forces were responsible for the murderers of *cacos* and they knew them as men who harmed innocent Haitians. Another Haitian, a Mr. Duchesne, testified that Colonel Hooker's violent behavior toward him resulted in his own imprisonment. Duchesne shared: "He told me that if I did not tell him the truth at this time, I would tell him to-morrow, and I would be in front of two squads of gendarmes who would fire on me."[43] Duchesne's testimony revealed the violence used during the invasion, especially when Haitians disobeyed. Major General Commandant George Barnett disclosed his awareness of these crimes in a confidential report dated September 27, 1919. Barnett wrote:

> It appears from the testimony in the general court-martial cases of Privates Walter E. Johnson and John J. McQuilkin, Jr., Marine Corps, and from the argument of the counsel for the defense in the case of Private Johnson, First Lieutenant F.L. Spear, that unlawful executions of Haytiens, called Cacos, have occurred in Hayti. You will issue immediately necessary and proper instructions regarding these unlawful actions. . . .

> Such unwarranted and unlawful actions on the part of officers and men of the Marine Corps, or of the Gendarmerie d'Haiti cannot be tolerated under any circumstances.[44]

U.S. Intelligence

Judging from the comprehensive knowledge U.S. forces obtained, it appears that they stepped up their surveillance of *cacos* armies. They intercepted a letter from Batraville to Charlemagne about an attack on Port-au-Prince. The foreigners noted that Péralte always had a division of about thirty-five men and that the *cacos* chief "never goes near the fighting."[45] The troops reported that Péralte's routine was to remain in an area a maximum of two or three days. Additionally, *cacos* women gained intelligence from the market people, who would disclose the strength of U.S. forces. The mention of *cacos* women and market people, who also tended to be women, reveals that the former were fighters. Despite their detailed tracking of leaders from Rameaux to Péralte, the archives do not list the names of these *cacos* women. U.S. officials reported that Benoît and Charlemagne often communicated through letters sent by "camp women," as the two men were rarely in the same place. There is a distinction here between *cacos* camp and market women. The former traveled with the male *cacos* and the latter were a steady intelligence-gathering team. They were likely mothers like Madame Masséna, wives, sisters, and girlfriends. They entered and remain in the historical record as "camp women" not *cacos* leaders or fighters, even though the information they provided was of paramount importance. The U.S. troops listed the names of other Haitians—like Jancy, Charlomise, Exuel, and Celestin—who feigned support of the U.S. forces but who were really *cacos*. Finally, they reported on one *caco* chief, Hello, who was stationed at Jaco with thirty men and had a camp in a cane field. Hello's locale was a smart choice given the coverage that the tall fruit plants provided.[46] During this anti-invasion fight, the *cacos* used the geography as their resistance zones (Figure 6).

Sometimes U.S. forces interrogated Haitians to gain intelligence. Private Kelly, who served as captain of the gendarmes, questioned a Haitian who participated in the *cacos* revolt. This Haitian presented Private Kelly with two letters sent by Charlemagne, one of which stated that the revolution had spread across Haiti. He was chosen to lead in his area as chief. He admitted accepting this role voluntarily. Often, the U.S. military argued that the *cacos* coerced Haitian participation. Kelly inquired about the number of arms, munitions, and machetes the *cacos* possessed. He also demanded the name of the supreme chief of the revolution. The Haitian replied that, in Hinche, they say it is Charlemagne.

Péralte aggravated U.S. forces because he would not back down and he led a successful network of guerilla fighters. It was not long before the U.S. forces made plans to execute the *cacos* leader. On May 2, Henry Montas sent General Catlin, the chief of the American occupation in Haiti, a confidential letter:

> Allow me, Honorable General, to say that the part to be played by me, with your kind authorization, will be carried out with the greatest secrecy that is to exist between your office and the five members of the future Peace Commission that I beg you to appoint. . . . If the insurgents or anyone connected with them should by any chance have any suspicion of the plan of pacification that I have the honor of submitting to you, it would then be impossible for me to accomplish any good. . . . It will not be possible for me to get acquainted with you before the successful issue of our enterprise, because the tactics to be employed by me would thereby be made non-effective. If I could not carry them out in a manner to take the enemy by surprise and to proceed in such wise as by the help of God, to be able to lay hands upon Charlemagne Péralte and his companions, by a subtle work consisting of making their men to fall away from them before they have quite realized it.[47]

They infiltrated his *cacos*.

In order to topple imperialism, Péralte publicly lambasted the invaders. By openly displaying his anger at President Wilson and the gendarmes, Péralte maintained the U.S. forces' attention. In June 1919, he appealed to the British acting chargé d'affaires in Port-au-Prince:

> Since, today, the revolution in Haiti has spread all over the country. . . . You can, Consul, in order to be informed as to the strength of the revolution, send a Commissioner to visit my troops and, on his return, render you an exact account of what he has seen, for we are more than thirty to forty thousand men

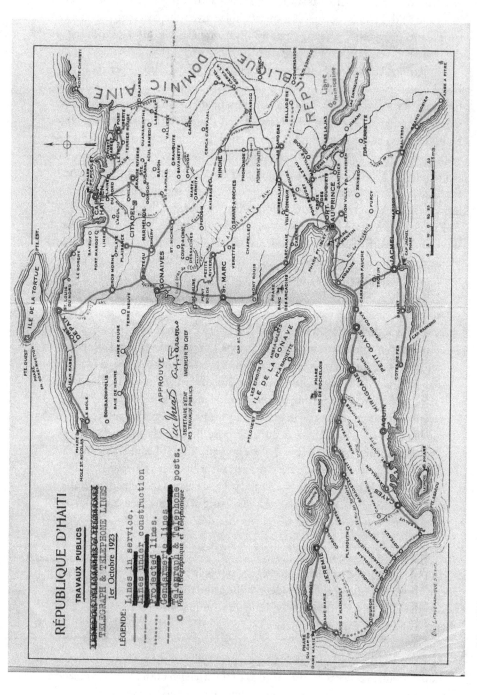

FIG. 6 Map of Haiti. By 1923 the U.S. military had created this map of the nation. It offers a clear picture of *cacos*' various resistance zones (Reference Collection, Marine Corps History Division, Quantico, VA)

on foot. . . . We are fighting valiantly with the help of Providence only: For God feeds the little birds. But we had thought that the Americans who are defending the government of the famous Sudre Dartiguenave would have been braver and more gallant to fight us with equal arms, rifle to rifle, albeit that they are superior to ours. . . . Soon it will be nine months since we have been fighting against a great nation, and no other nation has as yet come to look into our situation and fate, notwithstanding that we are living in an age of light and progress; notwithstanding that everywhere the nations are preaching justice. I, therefore, make it my duty, Mr. Consul, to write to you to claim your kind and humanitarian help for the poor, feeble Haitian people who are aimed solely for the defense of their territory and their flag.[48]

It is unclear why Péralte dated the *cacos'* movement as nine months old, especially because the U.S. forces had imprisoned him in 1917–1918 for his participation. Perhaps he only counted his leadership of the guerrilla fighters. Nevertheless, Péralte critiqued the military by employing the U.S. Americans' own ideological tools. U.S. Americans freely promulgated ideas of freedom and democracy, especially during the First World War. As Péralte challenged: Why then were there so many occupied nations? Meanwhile, the *cacos'* battles continued: on June 19, 1919, at Trou Cayman; on June 20, at Acul Samedi; on June 22, at Arcahaie and Saint-Marc; and on June 28, at Thomazeau.[49] A month later, Péralte appealed to the French minister.[50]

By October, U.S. forces stationed on the ground sought additional help. Colonel John H. Russell arrived in Haiti on October 1 and met with General Catlin. Russell wrote:

I saw General Catlin who informed me, much to my surprise, that conditions in Haiti had greatly changed during the past few months and that a certain section of the country was filled with bandits and that he had placed Marines in the field of operations as the Gendarmerie had been unable to handle the situation without assistance. . . . My inspection convinced me that immediate and intensive measures were necessary, first, to reorganize the supply system and provide better accommodations, food, clothing, comforts, and recreation for the men in the field, and by well-organized and intensive campaign to stamp out any organized bandit or revolutionary force that appeared to be growing greater as time passed. The total number of Marines under my command at this time was only 1253. The estimated number of bandits actually in the field was conservatively placed as: in the northern Haiti, 3,000, in central Haiti, 2,500 or a total of 5,500. This number was continually being augmented by recruiting parties, so that the number available to the different chiefs as evinced by surrenders, was much greater being placed as high as 17,000.[51]

This missive highlights several facts. First, the number of *cacos* was growing. Second, they put up such a formidable fight that the invaders had to restrategize in their dealings with the guerrilla fighters. Third, they acknowledge through their surveillance of numbers, space, and the use of the word "chiefs" that the *cacos* were not a haphazard group of bandits. The U.S. military had a legitimate war on its hands against the *cacos*, and it strategized for the guerrilla fighters' demise and the end of their movement.

Russell's words are consistent with the U.S. policy of doublespeak—the resistance fighters are at once merely "bandits" and at the same time a "revolutionary force." His missive continues in lockstep with other U.S. narratives: it denies the justified motivation of Haitian fighters to resist foreign takeover by calling them merely bandits. Yet it also admits that there was a real and significant resistance force the United States had difficulty managing. Here, we have a U.S. account of high numbers that shows Péralte was not exaggerating the size of his forces as merely a strategy—Péralte had an army and he was at war. The United States knew this. Russell next identified Charlemagne's role as leader of this resistance and detailed what would be the U.S. forces' attack.

> The bandits were fairly well organized under the leadership of Charlemagne Péralte, a man who showed some ability as an organizer and leader in the field and to these were added some of the best brains from Port-au-Prince and Cape Haitian, who gave advice and assistance. Charlemagne, as supreme chief, had his cabinet of ministers, issued commissions to his officers and carried on a campaign with the object of overthrowing the de facto government and driving the whites out of Haiti, either by force or discouraging them to such an extent that they would withdraw.
>
> The system of supplies and information of the bandits was mostly carried to show that a regular system of espionage and supply consisting of men and women was established at Port-au-Prince.
>
> After a careful and exhaustive estimate of the situation, I decided that the best method of breaking up the well-organized bandit groups was to first completely reorganize the brigade under my command, paying particular attention to the system of supply, and then to begin a campaign of great intensity, keeping all bandit groups continuously on the move, thus giving them little or no time to rest or reorganize after contact with our combat patrols. At the same time, I informed all the Magistrates or Mayors of the towns I visited, as well as the Priest at Hinche, Charlemagne's birth-place, that unless Charlemagne surrendered immediately, he would surely be killed, as I intended to use every effort to get him.[52]

The U.S. military acknowledged over and over that the *cacos* were soldiers and not bandits. Yet, the official narratives that draw from their primary sources lie about their sense of control and of *cacos* being mere bandits. The U.S. military's reorganization of how to deal with these *cacos*, including the market women who were part of the guerrilla fighters, and their conference with people who knew Péralte reveal their weak positions. Despite seizing Haiti, they had not captured the Haitian people as a whole nor convinced all of them that the invasion was just. In fact, not only do the *cacos* have well-developed strategies, they have cultivated patriotic kinship. The record's mention of the priest, mayors, and others suggest that the military needed to interact with these people personally to convince them to betray Péralte. Finally, their mention of Port-au-Prince, the seat of their power in Haiti, proves that the *cacos* were not operating in rural hinterland areas solely. They were in major cities that had a strong U.S. presence and the *cacos* battled these foreigners in these spaces. The *cacos* movement sent a message to its fellow citizens that *cacos* were present almost everywhere and that they would defend Haiti. A rereading of the U.S. military's sources about the invasion shows that Haitians resistance was in full effect and was successful.

Six days from the above attack, the *cacos* struck again. They apprehended gendarme Adam Bristol and seized his rifle and ammunition. As the *cacos* departed from Bristol, he heard them declare, "Long Live Charlemagne!"[53] That very day, on October 7, over 200 *cacos* surrounded Port-au-Prince. It was a bold surprise attack on the nation's capital. U.S. forces reported on Benoît's activities and identified several other leaders of "the movement."[54] Their surveillance of all the *cacos* became a priority. In their attempts to capture Péralte, whom they labeled, a "very slippery individual," U.S. forces increased their surveillance. One report indicated that Péralte was last seen in Fort Capois wearing a "blue suit, Panama hat, [with an] unkempt beard."[55]

In their ongoing efforts to catch Péralte, U.S. forces again tried to recruit Haitians to assist in their anti-*cacos* operation. On October 13 and 15, they wrote:

> All good citizens of Haiti will be fully protected, and you are informed that the necessary military measures have been taken to this end. On your part, any suspicious strangers, unusual gathering or rumors which you hear and which you think might tend to destroy the peace you at present enjoy, should be reported to the nearest gendarme post. You are informed that 2 nights ago, 12 gendarmes entered the largest bandit camp in your district and scattered vagabonds in all directions including the outlaw Benoît.[56]

On October 15, Colonel John H. Russell once again addressed the *corvée*. In his "Address to the Population," he reported another abolition, its fourth.

> Citizens you are all aware by this time that the *corvée* system has been definitely abolished. . . . The occupation is determined that the laws of Haiti shall not be as violated and that all good and peaceful citizens shall be fully protected while the lawless element will be rundown.[57]

Just like their eighteenth- and nineteenth-century predecessors, U.S. forces never acknowledged the original violence of their actions. In this document, they try to explain that the *corvée* system was abolished—even though there is evidence that it continued past official efforts to end it—without mentioning that the unjust system was itself of their own creation. Their effort to convince Haitians of their supposed goodwill falls in line with all of their communication about the invasion—that somehow good was bad and bad was good. The U.S. military addressed Haitians as citizens in this document but discuss how they treated them as nonpersons. Furthermore, they mention their fourth abolition of the *corvée* in a paragraph about the *cacos*. They purposefully address both as if they are one and the same disorderly, criminal actions. The continual lies about the *corvée*, its purpose, and its end were a trend of the U.S. military articulating one thing and practicing another.

"Banditism Is a Thing of the Past"

The invaders' hunt for Charlemagne Péralte and his subsequent assassination reveal both the sheer brutality of the invasion and the formidable resistance that Haitians like him waged. Under Péralte's leadership, *cacos* activity not only escalated, it spread to the "entire center of the country and [was] active in the mountains of the North."[58] The United States listed the towns of Lascahobas, Mirebalais, Grand Bois, Maissade, Cerca-la-Source and a place they referred to as Lo bas Canton Ravine. The United States recognized the expansive network of resistance, this patriotic kinship, and that there was a connection between the war fought in Haiti and the one in Europe. A report explains:

> Charlemagne's revolt was receiving potent aid from Port-au-Prince. Certain Germans, with whose country the United States was then at war, and various Haitians who could always be relied upon to participate in any movement no matter how debased, provided they saw a chance of profit, were sending money and food to Charlemagne. Improved rifles and ammunition were noted among articles captured from bandits.[59]

Again, the U.S. military both acknowledges the *cacos'* vast reach in Haiti and slyly dismisses their inroads with its allegations that Haitians would participate "in any movement no matter how debased."[60]

U.S. forces had kept heavy surveillance on Péralte and his immediate army for quite some time. They reported on the *cacos'* chain of communication, by stating that "the system of supply and information of the bandits was mostly carried on by means of market women but evidence has been produced to show that a regular system of espionage and supply consisting of men and women was established at Port-au-Prince."[61] For three months, U.S. forces, led by Hanneken, colluded with Haitians Jean-Baptiste Conzé, gendarme Jean Edmond François, and Cherubin Blot. Conzé was a chief of police at Grande Rivière, whom they enticed with the promise of U.S. $3,000, the equivalent of 15,000 Haitian gourdes. Conzé partnered with someone who could correspond with Charlemagne in French. Their names were not made public, especially after Charlemagne's death. Perhaps because they were aware that patriotic kin would revolt against them, they concealed their names.

In August, the U.S. forces infiltrated the *cacos* by setting up their own camp at Capois. When other *cacos* suspected them of falsehood, the Conzé/François/Blot group simulated an attack, and U.S. soldiers acted as if they had been harmed. Hanneken reported on one such attack, in which he "played the part of being shot in the shoulder, and I had bandages, and I had red ink to show; it looked like blood." Hanneken purposefully rode through the market in Grande Rivière, making a point of appearing hurt. The rumor circulated that Conzé had shot Hanneken, for which Charlemagne reportedly "praised Conzé for joining the revolution . . . the revolution against the United States Marines." The theatrics and military strategy involved in this faux attack shows the tenacity of the *cacos* movement. Furthermore, the traitors use of the market underscores the importance of that space. There, *cacos Ayisienne* and patriotic kin gathered and disseminated information for Péralte.

On October 26, Charlemagne arrived in Capois with his brother, Saint-Rémy, other chiefs, including, Adhémar Francismar, Estravil, Papillion, and close to twelve hundred *cacos*. U.S. forces and their Haitian infiltrators planned to attack the *cacos* on October 31. Marines and gendarmes stationed men at different towns, including Saint-Raphaël, Ranquitte, Grosse Roche, Vallières, and Maissade, in case their plan went awry.[62] Hanneken offered his men a shot of rum to brave the attack. He reported:

> With our faces blackened, and twenty gendarmes all in old dirty clothes, dressed as civilians, and with one machine gun, [we] took up position. . . . About seven hundred bandits passed en route to attack Grande Rivière at about ten p.m. . . . Charlemagne had changed his mind and remained up in the mountains between Grande Rivière and Fort Capois on the top of a high hill. . . .

> Charlemagne had arranged with General Conzé that after Conzé had captured Grande Rivière that he, Conzé, should send up a detachment of bandits to come and notify him. . . . So, after our first plan was frustrated, the following was decided upon. We would be the detachment that would go and tell Charlemagne that Conzé had captured Grande Rivière, and it would be safe for him to come down. . . . The Secretary thereupon returned to us and swiftly told me what Charlemagne had said, and that was dangerous, as we had to pass six different outposts to get to Charlemagne. . . .

> The sixth outpost was the immediate guard over Charlemagne. . . . Button and
> I advanced to within fifteen feet of Charlemagne, who was standing over a fire
> and was speaking with his woman, when two men halted us and worked the
> bolts of their rifles. The undersigned said to Button, alright and immediately
> raised his 45 automatics and took deliberate aim and fired at Charlemagne. . . .
> The undersigned found Charlemagne's body shot through the heart.
>
> All invaluable articles which were not deemed necessary to transport were
> burned. Charlemagne's body arrived in Grande Rivière at 9:00 a.m., Novem-
> ber 1, 1919. It is requested that the reward offered for Charlemagne, plus $1,000,
> be given to Mr. Jean B. Conzé, who has performed a wonderful piece of work
> in the killing of this man, risking his life every moment that he was in the
> hills.[63]

The fact that the U.S. had to find collaborators to get to him proves Péralte's
excellent leadership skills. Only those closest to Péralte would have been in his
camp. The woman they noted above was also a key figure in the resistance. Either
she was an informant, a fighter, or both, demonstrating that not all the fighters
were men. Her presence in his camp already proves that she and Péralte were inti-
mately connected. The U.S. Americans' noting that she was his woman suggests
that they had information about her and/or her relationship with the *cacos* leader.
Charlemagne knew his death hovered close. His previous hesitation at Grande
Rivière and his instructions to Conzé demonstrate his awareness that something
was amiss. And on the evening of October 31, the invaders and the Haitian traitors finally got to him.

On November 1, 1919, the radio announcement came on the U.S. Naval Radio
and sounded as follows:

> RUSH CHARLEMAGNE PERALT KILLED BY CAPT HANNEKIN TWELVE
> MIDNIGHT NEAR GRAND RIVIÈRE STOP. JUST BROUGHT INTO CAPE
> HAITIEN AND POSITIVELY IDENTIFIED BY PRIEST OLD PRISON SERGEANT
> AND OTHERS WHO KNEW HIM PERSONALLY. DETAILS WILL FOLLOW.[64]

Hanneken had been on a hunt for Péralte and other *cacos* for a long time. He
succeeded only because of some Haitians, the very people whom he and his comrades dismissed and belittled. The extensive plot to murder Péralte exposes the
invaders' lies about *cacos* resistance. U.S. soldiers had used blackface before in
minstrel shows in the Dominican Republic and in Haiti.[65] This time the alleged
blackface was to effectuate Péralte's death. Their murder of Péralte and display
of his body was a performance. Their strategies of using blackface, finding Haitian traitors, speaking the native language, *and* operating at night showcased
their extensive operation against the *cacos*. The invaders narrative was that they
blindsided and dominated the *cacos* leader. Yet what is made clear in their

various strategies is that it was the *cacos* who were succeeding. Rather than capture Péralte and imprison him, Hanneken assassinated the *cacos* leader with a shot to his heart. As Hanneken reflected decades later in an interview, the ultimate goal with Péralte was to kill him. Hanneken recalled that, in addition to the fatal shot, he fired two more into Péralte's heart for assurance. In a manner that continued the U.S. violence on Péralte and his memory, officials transported his body to a public square to display it. The invaders assumed that cutting off the head (Péralte) would end resistance. It was a temporary feeling. In reality, the invaders actions of murder, confirming his death, and displaying Péralte's cadaver, served the contrary. They had killed a celebrated politician and *caco* who had amassed patriotic kin who would continue the fight.

Many Haitians believe that there is an honor in the sacred act of death, of passing to the other side. It is often described as a reunion with African ancestors. As a sign of respect for this sacred moment, burials are prompt. The United States had no intention of respecting this honorable tradition because it never acknowledged the humanity and justified rage of the *cacos*. Péralte, to the Americans, was merely evidence of the fallacy of their "peace building" narrative. Showing his mangled body to the others was a cruel tactic to ensure compliance with an illegal foreign occupation. Instead, the invaders publicly communicated with Péralte's patriotic kin by using his body as a warning.

Though Péralte's history, written by his oppressor, was one of supposed "banditry" and defeat, the U.S. military's use of his murdered body and its image is the most blatant example of the fallacy of their version of events. Moreover, the fundamental racism of the dehumanizing act witnesses to a shared experience among Blacks in Haiti and the United States. Black people were murdered and hung from trees—their assassinated bodies were reason to gather and celebrate. Similarly, marines boarded a plane with the photographs and disseminated the pictures that announced the death of the *cacos* leader to Haitian citizens. This was reminiscent of the pictorial images and commercial postcards of lynchings in the United States. In one report, they admitted photographing Péralte's body so that "there could be no claim made by Haitians that the body had been in anyway mutilated."[66]

U.S. forces also called in a medical inspector to identify the body. A major, two lieutenants, and the prison record confirmed that the deceased was in fact Péralte. Using his prison record at the civil prison in Cap-Haïtien, the report provided this description:

> Age 32 years, born in Hinche, former occupation cultivator, citizen of Haiti. Complexion Black, hair Negro, eyes Negro, weight 140 lbs., height 59.5 inches. Large scar over left shin, six lance scars over right buttock, three lance scars over left buttock. Under remarks—escaped September 3, 1918, about 8:30 a.m. . . . Body shows two bullet wounds on left chest, both bullets passing through the body, leaving it with small clean wounds in the back, both bullets having

penetrated the heart. There is no body or facial disfigurement.... Face is clean shaven, except a rather large mustache.[67]

The omission of Péralte's public service record illustrates another act of symbolic violence, this time on Péralte's legacy. Despite his diverse political roles, the authors of the report omitted his service to the Haitian state. Rather than list him as a politician, they documented his acts as a cultivator and a convict, as peasant and thug! The specific display of Péralte's body demonstrated the U.S. forces' brutal triumph in executing the supreme *caco* leader. U.S. troops hoped this would signal an end to Haitian resistance. They reasoned that, without their leader, the *cacos* would buckle. In fact, Péralte's death had the opposite effect. *Cacos* and other Haitian resistance only escalated.

Toussaint L'Ouverture, who led the Haitian Revolution but who was also imprisoned by French forces and left to die in a prison in the Jura Mountains, famously declared: "In overthrowing me, you have overthrown only the trunk of the tree of Negro liberty in Saint Domingo. It will rise again from the roots because they are many and deep."[68] Péralte, who drew connections between the *cacos*' fight for resistance and ancestors from L'Ouverture's and Dessalines's era, was also only part of this group that had a deep desire for freedom. As the invasion continued, even though the U.S. troops had assassinated Péralte, the roots of the *cacos* ran deep, thanks to the Haitian patriotic kin. The marines' claim that "banditism is a thing of the past," was, in fact, premature.[69]

5

Violence (Vyolans)

● ●

After Péralte's murder, U.S. troops, still articulating their message as one of democracy building and peace keeping, continued to violently oppress Haitians. From 1919 to 1921, the foreigners normalized aggression through a variety of means, including celebrating *cacos'* deaths, patrolling the nation, and spying on citizens. The guerilla fighters, even without Péralte, continued to wage a strong resistance movement—one that the United States countered with air patrols and bombs. The network of patriotic kin, including women whose stories often went untold, also continued its support of the *cacos*. Despite the 1920 Navy Commission's conclusion that the invaders had resistance under control, *cacos* and other Haitian protests remained in 1921.

Violent Machinations

Violence was a tool for the invaders. It allowed them to keep their control over the country, all while denying the immorality of their actions. U.S. troops were, of course, brutal to *cacos* leaders who resisted their control, but they also violently oppressed average Haitian citizens. From invasive surveillance to outright torture, a system of brutality kept the U.S. invaders in control. At best, market women, farmers, and editors had to live under the watchful eye of the invaders; at worst, innocent people were imprisoned and murdered.

A racist ideology, so engrained in U.S. culture, dominated the way that troops interacted with Haitians. This racism was blatant because it was often stated openly by high-ranking U.S. officials. The secretary of state William Jennings Bryan (1913–1915), for example, called Haitians "niggers who speak French." The statement juxtaposes a racist term with the language of a former colonizer—assuming the superiority of the latter. His words witness to the mistaken U.S. belief that Haitians were supposedly inferior and somehow deserving of the U.S.'s illegal invasion. His comments echo those of his predecessor Robert Lansing, who thought Africans unable to govern themselves.

In the culture of the country that the U.S. troops called home, their legal structure buttressed Jim and Jane Crow's fallacies about Black inferiority and White superiority. This mentality was so embedded in U.S. culture that the irony of their own actions often went unnoticed. Former president Woodrow Wilson, a historian, seemingly conceded to this racial ideology when he permitted the premiere of *The Birth of a Nation* to play at the White House in June 1914. The showing of a film presenting Black people as threats to White society inside a building constructed—not once, but twice—by enslaved Black people was in line with the doublespeak of U.S. history about the Haitian invasion. During this time, as Ida B. Wells and other antilynching activists meticulously documented, White Southerners regularly displayed black people's dead bodies suspended from the trees on which they hanged them. *This* was the society that formed U.S. troops such as John Houston Craige, Herman Hanneken, Alexander Williams, and Smedley Butler.

This ideology informed their actions in the Caribbean. U.S. troops dressed in blackface at a minstrel show in front of a fort in the Dominican Republic. Over twenty marines donned clown and butler costumes in direct imitation of White minstrel show performers who perpetuated stereotypes of African Americans as cowards, lazy, and ignorant. The soldiers reproduced their racist stereotypes of what Black people looked like with their darkened faces, their exaggerated lip sizes, and their performance of "blackness." Just like back home in the United States, these soldiers' minstrelsy of Caribbean people contained within it violent ideas about people of color. As African American and Theatre Studies scholar Daphne Brooks argues: "There are different ways in which blackface becomes weaponized as a form of white supremacist propaganda."[1] Against the backdrop of segregation, the soldiers' actions appeared the norm. Minstrel shows became commonplace in the Dominican Republic and Haiti.[2] One of the soldiers' programs, "The Marine Masqueraders present Coontown Nights" by the "Burnt Cork Company," is also preserved in their archives about the invasion period.[3] Thus, soldiers who patrolled a nation as an act of democracy, per their reasoning, acted in racist fashion. In its formation and execution, the invasion of the Americas by a fellow member republic buttresses the myth of white superiority and black and brown inferiority. Additionally, the preservation of their actions in the U.S. military archives screams power and privilege. The troops were not acting surreptitiously. Rather, these were intentional and public acts of nonphysical violence and intimidation. Racism was at the core of their seizure of Haiti and all interactions with Haitians, whether in the White House, in Haiti's

National Palace, or on the battlefields in rural Haiti. They had used blackface to effectuate Péralte's death.

Public Spectacles of Death

Two weeks after Péralte's death, U.S. forces and President Dartiguenave publicly celebrated his assassination. Military honors were bestowed upon the men who killed Péralte. On November 10, *Le Nouvelliste* informed readers that "a few officers and gendarmes [who] attacked and killed the famous leader of the *cacos* will receive the head of state military medal of the Gendarmerie."[4] Indeed, on Sunday, November 16, the band of the gendarmerie played the Presidential March as Dartiguenave entered the public square in Champs de Mars. In the company of U.S. Colonel Russell and General Frederic M. Wise, the president of Haiti decorated the men who had assassinated one of its citizens. He acknowledged four U.S. officers, including Colonel James J. Meade, gendarme and USMC; Captain Herman Hanneken, gendarme and sergeant USMC; Second Lieutenant William R. Button, gendarme and corporal in the USMC; and Second Lieutenant H. R. Woods, gendarme and sergeant in the Marine Corps, with the medaille militaire for "destroying Charlemagne Péralte and his band."[5]

U.S. troops played "Semper Fidelis" for their fellow marines. Following the ceremony, the awardees attended a small reception at the Palais Nationale.[6] It is possible that the ceremonies were segregated, as neither Cherubin Blot nor Jean-Baptiste Conzé was present. But it is also possible that these two refused to publicly associate with the killing of a fellow Haitian. With Conzé, and originally the gendarmes in Haiti, the U.S. military purposefully recruited fellow Haitian citizens to police, harm, and execute one another.[7] The same day, the headquarters of the gendarmerie issued a memo expressing gratitude to all the men involved in Péralte's death.[8] The brigade commander especially commended Hanneken for firing the revolver into Péralte's heart. He requested that Washington, DC, acknowledge the marine giving him "unstinted credit for his initiative, good judgment, tenacity of purpose, and courage in this brilliant affair."[9]

The United States used ceremonies to legitimize violence. The practice parallels the violent actions of racist White U.S. Americans against Blacks. Postcards and public ceremonies—while not part of the state—displayed civilians harming fellow citizens because of their race. The popular memory of Blacks discussing how Whites would sometimes picnic at these sites of death not only normalized the violence of "strange fruit" hanging from trees, but it also inoculated future generations of White and Black children.[10] In Haiti, after Péralte's death, the band and officials who marched at the public assembly provided a veneer of discipline and order to a Haitian state that was truly in the throes of chaos and rebellion. The use of the Haitian president in this and subsequent public celebrations of death was intentional. The image of President Dartiguenave flanked by U.S. administrators—Russell as the head of the invasion, and Wise as head of the military force—all communicated nonverbally with the Haitian public. For Haitians involved in the anti-imperialist movement, the event in Champs de Mars further demonstrated that Dartiguenave was allied with U.S. forces over citizens attempting to free Haiti of foreign rule. The ceremony also sent a subtle message that the Haitian state would not—or could not—protect its citizens who rebelled. It demonstrated that Haitians who resisted—rather than the foreigners—were the true enemies of the state in 1919. The public ceremony about Péralte's death was a distraction. It diverted attention away from the brutality of what they had convened to celebrate. Péralte's murderers then had the nerve to attend a reception. The murder of Black people, especially those who resisted White supremacy, became casual and its violence was erased. In addition to the United States' seizing Haiti and her political and economic institutions, the murders of citizens who were or were not *cacos* was normalized and absolved. The U.S. military's lies about the votes for the 1918 constitution not being a coerced display of obedience; the *corvée* being work rather than enslaved labor; its actions being peacekeeping rather than murder; and now staging a medal ceremony as a celebration rather than an official display of the government support for murder: these all exposed who were the vagabonds and criminals.

Cacos and Benoît Batraville

The *cacos* had prepared for their leaders' deaths. Days after Péralte's demise, they regrouped. The *cacos'* ministers of war and finance selected Benoît Batraville as the "supreme chief in Charlemagne's place."[11] Batraville was born in Mirebalais in the late nineteenth century.[12] He and Péralte were cousins by marriage.[13] The Batraville's family connection to the Péralte family, including how members of their families participated in *cacos'* struggles, helped cement their bond. Batraville's familial class origin as peasants, his work as a schoolteacher, and his role as an *houngan*, all contributed to his ability to galvanize and sustain *cacos'* support.[14] In their written communications, Péralte and Batraville had often discussed strategies.

Still angry about the death of his comrade, Batraville grouped his fighters into "strengths of about 150–300" to avoid ambush. He engaged U.S. forces across Haiti.[15] Saint-Rémy Péralte, who worked as a minister, had accompanied Charlemagne the night the U.S. forces killed his brother, and escaped with injuries. Months later, however, gendarmes killed Saint-Rémy as they patrolled Habitation Cercady near La Victoire.[16] By the end of 1919, Masséna Péralte had buried three of the Péralte boys, including her beloved Charlemagne.

The *cacos'* anger increased their mobilization against U.S. forces. On November 4, just days after Péralte's death, the guerilla fighters killed Private Clarence E. Morris of Squadron E, First Division Marine Aviation Force.[17] Private Morris had armed himself with his Lewis air machine gun and three ammunition drums before leaving his plane. He trusted three unnamed Haitians as guides, and even allowed one to hold his weapon. When Private Morris took a rest, the guides revealed that they were *cacos*. After striking him with a machete, they stole his gun, his ammunition, and his clothes. Later, patrols found Private Morris's body and helmet.[18]

The *cacos* also channeled their grief for Péralte into anger toward Haitians like Conzé and Blot who had betrayed their leader and the anti-invasion movement. Days after the celebration of Haitian independence on January 1, 1920, *cacos* chief Papillion Fils issued the following proclamation to "Young Haitiens." Similar to Péralte's method, Fils's letterhead read "Liberty, Equality, Fraternity," an overt reminder of the *cacos'* mission.

> Gendarme, when the white man shall have gone away, what will you do. Try and find some way to join us as soon as possible. It is still time to do so. Nothing bad will happen to you. We are all Haitians and we are not led by any ambition for money or by any desire to kill our brothers. I cry: Long live the young men of Hinche; long live the Gendarmes of Hinche and of St. Michel. You should understand that you are considered like dogs by the Americans. And know too, that the Americans will soon be leaving. While you are expending all your forces against me.[19]

Fils appeals to Haitian gendarmes who were not yet allied with the *cacos*. He reminded them that they, too, were connected as patriotic kin. The second half of his letter was not so tolerant. In the first half he reassured his readers that they would not get hurt as *cacos*; subsequently he cautioned them about the risks of not joining their brothers in the struggle:

> When the day of my deliverance shall come, you will be severely punished; you will be held in contempt. We cry "Vive Dessalines." Do you not intend to lay down your arms? If you think that the *Cacos* are not going to win, if you do not lay down your arms and come and join me, you shall have no part with me. But if you lay down your arms and come and join me, I can promise you in advance that you will be given employment, I am in a position to hold out two years; or to die or succeed at the risk of my life. P.S. I forgot to inform you that I have 17 Gendarmes with me. Some have been appointed Chiefs of divisions; others, Chiefs of Brigade. They are well thought of and protected. There are also two white men with me. Papillion Fils, Revolutionary Chief of the North.

Fils employed a familiar *cacos* strategy. He used historical memory in naming Dessalines, a reminder of the founding father's mission for a free Haiti. His employment offer reveals how the U.S. military sought to negotiate with *cacos* in prior years. The *cacos* were effective at recruiting soldiers; and this call for them to behave like these gendarmes who had defected, highlights their success.

Smedley Butler spoke openly almost two decades after Péralte's death about the nefarious motivations of U.S. military invasions. He blamed his own training to simply follow rules and not think—and stated that this was how the U.S. military succeeded.

At speaking engagements in the United States, he admitted to contributing to U.S. imperialism across the world: "We always declared war on everybody else first, but it has always been in our defense. . . . War is a racket. [The U.S. government is] glad to create some incident and exaggerate it to attract attention and get everyone to want to know what it is all about. I have helped to start wars."[20] Even with his change of heart, however, Butler fails to mention that the fundamental racism of U.S. culture made the unthinking attacks of the United States even more likely. He often used racist epithets when referencing Haitians.[21] In this reflection about his time in the nation, Butler makes no apology for the Haitians that he killed who were defending their nation. Rather, he indicated he sought absolution for himself and other soldiers who obeyed U.S. commands.

> I would not under any circumstances leave the continental United States to fight another war. . . . I spent 33 years of my life collecting for Wall Street making ravishing expeditions to Central America. Nine ravishing expeditions—that's what they were. The Marine Corps is the greatest collection agency in the works. Fortunately, the present administration has put a stop to that. All school children are taught that an American citizen has a perfect right to go anywhere at any time and be protected by the flag of his country. That makes it hard on three or four million soldiers, because some person with a selfish motive feels at liberty to do whatever he pleases, because he will be protected by the American flag. . . . When you get into the service, you don't think. You just do as you're told. You can't think and it's a good thing. Don't blame soldiers and sailors.[22]

Butler declined later requests for interviews, so any shift in opinion about Péralte and the *cacos* in particular is not recorded.

The uninterrupted resistance between the time of Péralte's demise and Batraville's rise as chief of the *cacos* surprised the U.S. forces. Briefly, the United States reinstated its previous nonviolent approach to counter *cacos'* activity. First, the soldiers partnered with the financial advisor to Haiti, the engineer of Haiti, and representatives from the United West Indies Corporation and the Haytian American Sugar Company to offer *cacos* an employment incentive not to participate in the "revolutionary movement."[23] They continued to misconstrue the *cacos'* cause by suggesting that poverty or unemployment drew them to this fight. Second, they offered amnesty to *cacos* who surrendered—on the condition that they police one another.[24] To qualify for this option, a *caco* could not be an escaped convict (a direct reference to Péralte's story), could not be involved in the murders of Privates Mike Morris and Lawrence Muth, and must be willing to assist U.S. troops on their patrols. These nonviolent methods of dismantling the resistance after its leader had been violently taken down were met, however, with disdain. The *cacos* refused this offer, a testimony to the fighters' unity and intelligence. In fact, these acts of defiance added to the *cacos*' strength. Their steadfast devotion to their cause and their ongoing protests demonstrate the fallacy of any idea they were disorganized or ineffective.

In fact, months into his leadership, on January 25, 1920, Batraville and an estimated three hundred *cacos* attacked Port-au-Prince.[25] On a patrol of Mont Michel, Lieutenant Lawrence Muth and others fired on the *cacos*; Batraville and his guerrilla fighters ambushed the invaders from the flank and rear. Muth was shot fatally in the stomach and head. Private Stone, next in command, suffered injuries to his neck, face, and left eye. He escaped with his remaining troops. According to U.S. reports, the *cacos* then mutilated Muth's body.[26] The murder of individual U.S. troops likely felt like a small victory in an ongoing war against a giant imperial power. The *cacos*' mutilation of Muth exemplified their rage. The guerrilla fighters had lost leaders and soldiers in the most savage ways, and they responded in kind. While Marine Corps Lieutenant Frederick Spear claimed that "those Cacos were very savage men, and if they had captured one of our marines they would probably have skinned him alive," he also disclosed that in actuality, "all Cacos were to be killed."[27] The *cacos*' murder of Muth was potentially in reaction to the display of Péralte's body. At this stage, most of the Péralte family was dead, along with several hundred Haitians. This was a small war with significant consequences—physical and psychological warfare, seizure of lands and properties, and brutal deaths. Haitian resistance continued—despite countless cases of brutalization and assassinations. It was never on the same scale because they did not have the governmental power that the United States did. It was in reaction to the war waged on them, but because of racism, their act was always viewed as violent and was further used to demonstrate the need for their oppression. It was turned against them, whereas the invaders' murder and display of a dead body was celebrated with medals.

Unlike their covert operation against Péralte, the U.S. soldiers widely publicized their vendetta against Batraville. They needed the *cacos* problem to resolve quickly and completely. The guerrilla fighters' quick regrouping after Péralte's death hastened the invaders zeal to end the *cacos* for good. A livid Colonel Russell launched a comprehensive plan to rein in the *cacos* leader. The U.S. military enacted martial law. It tried protestors in military tribunals. U.S. forces visited officials and clergy in towns. One report stated that the aim was fostering cordial relations with "natives" and "at the same time gathering any information which might be of service."[28] In doing so, they intercepted letters from Batraville to residents in Hinche. Further, they asked the Haitian public to help capture him. They posted a proclamation in French that read:

Citizens of Haiti: All good citizens who love their country should work to put hold on the disorders that have existed since last year. The time of bandits is finished. Most of the chiefs engage in battle with the invasion forces daily . . . to obtain complete security. . . . There should be no rest until the capture of the malefactor, the one who brought us acts of pillage and brigandage, Benoît Batraville. Every good Haitian should bring all information to help us capture Benoît Batraville, and we will give a compensation of five gourdes.[29]

The rhetoric echoes the U.S. characterization of Péralte. U.S. forces attempted to defame the *cacos* as criminals, cannibals, and bandits—anything but libera-tors. The use of the phrase "every good Haitian" presents the idea that those who rebelled against the United States and desired self-rule were "bad" Haitians. Hai-tians did not respond to their monetary offer. The memory of what the U.S. soldiers did to Péralte had solidified their distrust of the foreigners. Many Haitians had received a photograph of Péralte when the invaders dropped the picture of his cadaver from their planes. It is impossible to imagine that Haitians felt warmth and solidarity for people who would behave this way. Furthermore, as Batraville and the *cacos* continued their mission to free Haiti of foreign rule, U.S. forces reacted violently against Haitians. They suspected all people of har-boring, aiding, and abetting the guerrilla fighters.

An Encounter with a Haitian Woman

Muth's death in particular incensed the U.S. troops; and they spared no effort in their hunt for Batraville and other Haitians. While on *cacos* patrol, Captain J. L. Perkins, six marines, and a visiting U.S. reporter, Herbert J. Seligmann, encoun-tered an unnamed Haitian woman. Out of respect, I have named her Madame Gislaine. Though our own records of her interaction with the U.S. military are from a hostile source, the account of her actions offers a window into the way that women resisted the invasion. Captain Perkins dated his report of their interaction from April 3 to April 7, 1921, the days they patrolled the northern areas between Morne Petite Bois and Morne Pierre. There are two versions of this encounter. Per-kins first explains that he ran across a woman and intimidated her to get informa-tion about the *cacos*.

> While searching for information as to the trail I found a woman gathering
> food in a deserted garden. Upon seeing me she ran but failed to escape.
> Mr. Seligman and myself questioned her considerably regarding the trail to
> Morne Michel, but she said there was no such trail, which I personally knew to
> be a lie. During the questioning, she contradicted herself four times and tried
> repeatedly to escape. A native passerby informed us that her husband was
> among the bandits and that she was probably supplying them with food. I then
> resorted to some means of frightening her because it was of paramount
> importance that I find that trail immediately in order to save that entire
> section of the country from devastation at the hands of Benoit. I passed a small

four-foot cord around her neck and tree, over a six feet limb from the ground
and threatened to hang her in case she further refused to lead me to the trail or
tell me of someone who could. She persisted in her refusals and failure to give
us a bit of information, an attitude so truly characteristic of the bandit
sympathizers. Mr. Seligman then lost his temper and exclaimed, "shoot her
God damn her, she has lied to you four times now."[30]

This version of the story demonstrates that the behavior of U.S. troops in Haiti
mirrored *exactly* the racial oppression that was normal and widespread in the
United States. U.S. imperial power relied on a model that it had set up, practiced,
and even perfected in its own land—the dehumanization and brutalizing of
people of African heritage. Perkins's report continued, claiming that he was actually avoiding cruelty:

> However, I restrained him [his fellow officer] and explained that any cruelty
> was out of the question because it was not in keeping within our policy in
> dealing with such natives, who were little more than children mentally.
> Then Mr. Seligman requested me to allow him to photograph the scene, but
> as a photograph appearing in a magazine would give the American public a
> false impression of our methods in dealing with the Haitians, I refused to
> permit any such photographs. The woman was released and allowed to return
> to her home. She had not been strangled or mistreated in any respect
> whatsoever.[31]

In the mid-1920s, Seligmann had published a series of articles in *The Nation*
against the invasion.[32] In one article "The Conquest of Haiti" dated July 10, 1920,
Seligmann criticized the U.S. for its doublespeak about democracy and being
peaceful in Haiti.

> To Belgium's Congo, to Germany's Belgium, to England's India and Egypt, the
> United States has added a perfect miniature in Haiti. Five years of violence in
> that Negro republic of the Caribbean, without sanction of international law or
> any law other than force, is now succeeded by an era in which the military
> authorities are attempting to hush up what has been done. The history of the
> American invasion of Haiti is only additional evidence that the United States
> is among those Powers in whose international dealings democracy and freedom
> are mere words, and human lives negligible in face of racial snobbery, political
> chicane, and money.[33]

In December 1921 Perkins recounted a second version of the event in which
his story changed significantly.[34] The soldier was suspicious of Seligmann, given
his publications that painted the invasion in an unfavorable light. After reading
one such article, Perkins questioned whether Seligmann's visit had been a ploy

to defame the invasion of Haiti. He more forthrightly accuses Madame Gislaine of being a *caco* and downplays his own aggression toward her.

> We saw a woman gathering food in a deserted Garde; we were unobserved by her. After watching her actions for a moment, I could see that she was in great haste, that her movements were guarded and that she was very wary. As soon as she had gathered a load of potatoes, she would pass them to a child back in the weeds and run back for more. In fact, it was clear that she was gathering food for the "Cacos." We crept as closely as possible, and then rose up and made our presence known in a gentle way without any attempt to alarm her.

Perkins continued:

> We quieted her down and told her we were simply searching for food and would like to buy some. But she was still very excited and still attempted to escape. Then I asked her to tell me where the trail to Morne Michel was, and she told me there was none, which I knew was a lie, as I had heard of it a dozen times. Persuasion obtained nothing, so I resorted to fear. Then she promised to take Seligman and myself to a man who would show us the trail and wanted to carry the Browning Automatic Rifle. She led us up hill and down for about an hour, not to man nor to any house, finally attempting to escape again. So, we led her back.

Perkins's comment on "persuasion" and "I resorted to fear" were threatening.

> Seligman was exhausted. He spoke to her in French for a few minutes, and finally losing his temper turned to me and said, "Shoot her, God damn her, she has lied to you four times now"—which was true. I replied that shooting her was not only forbidden, but it would accomplish nothing, and would also arouse the whole countryside and betray our location, and also that there was a shadow of a possibility that maybe after all she was too afraid of "*Caco* revenge" to tell us. Then I told him I would try to scare her by tying a small cord around her neck and pretending that I was going to hang her, which pleased Seligman immensely. But I did not attempt to string her up. He begged me to as he said wanted to take a Kodak picture of the scene; he wanted as many of the Marines in the picture as he could get. I asked why he wanted that, and he replied that he wanted simply as a souvenir for his own future amusement, etc. I released the woman at once; no picture was taken.

Madame Gislaine was a victim of the normalcy of violence under the U.S. regime. Upon hearing news of the death of Lieutenant Muth, Perkins had unleashed his anger on her. His casual recounting of this encounter shows the ordinary nature of brutality and their fundamental mistrust of any Haitian, regardless of what they were saying or doing. A U.S. officer threatened to lynch a woman if she did not provide him with information. Even the presence of a newspaper reporter did not alter his behavior or give Perkins pause. Perkins downplays the violence of his intimidation, while also acknowledging it occurred. Madame Gislaine was terrified given her hasty movements and attempts to escape. Yet Perkins read her demeanor as disobedience. Perkin's comment that "we caught her" inform us that Madame Gislaine was sexually intimidated by the eight White foreign males, seven of whom were armed, who surrounded her. Indeed, various investigations discussed the excessive use of force against Haitians, including the killings of unarmed Haitian prisoners and those who fled the *corveé* as well as the sexual harassment of Haitian women.[35] Madame Gislaine requested the rifle to protect herself from these men.

Both the race and gender of Madame Gislaine were central to how this event unfolded.[36] Perkins could have arrested her. Further, the preservation of this record, as written by him, attests to his power and privilege. The U.S. military documented its acts of racism, sexism, and xenophobia meticulously. Perkins's race and U.S. American nationality afforded him a right to recall this violent encounter casually. Perkins's conclusion that his forces had treated her with respect illuminates the attitudes of U.S. troops toward Haitian citizens. It is true that they did not hang Madame Gislaine from a tree, but placing a cord around her body and threatening to perform this act was violent enough. Perkins did not conceive of this act as a harmful move. Although he did not kill her, Perkins aggressively demonstrated his power. Additionally, in his second version, Perkins positions the *cacos* and Seligmann as the violent agitators, although Perkins's actions demonstrate that even he did not believe his assertion that the woman was afraid of *cacos'* revenge. He intimidated her. The previous four-foot cord is now a smaller rope. Perkins concluded by suggesting that Seligmann be placed on the Department of Justice's blacklist.

While Perkins is an unreliable narrative, his two version of events do provide us with some important details about Madame Gislaine, women's political participation, and life under the invasion. It is possible that she was simply gathering food and was rightfully afraid for her life when she encountered the foreigners. If so, it is likely that no matter how she responded to their questions, they would not have been satisfied. Further, none of the soldiers communicated with her in Kreyòl, noting instead that Seligmann tried without success, to speak to her in French. Due to the fundamental racism of the U.S. troops, they always understood her as a threat. On the other hand, it is also possible that Madame Gislaine was working for the resistance and that she, like many of her predecessors, refused to cooperate by giving no information. If it is true that she misled the troops, then her efforts show that she was a *caco* or patriotic kin, both of which would have taken great skill and calm, especially if she did, indeed, have a child with her or nearby for whom she was caring. As Captain Perkins unleashed his anger and as Seligmann reportedly ordered her death, the Haitian woman brandished silence and feigned ignorance as resistance. While records of female *cacos* leaders are sparse, women did fight. Present at *cacos* camps and taking roles as letter carriers and informants, women participated in the anti-U.S. struggle in many ways.

And yet, although we learn the names of the male *cacos* chiefs (Rameaux, Batraville, Péralte, Bobo, and so on), this woman enters the historical narratives as Madame Gislaine. Why were there no named women *cacos* leaders, even though they also fought? As Haitian feminists continue to ask: "Kote Famn yo? Where are the women?" Haitian women took up arms throughout Haiti's formation, from 1697 to 1804. Historian Grace Louise Sanders Johnson analyzes Haitian women who formed feminist groups during the invasion and who fought hard for suffrage.[37] It is quite possible that women who refused to cooperate with U.S. troops, like Madame Gislaine, were *cacos*.

In my research, I secured only one picture of a Haitian female fighter. She also enters the text nameless. The caption reads "a *cacos* wife *caco* herself" (Figure 7). The unnamed guerrilla fighter holds her rifle in an intimate manner and with a sense of poise and grace. Both her stance and her grasp of the weapon convey the knowledge of a soldier who has fired it before.

Until I locate her name and her story, her name is Madame Agathe. Madame Agathe's photo is certainly rare, but its inclusion in the archives reveals that women did indeed participate in the resistance movement. Though few details exist, historians can respond to the erasure of women's history by examining photos like these and stories like those of Madame Gislaine.

Madame Agathe appears fully clothed and in a position of authority. The ease with which she holds her rifle suggests confidence in battle. Madame Agathe looks unintimidated and aware of her equality to men. Too often, images of women during the invasion depict them without the women's consent, which further dehumanized them. One finds images of women bathing and foreign troops gazing at and photographing them. In fact, Madame Agathe's representation as a fully clothed woman is a rare find in the invasion's archives. Her ownership of a gun suggests protest and her claiming her power. Furthermore, she stands in front of two men, who languish in the background, which evokes an impression of command and power. Madame Agathe's photo tells a story rarely told: women were resistance fighters. They, like Madame Gislaine, encountered U.S. soldiers and fought back, either by silence or force. They had power, even if no one remembered to ask their names.

(Non)physical Battles

In addition to their battles with the *cacos*, the collaborating Haitian government also led an initiative to favorably present the invasion. Haitian president Dartiguenave went on a pro-invasion tour. In the company of U.S. troops, Dartiguenave targeted areas that could hold large numbers of Haitians at one time,

FIG. 7 Femme *cacos*

primarily marketplaces. He spoke to the people who lived predominately in areas of a *cacos* stronghold. On April 15, for example, U.S. troops reported the following: "The people listened with intense interest to a very earnest speech made by the President, in which he told them that Benoît Batraville was an outcast, a man of no education, who even could not read or write, and yet that he aspired to the presidency. That he, the President had five years ago signed a convention with the United States, that he was a Haitian and loved his country."[38]

The content of Dartiguenave's speeches on this circuit promoted him as a Haitian patriot *and* an ally to the U.S. administration of his nation. He worked with U.S. forces to counter Péralte and painted the *cacos*' critique of the invasion as the antithesis of democracy and liberty. Dartiguenave met Haitians where they were, rather than at the capital in the Palais National. The president and the invaders probably walked this ground to assess the range of the *cacos*' reach in the markets and at newspaper offices. As Dartiguenave expressed his support of the U.S. troops, they also kept watch of his rhetoric. President Dartiguenave and the U.S. administrators' presence up north informed the Haitian public that these officials were ever present, in the cities and hinterland areas. They also attempted to incite Haitians against Batraville and the other *cacos*.[39]

In order to eliminate Batraville and stifle his influence on the Haitian population, the United States mobilized seventy-five soldiers under Captain J. L. Perkins during the month of May. From one marine's report, twenty-nine marines traveled to Marche Canard where Batraville was stationed. Before month's end, Perkins led them on a surprise attack on Batraville's camp. On May 19, a day after Haitian Flag Day, the new leader of the *cacos* lay dead.

Unlike the murder of Péralte, the U.S. forces did not display Batraville's cadaver. It is unclear if they buried him. Rather they remained in this northern locale and escalated their surveillance. While morale may have been low among the *cacos*, they were still able to regroup. This time *cacos* leadership involved multiple people. U.S. forces noted the presence of four *cacos* leaders after Batraville's death. The new *cacos* chiefs included Leger, Norde, Castine Feder, and a discharged gendarme named Justice Civil. It is unclear how long Civil had masqueraded as a gendarme, but the knowledge and training he received in that military wing of the U.S. administration were invaluable. As an insider to the U.S. military, he was privy to their topics and behavior. The guerrilla fighters' continuous resistance inspired other Haitians to rebel. The "*cacos*' infection"— as the U.S. troops called it—was exactly what they feared. Varied forms of protests and U.S. containment of these activities erupted from 1920 to 1934. The U.S. military could not counter Haitian protests despite their violent and nonviolent methods. Because of the *cacos*' success, Colonel John Russell now gave his troops a three-pronged mission. Colonel Russell dispatched high-ranking marines to the northern countryside and they visited the "infected districts in Haiti."[40] The officers in this case were being promoted as accessible to the natives. This move also gave the troops the opportunity to patrol *cacos* hubs. For example, Colonel Russell noted that he was installing a radio station and troops in Hinche to "crush any uprising in the north of Haiti." Navy Rear Admiral H. S. Knapp routinely visited the northern towns of Mirebalais, Lascahobas, and Hinche. The troops' presence across Haiti—especially in *cacos* towns—signaled to Haitians that the foreigners were prepared to uproot resistance.

Yet the escalation of U.S. military tactics also plainly revealed the *cacos'* success. Whether or not the *cacos* actually won this war is irrelevant to the fact of their persistent resistance. In fact, the *cacos* were victors given the size of their regiments compared to those of the U.S. military and in relation to the population: their force and skill kept a massive imperial power on the move, guessing, and ready to use the most inhumane tactics to get their way.

The second goal in their operation had U.S. administrators sending President Dartiguenave on another speaking tour across Haiti.[41] They hoped that parading the president before the public would generate favor among both the elite and the peasantry, which were their two designated classes of Haitians. Dartiguenave was to contribute to the U.S. discourse that law and order prevailed in Haiti because of their military presence. In 1920, President Dartiguenave travelled to Mirebalais, Lascahobas, Saint-Marc, Gonaïves, Hinche, and towns in between Saint-Michel and Maissade. His actions during his visit to Hinche demonstrated the type of obedience U.S. administrators hoped this method would enforce. Russell noted:

> At Hinche, the heart of the bandit district, the President made a very excellent speech in Creole, and at the close, he asked the country in this neighborhood is devastated, your houses have been burned, your women have been ravaged your cattle stolen, your gardens destroyed. Who has done this? Was it the Occupation?" They all answered, "No, M. le President." "Was it the Gendarmerie?" "No, M. le President." "Then who was it?" And the answer came "It was our own people."[42]

Their comment that women had been ravaged was evidence of the rape that *Ayisienne* endured during the invasion. The U.S. soldiers casually included this assault of women's bodies in a list that described lost property, indicating that this harm was not taken seriously nor discussed at length. Additionally, the "head" of state flanked by foreign military figures asked questions of his citizens that created a false narrative. Much like the U.S. military, Dartiguenave blamed Haitians for the destruction and chaos of the invasion. He knew that Haitians could not answer honestly that the invasion caused disorder. He himself had experienced reprimands from the invaders when he offered an opinion about the invasion. Dartiguenave could not protect his citizens and neither was he protected in his role as a puppet president. Violence and martial law prevented them from telling the truth. It is quite possible to read the response of the crowd as another resistance tactic. Rather than laying blame on the *cacos*, their answer articulated that they were patriotic kin who all took the blame.

By the end of 1920, Dartiguenave was no longer complicit in this pro-U.S. propaganda tour. In a confidential report in November between the brigade commander and the chief of the naval operations, Russell reported on the political situation. Russell warned that President Dartiguenave had shifted his allegiance against the U.S. administrators. Russell reported, "His [Dartiguenave's] entire attitude changed. He virtually threw off the mask, stepped into the arena, fought fiercely as the so-called champion of the Haitian people and with evident intention of posing as a martyr."[43] Russell's use of the word "mask" suggests that Dartiguenave had feigned cooperation all along. But it is not clear how he advocated for nor protected Haitians.

Dartiguenave probably changed his views as he accepted that he did not govern his homeland. The United States had appointed him president, and under his watch he observed their abuse of Haitians and misuse of Haiti's land and resources. But Russell blamed U.S. "American radical writers" for Dartiguenave's shift, as if the Haitian man could not think for himself. These types of quip and belittling of Haitians' intellect were another type of racism. U.S. forces could only conceive of Haitians as children. Additionally, letters calling for the invasion's end from U.S. Americans to the secretary of state and the president became commonplace as well.[44] Feeling blindsided, Russell commented, "The Haitian Government, the Haitien newspapers, and the many political agitators in Port-au-Prince now exerted every effort, apparently, to encourage a dislike among the Haitiens for Americans."[45] The foreign soldiers had previously admitted to selecting Dartiguenave and keeping him in line. And yet, his position against them suddenly generated surprise. Haitian criticisms of the invasion—either from *cacos* or from nonguerrilla fighters—contradicted the U.S. façade of law and order and their doublespeak.

Despite the *cacos'* activities from the onset of the invasion and the diverse group speaking out against it (politicians, newspaper editors, market women, and soldiers), U.S. administrators failed to make the connection that these different classes of Haitians were unified against them. U.S. administrators assumed that with assassinations of key *cacos* leaders, Haitian resistance would end. But the *cacos'* unrelenting activities comprised a multiheaded hydra. For example, in the case of Auguste Magloire, brother of the owner of *Le Matin*, his resistance went unnoticed for a significant period. Magloire had written articles against the *cacos* in the journal. Yet he regularly communicated and was seen with the Péralte brothers, Saül and Charlemagne. It took some time for U.S. administrators to piece together that Magloire's anti-*cacos* editorials were a ruse and that he was one of them. Writing to the Major General Commandant Headquarters in Washington, DC, Russell remarked, "It is my impression, however, that this contra bandit activity on the part of Mr. Magloire was undertaken with the purpose of allaying any suspicion that might be directed against him." Russell requested that the military commission place Magloire on trial to act as a deterrent to any "ambitious and anti-American Haitians."[46] While they collected Magloire's writing, they had no sufficient cause to try him. Russell concluded:

It has been generally known that a large percentage of the population of Port-Au-Prince, namely those not making money at this time and including disgruntled politicians and most of the lawyers, were at heart in sympathy with the bandits and their activities, but the cleverness with which they communicated with bandits and gave them advice and assistance has been such as to preclude their detection.

U.S. troops' separation of Haitians into two classes—elites and peasants, with no other groups in between—limited their vision for ending resistance. They described the former as "the class that thinks the most nearly white. Many of its members have travelled and lived abroad. . . . This class has been divided in its opinion regarding the occupation."[47] These types of casual commentaries signaled how the United States interacted with Haitians from positions of authority and a false sense of superiority. Their lack of cultural competency was a disservice to the troops' mission. U.S. forces assumed that these two groups did not form alliances. Russell concluded his report with interesting musings about Haitians' lack of unity.

> The question naturally uppermost in everyone mind is where [this] will lead the United States. Two people can ride a horse, but one must ride behind. Is the United States in its dealings with Haiti going to ride behind? If so, it will soon be ready for a fall and it would be much better to get off now. It is beyond the question of doubt that it would soon mount again or allow someone else to do so and take the reins but half way measures among a people who are over 97% illiterate, who have not even the tribal relations of jungle Africa to bind them together and among whom the literate class have solely their own interests at heart cannot be considered.[48]

Russell shows his outright disdain for the majority of Haitians, which is based on racist assumptions about their intelligence and education. Defining literacy as an indication of intelligence, he suggests that somehow this means the United States should control Haiti. The assumption of a lack of cohesiveness erases Haiti's colonial history. A dedication to national sovereignty binds Haitians together—any differences based on regional ancestral origins are due to the history of colonial slavery. Yet again, he blames Haitians for a violence enacted upon them by Whites. The privilege of White domination permeates his last sentences. The U.S. military themselves barely spoke Kreyòl and French. Further, despite thousands of miles away from both Haiti and the United States, "Africa" is imagined derogatorily: half, barbaric, Other. The racism at the foundation of U.S. opinion and action in Haiti was certainly not new, and it influenced everything that they did, good or bad. It prevented the U.S. from fully understanding those who resisted them, but it also dominated the history that was told about the *cacos*. Focusing on the *cacos' nasyonalis* vision, strategies, regrouping, and their longer timeline of resistance from 1915 to 1922 proves how inaccurate and racist the invaders' narratives about them were.[49]

The United States also sought to counter any criticism by its own citizens of its invasion. Many in the United States had long questioned the purpose of their country's interventions in Caribbean states. With increasing reports of U.S. soldiers and Haitians dying, opposition in the United States increased.[50] The formation of the Society for the Independence of Haiti and the Dominican Republic attests to the burgeoning U.S. movement against its nation's invasion. The society's explicit use of the term "independence" both recognizes the invasion as an outright attack on Haitian sovereignty and defines its objective as assuring an end to the denial of Haiti's right to self-governance.[51] The leadership of the NAACP, including James Weldon Johnson, was galvanized against imperialism. African Americans felt that the existence of U.S. military republics was a jarring sight, especially those who fought in a world war for democracy.[52]

The 1920 Navy Commission marked the beginning of three state-sponsored inquiries about the invasion. The best consequences of these commissions are that we "hear" from Haitians of this period, and the records are filled with rich prose to analyze. Their existence and frequency, however, articulated their ineptness.

In the 1920 investigation, the Navy Department dispatched Major John A. LeJeune to Haiti to observe the military situation.[53] LeJeune's reports provide a valuable glimpse at the nation's sociopolitical state and the U.S. troops' willful misunderstandings of Haitians. Initially, LeJeune's reports were optimistic. He opined that the country's mountainous landscape made it especially suitable for banditry, and he praised the command of Colonel Russell, as "able, just, and humane." He boasted of U.S. troops' maintenance of "good order," stating that "we traveled through the country without a guard and found no evidences of hostility on the part of the natives."[54] However, within that same report, he documented the stabbing of two marines. He reasoned that this type of violence was commonplace at "home or abroad." Finally, LeJeune noted that marines had killed "Louisnord, the last important bandit leader in Haiti."

LeJeune also assured the State Department that U.S. troops completely controlled the nation. In fact, months after his visit, U.S. troops drafted a list of the remaining *cacos* they sought to exterminate. After capturing a *cacos* chief, "Minister Yeus," they expressed consternation about locating other *cacos* chiefs, such as Estravil, Estifable, Telemoque, and Jean Alcius. U.S. troops attempted to convince themselves and State Department officials that this was only a "light form of banditry-petty thievery" that "will continue indefinitely."[55] The words of the newcomer follow the U.S. story precisely: everything was under control and resistance was merely minor theft. This was, of course, not true when LeJeune said it, just as it had not been true when his fellow countrymen had said it before him.

In 1921, for example, U.S. troops stationed gendarmes in "affected areas to gather intelligence."[56] These U.S. and Haitian soldiers provided information on select areas in Haiti and described the landscape, residents, and their occupations. The city of Cap-Haïtien was surveyed because of Péralte's jailbreak, and the unwavering *cacos* presence in this location. In fact, for that town's report, they charted whether inhabitants were in favor or against the invasion. Philomé Obin, the artist who later memorialized Péralte in two paintings, resided in Cap-Haïtien. The U.S. forces listed Obin's sentiments about the invasion as unknown.

In their surveillance of Péralte's hometown of Hinche, U.S. troops noted it was "within striking distance of the mountains, which are the usual lurking places of bandits."[57] They collected information about the town's population of fifteen hundred, listing them as agriculturalists, artisans, masons, and carpenters—people whom they stereotyped as "uneducated and not very prosperous."[58] They generalized that the town's population was pro-U.S. rule. Their racial bias concerning Hinche residents in particular and Haitians in general dominated their descriptions of their time, their presence, and their military efforts:

> The race is Negro in every particular. The people are very simple-minded, with exceptions, uneducated. They have a native shrewdness, however and can lie as fast as they can talk, if by doing so they can keep themselves out of trouble.... They have absolutely no sense of honor or regard for what they say. They will all steal. This is sometimes a matter of necessity among the poorer classes in order to keep from starving. Very valuable information of military importance has at times been given by the natives, but for the most part, information given by them, has upon investigation been found to have no foundation.[59]

Irrespective of the cultural and lived differences between Africans, African Americans, and Afro-Caribbeans, U.S. troops homogenized Blacks as a race that exhibited simple-minded behavior. This racist rhetoric informed their behavior in the United States *and* the Caribbean.

The United States used its racism to justify its oppression of Haitians, but their racism also made its forces oblivious of the fact that these Haitians engaged in everyday resistance. Hinche residents aided the *cacos* as participants or as silent witnesses to their affairs. A contemporary resident of Hinche assessed the local people's participation: "But when they [U.S. troops] did enter, it took some time for them to assume control because people in the area did not relinquish and accept any domination. In Péralte's era, they were not willing to accept this domination.... They always had a mentality of association—putting heads together to defend the community."[60] This statement testifies to how citizens acted during the *cacos*' struggle. Their actions were, as James Scott notes, "ordinary weapons of relatively powerless groups," which included false compliance.[61] These "hidden" tools, as practiced by Hinche residents, pushed the *cacos*' struggle forward. The United States' underestimation of Haitians in general kept it in the dark.

The ongoing battles in 1921 exasperated Colonel Russell. In one report, he conceded that banditry would continue and reasoned that it "is difficult to conceive further reduction when the terrain affords such favorable opportunity for an easy existence among the so inclined."[62] By the year's end, *cacos*' chiefs, such as Estravil and Alcius, remained at large. Both routinely traveled to the neighboring Dominican Republic, where the invasion continued.[63]

Beginning in February 1921, the remaining *cacos* resistance motivated the United States to try different courses of action. In addition to organizing two regiments, the Second and Eighth Brigades, against these guerrilla fighters, Russell appointed Louis McCarthy Little to command the marines' and gendarmes' operation against the *cacos*. Also, veteran officers, particularly those who had just served in France, replaced short service enlisted troops. Troops now included members of air squadrons.

Patrolling by foot took a toll on U.S. soldiers. In one report, Russell described the perilous conditions his soldiers endured:

> The hardships that the men underwent on these patrols, where they were subjected to tropical rains and sun, where the trails were mountainous and rocky, living off the ration which they carried with them, having to be constantly on the alert for fear of ambush, made this work most trying. . . . Often men would return to camp after ten days patrol, suffering with fever, and as soon as they had been taken off the sick list would have to go out again on another patrol.[64]

Thus, air surveillance became necessary. One soldier explained:

> The lack of good roads and means of transportation to overcome the hardships of fighting bandits in the high mountains and many valleys has brought our squadron of the "eyes" to Haiti. We are here to observe the movements and hiding places of the bandits and to report by radio and wireless telephone their location to troops operating on the ground; and to transport military passengers, freight and mail to all the principal towns in Haiti. . . . We are very proud of the fact that this is the first aviation squadron, flying both land and water machines in the history of the Marine Corps.[65]

The final initiative involved mapping the nation.

These new U.S. strategies reveal *cacos'* success. Despite efforts to publicize the guerrilla fighters as criminals and ineffective, the U.S. administrators' concerted and costly efforts to eliminate the *cacos* proved otherwise. The source further elaborated on how they sought to extinguish the Haitian rebels: "When bandits have been located by troops in dense, inaccessible areas, the aviators fly over and drop a few bombs in their midst. As they come out of the jungles they are seized by the ever-ready Marines on foot."[66] U.S. troops now resorted to bombing suspected *cacos*. The source did not detail the number of casualties or survivors of this violent act. This terrorizing act though was unnecessary. There were battles between the *cacos* and U.S. forces in Gonaïves on September 21 and in Petite Rivière on September 26. As 1921 came to an end, the invasion, and resistance to it, remained.

6

We're Still Fighting
(Nou Toujou ap Goumen)

● ●

Contrary to the United States' assertion that it had stifled resistance, Haitian resistance remained and took on new forms; and women participated, even if their contributions were not noted as clearly. That the United States did not leave after the First World War and after the 1920 naval inquiry demonstrates what a useful role Haiti played in the building of the U.S. empire. The violence, so fundamental to the U.S. invasion, remained consistent throughout the U.S. military's time in Haiti. The Senate inquiry of 1921–1922 recorded the invasion's wrongs more extensively but also did not result in the invasion's end. The *cacos*' fight inspired a new generation of protest from 1922 to 1934. The United States responded with imprisonment, abuse, martial law, and spies. Despite the United States' firm and violent grip on Haiti, Haitians loosened U.S. control of their nation through ongoing resistance. The military invasion ended in 1934 without accomplishing its goals. As the U.S. military evacuated, Haitians remembered Péralte's *nasyonalis*' fight.

Violent Retellings

Life under the U.S. invasion was difficult for Haitians because violence was a way of life. Even though U.S. troops were cautioned against committing war crimes, the possibility of prosecution was slim. Furthermore, Haitian women lived in constant threat of rape from off-duty soldiers who suffered no consequences from their violence. As military historian Allan R. Millett explains:

> While the campaign was not organized to spread general death and destruction, some atrocities were inevitable. The combo of racism and revenge, fueled by stories of mutilation and cannibalism performed on two captured Marines, affected some of the Marines. The Gendarmeries too were still inclined to shoot prisoners. A Marine colonel recently arrived from France thought there was entirely too much shooting of "fleeing prisoners," and an officer saw Lt. Louis Cukela personally execute one group of prisoners in the middle of a Marine camp. A Congressional Medal of Honor winner as a sergeant in France was transferred but not court-martialed. The majority of incidents however involved enlisted men in off duty hours prowling for liquor and women and was not part of the pacification. When witnesses would testify, Russell had offenders court martialed, and he cautioned his commanders not to allow violations of the rules of warfare.[1]

Marines coming from other war zones, like France, commented on the particularly high level of aggression in Haiti, which indicates that, even among experienced military officials, the violence of the U.S. invasion was unnecessarily harsh. The threat of rape for *Ayisienne* in particular meant they were in constant danger—and it was doubly infused with racist hatred. The term "prowling" suggests a justification for the men's animal-like behavior. Moreover, many of the U.S. military even boasted that forced assault and the resulting pregnancies were good for Haitians. One marine, John Houston Craige bragged he had fathered over 200 children in the republic, "whitening the race."[2] In 1920, an African American reverend of a church in Haiti, S. E. Churchstone-Lord, noted how children were fatally harmed by this sexual violence: "In one night alone in the 'Bisquet' section of Port-au-Prince, nine little girls from 8 to 12 years old died from the raping of American soldiers."[3] These women and children remain nameless and voiceless in the invasion's archives even when acted upon by foreign soldiers. The appearance of their oppressors' name in historical records, archives, and narratives reinforces power, privilege, and dominance. Noting the singular and incredibly difficult position that Haitian women found themselves in—having to live not only with the threat of death that all Haitians lived with, but also the threat of rape—gives more insight into their experience and what it means for them to resist.[4]

The 1921–1922 Senate inquiry (undertaken by the Select Committee on Haiti and Santo Domingo) included Haitian women's testimonies of this violence. A combination of factors led to the inquiry, including leaked confidential reports that had circulated among the U.S. military about the indiscriminate killings of Haitians, U.S. Americans' criticisms during the 1920 presidential election about their country's control of Haiti, articles in newspapers like *The Nation* about marines' violence, and the collaborative work of African Americans and Haitians against the invasion.[5] Originally, the select committee of three senators and its chair, Senator Medill McCormick, planned to meet solely with the invasion's forces rather than Haitians, demonstrating early on that the inquiry was not designed to bring the invasion to an end nor to discuss its harm on citizens. Some Haitians, however, aware of this plan, greeted the committee with protest signs upon its arrival, eventually resulting in the committee hearing testimonies from citizens. The inquiry took the same approach that the U.S. forced on President Dartiguenave: blame the *cacos* for U.S. destruction. When faced with the stories of Haitian suffering, the committee tried to suggest that the United States did not commit these acts.

The inquiry offers rare insight into the experiences of named Haitian women. Madame Celicourt Rozier testified that U.S. marines and gendarmes shot her, killed her eight children, pillaged her home, and set it on fire. When asked who committed these infractions, she named the U.S. trooper as either Baker or Becker. Rozier, like many of the Haitian witnesses in these volumes, disclosed that she did not make a complaint to a magistrate prior to these hearings. Her words recall the intimidation during the passing of the 1918 constitution *and* the call and response whereby President Dartiguenave quizzed Haitians while he himself was flanked by the U.S. military. These separate instances amount to a thick documentation of the U.S. military violence on Haitians. Many Haitians expressed fear of being hurt or killed if they had reported these infractions. When Senator Oddie asked her, "Are you sure that they were Americans?" she responded, "They were white men. It was a white man whose name I gave you who did that." During these testimonies, the interrogators often drew a distinction between Haitians and U.S. Americans, asking if the offenders were marines or gendarmes, or if they were White men or Haitians. White in this instance meant the U.S. military. When Senator Oddie asked Rozier about Becker's role in the violence, she responded: "It was he himself, I told you, who put the fire in the house. He broke up the beds and furniture and set fire to the houses."[6] Rather than respond to her claim, Senator Oddie asked: "Were the *cacos* around at that time?"[7] The following was their exchange:

MADAME ROZIER No. When they [U.S. troops] came they didn't find anything there.
SENATOR ODDIE Were they [U.S. troops] afraid of the Cacos coming at that time?
MADAME ROZIER No.
SENATOR ODDIE Did they come later?
MADAME ROZIE No.[8]

The number of Haitians who came forward to speak to the commission was plentiful. Rozier's voice was captured, but the types of resolution were not.

From Madame Philoscar Joseph's case we learn that a U.S. troop beat her to the point where she felt she would die. She named Williams—along with the gendarmes—as the culprits. Asking for further clarification, Senator Oddie asked, "the gendarmes or the marines, the white or the black?"[9] When asked if this was "the time the Cacos were making trouble," she flatly rejected this and said, "No, it was a white man, this same Williams who was going around killing people. The Cacos had not yet come."[10] She testified:

MADAME JOSEPH   He [Williams] gave me 15 blows with a stick on the arms and the head, and I was bathed in blood, and he asked Marcial [commander of Maissade] if he was not going to kill anybody, and Marcial said, "no," he didn't want to kill anybody.

SENATOR ODDIE   Did the Americans know anything about this?

MADAME JOSEPH   Yes; all the whites knew it.

She also stated that she kept the violation to herself, "because if I had made complaint, I would have been killed."[11]

In these recountings, Haitians employed by the U.S. state—such as the gendarmes—were also complicit. Even if there was no blood on their hands, they accompanied U.S. Marines and witnessed these violent acts. Just as with Madame Rozier, Madame Joseph's voice is recorded, but there is no resolution.

Madame Michel Maxine alleged that U.S. Americans had killed her mother. She also said that they arrested her brother, who subsequently died from mistreatment in prison. She found her mother with bullets in her side and breasts. Senator Pomerene inquired: "Did you see the man who did the shooting?" to which she responded, "Yes; I saw them; I saw three white men."[12] The chairman made the following acknowledgments:

The American authorities, civil and military, are opposed to the ill treatment of the people. The American officers of the gendarmerie and of the Marines are under instructions from their chief to assure the good treatment of the people and to receive complaints. . . . Any further investigation which is made will be forwarded to the commission at Washington.[13]

The volumes read as a Truth and Reconciliation collection, except there was no reconciliation. The inquiry offered Haitians a platform to speak, but the U.S. government never acted. The invasion's continuance proves that there were no real resolutions for Haitians harmed by the invaders.

The commission learned that U.S. Marine Captain Kelly stole Madame Exile Onexile's mule. When she filed a complaint, he imprisoned her overnight. Horrifyingly, she went on to assert that Kelly then hanged her husband and set fire to their house. The following was their conference:

SENATOR POMERENE   What did you do or say to Captain Kelly?

MADAME ONEXILE   I said nothing.

SENATOR POMERENE   At that time were there Cacos here in Hinche?

MADAME ONEXILE   There were no Cacos at the time.

SENATOR POMERENE Did your husband belong to the Cacos?
MADAME ONEXILE Never.[14]

As in many of these testimonies, the Senate wanted to redirect attention to the *cacos*. The senator does not seem moved by Onexile's account of brutal injustice. Instead, he asks about her husband's political actions, as if somehow his resistance against the foreign invasion would have justified his murder.

During Madame Tilus Fortuna's testimony, she charged Becker with firing between five and six fatal shots at her husband and burning her house. This was an act of violence against Haitian families. To Mr. Angell's question about whether or not there were Haitians with Becker, she responded yes, but no gendarmes. She identified a Solomon Neuve as the man accompanying Becker. Again, the line of questioning ended with Senator Oddie asking if there were any of the guerrilla fighters causing trouble in the area. She replied that there were not.[15]

Mercilia Raphael documented the sexual threat that a U.S. troop posed to her. Williams approached while she was coming from a market and inquired if she saw *cacos* in the area. After she said no, he took her money, a total of 13 gourdes and 75 centimes. When she attempted to retrieve the money from him, he reportedly stated, "If he was to give me the money, I was to live with him." The next day, Raphael asked Williams again for the money, and he reiterated his previous response. She concluded by saying, "I did not ask him any more."[16] Her testimony reminds us of how vulnerable Haitian women—single, wed, young, and old—were during the invasion. In this exchange, we see how a U.S. military man allegedly attempted to barter with a citizen. In addition to seizing her money, he tried to coerce her into his residence. Ms. Raphael feared this soldier. These Haitian women had no recourse against these foreign police who harmed them.

The women's voices in this Senate inquiry are a rare find that richly articulates the invasion's violence. Given the surveillance under the invasion, these women's acts of testifying and documenting their stories in a public way were brave acts. They put their voices on the record.

In a report about the Senate committee's visit in 1921–1922, the U.S. military acknowledged its futility.[17]

> This Commission of investigation resulted from a number of cumulative causes. It received impetus when politicians in the United States seized on lurid, imaginative tales recounted in yellow journals . . . relative to the cruelty of marines on duty in Haiti as an excuse to embarrass the administration then in power and as a political campaign issue. A hastily formed patriotic society in Haiti headed by politicians, . . . hurriedly gathered alleged witnesses of unparalleled barbarous acts.

> Many of these witnesses were plain liars, and others spokesmen for prepared propaganda. A very few were victims of real injustice. After months of taking

testimony, the committee made its report, in which the Gendarmerie and the Marines came off with flying colors.[18]

This statement makes it clear that internal U.S. politics played a role in the decision to hold the Senate inquiry into the abuses of the U.S. invasion. While politicians might have tried to use domestic rivalries to dismiss the stories of injustice, the records of Haitian experiences gathered from this event are too numerous and specific to be disregarded. Furthermore, the United States' consistent dismissal of Haitian sovereignty, agency, and humanity regardless of political party makes it clear that no U.S. account was fully accurate. What is clear is that members of the committee recorded a number of claims of military abuse. The number of Haitians who testified at this "truth" collecting was large; the result encompassed two volumes. There are over 800 testimonies. This assertion, however, emphasizes the deep and consistent way that a racist ideology influenced a majority of the U.S. perceptions of its invasion of Haiti. It redirects attention to the plight of the invader and dismisses the horrific injustice of their actions. The inquiry perpetuated false stories about the *cacos*. At every turn I wish to dismantle the dominant, false narrative that the United States was doing a good thing, a narrative that the invasion officers and their supporters stuck to.

The Invasion Remains

The commission that listened to countless cases of U.S. military abuse and violence in both nations—the Inquiry into the Occupation and Administration of Haiti and Santo Domingo—did not advocate for the invasion's end. Rather, it proposed the contrary. Before it arrived in Haiti, the congressional group had already decided that it would reorganize and rationalize the invasion.[19] It suggested that power be consolidated into the hands of one U.S. military official. This official would serve as high commissioner to whom the gendarmes, civilian officials, and marines would all report. They selected Colonel John Russell for this task, and he served as high commissioner from 1922 to 1930.[20] The United States was not ready to relinquish Haiti as a territory. From the U.S. Americans' point of view, leaving Haiti would not be politically expedient.

Controlling Haiti politically was ideal for U.S. American creditors and banks. A U.S. presence increased U.S. investments in the nation as it eased the financial sector's conscience about its investments. In 1920, the U.S. National City Bank negotiated a deal with French stockholders, which left them with complete rights to the Banque Nationale.[21] U.S. American creditors offered Haiti a new loan, which would transfer all of the nation's debts to the United States. President Dartiguenave objected to these economic concessions. In the final years of his rule, Dartiguenave appeared fed up with the invaders. He increasingly dismissed cabinet members who supported U.S. policies at the expense of Haiti.[22]

U.S. administrators tried to manage the president, first temporarily withholding his and his cabinet's salaries. Subsequently, they replaced Dartiguenave with Louis Borno, a former minister of finances and foreign affairs.

U.S. administrators made Borno president, and he abided by their commands during his administration from 1922 to 1929. Borno proved just as eager to please the U.S. government as Dartiguenave had been during his initial years as president. Arthur C. Millspaugh, financial advisor to Haiti, once characterized the period of Russell's and Borno's rule as a "joint dictatorship." And yet it is clear that Russell governed Haiti while Borno became another puppet. In an attempt to assuage H. B. Baker and his group's consternation about investing in Haiti, Russell said:

> Haiti is but a waif on our doorstep. We could not see her lying there diseased, suffering. It was our duty to assist her. President Borno is a man whom you would all be delighted to meet. He is a man of culture, a man of intelligence, and a thoroughly well-grounded lawyer. He has received his education in France, speaks beautiful French, Spanish, and English fairly well. . . . You will remember how quickly the Loan Law was passed after he assumed his seat as President of Haiti, which was on the 15th of May, and the Loan Law was passed on the 26th of June. . . . I believe that if we can bind Haiti commercially to the United States, it will be a very strong factor in keeping the Government absolutely stable in future years. To that end, we are encouraging United States or American capital investing in Haiti.[23]

Russell continues to rely on the same narrative trope that characterized all U.S. stories about its invasion of Haiti: somehow the U.S. was doing a positive thing. Of course, this was not true. Haiti was not in need of a brutal invasion and foreign takeover, but the story that it was had a lot of power and was therefore told time and time again. Russell endorsed Borno because he supported this story. During his presidency, Borno imprisoned several Haitians—such as C. R. Moravia—for their diatribes against him. "Free" speech was permissible only if it supported the U.S. state in Haiti.[24] Yet, whenever President Borno failed to cooperate with U.S. officials, he, like his predecessor, suffered consequences, which ultimately explains who dictated policies in Haiti.[25] Politically and economically, Haiti was a beneficial imperial entity. It was important to the U.S. that this control remained with Russell. Any reference to Haitian control was an illusion meant to support the false narrative of benevolent leadership rather than hostile takeover.

Haitian Protests and U.S. Surveillance, 1921–1934

As U.S. control and its violence remained, Haitian resistance also continued. Péralte and the *cacos* were trailblazers and pioneers in this fight for Haitian liberty. In 1922 several *cacos* leaders, such as Estravil and Jean Alcius, remained and fought the U.S. military. In his work, Millett reflected on the *cacos*:

> Between 1918 and 1922, two Marine brigades and their stepchildren, the Gendarmerie d'Haiti and Guardia Nacional Dominicana, fought a tiring brutal anti-guerrilla war against the *cacos* and the Dominican bandits. Even if the rebels were ill equipped and poor tacticians, their initial advantage in mobility and use of the inhospitable terrain was substantial, and their ability to fade into the population gave them an anonymity that frustrated the Marines.... The *cacos* drew blood and retained enough confidence to stay in the field, the number of jungle battles soared to more than eighty in July through September.... The attack on Port-au-Prince jarred the Navy Department and focused public attention in the United States upon the war for the first time.[26]

The military had not captured all *cacos* leaders—which is made clear from this note. Yet this 1922 description is the last U.S. mention of the group and its chiefs. It is unclear if the guerrilla fighters ceased or if the *cacos* morphed into new protest avenues. Undoubtedly, the *cacos'* fight, which spanned 1915 to 1922, their leadership and vision, their unity, and their sacrifices inspired other types of protests from 1922 to 1934. The final years of the invasion witnessed a transformation of Haitian resistance that incorporated Péralte's and the *cacos' nasyonalis* strategies. Their protest example and legacy lived on through Haitian writers, strikers, members of the Ligue Patriotique (also known as L'Union Patriotique), and those who globally petitioned international allies for the invasion's end.

The Haitian press was particularly agitated about continued U.S. control.[27] The U.S. administrators kept a close watch on Haitian newspapers and listed several as against the invasion, including: *L'Essor, Courrier Haïtien, Le Matin, Le Moniteur,* and *L'Étendard.* In one issue in 1921, *Le Nouvelliste* reminded its citizens of the obvious, that Haiti remained invaded. The editors reported that U.S. rule would continue in both nations of Hispaniola until the nations proved that they were capable of self-governance. Two days later, *Le Matin* reiterated that Santo Domingo and Haiti remained invaded. On May 17, 1921, the journal announced that Haitian presses would use Haitian Flag Day, May 18, as a protest day. They criticized what they called an illegal invasion of the republic.[28] Their strategic use of Flag Day engaged with U.S. troops' daily ritual of public showcasing their own flag, the stars and stripes, across the nation. One U.S. troop's record reminisced about the flag's display: "Wherever 'old Glory' flies you will find Marines. Every morning at 8 o'clock there is the ceremony of raising the flag. This time the flag is flown high above the palms in Haiti."[29] The act of flying the U.S. flag and not the Haitian reinforced U.S. control. Thus, the Haitian press used Haitian Flag Day to encourage more protest for Haiti's liberty.

After the presses' protest on May 18, Fernand Naudier in *Le Matin* charged the U.S. administration with lying. He argued that Haitians' loss of freedom was legitimized by the invasion's illusory pieces of legislation.[30] Nine days later, High Commissioner Russell issued a proclamation that restricted the Haitian press from speaking out against the United States.[31] Both *Le Nouvelliste* and *Le Matin* consistently reminded their readers of Haiti's and neighboring Santo Domingo's invaded fates. Given the marines' regular monitoring of Haitian journals and their arrest of editors who challenged the invasion, these postings to the public were brave.[32] Haitian newspapers kept their citizens informed, regardless of the harm to them.

In a manner reminiscent of Péralte's and other *cacos'* strategies, *Le Matin* also deployed historic nationalism. On July 4, 1921, the editors mused: "Hayti and 800 of her freedmen fought for America in 1779.... The generous Haytian contribution to the cause of the independence of the U.S. is scarcely known in this country, as American historians make no mention of it."[33] Their disclosure of this fact was strategic, since U.S. troops in Haiti were celebrating their Independence Day. This move was reminiscent of Péralte, who critiqued the idea of the United States as the definition of democracy.

Midway into U.S. rule, Haitians began to flee their homeland in protest. If fighting back against a brutalizing regime was not possible, then refusing to live under the regime by physically leaving was another form of resistance. Between May 19, 1921, and June 23, 1921, *Le Matin* covered the large migration of Haitians to Cuba, which continued through 1923.[34] Haitians' willingness to transport themselves by boat to Cuba and nearby to the Dominican Republic testifies to the continued instability under U.S. rule. These Haitians traveled to both sites out of necessity, in search of better living and working opportunities.[35] *Le Nouvelliste* reported, "The Emigration Scandal Is about to Break Out again in Hayti." The editorial made an appeal: "The Cuban government edited a law declaring Haytian laborers undesirable. We beg M. Borno to keep his eyes open and to pay attention. Public opinion knows the underside of the matter and will not allow Haytians to be driven to shame."[36] Even though they were resisting by leaving, Haitians faced discrimination abroad.[37] The path to a better life was a challenge—but their determination to resist the brutal invasion like Péralte was firm.

At home, the Haitians who decided that physical departure was not an option found other ways to carve out an existence under the U.S. invasion. Freemasons, for example, just like Péralte, framed the invasion as a global issue. On June 14, 1923, members of the Masonic Lodge of Cap-Haïtien appealed to all the Grand Oriente, Grand Lodges, and Masonic Powers: "We address this cry to you in favor of our oppressed fatherland, and entreating you to transmit it to the Or of the Masonic world, Nearly eight years ago, without a declaration of war, while our Government maintained the most cordial relations with the Federal Government, American military forces, arbitrarily occupied Haitian territory, and still do so, in violation of all principles of the rights of those who administer and direct relations among the people."[38] The masons reached out to international allies. Their timing was fortuitous, given that there was a developing international discourse on progressive ideals and the rights of "small" nations.

This move toward examining international options—either through emigration or by forming alliances—extended to those in the African American community in the United States, who compared their fates with those of invaded Haiti. James Weldon Johnson, a prominent writer and secretary of the NAACP, met with Haitians in the States and in Haiti. Haitians, including Georges Sylvain, Jean Price-Mars, and Sténio Vincent, revived L'Union Patriotique (also known as the Ligue Patriotique). Sylvain had founded the Ligue in 1915 as a patriotic organization against the invasion, but U.S. martial law prevented its operation. Sylvain, in conjunction with the NAACP, revived the Ligue and ensured that the Senate inquiry heard from Haitians.[39] Like Péralte, members of L'Union Patriotique invoked images of Dessalines and L'Ouverture in their call for Haiti's liberty. According to U.S. notes, speeches by Mr. Morpeau of Port-au-Prince called on the legendary national figures, Dessalines and L'Ouverture. This continual call to carry on the legacy of Haitian independence leaders inspired long after Péralte's murder. Both speeches were received with loud cheering, and during the second speech the entire house shouted "Vive la liberté!" A collection was taken at both meetings for the support of the delegates of the Ligue Patriotique, who traveled to the United States.[40] L'Union Patriotique's recollection of the 1791 founding revolutionaries reflected the guerrilla fighters' strategy. Though not named as *cacos*, the inspirational strategy of the *cacos* is clear in these words.

L'Union Patriotique members traveled to Washington, DC, to express their objections to U.S. rule.[41] Madeleine Sylvain-Bouchereau, writing of her father's role in L'Union, also discussed how *Ayisienne* participated in the "national struggle." Their fund-raising helped send L'Union "delegates to the United States to advocate for the Haitian cause."[42] At select points, members of L'Union Patriotique, the NAACP, and the Society for Haiti-Santo Domingo Independence in New York collaborated to work against the U.S. empire.[43] One of their main objectives was to keep the issue of Haiti's invasion in the media, just like the writers in *Le Matin* and *Le Nouvelliste*.[44]

The U.S. invaders noted all of these protest forms. U.S. patrol reports in 1923 regularly commented on the activities of L'Union Patriotique. In November 1923, Second Lieutenant Ernest E. Linsert noted in his report that "Members of the Union Patriotique seem to be increasing." By year's end, he had created a list of twenty-three Haitians in the Saint-Michel and Maissade areas who were known to be members of the group.[45] Surveillance of the group spanned a decade. In 1933, Second Lieutenant Roland E. Simpson recorded that the "activities of the Union Patriotique seemed to be at low ebb."[46]

Further, U.S. troops diligently patrolled and reported on Haiti's state of affairs. The titles of their reports included: "State of Territory," "Friction between

Natives and Military Forces," "Other Military Movements Noted," "Economic Conditions," "Attitude of Citizens," "Roads," and "Prominent Citizens and Officials of Towns," among others. These meticulous notations demonstrate the intensity of efforts to track Haitians' sentiments and actions against the invasion. The intelligence department within the gendarme reported on their initiatives. They had mapped the location of "former bandit camps," and ascertained the whereabouts and attitudes of "all ex bandit leaders."[47]

U.S. tactics to maintain control remained consistently focused on minimizing and denying Haitian resistance—and Haitian writers recognized this continued injustice. The literature of the time takes up the tradition of the *cacos* by reminding readers of a glorious African past and using stories of a fight for national independence to inspire. In his book *Ainsi parla l'oncle* (*So Spoke the Uncle*), written just a few years after Péralte's murder, Jean Price-Mars demonstrates the power of the *cacos*' message as he clearly articulates what life was like during the invasion. For the Haitians who idealized the French component of their identity, Price-Mars challenged them to redirect their adoration to that continent. His ethnological work was an early precursor of négritude and Pan-African ideologies. It bore similarities to Anténor Firmin's scholarly strategies from earlier. Price-Mars and other Haitian writers were witnesses to the fate of the *cacos* who had fought against the invasion. At a time when U.S. troops deemed Haitians incapable of self-rule because of their African heritage, Price-Mars rejected their reasoning. For Price-Mars and other writers, words became their weapons in the anti-U.S. struggle. In the spirit of the *cacos*, these writers emphasized Haitian *nasyonalisme*. Péralte had used Haitians' collective past to inspire a movement against their invaded fate. Price-Mars engaged these same ideals. His argument was not simply against U.S. rule; it proposed the building of a pro-Haitian self, which Péralte and Price-Mars had both hoped would spill over into a reconstruction of the Haitian state.

Other Haitian writers, including Jacques Stephen Alexis and Jacques Roumain, centered the experience of life under U.S. domination in their writings of the 1920s. Their works criticized the repressive U.S. regime and its impact on all classes of Haitians.[48] These authors addressed themes of sexual abuse, racism and colorism, and class. For example, in 1929, Jacques Roumain, then president of the Ligue de la Jeunesse Patriote Haïtienne, wrote an article in *L'Action*. He raised concerns about the abuse of Haitians and his female counterparts at the hands of U.S. soldiers.[49] Other contributors to *L'Action* appealed to Haitian's patriotism. Writers often called for a "deliverance of the homeland," and espoused the idea that the "national soul is not yet dead, it is living in all of us."[50] Literature became a forum for Haitians to critique continued U.S. rule. These writers carried on Péralte's and the *cacos*' legacy. The authors contributed to the *cacos*' cause and were inspired by them. Indeed, the timing of Jean Price-Mars's academic publication and Péralte's death emphasizes the influence of the *cacos* leader on the intellectual resistance percolating at this time.

Even though much of the guerilla fighting that the *cacos* led died down in the 1920s, the U.S. continued to dominate by violence—and this meant that even the transformed resistance of literature was a dangerous endeavor. As some Haitian women testified bravely at the Senate hearings, some elite Haitian women turned to fiction. Their novels corroborate their patriotic kin's experiences. Elite women such as Anne-Marie Lerebours Bourand, who wrote under the pseudonym Annie Desroy, and Cléanthe (Virgile) Valcin, created fictional works that offer other useful analytical terrain. As Haitian women and men experienced the invasion and could not articulate their frustration and harm to officials, they wrote. Writing became a space to vent and repair. In "The Occupied Novel," Nadève Ménard explores the written works of these two women in particular, Valcin's *La Blanche Négresse* and Desroy's *Le Joug*. Both Haitian authors published as the invasion drew to a close in 1934.[51] The voices of Valcin and Desroy were also invaluable records of Haitian women's resistance. As the United States patrolled the Haitian state and kept its citizens under strict surveillance, these women addressed issues of sexism, classism, and racism through a literary lens. They used fiction as a medium of protest. Because of martial law and the proclamations preventing discourse against the invasion, the fictional text become an outlet for *Ayisienne*.

Americans in Haiti articulated their stance as either anti- or pro-U.S. rule. Napoleon Bonaparte Marshall was an African American lawyer and clerk in the U.S. American consulate at Port-au-Prince from September 1922 to January 1, 1929. He published his reflections on his post and his nation's position in Haiti in the newspaper the *New York World* in February 1929:

> In consequence of the annual reports of Gen John Russell, the American High Commissioner to Haiti, and a press bureau, the American people have the notion that Haiti is prospering under the American occupation. Nothing could be further from the truth. I have spent six years in the United States Legation at Port-au-Prince. . . . When I left there a few days ago misery prevailed everywhere. If the purpose of the occupation was to crush the spirits of a free and sovereign people and reduce them to a dependent state, that purpose has been brilliantly achieved. . . . It seems that many Americans the Government has sent down to Haiti look with disfavor and contempt upon the cultural side of the Haitians. Perhaps this attitude springs from the fact that in education and refinement of manners, as well as in personal appearance, the Haitian society is immeasurably superior to anything this brand of Americans has exhibited there.

Marshall's views, especially as an African American stationed in Haiti, are a valuable find. The United States had dispatched an all-White regiment to Haiti in 1915. Marshall's role as an administrator gave him a different lens from which to critique the invasion. He presumably interacted with the likes of Russell as head of Haiti and Smedley Butler, who killed the *cacos*. Despite his power, Marshall could only critique his nation's control of Haiti, not bring it to an end, but his assertion that the dominant U.S. "peacekeeping" narrative was false exposes the doublespeak. Marshall's words articulated what Haitian resisters like Péralte and the *cacos*, and those who came after them, proved—the U.S. empire was failing in Haiti.

In his 1929 article in *New York World*, Marshall made it clear that the U.S. racist attitude toward Haitians had not changed and still dominated their approach to the entire invasion. He wrote: "From top sergeant down to buck private one can hear the boast: We done this; we came here to train these Haitian Niggers."[52] Each soldier believed, with every interaction, that he was somehow superior to Haitians. This false and harmful attitude shows up even more explicitly in the words of other soldiers. For example, an official in charge of the Department of Public Works stated: "While we are in the process of permitting the Haitian engineers actively to direct the work, I must say that in the one instance above reported of placing a Haitian engineer in charge of an important department, it has not resulted as satisfactorily as I would have wished. It is my opinion, after long study of the Negro race, that they will always require inspection by white men."[53] These quotes demonstrate that throughout the U.S. military, an ignorant, false idea of racial superiority influenced not only broad policy decisions but everyday interactions. Haitians were, of course, not in need of "inspection" or "permission" from any foreign power—but the story that they were continued to hold power even a decade after Péralte's death. Marshall's writing about "crushed spirits" describes what life surrounded and dominated by dehumanizing racists must have been for Haitians under U.S. rule. To resist was to counter the story of one's own inferiority—and Haitians had to do this time and time again.

1929–1932: Elections and Additional Resistance

During Borno's and Russell's rule, Haitian agitation escalated. The duo decided on October 5, 1929, that the upcoming election on January 10, 1930, would be postponed. They delayed the elections for delegates and the Senate until January 10, 1932. Per the 1918 constitution, legislative elections were to be held only in even-numbered years. Haitians reacted against what they saw as constitutional abuse. Strikes erupted across the nation. The students of the Damien School of Agriculture, who were upset with the school's administration—namely Doctor George F. Freeman, also head of Service Technique—began a strike on October 31, 1929. These peaceful demonstrations continued to the year's end and eventually escalated into violence. Haitians in the law and medical schools also went on strike. On November 8, students, upset about the reduction in their scholarship, stoned Freeman's house. U.S. troops arrested fourteen of the strike's identified leaders.

On November 18, in an attempt to manage his citizens, Borno issued a statement that he would not seek a third term. Haitians dismissed Borno's effort to maintain calm. For many Haitians, President Borno's statement was a nonissue.[54] Haitians were tired of continued foreign rule and the accompanying abuses it brought to their lives. Demonstrations continued in the aforementioned departments and spread to Gonaïves and Saint-Marc. Another strike by students took place on November 28. Subsequently, the customs service employees threatened to strike, which they did, starting on December 4. Initially, these demonstrations centered in Port-au-Prince, but they quickly extended across Haiti, in places like Cap-Haïtien and Jacmel.[55] These displays of Haitian agitation were reminiscent of the *cacos'* battles. Like the guerrilla fighters, these strikers coordinated their protests, and they erupted in multiple sites. The disruptions to the Haitian state propelled Russell to reinstate martial law on December 4.

Two days later, on December 6, Les Cayes residents, an estimated 1,200 people, confronted Captain Roy C. Wink, Lieutenant Blanchard, and other U.S. forces with machetes and clubs. Haitian and U.S. accounts differ. According to some U.S. records, their men were "forced to extremity" and fired on the Haitian demonstrators.[56] Yet, while no U.S. troops were harmed, twelve Haitian citizens died and twenty-three suffered injuries. Haitians memorialized this incident in Aux Cayes as a massacre. The disparity in the number of casualties on each side buttresses their reading and analysis of this event. In another version of this incident, a U.S. official wrote the following:

> Here on December 6, 1929, a small Marine patrol reinforcing the local Garde
> d'Haiti was surrounded at nightfall by a mob between 1000 and 1500 male
> rioters bent upon overcoming the police and looting the town. The patrol, after
> a display of remarkable self-restraint under blows dealt by individuals of the
> mob, and after firing over the latter's heads without success, then in self-defense
> delivered fire for effect, but only in sufficient volume to turn the rioters, several
> of whom unfortunately were killed and others wounded, as previously reported
> to the Navy Department.[57]

The troops were aware that Haitians prepared to demonstrate. In response, hundreds of marines had been stationed in Virginia the day before, ready to leave for Haiti in case reinforcements were necessary. The U.S. troops' plans to stifle this protest reveal that they had time to coordinate the attack. Additionally, in an extreme measure, they used planes to bomb Aux Cayes residents at this confrontation. This blatant use of a destructive weapon was in line with all U.S. policy in Haiti—it was excessively violent. The U.S. official's deliberate use of the words "mob" and "rioters" does not consider why Haitians were agitating, using democratic means—freedom of speech and the right to assemble.

As in the celebration of Péralte's murder, the Navy Department awarded the U.S. marines involved in the massacre the honorable Navy Cross for their supposed courage.[58] These ceremonies reinforced the use of violence against Haitians. Furthermore, U.S. actions averted attention from the causes for which these Haitians fought.

Between December 4 and 15, U.S. troops arrested 268 Haitians in Port-au-Prince, the majority of whom—229 of them—were curfew violators. The United States later released these individuals. By December 16, Russell lifted some of the martial law's restrictions, including suspending the curfew mandate. Meanwhile, the December 6 massacre remains a part of Haiti's cultural memory of life under the invasion.

The Invasion's End

Back in the United States, President Herbert Hoover, triggered by these latest events in Haiti, authorized another commission to the nation. W. Cameron Forbes served as the chairman of the Hoover Commission. Forbes was a questionable choice to evaluate the conditions of Haiti.[59] He was an agent of imperialism, the former governor of the U.S.-occupied Philippines. The 1898 U.S. seizure of the Philippines during the Spanish-American War began the military component of imperialism. At the war's conclusion, U.S. military men, including Forbes, arrived in Cuba, Puerto Rico, Guam, and the Philippines.

On February 25, 1930, the five members of the Forbes Commission set sail aboard the USS *Rochester* and arrived in Haiti on February 28. Haitians eagerly awaited their arrival. Less than a day into their stay, on March 1, *Ayisienne* greeted the commission members with a march, urging officials to end the invasion. Organized by Mrs. Perceval Thoby, Thérèse Vieux-Clesca, Justinien Ricot, and other women, the march proceeded from the Sacred Heart Church to the hotel where members of the commission lodged. Sylvain-Bouchereau recalled that the peaceful demonstrators sang songs for "the liberation of Haiti."[60] The commission remained in Haiti for fifteen days. In their daily sessions, they heard from Russell, Borno, and a number of Haitians. The Forbes Commission acknowledged the failures of the invasion.[61] Their deliberations with the people and discussions with Russell and Borno resulted in a U.S. evacuation plan.

The commission, in conjunction with a Federated Commission of Haitian political parties, Borno and Russell, selected a temporary president, which would be followed by the election of a permanent president of the republic for a six-year term.[62] From the five names submitted by the opposition for temporary president, President Borno agreed to the selection of Eugene Roy, a businessman. Both sides agreed on Roy's selection on March 15, and the members of the commission left the next day.

Some U.S. Americans, however, genuinely believed that Haitians were incapable of self-governance and always grounded this perception in race. Days after the commission left, the author of *Black Democracy*, H. P. Davis, declared:

> The American occupation of this little negro republic [came] to the attention of the American people.... The great peasant mass, probably ninety-five percent of the population, is little removed from the primitive condition of their African ancestors. They are pitiably poverty stricken, indescribably ignorant, but simple, subservient and kindly ... as the situation now stands, there is practically no participation by Haitians either in the preparation of the budget or in the administration of the spending departments of the government.... Borno's ministers have been figureheads with little influence in the policies or conduct of their departments. They are complaisant tools.[63]

Even in its departure, the United States stuck to its false narrative about the reasons that it had invaded Haiti and how it had dominated the people of the nation brutally for nineteen years. The story was so engrained in U.S. thinking that it influenced historical writing about the invasion for years to come. Further, Davis does not comment on the lack of preparation by Russell for Haitians' regaining their self-rule.

Despite this hesitancy about U.S. withdrawal, plans were underway. When President Louis Borno completed his second term in May 1930, Eugene Roy succeeded him. Russell resigned after his eleven-year service in Haiti.[64]

After the strike and the Hoover Commission, U.S. troops continued their surveillance on Haitians, especially those they considered part of the revolutionary element. They listed Antoine Pierre-Paul as a "dangerous element." Earlier, Pierre-Paul had participated in an attack at the Port-au-Prince penitentiary that freed Haitian prisoners in the illustrious "Codio Affair." He served ten years of a twenty-seven-year sentence. After his release, Pierre-Paul formed the Labor Party, which the United States observed did not have a large following. It noted that during the commission's visit, Pierre-Paul had asked for the "reestablishment of a duly elected legislative body and withdrawal of the Intervention." Additionally, the United States identified Antoine Rigal as the chairman of the Federation of Opposed Political Groups and president of L'Union Patriotique. The former was a number of different groups opposed to the U.S. invasion. The United States charged that the group L'Union Patriotique had "red" affiliations. Due to Rigal's speeches and positions on the invasion, the United States profiled him as anti-American. Because of the content of one of his speeches, the provost court tried him and assigned him a prison sentence. U.S. troops did not believe Rigal's statement that his federation had 200,000 Haitian members, and they set the number at 25,000 instead. These efforts demonstrated the lengths they sought to snuff out the Haitians' ongoing fight against them. Further, the claims of communism and "red" affiliations echo similar moves to repress freedom of speech and choice in their own homeland. After the Second World War, the United States patrolled its citizens because of the ideological battle of democracy and capitalism versus socialism and communism.

The U.S. commission had identified Justin Sam as one of the student strikers at the École Centrale at Damien. Sam demanded an end to both Russell's post and U.S. rule. The U.S. troops cautioned that if it had not been for their presence, Sam and other "agitators" would have incited a revolution in the nation's capital on December 4. U.S. troops also listed Emmanuel Cauvin, Emmanuel Rampy, M. Gilles, Eugene de Lespinasse, and Jacques Roumain in their profiles.[65] They commented on Roumain's challenge to Articles 35 and 39 of the 1918 constitution. Their notes on Victor Cauvin illustrate the other protest methods in which Haitians engaged. As a member of the L'Union Patriotique, Cauvin communicated with unidentified persons in Mexico City. They discussed a boycott of U.S. American goods. This is significant on several counts—first, the transnational dialogue, and second, the use of democratic means to protest.

Until the actual departure of the U.S. military, however, Haitian resistance continued. Haitians set fire to key places in protest, including burning Colonel R. M. Curtt's house. Others protested against the taxes on tobacco and rum. On May 12, several Haitians confronted the Garde in Abricot. In the meantime, beginning on May 14, Eugene Roy served as provisional president, a post he held until November. U.S. troops noted the presence of *La Garde,* who produced a play that critiqued Borno.[66] As they did at other key moments, Haitians turned to newspapers in order to voice their frustration. They also put on a play, entitled *Croix Marche à Terre,* that criticized the United States. Some Haitians memorialized the *cacos.* Louis Diaquor authored an article, "Tombes de Cacos." In his reflection, he recounts witnessing the gruesome torture of the *cacos* in Gonaïves. After their deaths, he noted the community's search for the *cacos'* bodies and lighting candles in observance of their deaths.[67] In 1931, the marines briefly mentioned the presence of "bandit activity" but neglected to provide details on these figures.[68] Given their use of the word "bandit," which had become synonymous with *cacos,* the interaction may have involved the guerrilla fighters. The Gonaïves community's response to the *cacos* illuminates the reverence that these guerrilla fighters and their movement commanded in parts of Haitian society.

In a move reminiscent of European imperialist policies in African and Caribbean nations, the United States gradually transferred Haiti back to its citizens over a four-year period, from 1930 to 1934. In theory, there was to be a "Haitianization" of the nation's governing branches to allow full Haitian governance. On November 15, 1930, Haitians elected Senator Sténio Vincent as their president for six years.[69] President Vincent had worked for the invasion's end, in spite of the restrictions the United States placed on him.[70]

In a major change, the United States appointed Dana Munroe to serve as civilian official in place of Colonel John H. Russell. Despite the fact that Vincent was elected president, Munroe effectively supervised him. Haitians impatiently

FIG. 8 "Haiti Says Good-bye: Natives gather at Cape Haïtien to bid farewell to the U.S. Marines," August 6, 1934 (Reference Collection, Marine Corps History Division, Quantico, VA)

awaited the "Haitianization" of several departments in the country. By 1932, acts of arson against U.S. American clubs and stores had become commonplace.[71] Even U.S. troops expressed doubts about Haiti's separation from the United States, as they wrote in their records: "Treaty Signed to 'Free' Haiti."[72]

Ayisienne saw their country's liberation as a moment to assert their own authority as well. They had worked hard for the invasion's end, and in 1934, they assured that their rights would also be heard. On February 22, 1934, *Ayisienne* who predominately were "intellectuals and social leaders" founded an association for "the political and social emancipation of women."[73] These women, including Mrs. Pierre Hudicourt, whom they elected as president, advocated for educational access, equal pay, economic freedom for married women, civil and political equality, among other causes. Two months after their forming, the government banned them from operating, taking issue with the women's proposals. Yet a select group of these women navigated their way around this preclusion. On May 10, *Ayisienne* including: Madeleine Sylvain-Bouchereau, Alice Garoute, Fernande Bellegarde, Olga Gordon, Thérèse Hudicourt, Marie Corvington, Alice Teligny Mathon, Esther Dartigue, Maud Turian, and Georgette Justin, reorganized their association. Their promise to study the aforementioned issues for two years appeased the invasion's government. On June 3, 1934, the inaugural session of the Ligue Féminine d'Action Sociale's (Feminine league for social action) took place.

A month later in July 1934, President Franklin D. Roosevelt arrived in Cap-Haïtien to assist with the invasion's end.[74] It was an ironic moment, given President Roosevelt's earlier role in the invasion in 1918 as assistant secretary of the navy. As the new U.S. head of state however, he now effectuated its end. At Cap-Haïtien, President Roosevelt acknowledged that his nation had restricted Haiti's sovereignty, and he stated: "I am glad to come back especially at a time when the relationship between the Republic of Haiti and the Republic of the United States will be resorted to a basis of complete independence."[75] President Roosevelt's visit occasioned an abundance of "receptions, speeches, and champagne."[76] By August, a new type of celebration was in the air. At a ceremony in Champ de Mars, U.S. troops transferred the supervision of the Garde d'Haiti to the local government.[77] That month, the United States lowered its flag in the nation, and U.S. troops gradually departed (Figure 8).[78]

Péralte's heroism of 1915–1919 worked its way into the Haitian cultural imaginary in the twentieth and twenty-first centuries. Haitians apotheosized Péralte as their *nasyonalis* fighter. The *cacos* had organized a movement, launched successful battles, and inspired generations of Haitians to protest from 1915 to 1934. As the United States continued to encroach on Haiti's affairs after 1934, Péralte took on a new life because his legacy held such sway. Like other leaders before him, his was a story of injustice—the story of a man dedicated to freedom and equality whose efforts were tragically cut short. His murder, in fact, gave him a second life. Studying this legacy not only demonstrates the success of the *cacos*, but how injustices only strengthen Haitians resolve to ensure its own national sovereignty.

7

Second Revolution
(Dezyèm Revolisyon)

● ●

Haitian resistance continued throughout the twentieth century because the United States never truly supported Haitian sovereignty. During that time, Péralte took on a new life. His legacy served as an inspiration for many and, for many politicians, was a tool to claim legitimacy, even if their policies fell short of his ideal. Analyzing Péralte's effect on his country after his death offers a glimpse into the various forms that Haitian resistance took during these years.

Péralte was murdered and never given a proper burial. Perhaps the first and most important step in the building of his legacy after the U.S. invasion was President Sténio Vincent's move to memorialize Péralte in 1934. He held a posthumous funeral for the *caco*. Fifteen years after his death, the president publicly acknowledged the guerrilla's role in fighting U.S. imperialism. Vincent's work with L'Union Patriotique was an extension of the *cacos'* sacrifices. His memorial service for one of their chief fighters in Cap-Haïtien conveyed his historical consciousness and gratitude. Cap-Haïtien had been one of the hubs of guerrilla fighters' resistance. The president acknowledged the area's significance to his citizens who had been *cacos*, imprisoned, *corvée* workers, and those who had experienced the invasion's violence. Neither the Péralte brothers nor Batraville lived to witness their work's success. Vincent's generation inherited his patriotic kin's revolutionary victory. The president, in that moment and through this action, framed *désoccupation* around the memory of the *cacos'* movement, honoring the *caco* for the first time.

The Haitian artist Philomé Obin captured this national euphoria for Péralte in a painting dated November 26, 1934. He descriptively called the work *Les Funeralles du Héros Charlemagne Péralte* (The funeral of Charlemagne Péralte, the hero).[1] His vivid use of colors captured Cap-Haïtien's urban landscape and Haitians' different chocolate skin tones. The artist beautifully illustrated Haitians from all walks of life—young, elderly, female, and male. Symbols of Catholicism abound, reminiscent of Péralte's school years at Saint-Louis Gonzague. Nuns walk alongside fellow Haitians, and the clergy and altar boys walk in between Haiti's armed forces and President Vincent. Through Obin's eyes, one sees a nation mobilized for the *cacos* leader.

The artist captured a scene of homage. In the artwork, Haitians both near the procession and afar gaze reverently at Péralte's remains. Everyone—from members of the armed forces to civilian onlookers—dons immaculate suits, dresses, hats, and uniforms for the occasion. Musicians hold their horns and officers clutch their artillery by their side. Obin's artistic processional occurs on a city street. The doors and windows to the residential and commercial spaces in the background are shut, as if all of Cap-Haïtien's residents attended Péralte's eulogy. Indeed, no single head peeks from either a window or a doorway. Those who observe this pageantry do so front and center. They stand as the procession goes by. It is unclear if Péralte's surviving family—like his mother Madame Masséna—was present at the belated funeral. Obin did not include Madame Masséna in this painting.

Unlike the actual image of Péralte's naked and abused corpse in Grande Rivière in 1919, this 1934 artwork portrays Haiti's farewell to a dignitary. Obin's work reframed the circulated image of Péralte's dead body. When President Vincent eulogized Péralte fifteen years after his assassination, Obin's art captured a nation that was still in awe of the *caco* and his sacrifice. This and subsequent paintings of Péralte represented Obin's ode to an unforgotten figure. During the invasion, the military had marked Obin as a neutral Haitian in their intelligence gathering. Unbeknown to them, Obin was a *nasyonalis*. He was a member of the Cap-Haïtien masons who issued the international appeal to other brothers. The artist hid in plain sight. Obin, like many other Haitians, articulated that Péralte was a hero; they would reclaim this fact over and over.

Vincent and Obin began a tradition of counternarrating Péralte's story. They were the authors of two different legacy uses. Vincent used it to indicate his authenticity—even if it was not true—and Obin to protest what was, to remind people that the ideals to which Péralte aspired were not met. Péralte's legacy meant fighting for Haiti and Haitians' sovereignty at all costs. Global powers, especially the United States, whom he worked hard to resist were not to invade nor govern his nation. Because of Péralte's ultimate sacrifice—his life—this legacy grew larger than life—Christ-like, so no one could adequately live up to his legacy.

Despite the apparent moral righteousness of Vincent's memorial, it was also a self-serving display. President Vincent deployed Péralte's memory for his political agenda. Vincent symbolically linked his presidency to the *cacos* fighter. At first glance, Vincent's move appeared militant. Rather than honor nonviolent Haitians, Vincent chose Péralte. His ode to the fighter communicated with Haitian citizens that their needs mattered. Péralte had placed his citizens' freedom above his and, therefore, many could have perceived Vincent's use of him as doing the same for them. Vincent's constituents were a generation reared under the nineteen-year invasion. Having their needs placed above that of the former invaders signaled a refreshing change.

Many Haitians understood the U.S. exit as a second independence. The year 1804 had seen the departure of the French. The year 1934 was the departure of another colonialist imperialist force which espoused the same type of racist ideology. There was a collective euphoria.

Early in his administration, Vincent sought to mobilize Haitians under a Péralte banner and his symbolic gesture in Cap-Haïtien was tactful. Vincent's action echoed the sentiments of those Haitians who understood the *désoccupation* as a second independence. The *cacos* fought long and hard for this victory, and many witnessed their successful defense of Haitians' freedom. During the *désoccupation*, Péralte emerged as a *nasyonalis* martyr. The president's use of the *caco* communicated that he would sever imperialist ties with the United States.

Vincent's memorialization of Péralte was a first step in recognizing the leader's significance in the history of the long fight for Haitian national sovereignty. It was, however, also the first example of the politicization of Péralte's legacy. Vincent used an anti-imperialist leader to define what his presidency would be after the U.S. departure, but his actual administration proved to be the opposite of what Péralte, the *cacos*, and he, as a L'Union Patriotique member, fought for during the invasion.

Vincent signaled to the Haitian people that his attitude toward the United States would be harsh by evoking the legacy of Péralte in 1934. However, his policy toward the United States was not one that asserted Haitian independence.[2] Vincent signed a reciprocal trade agreement in 1935 and other agreements with U.S. businesses that prioritized profit over national independence.[3] For Haitian citizens, their nation remained controlled by outsiders, rather than by and for them.

Three presidents took power in Haiti during the first sixteen years of its supposed independence. Though this period began triumphantly with Péralte's belated funeral, so beautifully celebrated as national euphoria in Obin's art, any real assertion of Haitian independence remained elusive. Haitians understood these administrations as merely extensions of U.S. rule. They characterized a new type of invasion in the form of economic imperialism, which meant that any of Vincent's efforts to call on Péralte for inspiration rang false.

During his administration, President Vincent granted twenty-five year contracts to both the Standard Fruit and the Steamship Company for banana cultivation.[4] His move was reminiscent of the invasion's final years, with Borno's economic concessions to U.S. companies. But the U.S. military had flanked Borno. President Vincent did not protect his citizens as producers when he conceded to a U.S. monopoly on a Haitian agricultural product.[5] What is more, Vincent leased Haiti's lands to these foreign companies, which prevented agricultural laborers from cultivating and owning their land. These grants locked some Haitians into unfair labor contracts with foreign companies. Thus, although the U.S. military had no presence in Haiti, Haitians nevertheless felt occupied economically by the United States.

Politically, many Haitians felt unprotected by President Vincent. Dominican president Rafael Leonidas Trujillo's 1937 genocide of Haitians and darker-skinned Dominicans proved this lack of security. Despite the estimated fifteen thousand Haitians massacred by Dominican soldiers because of their race, the international world did not respond. In addition, Haitians witnessed President Vincent's inaction. Their president failed to prosecute Trujillo for the genocide. In fact, Trujillo's presidency continued until 1961. Vincent's passivity in the face of the racial violence disillusioned Haitians.[6] Many experienced traumatic feelings from the massacre after 1937, partly because this inhumane crime went unpunished. For a man who initially linked his rule to Péralte's memory, Vincent's economic and political choices failed the very citizens whom Péralte protected. Ten years of Vincent's inept rule was enough for Haitians.

The next postoccupation president, Élie Lescot ruled similarly from 1941 to 1946. Lescot pledged Haiti's support to the United States during the Second World War in 1941.[7] Haitians commended Lescot's move against Jewish genocide. Yet, their president took his allegiance to the United States even further, at the expense of his citizenry. He opened the country to rubber and sisal cultivation.[8] This material assistance to the global war hurt Haitians. It dispossessed many Haitian peasants of their lands. Disgruntled Haitians objected to the seizure of native land for foreign cultivation. Furthermore, these industries polluted Haiti's terrain. The burning of rubber and tree cutting were environmental disasters. Haitians—already incensed by Vincent's rule—became even more outraged by President Lescot's choices. For these and other political and economic wrongs, Haitians protested in artistic and political form.

In 1946 Haitians forced out Lescot and welcomed Dumarsais Estimé as his successor.[9] President Estimé's rule from 1946 to 1950 mirrored that of his predecessors. Like Vincent, he accepted deals with U.S. businesses that compromised Haiti's economy.[10] And like Lescot, he became a pawn in U.S. economic imperialism in his nation.[11] By 1948, Haitians charged Estimé with practicing "Yankee imperialism."[12] The term conveyed their sensibility about the Haitian administration and their vulnerability about their nation's economic state of affairs. In 1950, Estimé's rule ended.

Obin's Art against the Haitian State

Obin's dramatic painting memorializing Péralte's funeral captured the feeling of hope that Haitians had after the departure of the United States. They hoped that their country's national sovereignty would be respected, as Péralte had so passionately fought to ensure. As the years passed and this dream seemed less and less a reality, artists like Obin turned to their work as a form of protest. Péralte inspired Obin. Like the *cacos* leader's adulation of Dessalines and Pétion, Obin produced art that promoted historical memory. During *désoccupation*, Obin painted two works, in 1934 and 1944, that reminded his patriotic kin of Haiti's experience with the invaders. With his paintings on Péralte and his art that depicted the 1915–1934 period, Obin intentionally stirred up memories about the invasion in order to assert that the quest for Haitian sovereignty during the invasion and *désoccupation* was ongoing and often unfulfilled.

Though Obin has not been the subject of extensive historical research, his experience as an artist-activist and archivist-artist during these crucial periods of Haitian history makes his work a rich source of detail about Haitian cultural memory and political action at the time. Born in the north in 1892, Obin was one of seven children of Obénard Obin. His mother's name is not recorded. At the invasion's onset in 1915, Obin was twenty-three years old. Professionally, he worked as a barber, financial clerk, and later on a sisal plantation. As a Cap-Haïtien resident, Obin was aware of the *cacos* and Péralte. Moreover, Obin understood the invasion's deleterious effects on Haitians.

Obin was in fact, quite politically invested in supporting Haitian sovereignty. The artist witnessed the endless public battles between the *cacos* and the U.S. troops. The subsequent capture of Péralte had become a public spectacle. Further, the painter watched the prison construction in Cap-Haïtien, often by *corvée* laborers. These jails were built to contain the nationalist Haitians who rebelled. Obin was a fraternal member of the Cap-Haïtien Freemasons who delayed the U.S. troops' purchase of their lands for prison construction.[13] The U.S. military's records about the Masons noted that Obin painted art for the Masonic Hall and was their bookkeeper. These were the same Masons who issued a global plea against the invasion in 1923.

Through his art, Obin documented President Franklin D. Roosevelt's arrival in Haiti (*Visite du président F. D. Roosevelt au Cap Haïtien le 5 juillet, 1934* [Roosevelt's visit to Cap Haïtien, July 5, 1934]), recounted *cacos* history (in *Les Cacos de Leconte* [The *cacos* of Leconte]), and captured the mock funeral *Les Funeralles du Héros Charlemagne Péralte*. Obin's paintings were a platform for historic *nasyonalisme* and political awareness.

Obin's works were crucial commentaries on the political situation of his day. He produced them at strategic times, as cultural memories and reminders of Haitian independence. On one occasion, Obin insisted that Selden Rodman and his colleague DeWitt Peters, who helped create Haiti's Centre d'Art in the 1940s, visit Péralte's tomb.[14] Another Haitian artist, the poet Christian Werleigh, inscribed the following on Péralte's grave:

Dead at 33 years old, betrayed like the Lord,
Exposed on the flag crucified;
Like there would be a day like we promised,
For the country, he made sacrifices
Faced with the American, he alone cried halt:
Before you is Charlemagne Péralte![15]

This epitaph clearly indicates how grandiose the legacy of Péralte became after his death. Like Toussaint before him, his untimely death—before the goal of Haitian independence could be achieved, was a tremendous tragedy. Werleigh evokes the image of Christ while honoring Péralte, suggesting that a second life of inspiring future Haitian leaders is possible for Péralte. Indeed, Obin found this legacy inspiring, especially when he portrayed the religious imagery of this poem in another painting of Péralte entitled *Crucifixion de Charlemagne Péralte pour la Liberté* (Crucifixion of Charlemagne Péralte for freedom).[16] Obin intentionally exposed the U.S. Americans to Péralte's tombstone, keen on showing them the poet's accolade. The artist equated his work to that of a historian: "As I see it, painting should be considered in part like the Holy Book, in this way: by means of painting, that is, a picture, one is able to learn something about the past in every part of the world, one can get an idea of a foreign country, and with paint one can leave documents for future generations that writing alone would not provide."[17] Through his art and his visit to Péralte's tomb, Obin educated observers about the *cacos* movement. His paintings on the invasion and of the *désoccupation* period became his political platform, useful in continuing Haitian protest against foreign invasion under succeeding presidents who seemed to allow the United States free rein.

In 1944, two years into Élie Lescot's administration, Obin painted the second of two invasion-themed works. The piece, *Visite du président F. D. Roosevelt au Cap Haïtien le 5 juillet, 1934*, depicted the U.S. president's arrival in Haiti, ten years before. Given Obin's self-perception as a historian, this particular painting was a form of archiving. He inserted into this art piece both the date of completion in 1944 and the date of the event. The painting depicts a festive day. Obin paints Roosevelt at Cap-Haïtien surrounded by both countries' flags. The artist captures Cap-Haïtien's port location at the Atlantic Ocean and amid the U.S. fleet. Obin portrays the president as respectful, greeting the onlookers with his hat off. They eagerly await Roosevelt's speech for the invasion's end. Obin painted mostly males in this artwork. He displayed how the invasion's end involved a small group of Haitian and U.S. males, despite Haitian women's contributions. Through Obin's gaze, one sees this historic moment. The painting is an important document situated among actual photographs of Roosevelt's visit.

Despite the invasion's end in 1934, Obin witnessed the economic ties that still bound both nations. As noted, Obin himself worked on a sisal plantation. Both presidents Vincent and Lescot had acquiesced to concessions that favored the United States above citizens like him. Obin intentionally produced this artwork in 1944. As Haitians experienced economic imperialism under postinvasion presidents, Obin protested. The artist painted two works on Péralte and three on Roosevelt during his lifetime, including *Apothéoses de F. D. Roosevelt* and *Franklin D. Roosevelt intercédant dans l'au-delà pour l'union Amériques et la paix mondiale*. Placed together, the subjects of his art speak about Haitian sacrifice for citizen and nation and an end to the U.S. empire. Despite FDR's previous involvement in the early years of the invasion, the artist does not malign him. Rather, in each of these paintings, he portrays Roosevelt in a progressive light. For Obin, Roosevelt's administration signaled a restoration of Haiti's liberty and a new type of diplomacy.

Obin's timing with his painting was purposeful. Ten years after the invasion's end, Obin's artwork sent a cautionary message. Through this art piece, Obin probed at Haitians' memories about the invasion. His art seemingly asked: Is Haiti really unoccupied? Obin was not alone in wondering what the nation's leaders had really accomplished in support of Haitian sovereignty. These questions make his art part of a larger resistance inspired by Péralte.

Obin's painting suggests that the moment of FDR's arrival in Haiti in 1934 should have indicated a more appropriate and recognizable separation between the two nations. Many Haitians agreed. Citizens in the 1946 populist revolt, including students, Marxists, and communist groups, framed part of their appeals around these political and economic abuses.[18] *Ayisienne* like Lilli Fortuné, Jacqueline Wiener, and Léonie Madiou were on the front lines of this struggle. Others, like Lydia and Pauline Jeanty, in the tradition of patriotic kin, hid the conspirators in their home.[19] *Ayisienne* like the revolt's leaders articulated what Obin's art conveyed. One leader, Theodore Baker, argued: "We are anti-imperialist. We fight against all forms of imperialism. For more than thirty years we have been controlled by America and have not seen the benefits. When we vote in a few months it should be against all those who since 1915 have worked toward our ruin."[20] The populist revolt's participants framed their protest as a crusade against imperialism. Baker's dating of imperialism to the invasion's start in 1915 dramatized a general Haitian sentiment: the United States dictated the nation's affairs, with the permission of Haiti's leaders. For them, Haiti was still not free and Haitian presidents were too complicit. In an interview about the 1946 revolt, René Depestre, another architect of the uprising, charged President Lescot with being a "faithful reflection of North American foreign policy." Depestre commented on how rubber cultivation affected Haiti:

With SHADA [the Societe Haitiano-Americaine de Developpement Agricole, which oversaw the rubber cultivation], Lescot demonstrated he would dispose

Haiti once again to US imperialism, abandon the nation's political sovereignty, and completely open Haiti to the entry already advanced in the US in our affairs, to reduce our homeland to a neo colony state of the US.[21]

These Haitian radicals ended Lescot's rule. Obin is part of this canon of protest. His artwork reminded Haitians about the invasion's dangers and provoked national memory about Péralte and Roosevelt during *désoccupation*.

Ayisienne, 1934–1950

Haitian women pressed for change continually during the *désoccupation* and postoccupation period. Fighting for a variety of causes, *Ayisienne* articulated the obvious to their fellow citizens—that they were vital to the health and progress of the nation. Just like Péralte, their desires linked to the ultimate goal of sovereignty. They created several associations, such as L'Association des Femmes Haïtiennes pour l'Organisation du Travail (Haitian women's association for the organization of labor) in 1935 and La Ligue pour la Protection de l'Enfance (League for the protection of children) in 1939. Because of their efforts, in 1942 the government finally overturned a law stripping citizenship from *Ayisienne* who married foreigners. A year later, in 1943, Résia Vincent helped found L'Œuvre des Enfants Assistés (Child welfare works), and urged her relative, President Vincent, to create boarding schools and asylums. That same year, they won part of their long struggle for women's educational access with the establishment of a high school for girls in the nation's capital. In 1944, *Ayisienne* made notable strides. The year commenced with the government finally granting married women the right to keep their salaries. Additionally, the women's amendment to the 1935 constitution granted them access to civil and political jobs, with the exception of the presidency. This came with an interesting catch, though, as the government still denied *Ayisienne* suffrage. In 1946, the women of the Ligue Féminine d'Action Sociale continued their campaign for suffrage and gender equality. Their presentation to the 1946 constitutional assembly was met with both support and derision. Sylvain-Bouchereau describes these contentious moments, including some men blaming them for the nation's ills and the Ligue women being pursued by a hooting crowd. Undeterred, the women increased their activities in the Ligue Féminine and publicly shared their experiences at the assembly in a published pamphlet entitled *La Femme Haïtienne répond aux attaques formulées contre elle à l'Assemblée Constituante* (The Haitian Woman Responds to the Attacks against Her at the Constituent Assembly).[22] Haitian women were demanding a new type of national sovereignty—and the lessons learned from surviving the humiliations and abuses of the invasion period were key.

By the time of the 1950 constitutional assembly, the Ligue women were prepared on all fronts. To date, their efforts had included collecting thousands of petitions from both sexes that demanded equal civil and political rights and mobilizing a mass with their various speeches and presentations. Sylvain-Bouchereau describes the opening day of the assembly's meeting:

> On the 4th of November, the day of the Constituent Assembly's opening, more than a thousand women of all social classes from different parts of the country marched to Gonaïves with calm and discipline. Strangers deployed, carrying placards demanding their rights, the women traveled the streets of the city singing hymns; feminists and upright, under a blazing sun, they waited for two hours for the opening of the [meeting].[23]

Members of their women's rights committees stayed in Gonaïves the entire month to attend the assembly's sessions. Their ability to remain away from their families and reside outside of Port-au-Prince hints at the class and social positions that many of these women held. To allies like Dantès Bellegarde and Luc Fouché they credited the success of their work on Article 9 of the constitution, which finally deemed all Haitians equal before the law. The suffrage issue, however, came with restrictions. While Article 4 stated that "every Haitian, irrespective of sex," could exercise their political right, the same clause prevented women from voting in national elections until they had participated in municipal elections for three years.[24] *Ayisienne* thus voted for the first time in Haiti in the municipal elections of 1955.

By 1950, Haitians had endured sixteen years of postoccupation presidents. Now they could see that Vincent had bamboozled them with his symbolic ode to Péralte. He and his successors had not lived up to the *cacos'* fight for *liberté, égalité,* and *fraternité.* As the first head of state to showcase Péralte's legacy, Vincent misused the *cacos* leader. Haitians protested through art, a populist revolt, and by forcing the end of several administrations. Conversely, Obin used his art to elevate Péralte as a guide for a different type of Haiti. The artist envisioned national unity and patriotism. When that did not manifest from above in these administrations, Obin reminded them of the invasion's end through a painting of Roosevelt. Yet despite the protests of Obin and many other citizens, Haiti remained invaded. Their grim experiences darkened, for a moment, their hopes and dreams, which they had previously touted as Haiti's second independence. The complicity of Vincent, Lescot, and now Estimé, as well as the 1937 massacre, forced many Haitians to draw parallels between the 1915–1934 invasion and the 1934–1950 *désoccupation* and postoccupation period.

By 1950, Péralte had been dead for more than three decades. Yet all these years later, he still mattered. Haitians would continue to use Péralte in matters about Haitian sovereignty and resistance. They resurrected him to the annals of history because of his sacrifice to nation, and for their own purpose in nation building. Haitians used Péralte to communicate their angst and anger, as well as hope and vision for a better future. They would use art, political rhetoric, and political organization in lasting ways that preserved Péralte's spirit and legacy.

8

Péralte Resurrected
(Péralte Resisite)

● ● ● ● ● ● ● ● ● ● ● ● ● ● ● ● ● ● ● ●

Haitian politics shifted at the end of the presidential term of Dumarsais Estimé in 1950. A dramatic and terrible turn to dictatorship resulted in the rule of the Duvaliers until 1986. One of the Duvaliers' weapons was the U.S. government. U.S. presidents from Eisenhower to Reagan complied with this undemocratic state. They provided military training and financial assistance to Haiti in return for intelligence on Cuba's revolution and then its socialist state. The United States propped up authoritarian regimes in the Caribbean, including the Duvaliers and the Trujillos in the Dominican Republic, to spy on Castro's administration. Invoking its rhetoric from the invasion period, the United States justified its support of these dictators as peacekeeping and democracy building efforts. In reality, however, doublespeak permeated U.S. actions in Haiti at this time, including in how they supervised the Duvalier regimes' eventual end. Despite the brutality of these decades, Haitians fought back in ingenious ways. During this time, Haitian resistance had to take on new forms and became even more dangerous. For example, Obin's referring to Péralte in 1970 was a courageous act. Nevertheless, Péralte's legacy of protecting the nation and its citizens loomed large. International cultural memory also shifted with the opening of the Charlemagne Péralte Center in the 1980s in New York. The tragic and unfinished story of Péralte inspired continual recollections of him both inside and outside Haiti. By the end of the twentieth century, Péralte's demands for national sovereignty looked very socialist, as the Charlemagne Péralte National Liberation Front memorialized their *nasyonalis* martyr. They understood that without the U.S. military and financial support, the Duvaliers would have collapsed.

The Authoritarian Haitian State

From the middle to the late twentieth century the Duvalier family constructed an impenetrable, authoritarian regime. The Duvaliers were a new type of menace. Unlike the foreign invasion of the early twentieth century, Haitians now experienced terror from within their borders. Similar to the U.S. invasion period and postoccupation, the United States maintained its influence in Haiti's affairs through its support of the Duvaliers. Both François Duvalier and his son, Jean-Claude Duvalier, violently trampled on Haitians' civil rights. Haitians and the Duvaliers fought an ugly war. Haitians resisted both from within Haiti's borders and from abroad in Cuba, Bermuda, and the United States. The Duvaliers' multilayered terrorist state assassinated, brutalized, and imprisoned countless Haitians. U.S. Americans who traveled to Haiti were also left unprotected. The United States advised its citizens to cease travel to Haiti, and those who did travel there were left to their own devices. When the Duvaliers harmed U.S. Americans, the U.S. government departed from its previous actions. Previously, the United States would have invaded Haiti under this justification, but its Cold War paranoia shifted its agenda.

Haitians greeted 1957 on a seemingly progressive note. The year marked Haitian women's formal entry into the body politic, a huge feat after centuries of struggle to be equally recognized.[1] However, Duvalier's ascent to power cast a shade over this sunny horizon.

In an electoral standoff with at least three candidates—Daniel Fignolé of the Mouvement Ouvrier Paysan (MOP), Clément Jumelle of the Parti Nationale, and François Duvalier of the National Unity Party—the last emerged victorious. On paper, Duvalier appeared well qualified. He was an intellectual and a medical doctor with educational experience abroad and at home. During the invasion, he and two other Haitians had formed Les Griots. Their group articulated *noirisme* ideologies and advocated for Haitian sovereignty. Part of Duvalier's history suggested that he would lead Haiti away from imperialist practices and support his citizens. Yet the election of 1957, which reports indicate was a "calm and quiet affair," was also "rumored rigged."[2]

Three years into Duvalier's rule, the Parti Nationale of Haiti submitted an urgent report to the Organization of American States (OAS). Clément Jumelle charged Duvalier with imposing his authority on Haitian citizens. One Haitian elaborated on Jumelle's observations. He remarked: "The great majority of the people did not vote for him, but people were scared. [He] came by terror."[3] My interviewee described Duvalier's violent tactics, including random bomb explosions. Duvalier expelled clergy members between 1958 and 1959.[4] Jumelle also commented on Duvalier's prohibition of strikes and student demonstrations.[5]

By 1961, the president had placed a military censorship on incoming and out-going communication lines. Furthermore, Duvalier was the only candidate for the 1961 election. One woman reflected on his reelection: "But what can you do, or even say about it? . . . The best one can do about this situation is to whis-per or keep quiet . . . or you might wind up in jail or even dead."[6] By year's end in 1961, applications from Haitians seeking visas inundated the U.S. consulate. Fearing political execution, these Haitians traversed several continents, land-ing in Africa, Central and South America, and Europe. Their physical resis-tance mirrors some Haitians' protests during the invasion period, only now they faced the double threat of a brutal regime supported by their former invaders.

Duvalier fortified a police state during the early years of his rule. Both he and nearby dictator Rafael Trujillo sustained a threatening atmosphere through con-tradictory tools—fear and patronage. Both skillfully mobilized all sectors of their respective populations with such methods. Trouillot defined Duvalier's governance as a system of autocratic neutralization. In effect, Duvalier became the Haitian state through his citizens' compliance. Duvalier's three-tier law enforcement structure is based on autocratic neutralization.[7] First, there was the Haitian army. Despite his anti-U.S. rhetoric during the 1915 invasion, at the time of his rule Duvalier partnered with U.S. administrations. Using the Cold War and Cuba as pawns, Duvalier invited U.S. Marines to Haiti from 1959 to 1963. This marked the first time in twentieth-century Haitian history that a head of state had invited foreign intervention. The U.S. soldiers trained members of the Haitian army. In return, the United States gained another "anticommunist" ally in the Caribbean. The marines surveyed Cuba while stationed in Haiti.

In addition to the Haitian army, Duvalier created a civilian militia in 1962. He named the group the Volontaires de la Sécurité Nationale (VSN) (National security volunteers). Despite their benevolent name, the VSN functioned as Duvalier's private security. They protected the dictator by eliminating opposi-tion. Finally, Duvalier employed the Tonton Macoutes and Fiyet Lalo, men and women from all sectors of society who also guarded his rule. They worked as the eyes and ears of the Duvalier state. Haitians described how restaurant owners, judges, and taxi drivers were common members of Duvalier's Macoutes.[8] Soci-ologist Carolle Charles's groundbreaking article about the Fiyet Lalo discusses these terrorist women during the Duvalier period.[9]

Duvalier armed Haitians with the dubious honor of protecting the nation by guarding his rule. Between the terror, surveillance, and lack of free speech in the nation, Duvalier knew the matters of his state, at every level and at all times. One Haitian claimed proverbially that "one could not break an egg around him."[10] His state always had an ear out for protestors. Trouillot once described this period as "the polarization of the nation." He wrote: "By the mid-1960s, only two options remained: one was a Duvalierist or an anti-Duvalierist, a *makout* or a *kamoken* (the others)."[11]

A sense of normalized violence accompanied Duvalier's governance. The files on domestic terror during this time period are voluminous. Cases of beatings, kidnapping, acts of torture, wrongful imprisonments, rapes, and executions became epidemic. With the exception of kidnapping, the snapshot of Haiti under Duvalier reads like a charge sheet from the U.S. invasion period. Like the invaders, Duvalier especially targeted political opponents, union members, and journalists. In one example, union member Dacius Benoît became a "human torch."[12] Duvalier's agents lit him aflame and then imprisoned him after he survived this torture. One survivor wrote about the experiences in the Fort Dimanche jail, describing his time there as "Hell on Earth."[13] Mr. Sansaricq, another Haitian whose family endured abuse, cautioned the United States against its support for the regime. In a letter to the State Department, he warned: "The US is making a mistake using its military mission in Haiti to train men who use their weapons against peaceful Haitian citizens. In case of a change of the present regime, there would be left few Haitians bearing friendly feelings for the US."[14] Sansaricq's predictions came true.

As they had during the invasion of Haiti, U.S. officials engaged in doublespeak. Their support for Duvalier was about accomplishing their own agenda of winning the Cold War, rather than doing anything to help Haitians. Yet again, any relationship between Haiti and the United States turned out to favor the imperialist power. Supporting Haitian national sovereignty has and had always been about asserting the equality of Haitians in a world bent on dehumanizing them. Full separation from U.S. imperialism was Péralte's vision. When early presidents failed to assert national sovereignty, they failed to make the everyday lives of Haitians better. Yet, the dictatorship made conditions dramatically worse. That the Duvalier regime was supported by the United States came as no surprise for the Haitians who struggled to survive.

Haitian and U.S. diplomacy orbited around the Cold War. Two years into his rule, Duvalier let the United States build submarine bases and host training camps in Haiti in exchange for financial assistance and training of the Haitian army. On January 20, 1959, Colonel Robert D. Heinl, the chief of the U.S. naval mission to Haiti, arrived in the country.[15] By 1960, an additional three thousand U.S. Marines and navy personnel were in Port-au-Prince. Confidential correspondence circulated among the State Department staff about the pros and cons of their decision. Yet, only a year or so later, in 1960, Washington officials still trained the Haitian coast guard. For them, these efforts carried out "agreed hemispheric defense objectives."[16] The United States used the Cold War and communist Cuba as justifications for supporting François Duvalier.

In turn, Duvalier used both as pawns in his political game. He used the Cold War to negotiate U.S. aid for infrastructure projects. For example, on July 12, 1960, Duvalier wrote to President Dwight Eisenhower:

> May Haiti, my dear president and great friend, in the heart of the Americans and of the Caribbean, be a shining light in your administration marked by

cooperation, solidarity, and fraternity among men, to the glory of your
government and of the American people during these recent decades. . . . This
is my last and confident approach to you and your government, for aid for the
Artibonite Valley Project, malaria program, highway maintenance, etc.

In contemporary discussions about Duvalier the father, a minority praise him
for his political acumen of using the United States for Haiti's infrastructure benefit, pointing specifically to the above projects. President Eisenhower replied
two weeks later, but did not commit the United States to any specific plan: "Both
I and my advisors have taken an active interest in the difficulties which your people face in their efforts to obtain a fuller national life within the framework of
democratic institutions. . . . The U.S looks forward to continuing the close and
cordial cooperation which has characterized our mutual efforts in the past."[17]
Duvalier did not care for Eisenhower's delay tactics and escalated the pressure:
he threatened to put Haiti in the "Moscow camp," and he invited Haitian communists to participate in his administration, despite his previous persecution of
the group.[18] A month after Duvalier's ploy, he received letters from U.S. officials
that discussed the distribution of their aid in the form of "impact projects" in
Haiti that "would make something of a splash in Port-au-Prince." One such proposal involved the construction of homes in the capital. They almost named
this project the Cité Duvalier-Eisenhower. Duvalier had a diplomatic handle on
the United States and used it for his benefit.

Washington officials were aware of the abuses in Haiti, some of which jeop-
ardized U.S. citizens. In one case, Duvalier imprisoned Edmond Kouri, a U.S.
citizen who resided in Haiti. Kouri's family retained an attorney and petitioned
the State Department, elected officials in Florida, and the U.S. embassy in Haiti
to secure Kouri's release.[19] But Haitian and U.S. lives were not a priority to the
United States in the middle of the Cold War. A letter from Robert Newbegin,
the U.S. foreign ambassador to Haiti to Norman Warner, on November 28, 1960,
elaborates on this point:

My impressions of President Duvalier are anything but favorable. . . . As far as
his regime is concerned, it strikes me as one of the worst dictatorships with
which I have come in contact. He does not give any impression whatsoever of
being a "benevolent" dictator. I cannot see that he is doing anything at the
present time for the real advantage of his people and some of the brutality
which takes place is almost incredible. . . . Apparently, he has reached or
maintained his position through the worst type of Machiavellianism. It is
indeed unfortunate that we should be in the unhappy position of having to
support a regime headed by such a man. However, I have not at all changed my
viewpoint that this is probably still necessary until we can get the Cuban and
certain other problems out of the way. . . . We may find ourselves more and
more criticized by Haitians in general for cooperating with this regime.[20]

Just as Haitians and U.S. Americans criticized the invasion period, criticism about Duvalier also surfaced from across the Americas. The State Department received letters from ambassadors in Mexico, Puerto Rican citizens, and Haitians themselves. Francisco Vazquez Treserra, the Mexican ambassador to Haiti, characterized the Duvalier regime as "incompetent, immoral, dishonest, and a bunch of brutal opportunists in whom no one could have confidence but who had the local situation well in hand."[21] He—like Sansaricq before him—predicted a Haitian backlash. He concluded, "Our assistance to Duvalier, particularly the presence of our military mission and our military aid to the present government, was becoming the focal point of resentment among the elite, the middle class, the intellectuals, and the students."[22] In 1962, members of the exiled Haitian community protested against the $7 million that the United States gave Haiti. In 1963, Robin Frome, writing from Puerto Rico, expressed similar cautions:

> Under dictator Duvalier there is no democracy in Haiti and certainly the armed forces of that country could never be conceived in any way, shape, or form, as a non-political instrument. . . . This policy of supporting an oppressive dictator, just because he is not aligned with the communist bloc, seems to me most unwise. Haitian people are perhaps more oppressed under Duvalier than the Cubans ever were under Batista. . . . Our marines training Duvalier's army, the same army whose fundamental purpose is to suppress the people and keep Duvalier in power. . . . If the day comes when the Haitian people free themselves of this dictator, certainly they will not look towards the US in trust, but instead will turn in error, towards the neighboring island to the West.[23]

The United States was using Haiti as a tool as well. It supported the Duvalier regime while it plotted for its end. In May 1962, the State Department compiled a confidential list of ninety "Haitian Opposition Personalities" in Haiti and submitted short biographies on these individuals.[24] The department planned that those in exile could "form a cadre of democratically oriented people, opposed to Duvalier." In 1963, the national security advisor McGeorge Bundy sent a memorandum to the secretary of state, the secretary of defense, and the director of central intelligence that detailed the covert plan:

> Involvement in any program to unseat Duvalier should be limited, for the present at least, to encouraging and helping fund an effort by Haitians. Further consideration of the commitment of US prestige or US forces should be deferred until we have fully explored this approach. [The remainder of the paragraph was redacted]. Great care should be taken to ensure that we control the time frame of any revolutionary action that might involve the United States in any way. [Redacted] A determined effort should be made during the course of the next few months to encourage the development of an exile force

that might challenge Duvalier. (The manner in which this decision was reached did not preclude intensified efforts to achieve the same goal by working with oppositionists within Haiti.) It is extremely important that there be no discussion with the press about our plans for handling the Haitian problem.[25]

U.S. administrators never did resolve the François Duvalier problem. Through his law enforcement system, the dictator was always aware of U.S. efforts to unseat him.

Haitians versus François Duvalier

Despite the paralyzing fear Duvalier instilled, Haitians in the nation, and especially in the growing diaspora, tried to dismantle the Duvalier state. Like Péralte and the *cacos'* tenacity against the invaders, Haitians persisted against this internal and foreign threat. Their determination was brave given the violent police regime they faced. Indeed, some within Duvalier's administration resigned and others declined the dictator's political appointments. Subsequently, members from both groups fled their country.

In May 1959, Haitians objected to Duvalier's brutal assassination of three individuals whom the regime had suspected of antigovernment activities. These objectors both symbolically and literally attacked the president's deceased father, Duval Duvalier. They dug Duval's body from his resting place, destroyed his remains, and filled his gravesite with filth.[26] Their desecration of Duvalier's father symbolized the abuse that so many had suffered under his regime. This act warned François Duvalier of how far some Haitians would go to plan his demise. Additionally, college students and Haitian communists and Marxists demonstrated. The president imposed martial law in 1961.

Haitians in exile, while not completely free from Duvalier's reach, also protested. Some attempted several invasions to unseat Duvalier's regime and kill him. In 1958, Haitians in Florida, along with the Miami Dade County sheriff, devised such a plan. While records document their collaboration in the States, the trace runs cold about whether they landed in Haiti.

In 1960, the Parti Nationale of Haiti, operating in New York and Washington, DC, issued a fourteen-page report, "Memoire Relative to the Situation in Haiti."[27] This document publicly indicted the Duvalier state. It provided the ministers of foreign affairs of the Organization of American States and the U.S. secretary of state with an account of Duvalier's rigged election, his police state in Haiti, instances of kidnapping, political murders, and other types of "barbaric acts."[28] The document also explained the "state of siege" in Haiti, which prevented freedom of the press, freedom of religion, and protection against injustices.

Given Duvalier's authoritarian state, with eyes, ears, and military everywhere, Haitians in the diaspora had better opportunities to plot his overthrow. On

April 28, 1961, five Haitians, including the famous medical doctor, writer, and political actor Jacques Stephen Alexis, landed in northern Haiti from Cuba. Aware of their plot, Duvalier was prepared for those who sought his regime's end and his demise. His agents captured these five citizens and even today the Alexis family has no closure as to what happened to him or his remains.[29] Duvalier used the violent disappearance of the plotters as an example, reprimand, and warning to fellow Haitians. And for the international public, Duvalier defamed the group and their intent by labeling it as "an alleged Cuban inspired revolt."[30] The Haitian dictator justified disappearing and killing his own citizens using the necessity of defending against spreading communism.[31]

By 1962, Haitians had fled to various continents to escape Duvalier's wrath. A State Department report noted Haitians in exile in the Congo, Italy, Venezuela, Mexico, Colombia, Puerto Rico, and the United States. Haitians organized a number of groups in these new locales. In 1962, Gaston Millet and Kesler Clermont started the Union Nationale des Ouvriers d'Haïti en Exile in New York. In September 1963, Clément Benoît, leader of a group of thousands of Haitians in the Bahamas, formed the Haitian Revolutionary Party to resist the dictator.[32] In 1964, two exile groups, the Haitian Armed Forces for Revolution (FARH) and Young Haiti went to Haiti to try to eliminate Duvalier.[33]

In November 1966, a group of Haitians, Cubans, and U.S. Americans initiated a unique collaborative attempt. Carlos Martinez writing for the *Miami Herald* reported:

> This is the story of the Haitian invasion that never was. . . . The goal was to overthrow Haitian dictator François Duvalier. The players were Haitian exiles, Cuban exiles, US adventurers—with the big eye of the Columbia Broadcasting System beamed in as observer-historian. For the Haitians, it would have meant a homeland free of Duvalier. For the Cubans, it was a way to open a new base from which they could operate against Communist Cuba. . . . The real invasion plan, Villaboa said, was to land at an isolated point on the Haitian coast and capture and hold several villages.[34]

Cuban exile and former senator Rolando Masferrer and a Haitian priest in exile, Father Jean Baptiste Georges—who had previously served as a minister of education under Duvalier—orchestrated this scheme. They brought together former U.S. marines, Bay of Pigs veterans, and former Cuban rebel army officers. However, the plot ultimately disintegrated. Two years later, on May 23, 1968, another group of thirty-five people attempted to invade Haiti without success. In spite of these persistent efforts to end Duvalier's rule and his life—the dictator remained standing. Ironically, while these acts of resistance undermined Duvalier's authority, they also reinforced the image of Duvalier's regime as immune to collapse.

Charlemagne Péralte versus the Duvaliers

In addition to the multiple attempts to overthrow the dictator, artists also opposed Duvalier in both subtle and overt ways. Resistance in Haiti at this time looks different because of Duvalier's horrifying system of oppression, yet, in many ways, asserting the humanity and moral superiority of previous Haitian leaders like Péralte revealed the continuation of strong protest by patriotic kin. Moreover, this was also an effort to fight back against the hegemony of the United Sates because of its support for Duvalier. Philomé Obin, for example, was still painting during this period—and references to Péralte in his art continued.

In a unique protest, Obin produced another painting on Péralte in 1970. The artist repositioned the *caco* in Haiti's national discourse with his work *Crucifixion de Charlemagne Péralte pour la Liberté* (Crucifixion of Charlemagne Péralte for freedom) (Figure 9). Obin rendered a new interpretation of the 1919 picture of Péralte's body. The U.S. military had propped the leader's corpse on a door, as a half-nude, captured *caco*, an object of public display. With this painting of Péralte as a hero, Obin inverted the victim narrative. Obin added color to the black and white image of Péralte. He clothed him respectfully with a white sheath. The dead *cacos* leader leans on the door, flanked by both a crucifix and a Haitian flag. Through his art, Obin elevated Péralte as a Black Jesus figure, one who sacrificed himself for a noble cause. The art version of Péralte appears peaceful. Obin, perhaps cognizant of his close relationship to his mother, inserted Masséna Péralte in this painting, weeping at Charlemagne's side, a Black Mary figure. Mary in this instance represented perhaps the mother of Jesus or Mary Magdalene, to whom risen Jesus first announced his resurrection. In actuality, the U.S. military had not notified Péralte's kin of his death. Rather they used the image of the dead leader to warn citizens to cease protest. Finally, Obin rests Péralte's head on the Haitian flag. The patriotic symbol caresses Péralte's head and is displayed triumphantly as the reason for his resistance and death. Obin's artistic narrative reinserted Péralte's history into the national discourse. He fought back against the narratives of the *cacos* as bandits and apolitical. As patriotic kin, Obin inverted the depiction of Péralte as dispossessed to one who actively fought for his nation and citizens.

As before, Obin's artistic timing was strategic. By 1970, many Haitians were horrified by François Duvalier. Despite Haitians' and Péralte's fight against the invaders, a fellow citizen now terrorized all Haitians. Obin's painting called on Haitians to remember the country's heroes. He also warned Haitians by drawing parallels between the U.S. military invasion in the early twentieth century and the economic imperialism and authoritarianism in the mid-twentieth century. Obin powerfully used Péralte as a political memory project. For him, the *cacos* leader was a sacrificial lion whom Haitians needed to remember. Like his artistic work during *désoccupation*, Obin deployed Péralte as a weapon against

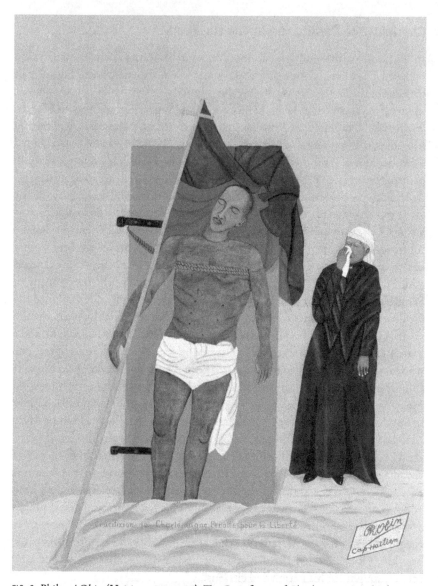

FIG. 9 Philomé Obin (Haitian, 1891–1986), The Crucifixion of Charlemagne Péralte for Freedom (*Crucifixion de Charlemagne Péralte pour la Liberté*), 1970. Oil on masonite, 19¼ × 15½ in. (48.9 × 39.37 cm) (Milwaukee Art Museum, gift of Richard and Erna Flagg M1991.139). Photographer credit: Efraim Lev-er

this domestic terror with its foreign allies. The artwork repositioned the ideas of patriotic kinship and liberation in Haitians' psyche.

A year after Obin painted Péralte, in April 1971, Duvalier died from natural causes. On his deathbed, the dictator ensured his political legacy. He named his then nineteen-year-old son, Jean-Claude Duvalier, rather than his adult daughters, as his successor. In making Jean-Claude Haiti's new president for life, he also did not choose democracy.

The continuation of the Duvalier dynasty from "Papa" François Doc to "Baby" Jean-Claude Doc endangered Haitians. Further, most of the Duvalier family served in governmental leadership ranks and in the armed forces. Within months of François's death, a *New York Times* article captured the fears of Haitians who lived outside of Haiti. Despite being in the Haitian diaspora community, interviewees in Queens, Manhattan, and Brooklyn chose anonymity in these interactions.[35] They knew firsthand that Duvalier's law and disorder extended beyond Haiti's borders. Some testified that the Macoutes routinely traveled to the United States to gather intelligence. In fact, through the 1970s, during Jean-Claude's rule, while Haitian immigration to the United States continued, a former Macoute in Miami said that many of the refugees in Florida were actually Macoutes. He disclosed that the "Duvalier family has an intricate intelligence network in the United States and even the Miami proceedings are under the surveillance of Haiti's secret police."[36] Thus, many of these Haitians in exile were not convinced that Duvalier's death would effectuate change. They feared repatriation because it resulted in retaliation. Similarly, Haitians at home felt repressed. Acts of torture and wrongful imprisonment continued with Jean-Claude's governance. Like his father, he continued to undermine Péralte's call for Haitians to protect one another.

Many Haitians fled their nation during the dictatorship years both as a means of protest and for their survival. By the 1960s, there was a sizable presence of Haitians in the United States. In particular, by the early 1980s, the Haitian diaspora community in New York had grown significantly.[37]

Though this Haitian diaspora was seeking asylum, many U.S. Americans rejected its presence. Unlike the government's classification of mostly fair-skinned, elite, and middle-class Cubans, the United States considered Haitians migrants, not political refugees. The Duvaliers' alliance with the United States precluded that distinction, the effects of which were deleterious for these refugees.[38] Many working-class and poor Haitian migrants found their "freedom" in the United States to be anything but free. The coast guard and other U.S. authorities imprisoned many of these immigrants in the Krome detention center in Florida. Authorities subsequently moved the refugees from Krome to Fort Allen, Puerto Rico; Lake Placid and Brooklyn, New York; and Big Spring, Texas.[39] The Krome detention center's intake sheets, however, were similar to the booking procedures for criminals. Imagine fleeing political execution, surviving a perilous boat journey, only to be detained at a custody center that is "reinforced with barbed wire and made secure as a prison."[40] Haitians routinely faced this ugly reality when they arrived in the States.

The close relationship between the Duvalier state and Washington indicates that the two parties found it mutually beneficial to support each other without regard to the health and basic rights of Haitian citizens. Duvalier's dedication to power at all cost led him to find ways to benefit from the United States' long history of disregarding Haitian life and its own anxiety about communism at the time. The United States, still demonstrating its ability to disregard Haitian suffering as it had done in the Senate inquiries of 1921, propped up the evil dictator.

Although the Haiti from which the refugees were fleeing was repressive, in respect to Washington's ongoing battle against communism the Duvalier state was "friendly."[41] In 1979, Jack Anderson, writing for the *Miami Herald*, argued at length:

> Immigration and State Department officials admit that a double standard exists for political refugees. Anyone from a Communist nation who seeks political asylum is assumed to have been persecuted; anyone from a right-wing regime is suspect, and the burden of proving political persecution is entirely on the refugee. . . . The Haitians misfortune is that Baby Doc's regime is considered pro-United States. This year, we will support the Haitian dictator with $40 million in aid.[42]

There was a difference in treatment for Haitian immigrants and Cuban immigrants—and later Vietnamese refugees. In addition to issues related to the Cold War, race was a major factor in how the United States received Haitians. The influx of predominately Black, non-English-speaking refugees fleeing a nation that the United States had propped up caused a stir.

The Haitian priest Reverend Gérard Jean-Juste led the Haitian refugee center in Florida. He actively pleaded for Haitian refugees' asylum. In an article describing Haitians derogatorily as "boat people," Jean-Juste pointed to this perilous oceanic journey and argued: "This shows that when these people make the decision to come, they are fleeing not just leaving."[43] In fact, one refugee attempted suicide at the idea of repatriation and another stated: "I would rather stay here and die, than go back to my country. They may kill me. I feel free here."[44] The freedom to be an independent nation and a free people was what both Dessalines and Péralte had argued and fought for. A Haitian engineer—who was later repatriated—endured four years in prison at three different jails, including Fort Dimanche. According to the Duvaliers, he betrayed and embarrassed Haiti.

In one of these Haitian prisons, 40 percent of the population of 300 inmates were repatriates. The Duvaliers charged them with abandoning their nation. As political retribution, the regime reserved a wing in Fort Dimanche for their executions.[45] Haitians who escaped Haiti were bold resisters who faced detention and discrimination in the States and/or repatriation and death in Haiti.[46]

Meanwhile, those permitted to stay in the United States faced the challenge of building new lives in a shockingly different culture. Many U.S. Americans discriminated against the Caribbean migrants because of language, race, and ethnicity, and stereotyped them as illiterate and poor. In New York City, Haitian immigrants and refugees developed diaspora communities, primarily in Brooklyn, Harlem, Queens, and Staten Island. Like their immigrant counterparts in Jewish, Irish, German, and Chinese communities, Haitians created ethnic enclaves in New York.[47] In these neighborhoods, Kreyòl and French remain the dominant languages. Here they built bookstores, barber shops, and churches. One 1984 article in the *New York Times* described these Haitian enclaves:

> The Haitian community is closely knit and elaborately structured with Haitian grocers and Creole restaurants as well as Haitian social, political, and cultural organizations, churches, bookstores, newspapers, and radio programs, lawyers and tailors and even voodoo [Vodou] groups. The largest such community in the city is in Brooklyn's Crown Heights-east Flatbush area, nicknamed "La Saline" for the slum district of Haiti's capital of Port-au-Prince. There are also communities on Manhattan's Upper West Side and in Cambria Heights, Queens, and in New Jersey cities of Newark, East Orange, Elizabeth, and Asbury Park.[48]

The dire state of life in Haiti did not make it easier for U.S. Americans to accept Haitian refugees. Once again, the United States seemed oblivious to Haitian suffering. These migrants who had escaped such horror and formed their own communities faced daily insults, including ones that demonstrated the complete ignorance of U.S. Americans, like "Go back to Africa." What is more, in a premature, xenophobic, heterosexist, and erroneous declaration, U.S. public health officials charged Haitians—along with hemophiliacs and homosexuals—as one of the "three Hs" of HIV carriers.[49] This association between disease and nationality at a time of HIV's initial outbreak further complicated life for Haitians, who had suffered severe violence at the hands of a regime the United States propped up. As a child, I vividly remember listening to the African American New York City mayor David Dinkins reiterate these falsehoods in 1988. That period marked the beginning of my *lakou* (Haitian diaspora community) and my marching across the Brooklyn Bridge to the mayor's office. Haitians protested against these stereotypes and its deleterious impacts on refugees and immigrants throughout the late twentieth century.[50]

The people who fled to the United States and formed new lives in such challenging conditions still dreamed of a better Haiti—of a world in which the first antislavery postcolonial nation thrived. Péralte loomed large in their cultural imaginary. In order to combat some of the isms they faced and acclimate to the United States, Haitians formed community centers. As François Pierre-Louis Jr. illustrates in *Haitians in New York City*, Haitians in Brooklyn organized for educational, political, and public health purposes in the 1980s. Some of these elders who founded these organizations were Haitian Fathers in exile because of the Duvaliers. These religious men helped formed the Charlemagne Péralte Center.[51] By 1982, the Péralte Center was one of six organizations in the Haitian Centers

Council.[52] The services rendered by the council sought to lessen Haitian immigrants' burdens.[53] The council provided job assistance, language courses, and counseling to Haitian refugees.[54] Haitian immigrants commemorating this historical fighter honored his legacy. Those from the 1980s who fled Duvalier's repression found solace in Péralte's story and his early twentieth-century patriot kinship example.

Péralte's image as patriot, savior, and *nasyonalis* served several purposes in Haitian New York. The center's founders saw in him a useful guide and one who protected his patriotic kin in their new, often hostile locale. They celebrated him during tumultuous times in Haiti and through their challenges in the States. Their use of his name on the Charlemagne Péralte Center was also a protest act. Their act shamed those back home who had caused Haiti's discord that resulted in so many of her citizens' decision to flee.

Haitian Protests against Jean-Claude and *Dechoukaj*

As was always the case, newspapers also fought back against the repressive regime—this time that of the Duvaliers. The administration had banned free speech and yet kept the nation's newspapers. To the international gaze, the nation's citizens appeared well versed in global happenings. Indeed, a review of publications during this period finds coverage of Congresswoman Shirley Chisholm's bid for the Democratic nomination and Black Panthers activities in the United States and African nations.[55] Nonetheless, under the Duvaliers' control, the Haitian domestic news predominantly covered the Duvaliers' ceremonies and speeches. In reading these papers, there is no obvious indication that Haiti was under siege from within. Yet, in 1983, after the pope visited Haiti, a Haitian religious radio station, Radio Soleil, became a vehicle for partial open discourse. Radio Soleil encouraged political engagement.[56] The radio station's very existence was bold. While the Duvaliers controlled the printed press, this broadcast station became an opening. This tiny crack of sunlight in an otherwise paved-over nation was the beginning of Jean-Claude Duvalier's end.

Between 1984 and 1986, Haitians, horrified with their state of affairs, created and disseminated the idea of *dechoukaj* (uprooting), the political and physical uprooting of the Duvaliers. *Dechoukaj* also meant waging a new liberation struggle, a second revolution. This desire for sovereignty engaged with the nation's past liberation struggles, including 1804, 1915–1934, 1946, and the suffrage victory in 1957. Haitians positioned *dechoukaj* as a weapon against their political, social, and economic ills. *Dechoukaj* conveyed a sense of pulling out these weeds from the top, with Duvalier and the U.S. influence on Haiti, and from its roots, with the cumulative effects of dictatorship and imperialism. The idea also conjured up an image of planting healthier roots once they had yanked out the rot. It was a nod to Toussaint L'Ouverture, who cautioned those who would be oppressors that they would always face resistance. The manifestation of *dechoukaj* then became a euphoric desire for change and a call for achieving Haiti's second independence by many means.

Haitians waged *dechoukaj* assertively and aggressively. This was a time of intense resistance. In Haiti, mass demonstrations exploded in the 1980s. This historical moment of Haitians openly fighting back was the culmination of multiple wrongs across decades. Frustrated by the effects of environmental disasters like the drought and hurricanes between 1977 and 1980 and the economic disparity between some Haitians' low finances and the Duvaliers' egregious spending, Haitians responded en masse.

Violence played a significant role in Jean-Claude Duvalier's uprooting. Whether the rebellion was launched against spaces or people, Haitians tore down what prevented their rise and stability. Some took to the streets and removed the vestiges of the Duvaliers, including the Fort Dimanche jail. They sought to rebuild a new Haiti that would work for all its citizens. In 1984, a food riot occurred in the northern town of Gonaïves. The people's shouts of "À bas Duvalier!" (Down with Duvalier!) and "À bas lamizè!" (Down with misery!) voiced their rejection of their political and economic hardships.[57] In 1985, the regime's army fatally shot four Haitian schoolgirls in the same town, which galvanized the people against the government. In 1986, the old *cacos* hub of Cap-Haïtien collectively demonstrated, with 40,000 out of 60,000 residents in protest.[58] The mass display of *dechoukaj* across different parts of Haiti helped force the regime's end.

Yet, articles in the Haitian newspaper *Le Nouvelliste* hint that others were also responsible for the Duvaliers' end. On February 8, 1986, the paper featured an article with the title "Les dramatiques journées des Jeudi, Vendredi, et Samedi" (The dramatic days of Thursday, Friday, and Saturday). It noted the presence of U.S. media for the departure from Haiti of Jean-Claude Duvalier, his family, and his close associates. A spontaneous coup d'état is never televised. Thus, Duvalier's "voluntary" departure from his nation and the media presence illustrated that Haitians had not yet seized control of their nation. His exit would have consequences for how Haiti recovered and restructured in the post-Duvalier years.

Nevertheless, by February 11, *Le Nouvelliste* noted the people's sentiments about his removal in an article with the title "La deuxième révolution haïtienne." Haitians saw the *dechoukaj* of the Duvalier state as an opportunity for the nation's second independence, much like when Haitians invoked similar hopes during the *désoccupation* period. One author, Emmanuel Buteau, wrote: "The life of a nation necessarily has certain violent and other times peaceful revolutions. There are profound transformations operating by different social classes who risked their lives for the notion of humanity."[59] After drawing parallels with Haiti's first revolution in 1791, Bateau continued: "The events of February 7, 1986 with the departure of Jean-Claude Duvalier can possibly be considered the second Haitian Revolution. The essential vindication of Haitians' rights and respect for its citizens. The government should recognize the national and constitutional rights of Haitians. The revolution is for the respect of Haitians by Haitians." The uprooting of a violent thirty-year regime seemed to bring this dream into focus.

Péralte's memory served as a symbol of defiance during the Duvalier period—at a time when any resistance was met with fierce oppression. Baby Doc Duvalier finally left power in 1986, nearly seven decades after Péralte's murder. The formation of the Péralte Center in New York indicates just how important the leader's memory was for Haitians who opposed their government's brutality and the way that the United States supported the regime. It was fitting, therefore, that when Duvalier left power Haitians turned again to Péralte. His push to rid Haiti of a brutal foreign force from 1915 to 1919 felt eerily similar to Haitians' push to rid their country of a brutal dictator supported by that same foreign force.

Once this horrific period in Haitian history came to a close, joyous Haitians, once again celebrating a feeling of hope for national independence, turned to Péralte as a symbol of the future they wished to create. By the end of the twentieth century, Haitians invested in a new idea of liberation recognized how Péralte's story could inspire them. As those before them, though, their actions often did not live up to the vision of national independence that Péralte had articulated. Nevertheless, Haitians reminded each other of the importance of *nasyonalisme* in their fight.

Remarkably, at the time of the dictator's demise, a minted coin and postage stamp featuring Péralte circulated in Haiti. The material reminders of the leader seem particularly fitting for the moment. They reminded Haitians of a long century of struggle and offered hope for a new start.

In a new type of historical public archiving and memory project, Haitians fashioned a new history, focusing on historical figures who had supported national independence and sovereignty, like Péralte. They uprooted Columbus's statute in Port-au-Prince and flung it into the sea.[60] Busts and monuments honoring foreign Whites were given Haitian names. For example, on Harry Truman Boulevard in Port-au-Prince, Haitians renamed the U.S. president's bust as Péralte. One Haitian passerby told Trouillot: "This is a statue of Charlemagne Péralte," even though the visage and nameplate depicted otherwise. Haitians behaved like lay historians in this period. At the Christopher Columbus wharf in Port-au-Prince, they inscribed: "Charlemagne Péralte Plaza."[61] The group said, "A bas Colon (ou Colomb) vive Charlemagne Péralte."[62] Through their rhetoric and actions, Haitians declared that they banned totalitarian rule and imperialism from their new Haiti.

Charlemagne Péralte Revived in a Political Party, 1986

Haitians also sought ways to create political entities whose work found inspiration in Péralte's original fight for national sovereignty. The Front Charlemagne Péralte de Liberation Nationale (FCPLN) (Charlemagne Péralte National Liberation Front) was such an effort. Founded in 1986, the party engaged the public's memory of Péralte and, like Vincent and Obin had before it, this memory was meant to criticize the nation's governance. The party made it plain that it understood that the United States persisted in terrorizing Haiti and Haitians through the Duvaliers. It is sensible that the first political party to call on Péralte after the Duvalier era was in direct opposition to the "the political theory—capitalism—that the United States had supported so strongly against Haitians' welfare. By the end of the twentieth century, Haitians in the FCPLN articulated Péralte's demands for national sovereignty as a socialist one.

The party's founders lived through the dictatorship's terror. In 1976, they formed a socialist organization, the United Front of Haiti, but changed the name due to the crackdown on Marxist and communist groups. In 1986, they were free to reposition themselves politically. Calling on Péralte at this time was not initially understood to be against the state. It was, instead, understood to be anti-imperialist. Most of the FCPLN's members were union members and communists. Gilles Hendrick, a medical doctor who served as the FCPLN's general secretary, was a political prisoner of the regime in 1965. Hendrick is the only one with a photograph and a short biography in the manifesto. Research on the others listed them as medical doctors, authors, and historians. For example, both René Theodore and Gérald Brisson were leaders of the Parti unifié des communistes haïtiens (PUCH) (Unified Party of Haitian Communists). In fact, the CIA monitored Brisson and his family.[63] Duvalier's security forces had harmed Brisson's family because of his communist beliefs. They fired on his home, arrested his wife, and sent her to the torturous Fort Dimanche jail. Between 1961 and 1969, the Duvaliers had harmed Brisson, Ambroise, Rameau, Rony Lescouflair, and Michel. In the FCPLN manifesto, members characterized them as deceased comrades. Others—Theodore, Laine, Bourjolly, and Hendrick—were political prisoners who had survived Fort Dimanche. Their militant manifesto criticized not only the Duvalier regime but its allies.

> For 29 years, and with the help of local and foreign secret forces, the autocratic regime of the Duvaliers spread terror within the hearts of almost every Haitian family in order to establish its political power and restore the hereditary Republic thanks to which the ruling class—at the service of foreign powers— was able to best carry out the shameless exploitation of the working and peasant classes, which represent more than 80% of the country's population.[64]

The manifesto explicitly named the Duvaliers, foreign U.S., and elite Haitians as the terrorists, while the victims were primarily Haitians from the working and peasant classes. The FCPLN reversed earlier U.S. narratives labeling Haitians as undemocratic and violent, and U.S. Americans as virtuous and even victims.

Though many of the FCPLN members came from the professionally elite class, as medical doctors and authors, they positioned themselves as the spokespeople and advocates for those without economic power. They emerged as patriotic kin to these Haitians and condemned the Duvaliers as enemies. They explicitly implicated the Haitian elite as accomplices in this tyranny.

The FCPLN founders attribute to these three groups Haiti's exploitation. The FCPLN listed all those culpable for Haiti's economically underdeveloped state in 1986. They intentionally listed the U.S. presidents who fostered this type of Haitian state:

> Since the rise of the Duvalier regime, the traditional methods of the age-old enemy have intensified and become worse: they are ready to try anything in order to maintain Haiti in the state of dependence that led it to become the most backward and its people the poorest in the western hemisphere. The Haitians must remember that the 29 years under the Duvalier dictatorship result from the support that it received from Uncle Sam, particularly under the administrations of Dwight D. Eisenhower and Richard M. Nixon. The impact of that support—whatever it may be—on the life of the Haitian people, should not be worrisome since it comes within the global frame of American interests to be defended. It is in the light of this sad realization that the FCPLN has undertaken to wage the struggle of liberation with the Haitian people.[65]

During François Duvalier's rule, Eisenhower supported his violence. And then, Nixon disbursed $26 million to Haiti under Jean-Claude's rule. The FCPLN and many other Haitians understood that without the United States' military and financial support, the Duvaliers would have collapsed. Eisenhower's backing of a regime that harmed Haitians and its own citizens angered those in the Charlemagne Péralte National Liberation Front. Many had warned that a U.S. alliance with the Duvaliers would foster Haitian resentment toward the United States, and these Péraltes used their manifesto to articulate that very resentment. Using the *cacos* leader's legacy, they vowed a liberation struggle with their fellow citizens.

Unlike his father, Jean-Claude lacked political acumen. His mother, Simone Duvalier, and later his wife, Michele Bennett Duvalier, directed many of his decisions for Haiti. Whereas François had manipulated the United States for mutual gains, during Jean Claude's rule, an asymmetrical relationship developed between the two nations. At the expense of his citizens, Jean-Claude attempted to lease Haiti's Tortuga Island to the DuPont Caribbean Corporation.[66] Further, the son did not limit U.S. companies' business interests in the nation. Trouillot documented the presence of 150 U.S. firms in Haiti in 1972. Merely five years later in 1977, that number had doubled. The FCPLN objected to the exploitation of Haitians that came with the presence of these firms. They understood that this exploitation was made possible and encouraged by the Duvaliers.

Ironically, Jean-Claude often boasted that he waged the economic revolution to match his dad's political one. In actuality, the son, unlike his father, failed.

Jean-Claude's version of economic development led to underdevelopment in a manner reminiscent of the invasion period and postoccupation presidents. While U.S. corporations could argue that they created jobs, the low wages and lack of health insurance and other benefits were inequitable and further added to Haiti's economic decline.

For the FCPLN members, Haiti no longer functioned as an independent republic that put the interests of Haitians at the forefront. To rectify the horrid political and economic conditions under the Duvaliers, they, like Péralte, called for a liberation movement. In their manifesto's preamble, the FCPLN declared:

> This struggle will give back the Haitian people its right to work, to a scholastic, civic and political education; its right to a better condition, to a decent lodging, to the promotion of [its] own national culture, capable of winning over the disquieting phenomenon of cultural void. This war is that which will put an end to the emergence of necessarily repressive puppet political regimes, to the exploitation of the nation's working class—in the majority—by the parasitical and pandering bourgeoisie and eventually to the subservience of the national patrimony by the enemy.[67]

Similar to the *cacos*, the party members positioned themselves as foot soldiers in a war. Unlike its predecessors, the FCPLN faced threats from within and without. Its namesake had envisioned and fought for a sovereign Haiti for all Haitians. And yet from 1957 to 1986, under the Duvaliers and their allies with the Haitian elite and the United States, Haitians were far from Péralte's vision. The FCPLN reissued Péralte's liberation in 1986. The topic of class as those who should inherit economic freedoms featured prominently for the FCPLN. Further, as outlined above, the FCPLN desired an independent Haiti that would offer all of its citizens education, housing, and basic rights.

The FCPLN members wrote a seventy-four-page multilingual "Manifesto and Political Program of the Charlemagne Péralte National Liberation Front." They presented their political program in three languages—French, Spanish, and English. Ironically, despite their defense of Haiti's working class, they did not offer a Kreyòl translation. This omission derived from the reality that until 1986, the language of engagement in schools, politics, trade, and media was French. With the year 1986 came the first national efforts to begin issuing Haitian publications in journals and elsewhere in Kreyòl. The FCPLN's multilingual presentation could, however, communicate with the party's fellow formally educated citizens and potential allies in Cuba and the Dominican Republic, as well as Guadalupe and Martinique.

The FCPLN pamphlet articulated its vision for a new Haiti in twenty-eight articles. It endeavored to formulate a complete national political and economic reconstruction. Its use of Péralte, its arguments, and its rousing language positioned it as the party that would realize Haiti's second independence. In 1986, it offered a blueprint to realize this ultimate goal. Similar to its namesake and the *cacos*, it relied on historical memory. The FCPLN attributed Haiti's underdeveloped state to the cumulative violence of colonialism, slavery, imperialism, and capitalism.

Just as Péralte fought against the actual presence of U.S. troops, the FCPLN framed its battle against the Duvaliers and the United States as a patriotic mission. It declared:

> Haiti's inheritance from colonialism is only but a deformed, dependent, and unfair structure. Up until now, the neo colonialist structure present in Haiti has only served the purpose of exploiting the natural resources and using our cheap labor in order to increase the local and foreign capitalist economies. . . .
> In Haiti, the foreign and local merchant bourgeoisie serve as middlemen between Haitian consumers and foreign producers and bear the responsibility—along with the traditional public service—for the barely existing local industry and agriculture. Imperialism, which is represented by multinationals with the collaboration of the local oligarchy, responsible for setting up the former, favors the exploitation of the country. We are left with an economy in which our working class does neither possess nor control the means of production. In fact, the local pandering bourgeoisie with the support of our reactionary and puppet governments strengthen the influence of imperialism and neo colonialism in our country.[68]

The FCPLN attributed Haiti's underdevelopment to colonialism. It accused Haitian administrations and the elite of permitting alliances with the United States that abused the nation and its citizens. It called out Haitians' complicity in this abuse.

The FCPLN advocated for a "socialist revolutionary government" that would "aim at the satisfaction of material, moral and cultural needs of the entire national community."[69] Its socialist vision fit with its previous existence as the United Front of Haiti. Previously, it could not articulate itself freely and without political consequence to its members and their families. But from 1976 to 1986, it openly positioned itself as Péraltiste and as a socialist movement that endeavored to govern the nation through this lens. The FCPLN—like other socialist activities in English-speaking Caribbean nations—envisioned a Haiti where workers controlled the capital and means of production. It was done with capitalism not working for all the people. Moreover, many of the organization's members had experienced the political use of capitalism waged against communism. The Cold War and the U.S. fixation with Castro's principles directly affected Americas' citizens. Drawing on Péralte's legacy, the FCPLN wanted a socialist Haiti that would benefit all Haitians.

As a result of its own history with the dictatorship, the FCPLN was adamant about Haitians' political, economic, and social freedoms. It promised that other political parties and affiliations could exist under its socialist revolutionary government. For domestic matters, it planned to (1) improve access to health care, especially among the disabled; (2) establish a second university and promote free education; (3) liberate women to participate in the state's political and civic affairs; and (4) support the rights of workers through unions. Moreover, the FCPLN's focus on particular "vulnerable" groups, including disabled people and women, was remarkable. Its inclusion of these citizens in its desires for a new Haiti was unique.

The FCPLN allied itself with other global liberation and anti-imperialist struggles. It promised support to the people's movements in Mozambique, Angola, Zimbabwe, Namibia, and Palestine in a manner similar to how Cubans participated in African liberation movements. It listed nations that the world typically ignored in diplomatic relations or peoples who were the underdogs, such as the Palestinians. Furthermore, the FCPLN pledged to open Haiti's diplomatic ties to "socialist and Muslim countries."[70] It disavowed both the Duvaliers and the U.S. isolationist polices toward nations in these two categories. Its revolution in Haiti would be part of a larger global struggle against the Cold War (outside its battle of democratic and capitalist nations versus socialist, Marxist, and communist states). Repeatedly, in its manifesto, it linked its critiques of classism, capitalism, and imperialism. For the party, each -ism divided the world into First and Third world divisive politics and realities.

The FCPLN mapped out a new type of sovereignty in Haiti that revolved around class and economic freedoms. It charged that multinationals in the nation and U.S. companies had caused "500 and more billion dollars of Third World Debt." The party would sever relationships with these sectors. In its place, it would grant foreigners' permission to invest in Haiti under one condition—that part of their profit remained in the nation for its development. The FCPLN's calls for economic and political justice echoed some of Dessalines's rhetoric for a nation free of economic or political chains, and they critiqued the Duvaliers, who offered no protection to Haitians. The murder of Péralte kept the fire going about national sovereignty. The party members declared that Haiti had a duty to "settle all political and economic matters without interference from any foreign nation."[71]

Similar to Péralte's recruit of *cacos* and patriotic kin, the FCPLN closed its manifesto with a call for unity and action. The manifesto declares: "The time has come for Haiti's second independence."[72] Haitians from the invasion period to this dictatorship era wanted a free Haiti. Additionally, like the *cacos* leader in 1915, the manifesto outlined who would be the recipients of this new paradigm: all Haitian citizens, including "men, women, intellectuals, executives, technicians, workers, peasants, traders, craftsmen, industrialists, officers, soldiers, blacks, mulattos, rich, poor."[73] It clearly expressed what type of unity the party called for and included members from these disparate groups under the common banner of being Haitian citizens. For the *cacos*, creating these relationships among disparate groups had allowed them to succeed.

In its conclusion, the FCPLN focused on every issue that it felt had limited Haiti by foreigners and insiders. The manifesto affirms:

> The FCPLN invites to rally under its banner in order to rush the complete collapse of hunger, social injustice, political repression, fratricidal fighting, and social intolerance to make space for material, social, and spiritual development. Long live Haiti, Long live democratic Socialism.[74]

The repetitious and exhaustive lists of Haiti's wrongs and the wrongdoers was intentional. The manifesto issued a platform and a plea. The FCPLN berated authoritarian regimes and also questioned the purpose of the U.S. "democratic" surveillance of "nondemocratic" states. The platform openly criticized democracy's failures, showing how the United States and allied Caribbean nation states did not permit other types of political governance in the Americas. The FCPLN used Péralte as a socialist critique of the capitalism of the Cold War that led the United States to support capitalism at all cost. In the late twentieth century, Péralte's legacy of anti-U.S. imperialism also became socialist.

The FCPLN members' indictment of the Duvaliers, the Haitian elite, and the United States was bold. With optimism, the FCPLN declared a people's revolution, led by and for the Haitian people. While the FCPLN never achieved this democratic socialist state, the Duvaliers dynastic power ended physically in 1986. Perhaps working under the cover of Charlemagne Péralte's name provided a safety net. The Duvaliers had targeted members of this group for their socialist leanings. And yet, as analyzed, the party's vision condemned the very groups who had harmed and could still harm them—the Duvaliers, the elite, and U.S. allies. The party changed its name but did not mince its political declarations. Rather, its platform was its rallying cry and conch shell.

The party's simple existence meant that people were articulating anti-U.S. imperialist and pro-Haitian sentiments. The United States remained an imperialist presence in Haiti over the course of the twentieth century, with its military invasion, economic imperialism, *and* support of an authoritarian regime. The policing of the Haitian press during the period 1957–1986 makes it difficult to analyze how the FCPLN disseminated its ideas and achieved its goals. Based on Articles 2 and 3 of its manifesto the FCPLN established its office in Port-au-Prince but it listed no address. It designed a symbol and slogan for the organization, "L'Union Fait la Force" (Unite for strength), that reiterated the message of the nation's flag. (Figure 10).[75] Just like Dessalines and Péralte, it uses the revolution and *nasyonalisme*.

Despite its absence from other archival records and contemporary memory, the Charlemagne Péralte National Liberation Front was a history-making party.

FIG. 10 Flag of the Charlemagne Péralte National Liberation Front, "Manifeste et programme politique du Front Charlemagne Peralte de Liberation Nationale" (Manifesto and Political Program of the Charlemagne P[é]ralte National Liberation Front), ca. 1986 (Latin American and Caribbean Collection, University of Florida, Gainesville)

In the heyday of sustained persecution, Haitian men and women united in a comprehensive liberation struggle. They sought to combat domestic and international terror in its many forms. Péralte was a useful patriot to uphold in a fight against the Duvaliers. He reminded Haitians that they had unified against the U.S. invaders and could unify once more, especially after the injustice of his murder. The United States supported the Duvaliers and it looked like Haitians were hurting Haitians, when in reality there was an international context that made resistance almost impossible. In some ways, this mirrors what Péralte was up against, including the betrayal by Conzé and others for money from the United States. The FCPLN's communicated that Péralte was Haiti's guide to Haitians' sovereignty. Péralte mattered to Haiti especially during the invasion, during *désoccupation* and postoccupation, and now during the dictatorship regime.

Post-Duvalier Violence, 1986–1988

A mural near the Palais National, just to the left of the nation's barracks, paints a vivid picture of the chaos that followed the departure of the Duvaliers. It featured Haitians from all walks of life with signs demanding this new Haiti. Though Haitians felt euphoric that the horrific leaders supported by the United

States had physically departed their nation, the injuries and scars of their actions remained. Beginning in February 1986, many Haitians' anxiety and fear for the past decades erupted as rage. They lashed out at any and all reminders of the oppressive dictatorship. They set fire to tires, turned cars upside down, and attacked members of the Tonton Macoutes, the army, and the Fiyet Lalo who had once brutally violated them. Haitian women and men from diverse classes organized demonstrations that called for equality and a reordering of the Haitian state.[76]

Thanks to a more open environment of ideas, many Haitians, including intellectuals harmed by the regime, published texts about their difficult life under the regime.[77] It was not only a time when Haitians began to look back on the long history of imperialism and its effects on Haitians since the era of Columbus, it was also a time of reflection on the ways that the United States had manipulated Haiti and Haitians for its own gain for nearly a century. What began as a tenuous relationship between one small antislavery nation and another proslavery major nation in the nineteenth century quickly spilled over into a U.S. effort to dominate and exploit Haiti and Haitians according to its need at the time.

This conversation about imperialism led Haitians to ponder Duvalier's bloodless exit. Unlike other Haitian presidents who, when deposed, fled to nearby Caribbean nations, Duvalier left the nation on his terms. Trouillot describes the dictator enjoying a final car ride around the nation's capital before boarding a private U.S. cargo plane with his followers to fly to France. The anthropologist concluded: "This was the most graceful exit of a dictator in Haitian history, . . . so much civility."[78] The image of Duvalier riding around Haiti before his political descent caused many Haitians to conclude that there was no coup d'état. Rather, they felt that the United States had orchestrated Duvalier's departure. They pointed to the presence of U.S. journalists who documented the president's "abrupt" exit.[79] The political shift that allowed Haitians such long-awaited freedom from an evil regime felt eerily simple—as they had learned from even before the time of Péralte. Haitians knew not to trust any action connected to the United States.[80] Calling on Péralte involved anti-U.S. imperialist sentiments. Haitians understood that in both 1915 and 1986, the United States exploited Haiti and blamed Haitians for their failure to thrive in a world set up against them. After the 1915–1934 invasion, Haitians used Péralte to fight back against these intrusions and demand sovereignty over and over again.

Even as Haitians celebrated Duvalier's departure, doubts surfaced about the feasibility of a new Haiti. One letter to the national minister of education expressed alarm at the "degraded socio-political situation in the country and the recrudescence of violence and repression."[81] He referenced the riots that had continued despite Jean-Claude's removal from office.

Writing the 1986 constitution provided a much-needed opportunity for change. Roger Savain wrote an in-depth analysis of the "Constitutional Project of 1986" in Le Nouvelliste.

The new Constitution of Haiti like the Haitian nation rests on fundamental principles: popular sovereignty, human rights, and social justice. These principles are democratic and ensure the participation of the public in the governmental process. It protects the entitlement to equal rights for all citizens [and] economic equality. In this light, we have the constitutional project of 1986. We seek important changes and invite civic participation. It retains lessons of the past, understands this disorder of the present, and anticipates the importance of a future to draft a precise and solid document that can survive assaults and ambitions of the time.[82]

Violence however, marred the constitutional discussions and its vote. In 1988, just two years after Jean-Claude's departure, General Prosper Avril, the former head of his presidential guard, seized power from President Leslie François Man- igat.[83] Uprooting the Duvaliers and their legacies of violent power was a chal- lenge. Yet, Haitians continued to push for Haiti's second revolution in the late twentieth century using Péralte's legacy.

9

Liberation with Péralte
(Liberasyon ak Péralte)

• •

The tumultuous period after Duvalier's departure led to an anti-U.S. and pro-socialist sentiment inspired by anti-invasion *cacos* leaders, like Péralte. Other leaders, however, also called on this legacy in their ascent to power. Jean-Bertrand Aristide was a Catholic priest who came to power at this time of political upheaval. He gained the support of the poor, but was not popular with the elite or the powers that be, because he initially evoked the legacy of Péralte. After only nine months in power, he was removed by a coup d'état and later returned to office with the help of the United States. Aristide used Péralte as a memory project that overtly discussed race and class in relation to Haitian sovereignty.

Aristide's Political Rise

Jean-Bertrand Aristide first introduced himself to the Haitian public in the 1980s as a harbinger of social justice and democracy. He, along with several other Catholic clergy, believed in the *Ti Legliz*, a liberation theology movement.[1] *Ti Legliz*, translated as "little church," was exactly that, a *Ti Legliz* within the larger Catholic Church. Aristide promoted this sociopolitical consciousness against the Duvaliers prior to their departure, and as a means for Haitians to recover from their impact.

As a priest, Aristide occupied an influential role. He emerged as a humble citizen who informed and inspired his congregation to become politically engaged.

On May 19, 1986, a Haitian newspaper reported on one of Aristide's protests against the Duvalier state and its remaining guard. He orchestrated a symbolic confrontation with one of the strongholds of the regime—the Fort Dimanche jail.[2] The priest led a group of Haitians in a memorial march to the prison as a homage to the thousands who had died inside those walls. The walk was a cathartic move, assertive and powerful for a population of people still carrying scars from the horrors of the Duvalier regime. Then, in 1988, members of this guard attacked Aristide's host church, leaving several congregants dead, leading to his resignation from the church. Within two years, Aristide reemerged as a politician who rode on Péralte's coat tails.

In Aristide's calls for unity after dictatorship, he decided to identify Haitians as "the people of Péralte." His statement indicates how powerful the memory of the *cacos* leader still was, and that there was a deep feeling of wanting to right the wrongs of the past. What better leader to evoke than the man who was murdered so young for simply daring to assert that no foreign power had the right to dominate and harass his fellow citizens? As one writer noted, Aristide "chose Charlemagne Péralte, the martyred hero of the American occupation, as his patron saint."[3] Aristide inspired Haitians to believe that this assertion of power, of national sovereignty in the interest of the good of the people, was possible. He declared: "After having banished the oppressive and corrupt regime of the Duvaliers on February 7, 1986, at the end of that long and courageous struggle, the people of Charlemagne Péralte had only one choice: to install, once and for all, a democratic regime in Haiti. In that light, 'liberty or death' is no different from 'democracy or death!'"[4] Aristide sought to incite patriotic kinship through the *cacos*' chief. His phrase, "the people of Péralte," was inclusive.

Aristide was similar to President Vincent in his use of Péralte's revolutionary image to help him gain Haitians' acceptance. In written and verbal communications with citizens, Aristide used the *caco* to articulate his anger and hopes. In one such address, he proclaimed: "As for the Haitian people, we again hail the heroic courage, crying, in the voice of Charlemagne Péralte, in the voice of Dessalines, in the voice of Lavalas [his political party]: It is better to perish with the people, than to succeed without the people, but with the people, we know no defeat, so, victory is ours!"[5] In Aristide's words, Péralte's fate was an injustice to correct and Péralte is a hero who has officially taken his place alongside the other national heroes of Haiti, like Dessalines.

Aristide's use of Péralte in his salutations to Haitians helped secure his presidential victory in December 1990. He uttered the equivalent of "Black Power," conveying unity and action to his citizens. Like the FCPLN, Aristide deployed Péralte's memory in his battle against international actors. In one 1987 speech, Aristide lambasted the foreigners who had wreaked havoc in Haiti. The following prose harkens back to Péralte's rhetoric, as well as to the FCPLN's manifesto. During the speech, Aristide received affirmations from audience members who shouted, "Amen, Aristide!"

We are asking if you acknowledge that you have stolen, that your countrymen have stolen during the process of colonization. If you want to call yourselves developed countries, you need to acknowledge what you have done to us. But we are not asking for your pity, no but for you to acknowledge that we have the right to recuperate a part of what has been stolen from us.[6]

Aristide implicated both the United States and France in Haiti's underdevelopment. Reminding his audience of the events of 1825 and 1915, he charged these nations with pilfering Haitian resources. Aristide, like the FCPLN, looked at the collective wrongs waged against Haiti, dating these infractions back to colonialism. He discussed France's exorbitant indemnity bill that took the nation centuries to pay. Furthermore, he reminded Haitians of the U.S. seizure in 1915 of their state and its institutions like the Banque Nationale. He challenged the use of the First World and Third World paradigm: "then they would not dare call a people you have exploited underdeveloped, when you are responsible for their lack of development."[7] Those in power created the paradigm of the First and Third Worlds. These terms often erroneously described nation states. The U.S. promotion of itself as a development hub fell on deaf ears in Haiti. Aristide charged the United States with having acquired its wealth through its roles as colonizer and imperialist. Aristide articulated what Péralte fought and died for—the long history of how the United States and France had obstructed Haitian sovereignty. In this late twentieth-century context Aristide carried the *nasyonalis* tradition of Péralte and Dessalines. Like both men, he exposed how global powers undermined Haiti and her citizens and he reminded Haitians to protect their nation.

Aristide's provocations continued. In an audio recording from the 1990s, Aristide evoked the memory of Péralte when communicating about domestic and imperialist wrongs. In a speech lasting less than three minutes, he proclaimed: "Charlemagne Péralte, man of Haiti who gathered fighters when they wanted power.... These men [perhaps marines, Haitians or both], Péralte forced them to eat dust.... They stand, while the Haitian people need food, education, and jobs."[8] Aristide's bold rhetoric echoes the FCPLN. Like the party, he sought patriotic kinship and access to educational, class, and labor equities. While his declarations incited many Haitians who voted for the priest, it failed to unify all Haitians around the same objectives. Part of the reason is that he berated his fellow citizens. He agreed with the FCPLN's analysis, the country's elite and army were culprits. He criticized these sectors repeatedly.[9] In one speech, Aristide implicitly charged them with being Tonton Macoutes. Aristide declared:

All powerful God, we are little before you, we do not identify with the imperialist Americans, neither with the Macoutes amongst us. We endure the blood, we are destroyed but you are one whom we understand and who can help us feel liberated of our sins and capable of freeing our country of the imperialist impression that suffocates us. . . . All powerful God, we incite a united march under the voice of anti-imperialism that can bring a grand revolution of love, of integral liberation, in the name of Jesus who walks with us always.[10]

He assertively stated the problems and used religious rhetoric to condemn those he called culprits. His rhetoric worked for many. In 1990 Aristide won in a violent electoral face-off against Marc Bazin, a former minister in Duvalier's administration. Working-class and poor Haitians overwhelmingly supported Aristide.[11]

Aristide aligned himself with the activism of a man that the United States murdered. Fittingly, he echoed the anti-imperialist message of the *cacos* leader and, like Péralte, Aristide found himself unpopular with world powers because of this message. His focus on "God before country" repeats Péralte's message of "God feeds little birds." Aristide interpreted supporting the poor specifically as part of his Christian message. Dupuy characterized Aristide's electoral style as the priest who saw his "candidacy as a messianic mission."[12] His leadership of the Lavalas Party drew from this style as well. Dupuy argues that he expressed democracy but did not practice it within his political party.[13] These collective issues of Aristide publicly indicting the Haitian elite, army, and the United States culminated in the coup of 1991 after a mere nine months in office. He sought exile in Venezuela and then the United States until 1994.[14]

During Aristide's time away from Haiti, he attempted to make sense of his removal. Some Haitians remembered how he had previously invoked both God and Péralte. Two months after the coup, *L'Union* reprinted a sermon that Aristide delivered at St. Jean Bosco, his church. During that mass, then Father Aristide first asked the following rhetorical questions: "God or Satan, whom do you want? Who is Satan? We or the Americans? Who is Satan, the government or the Americans?" He shouted:

Down with the American government! . . . Down with evil, die imperialism! Stay far away White Americans! My brothers and sisters, I salute you in the name of Charlemagne Péralte. This morning's meeting is one of brothers and sisters engaged in the same battle against a common enemy that is none other than American imperialism.[15]

For Aristide, the imperialist project persisted in the White U.S. American enterprise. He charged those involved with harming citizens across the Americas. He concluded with questions and a chant that recalled Péralte's legacy. His last sentence bears a direct resemblance to Péralte's rhetoric in 1918 in his letter to President Wilson:

Are the Americans really rich? Do they aid Haitians who are very poor? . . . Do the Americans love Haiti? They do not help us. The reason, there are too many

Judas amongst us.... Haiti is Haitians and not White Americans! Haiti is
Haitians and not White Americans! Haiti is ours and we are hers! Oh! Oh!...
Of the 705 invasions realized by U.S. imperialism, Latin America and Mexico
are victims 270 times, Cuba 92 times.... Never will we march heads bowed
before U.S. imperialism!... Today, we come to honor Christ, Charlemagne
Péralte and the forefathers.... The U.S. are already in Haiti. The local
U.S. A.I.D. [U.S. Agency for International Development] is the siege of the
government.[16]

Aristide's direct accusations repeat those of Péralte. He also overtly recognizes
the deep racism that guided U.S. imperial action throughout the twentieth century. Aristide's use of White U.S. Americans historically reflects on the soldiers
who invaded Haiti in 1915. Péralte also understood the actions taken against
Haiti as part of a larger U.S. plan for domination. He and Aristide both connect Haiti with its Caribbean neighbors in their plight against a powerful exploit-
ative nation.

A stern investigation of imperialism's lasting effects characterized this
euphoric and politically volatile period in Haitian history. Naturally, Péralte featured prominently—on coins, stamps, renamed busts, and in the words of the
popular—and brutally honest—political leader. Aristide's promotion of an anti-
imperialist figure who engaged the U.S. military for years was daring. Like
Péralte, he decried the United States as the antithesis of progress and democracy.[17]
Further, he reminded Haitians of the *cacos'* battles in their present struggles. His
phrases, "Haiti is us, and we are Haiti," sought unity, and his "Down with Americans" was militant. President Aristide communicated with urgent, simple, and
direct messages. And through Péralte, he posited thoughtful questions about
imperialism, classism, and sovereignty. One interviewee commented on Aristide's
initial allegiance to Péralte: "I think almost all of the presidents had a certain
respect for Charlemagne Péralte, but they were fearful of criticizing Americans,
so they did not speak much of it. But Aristide was in *bis bis* [conflict] with the
Whites, and he took a position supportive of Péralte."[18] Aristide discussed race
and class as part of Péralte's legacy. Aristide challenged the overt racism from
the U.S. invasion period and the fundamental racism that continued in U.S.
interactions with Haitians in the decades after the invasion. According to the
interviewee, Aristide gained political power through Péralte.

Aristide and the United States, 1994

In an ironic twist of events, the United States facilitated President Aristide's
return to Haiti in 1994 with its troops. Political scientist Robert Fatton's *Haiti's
Predatory Republic* meticulously details this "second coming of Aristide."[19] That
year, Aristide backtracked. Confrontational Aristide—who had been condescending toward the United States and combative toward the Haitian elite—mellowed

significantly. There was a dramatic and noticeable change in his speeches and tone. The former militant priest and president from the 1986–1991 period became less militant in 1994. He no longer denounced U.S. Americans' intentions for Haiti and instead allied with the Washington, DC, administration. Once the United States had helped him regain his seat, Aristide then celebrated one of Haiti's founders, Toussaint L'Ouverture.

Aristide's shift in rhetoric and historical affiliation, from a radical anti-U.S. leader to a revolutionary leader known for his diplomatic efforts with France, coincided with a different view of U.S.-Haiti relations. This shift shocked his supporters, who missed his honesty about the brutal and material effects of the United States' ongoing racism.[20]

Aristide, however, was politically astute in U.S. and Haitian diplomacy. He knew that past U.S. leaders—such as President Thomas Jefferson—had denounced Dessalines and other Haitian revolutionaries as vagabonds. Aristide probably reasoned that U.S. Americans viewed L'Ouverture's legacy as a safer narrative. His new allegiance brought him back to office. Despite Aristide's switch of political heroes, Haitians elected him twice more—in 1994 and 2000. Still, some members of the Haitian community in New York were not as forgiving. In one article in the *Haiti Observateur*, the author criticized Aristide's change: "The frenzy about Toussaint L'Ouverture underscores also Aristide's ungratefulness. How can we forget that he built his political fortune around Charlemagne Péralte?[21] An artist reflected on Aristide's shift:

> Well, once upon a time, when Aristide was president, he would speak of Péralte a lot. "We walk the testimony of Charlemagne Péralte," that is how he used to talk. However, he endured a coup d'état and was exiled. When he returned, he did not speak of Péralte. He started speaking of Toussaint L'Ouverture. I do not know if it is the work of the Americans, what they did to his spirit to have him return, but during his first time, he used to speak of Péralte a lot. During this second time, he never spoke of Péralte. He spoke of L'Ouverture. Hence, Péralte put a warning in Americans' heads and Americans do not like when you speak of Péralte. They probably said if we return you to the island, you have to cease speaking of Péralte and that is it. That is the way it is, he wanted to return to Haiti. Once upon a time, he also spoke badly of the Americans, but when he came back, he did not speak badly of them at all.[22]

The artist articulates a feeling that was common among some Haitians—somehow the United States was responsible for a second death of Péralte. Aristide revived Péralte in all his radicalness. Péralte had been the inspiration for Aristide's truth telling—U.S. Americans in power were racist, which had led them to dehumanize and dismiss the suffering of Haitians for decades. Yet again, however, the United States had demonstrated its unchecked power by moderating the political rhetoric of a Haitian leader. Toussaint L'Ouverture, even though he also met an untimely demise due to the inhumanity of colonial leaders, became a soft-spoken and moderate historical influence because he represented this disappointing political shift. While L'Ouverture was a radical figure, some have characterized his diplomacy and affiliation with the French as moderate and passive. Comparatively, these scholars pity him against Jean-Jacques Dessalines, whom they argue was militant and aggressive. Both men fought bravely for Haiti's Revolution in multifaceted ways and deserve to be characterized as radical figures for their sacrifices. At a time when Haitians felt hope with Aristide's rhetoric, they saw the United States stepping in again to moderate and deny its own culpability.

Aristide's change of outlook highlights Péralte's radicalism. His recollection of the *cacos* leader in all of these years shows Péralte's power. He like Vincent, Obin, the FCPLN, and Haitian lay historians reimprinted Péralte into national political discourse. He channeled the Haitian martyr as a reprimand to foreigners and an invitation to Haitians for patriotic kinship. His brave use of Péralte worked seven decades after the *caco*'s death. For Haitians who had never met Péralte, his fight and legacy were significant from 1986 to 1994.

10

Péralte Will Never Die; He Remains Alive in Popular Memory (Péralte p'ap janm mouri; li rete vivan nan memwa popilè)

● ●

Thanks to Aristide, by the end of the twentieth century, calling on the memory of Péralte became a sign of anti-imperial politics. That political position was no less radical or worrying to the United States in 1994 than it had been in 1915, perhaps because by then, it also meant a focus on the poor and the economic inequality that resulted in part from imperial domination. Like that of other Haitian leaders, Aristide's position did not remain moderated by U.S. interests. In 2000, he began to again assert his radical ideas. Reminiscent of the 1915 invasion, the forces of MINUSTAH (United Nations Stabilization Mission in Haiti) arrived in 2004, at the moment of the celebration of the 200th anniversary of Dessalines's declaration of independence. Understandably, Haitians turned again to Péralte as inspiration for their protest.

The Apotheosis of Péralte in Haiti in the Twenty-First Century

In Haiti, President Jean-Bertrand Aristide resumed his radicalism during his last term in office from 2000 to 2004. A year before Haiti's bicentennial, Aristide sent the French government a bill in the amount of $21,685,135,571.48.[1] The president demanded France's repayment of the reparations (with interest) that his ancestors had paid in 1825 and thereafter throughout Haiti's history. He boldly indicted France for Haiti's underdevelopment. The bill called attention to the reparations debate: whether and how former colonizers should repay their former colonies for the free labor they exacted and benefited from for centuries. President Aristide also embarked on a public history campaign. Haitians remembered L'Ouverture, Dessalines, and other Haitian patriots in preparation for 2004 bicentennial celebrations.

Haiti's bicentennial was a festive occasion for Haitians at home and abroad. Citizens celebrated the nation's glorious formation and commemorated its sheroes and heroes. Coinciding with this elation were serious reflections on the country's shortcomings in the 200 years since independence. Newspaper and journal articles and conferences proliferated on the topic of Haiti's inspiring revolutionary history and its bitter outcomes. Interlaced in these discussions were topics like colonialism, slavery, imperialism, authoritarianism, and the nation's experiences with coups d'état. The beginning of 2004 became a collective moment for some Haitians to celebrate their past and chart for a better, more prosperous future.

President Aristide's ouster or departure in 2004 put a damper on these national and international festivities. The subsequent arrival of U.N. troops in Haiti was unsettling. Haitians immediately likened the 2004 invasion of Haiti by MINUSTAH to the 1915 U.S. invasion. The irony of commemorating 200 years of independence with President Aristide's exile and the new supervision of the nation by MINUSTAH again called up sentiments of Charlemagne Péralte and sovereignty.

From the varied media coverage, Haitians likened their new reality to their ancestors' experiences during the U.S. invasion, with a few key differences. In the early twentieth century, the foreign officers were White males. Now in 2004 Haitians shared racial and cultural backgrounds with MINUSTAH soldiers recruited from Brazil, Argentina, and countries in Africa and the Caribbean. In 1915 the Haitian government of Vilbrun Guillaume Sam had collapsed in bloody turmoil. In 2004 Haitians questioned whether the United States had orchestrated President Aristide's exile. Based on their public objections, many Haitians accepted that explanation for Aristide's departure.

Both in Haiti and in the diaspora, a Péralte fervor emerged.[2] In my research of Haiti and its Haitian diaspora in 2004 and through my fieldwork in 2006–2008, I saw that Haitians memorialized Péralte everywhere. Despite his being dead for eighty-five years, they revived the *caco* in celebration and as a form of protest. In New York in 2004, a barbershop owner in Brooklyn renamed his parlor the Charlemagne Péralte Barber Shop. Asked why he had renamed his shop, his answer echoed that of the man who declared the bust to be one of the *cacos* leader: "It is Charlemagne Péralte." The declaration of his ongoing presence and importance was a message of hope at a time of another tragic attack on Haitian sovereignty. The barbershop owner's clear, succinct statement was commonsense

FIG. 11 Unknown artist, tug of war mural, Cité Soleil, Haiti, ca. 2006–2008

politics. There is a common slang that millennial Haitians use: *epi dats ett* (and, that is it). When I pressed him further about this choice of the *caco* figure's name and his twenty-first-century renaming, he repeated his response, "C'est Charlemagne Péralte." I added, "epi dats ett," or "'nuff said" (that is sufficient). In Haiti, Péralte's twentieth-century fight was relevant to Haitians' twenty-first-century present. Haitians' demonstrations were sometimes intellectual and artistic odes to the *caco*.

My conversation with the barbershop owner made me reflect on the portrait that I sat next to in 2006. Its bright colors were inspiring. Péralte's position next to Dessalines acknowledged that he was carrying his legacy into the future. The Haitian who painted the mural was sending the same message to Péralte—your fight for recognition and equality, embedded in the demand for national sovereignty, is not over. It will continue.

In another political mural, the muralist presented the nation's flag caught in a tug of war (Figure 11). A Black Haitian citizen pulls on one side of the flag, while a MINUSTAH soldier depicted as a White male, tugs at the other corner. The muralist's message was direct and clear, and it communicated with fellow citizens in a multilingual fashion. The image symbolically portrayed the flag as Haiti caught between citizens' liberation versus foreign invasion. Through these murals, Haitians roused questions about MINUSTAH's role in Haiti. They were powerful displays of Haitians fighting back.

In another artistic presentation in 2004, the musical artist Wyclef Jean released an album, *Welcome to Haiti Creole 101*, to commemorate the bicentennial and discuss national sovereignty. The LP featured the late agronomist and Radio Soleil's broadcast journalist Jean Dominique on the introductory track. Wyclef Jean intentionally used Dominque's recollection of the 1915 invasion of Haiti. Jean Dominique recalled his own father's protest against the U.S. flag:

> I was 4 years old when the marines left Haiti, the US marines left Haiti. I was a kid. And every time a battling marine passed in front of the house, my father took my hand and said, "Don't look at them, don't look at them!" And every May 18th, which is the Haitian Flag Day, defiantly, he put the Haitian flag in front of the house. And I said, "Father, what is that? What does that mean for you?" He said, "That means that you are Haitian, that means my great grandfather fought at Vertières, never forget that. You are Haitian. You are from this land. You are not French, not British, you are not American, you are Haitian!"[3]

Jean Dominique's passionate recollection of the invasion reinforces the analysis embedded in *Haiti Fights Back* about the use of memory, nationalism, and resistance in Haiti's long political history with the United States. The reflections on the significance of the flag were symbolic—both then and now. Dominique recalled his father's *nasyonalis* lessons. His father argued that their ancestors fought for freedom, and the ensuing generations—the beneficiaries of the Haitian Revolution—should continue this resistance. Just like Péralte and the *cacos*, Wyclef Jean used this historical nationalism to condemn MINUSTAH's presence in Haiti in 2004. The album's cover featured Jean in revolutionary military attire from the colonial days. The album sold in record numbers, making this public history available to listeners worldwide.

Interlacing history and nationalism, the Haitian commentators frequently recalled Péralte's actions in the early twentieth century to demonstrate against the state of affairs in the twenty-first. One individual described the *caco* leader as "President Péralte, a very highly respectable and respected person [who] is part of the soul of Haiti."[4] He characterized the *caco* as one of the founding fathers of the nation, a person who put a defining imprint on modern Haiti, and who was a "hope bearer for a new society." His point about a new society highlights Haitians' enduring quest for 1804's implementation of equality, liberty, and humanity for all citizens. Equating the presence of MINUSTAH with a military invasion, this Haitian expressed that the "soul of Péralte will be living... as an emblem of freedom and national resistance."[5] For the interviewee, his 2004 reality harkened back to his ancestors' fate under the U.S. invasion. He called for a *cacos* resurrection in this current neoimperialist fight. On walls in the nation's capital, Haitians urged the foreign soldiers' removal with slogans like "À bas MINUSTAH!" and invoked Péralte by simply writing his name.

Haitians remembered Péralte as an unblemished hero—his stance against U.S. imperialism was still of such relevance to their lives that his story naturally

FIG. 12 Unknown artist, Charlemagne Péralte Boys' School, Hinche, Haiti, 2008

lived on. Of course, Péralte was at one time human, like the rest of us, but his legacy grew to be almost godlike. From the Christ-like imagery of the 1930s to the oral histories of the twenty-first century, Péralte's second life was perhaps more powerful than his first. Many shared his granddaughter's sentiments that: "If we find liberty now, if Haitians find liberty, it is because of Charlemagne Péralte."[6] Haitians would not let him die. They credit his legacy with different political hopes throughout the twentieth century into the twenty-first. They have resurrected the *caco* time and again. In these continual reimaginings of Péralte at home and abroad, Haitians expressed their desire for sovereignty for all their patriotic kin.

As the nation remains supervised by foreign soldiers in 2019, fifteen years since its bicentennial, the invocation of the *cacos* leader is still useful. Haitians recall their patriotic kin in interviews, stories, newspapers, and murals, and they continue to use his coins and the public spaces in Hinche devoted to Péralte (Figure 12). In this enduring quest for sovereignty, Péralte's twentieth-century liberation fight remains significant for Haitians in the twenty-first century.

Epigraph

Charlemagne Péralte's movement and the collective remembrance of him in Haiti and the diaspora is a story about the power to resist *and* to be named.

Caribbean citizens have fought unrelentingly against intersecting oppressive institutions like slavery, colonialism, imperialism, and neoimperialism. Their ongoing survival is a form of protest against these violent systems. The freedom acts of Cécile Fatiman (Saint-Domingue), Mr. Tacky (Jamaica), and Queen Nanny's Maroons (Jamaica) during colonial times and the anti-imperialist liberation struggles of Lolita Lebrón (Puerto Rico), the *gavilleros* (Dominican Republic), and the *cacos* need fuller scholarly exploration and multilingual documentation. These underexplored and lesser-known Caribbean and African diasporan peoples, groups, and movements have contributed to a modern world history in their articulations of freedom, abolition, equality, and national sovereignty, all tenets of an evolving modernity.

In researching Péralte and the *cacos'* story, what became clear is the need to use interdisciplinary Africana and Caribbean methodologies. Documenting their roles in history became a study of the role of power in how individuals study the past. The military archives often framed many of the individuals named in this book as "bandits" in the pejorative sense. It takes a keen observer and thorough researcher, familiar with the fallacy of inherently racist narratives, to reveal a more accurate history of the consistent presence of resistance in Haitian history. Including my research subjects' traditional and alternative types of historical mapping—oral histories, art, music, silence, and murals—helps expand the archival borders used in historical narratives. As Dr. Lila Abu-Lughod argues, "Where there is resistance, there is power."[7] We can find power from the *cacos* manifestos, their politics of escape and using their feet (meaning using their bodies to protest in fight and flight), and the ruses and testimonies of *Ayisienne* during the invasion period, to the twenty-first-century murals that criticize the new MINUSTAH occupation of Haiti. Uncovering and recovering these individuals and also using their archival tools help tell the full story of Haitian Caribbean people. Many Caribbean people already know about these sheroes and heroes. It is time for official histories to tell the accurate story of brutal dehumanization and the consistent brave human refusal to accept it.

The stories of the Caribbean individuals appearing here, Péralte's family, and the *cacos* specifically, greatly matter. In another violent era where people of color continue to be overpoliced, undereducated, underresourced, targeted with extensive prison terms, and assassinated by state police forces, we need narratives of Black resistance. People of color, since their encounter with the European, whether on the African shores or the port locations in the indigenous Americas, have fought against oppression. Their *mawonage*, collective suicide, language creation (Kreyòl and Patwa), sustaining of spiritual pluralities (Santería, Vodou(n), Lucúmi, and Rastafari), battles, revolts, infanticide, homicide, legal cases, ongoing civil rights battles, and their sheer survival are all testaments to their resilience. Every single one of these acts is about Fighting Back. The doublespeak that is characteristic of all U.S. accounts of its invasion of Haiti continues to this day—and it prevents us from accurately seeing the true victim of a brutal system of dehumanization. From the scars on Dessalines's back to the raping of women to the murder of Péralte, time and again the suffering of Black people is ignored. The story of Western "civilization" is possible only if the fundamental dehumanization of an entire group of people does not figure into the history. Moreover, no appropriate attention has been paid to the ongoing intergenerational trauma of those who experienced enslavement, poverty, and other acts of dehumanization. Furthermore, the world's isms have only deepened and taken on new forms in Jim and Jane Crow, apartheid, genocide, prisons, and economic disparities. When Péralte and the *cacos* elevated their 1791–1804 ancestors, they reminded us that their anti-imperialist struggle was linked to the antislavery revolution. The U.S. empire was simply a continuation of unjust systems with new "masters and mistresses." By all accounts, a person has the right to self-defense. The *cacos* watched the invasion of their native Haiti and fought back. For them, this intrusion was illegal and a declaration of war. Péralte, his brothers, Bobo, Batraville, and many *Ayisienne* sacrificed their lives for homeland because national sovereignty was their protection against a vast system of injustice. The ongoing commemorations of Péralte today specifically underscore that the fight, whether it be against domestic terror or imperialism. Until the U.S. empire is completely dismantled, *Viv la Revolusyon!*

Acknowledgments

Researching and writing a book is a rite of passage. I am thrilled, relieved, and grateful to be at this stage of the journey. Praises to my Bondyé/God who keeps me alive and joyous. Mèsi anpil (thanks very much) to my family for always representing Ayiti and instilling pride in our heritage. My gran Charmante would entice me with the briefest stories about Haiti as she cooked her signature *diri pat* (mushy rice). As she delivered her tales in episodic form, she literally had me hungry for more. Thank you for being our family's foundation and for your deep love. When my *tante* Marie would moisturize my hair, she would rub the *lwil maskriti* (castor oil) on my arms as well, sharing the cultural idiosyncrasies as to why and so much more. Thank you for always honoring my father Yves Alexis and our roots. I hope the three of you are dancing in the afterlife. My maman Marie Agathe taught me *konpa* and the *Chants d'Esperance* hymns as she navigated her life. You embody resilience mum. Mèsi for all that you have poured into me and for always imparting your signature lesson with hands raised to the sky that "all will be well." My sys Guerda introduced me to black women's literature with classics from Mildred Taylor, Alice Walker, and Toni Morrison during elementary school (can someone say indoctrination?). Mèsi for encouraging my love of books, the cute do's, my summer retreats while you were in graduate school, advice about every avenue of life, for being present, and knowing me. Thanks to my bro Kevin Jean for our crazy laugh, our ceaseless talks and loud debates about everything and nothing, for carrying *akasan*/AK100 (cornmeal drink) and all types of patties on planes when I craved this Caribbean deliciousness. I appreciate your constant support and protective ways lil bro. Mèsi to my *cousine* Guerline Sanon Fravien for loving the way you do and for your nourishing ways. I appreciate your encouragement, witty Haitian sarcasm, prayers, and tasty food. I adore you fave nieces Tatyana Marie Graesser and Alexis Bryana Graesser! Thanks for the giggles, your exuberant energies, woke views of our world and contributions to it, as well as your love. Shout-out to my Nicolas and Alexis kin—uncles (Albert Nicolas et al.), aunts (Ma-Tante Gislaine et al.), cousins, fave nephew (Calvin Alexis), and step-pops Excellent Jean. Mèsi for the protests on the Brooklyn Bridge, finally admitting me to dominoes games, having to watch *fútbol*, teaching me Kreyòl, playing Tabou Combo's song "Lakay" on repeat through the decades, and our passionate talks about returning to homeland.

A heartfelt thank you to my graduate school advisors and mentors: Drs. Jane Rausch, Lowell Gudmundson, John Higginson, Joye Bowman, Françoise Hamlin, Bernie Jones, and Carlene Edie. Each of you model the type of scholar I aspire to be with your intelligence and passion. Thank you for your training, affirmations, advice, and support since then to the present! A special thank you to my graduate committee (Rausch, Gudmundson, Higginson, and Edie) for your insightful comments and questions, which helped shape the book. My sincere gratitude to the scholars in the History Department at the University of Massachusetts-Amherst and the History and Africana Studies Departments at Cornell University. Thank you to Margaret Washington and Ayele Bekerie for introducing me to African and African American women's history and the examples you set.

I greatly benefited from a fellowship in the Advanced Institute for Critical Caribbean Studies and Africana Studies Department at Rutgers. Thank you, Michelle Stephens, Gayle Tate, Yolanda Martínez-San Miguel, Mia Bay, Aldo Lauria-Santiago, and Patricia Lespinasse for your insights on the book and the profession.

A special thank you to Oberlin College. It has been a pleasure teaching bright, humble, creative, and thoughtful students. Warm thanks to my colleagues in the Africana Studies, Comparative American Studies, and History Departments, the Mary Church Terrell library, as well as the Arts and Sciences Dean's and Grants offices. Thank you, Renee Romano, for reading this entire manuscript during its early stages, providing insightful feedback, and being a warm presence. Pam Brooks and Darko Opoku: thanks for your helpful comments during revisions.

My deep appreciation to the community of people who cared about my well-being, provided cheer and encouragement, responded to my communication about Haiti, shared tips about surviving and thriving in this academy, and/or those who offered feedback on my scholarship. I am immeasurably grateful to the talented trio who bring their smarts, gut-busting laughs, levity, zoom Taboo games, and zoom work sessions. I appreciate your unconditional personal *and* professional support: Manoucheka Celeste, Casta Calixte Guillame, and Grace Sanders Johnson. Mèsi Harry Lorthe for your refreshing presence and optimism about all of life's matters. Gina A. Ulysse: Your scholarly and artistic expertise are profound. Mèsi anpil for your wise counsel, generosity, and warm, genuine mentorship. Mèsi anpil Chantalle F. Verna for your warmth, advice, and astute feedback on a chapter. Mèsi anpil anpil François Pierre-Louis for being the same scholar-activist whom I met as a graduate student throughout my tenure. I appreciate your check-ins, affirmations of this project, and last-minute reviews of my works in progress; you are an intellectual gem! Mèsi anpil, anpil Leslie G. Desmangles, Alex Dupuy, and Matthew Smith for your time as well as your valuable reviews and insights on an article and parts of this work! Big and warm thanks to Carolle Charles, Nadève Ménard, Ileana M. Rodríguez-Silva, Robert Fatton, Millery Polyné, Emmanuel Vedrine, Emmanuel Gay, Kabria Baumgartner, Patrick Bellegarde-Smith, Claudine Michel, Frantz Voltaire, Harry Franqui-Rivera, Rejoice Acolatse, Henryatta Ballah, Maria Paz Esguerra, Bonnie Cheng, Zeinab Abul-Magd, Pablo Mitchell, Gina Pérez, Wendy Kozol, Ann Sherif, Leonard Smith, Trecia Pottinger, Laurie McMillian, Myrna García, Julie C. Keller, Shelley Lee, Carolyn Fick, Evangeline Heiliger, Alexia Hudson-Ward, Rashida K. Braggs, Jennifer Vargas, Maggie Robinson, Pam Snyder, as well as Nadine Mattis and Jacquie Mattis and their Easton's Nook writing retreat space. Elizabeth Hamilton: thank you for rescuing my tenure document from my dramatic writing style. I appreciate your time and support. Dean David Kamitsuka, thank you for being an interlocutor. Mèsi to the founders of the Haitian Studies Association and the Journal of Haitian Studies for creating these spaces.

Researching in Haiti was invaluable to how I shaped this book. My sincere gratitude to everyone in Haiti who contributed to this project, including those who opened up their homes to me, the oral history participants, and the muralists and their art. Mèsi anpil anpil to Guillet Adolphe for your guidance, translations, and humor. Mèsi anpil to Charlemagne Péralte's family for welcoming me and sharing your knowledge about your *zansèt* (ancestors). Mèsi anpil to the staff at the Bibliothèque Nationale d'Haïti, Saint-Louis Gonzague, and the Musée du Panthéon National Haïtien for your great help!

Thank you to the staff at different repositories in the United States especially at the National Archives in Washington, DC, National Archives in College Park, the various New York Public Libraries, and the University of Miami's Cuban Heritage Collection. As corona hit during these edits and precluded travel to the archives, I appreciate your answers to my questions about archive groups.

Securing grants for this project has its own story. I am extremely grateful for the funding that made parts of my research possible. The United States Marine Corps Heritage Foundation's General Lemuel C. Shepherd Jr. Memorial Award provided resources for my graduate research. A big thank you to the staff at the General Alfred M. Gray Marine Corps Research Center and Marine Corps History Center for your generous assistance! I amassed useful primary sources due to a summer library travel research grant from the University of Florida's Center for Latin American Studies. Thank you to the staff at the UF Latin American Collection for your help. I am deeply appreciative of Oberlin College's Grant-in-Aid and H. H. Powers Travel Grants that facilitated key research in Haiti.

I have had my eyes on Rutgers University Press since graduate school because of its notable scholarship on Haiti. Kimberly Guinta: mèsi anpil for believing in *Haiti Fights Back* from the beginning. I am immensely grateful for your steadfast support and your calmness. A warm thank you to the Critical Caribbean Series editors: Yolanda Martínez-San Miguel, Kathleen López, and Carter Mathes for your helpful reviews. Special thanks to Jasper Chang and the staff at Rutgers University Press for your assistance. Thank you to the reviewers for your careful reviews, helpful suggestions, and critiques, which strengthened the text. Mèsi anpil Laura Helper-Ferris and Lesley Curtis for your editorial talents and support! Speaking to the both of you helped me own this story. Shout out to Kervin Andre for the book's cover!

Thank you to a network who have also inspired and encouraged me throughout my decades in meaningful ways: Margaret (Peg) and Gray Holbrook for being *famille*; Yvens (Chico) Fleurisme for your humor and support; Drs. Tanyka Sam, Shamieka Dixon, and Traci Parker for the laughter and sisterly check-ins; Sunera Schaller for being you; Pamela Ungar and Varzi Jean-Baptiste for being you, and for the food, braid styles, and dance locations; Drs. Bowman, Hamlin, and Higginson for being refreshing examples of humanity; Malis Loeung and family for feeding me in literal and figurative ways; and Isabella Moreno and Dr. RaShelle Peck for providing a warm space in deer-country and showing up. I am literally smiling at the irony that both of you sent encouraging texts as I finalize these copy edits this morning—thank you!

To my late nephew Robbie Ungar: I love you. May you rest in sweet peace, Robster. The whole crew and I miss you beyond measure.

I also reflect on those of us on this academic grind who are doing it in faraway, rural places with no loved ones around; for those teaching as adjuncts and visiting faculty; for single parents; for the many systahs whom I know who are managing elder care at an early age; and for each of you managing and winning against chronic physical and mental illnesses. To this group I say: Take a bow and carry onward!

Last but not least, onè ak respè (honor and respect) to my *zansèt* who paved the way and who along with my Bondyé walk besides, in front, and behind me daily: mèsi anpil!

Notes

Introduction

1 Robert Maguire and Scott Freeman, eds., *Who Owns Haiti? People, Power, and Sovereignty* (Gainesville: University Press of Florida, 2017); Maude LeBlanc, "Haiti Is No Stranger to War Crimes of the Former Colonial Powers which Now Make up NATO," *Haiti Progrès*, November 2, 2005.

2 "Security Council Establishes UN Stabilization Mission in Haiti for Initial Six-Month Period," United Nations press release, April 30, 2004, https://www.un.org/press/en/2004/sc8083.doc.htm.

3 As cited in Georges Michel, *Charlemagne Péralte and the First American Occupation of Haiti: UN Centenaire, 1885–1985* (Dubuque, IA: Kendall Hunt, 1995), 67–68. He cites *Le Nouvelliste* August 11, 1915.

4 Lexico, https://www.lexico.com/en/definition/nationalist.

5 In the 1801 constitution issued by Toussaint L'Ouverture, Haiti was still the colony of Saint-Domingue and the revolution's three goals had not yet been realized. Thus, the 1805 constitution is considered the first constitution of independent Haiti.

6 The entire text was geared toward multiple audiences (the French, natives of Haiti, and mixed-race Creoles).

7 Laurent Dubois and John D. Garrigus, *Slave Revolution in the Caribbean, 1789–1804: A Brief History with Documents* (New York: Bedford / St. Martins, 2016), 188–189.

8 Dubois and Garrigus, *Slave Revolution in the Caribbean*, 191.

9 Dubois and Garrigus, *Slave Revolution in the Caribbean*, 192.

10 Dubois and Garrigus, *Slave Revolution in the Caribbean*, 192.

11 Dubois and Garrigus, *Slave Revolution in the Caribbean*, 192.

12 Untitled four-page report on activities between March 14, 1919, and the summer of 1920, p. 1, Record Group 127, Records of the United States Marines Corps, National Archives, Washington, DC (USMC DC); Roger Gaillard, *Charlemagne Péralte: Le Caco* (Port-au-Prince: Roger Gaillard, 1982), 96. During his movement, Emiliano Zapata also critiqued President Wilson's intentions with Mexico, as cited in John Womack Jr., *Zapata and the Mexican Revolution* (New York: Vintage, 1968), 212.

13 John Garrigus, trans., *Le Code Noir ou recueil des reglements rendus jusqu'à present* (Paris: Prault, 1767; reprinted by Société d'Histoire de la Guadeloupe, 1980).

14 In both the antebellum and postbellum United States, there are a plethora of examples of this hypocrisy: the "Trail of Tears," the Jim and Jane Crow era, and various civil rights struggles for U.S. citizens of color in the twentieth century.

15 Michel-Rolph Trouillot, *Silencing the Past: Power and the Production of History*, 20th edition (Boston, MA: Beacon, 2015).

16 Trouillot, *Silencing the Past*; Brenda Gayle Plummer, *Haiti and the Great Powers, 1902–1915* (Baton Rouge: Louisiana State University Press, 1988); Joan (Colin) Dayan, *Haiti, History and the Gods* (Berkeley: University of California Press, 1995); David P. Geggus, ed., *The Impact of the Haitian Revolution on the Atlantic World* (Columbia: University of South Carolina Press, 2001); Sibylle Fischer, *Modernity Disavowed: Haiti and the Cultures of Slavery in the Age of Revolution* (Durham, NC: Duke University Press, 2004), Millery Polyné, *The Idea of Haiti: Rethinking Crisis and Development* (Minneapolis: University of Minnesota Press, 2013); and Laurent Dubois, *Avengers of the New World: The Story of the Haitian Revolution* (Cambridge, MA: Harvard University Press, 2004).

17 Spencer St. John, *Hayti, or the Black Republic* (New York: Scribner and Welford, 1889); J. G. Hopkirk, *An Account of the Insurrection in St. Domingo, begun in August 1791 taken from authentic sources* (Edinburgh: William Blackwood, 1833), http://digitalcollections.nypl.org/items/510d47e3-feec-a3d9-e040-e00a18064a99. For additional references on nineteenth-century scholarship about this topic, see Plummer, *Haiti and the Great Powers*.

18 In a conversation with the author on November 1, 2019, Marie A. Jean translated doublespeak as *Voye wòch, kache men*. A Kreyòl linguist offered similar translations: Michel Anne-Frederic DeGraff, email message to author, December 10, 2019.

19 Gina A. Ulysse, *Why Haiti Needs New Narratives: A Post-Quake Chronicle* (Middleton, CT: Wesleyan University Press, 2015).

20 Ulysse, *Why Haiti Needs New Narratives*.

21 Suzy Castor, *La ocupación Norte Americana de Haití sus consecuencias, 1915–1934* (Mexico City: Siglo Veintiuno Editores, 1971) and *L'occupation américaine d'Haïti* (Port-au-Prince: Société Haïtienne d'Histoire, 1988); Kethly Millet, *Les paysans haïtiens et l'occupation américaine d'Haïti, 1915–1930* (LaSalle, QC: Collectif Paroles, 1978); Plummer, *Haiti and the Great Powers*; Brenda Gayle Plummer, *Rising Wind: Black Americans and U.S. Foreign Affairs, 1935–1960* (Durham: University of North Carolina Press, 1996), and *Haiti and the United States: The Psychological Moment* (Athens: University of Georgia Press, 2003); Hans Schmidt, *The United States Occupation of Haiti, 1915–1934* (New Brunswick, NJ: Rutgers University Press, 1971); Mary A. Renda, *Taking Haiti: Military Occupation and the Culture of U.S. Imperialism 1915–1940* (Chapel Hill: University of North Carolina, 2001); Roger Gaillard, *Premier écrasement du cacoïsme* (Port-au-Prince: Roger Gaillard, 1981), and *Charlemagne Péralte*; and Patrick Bellegarde-Smith, *Haiti: The Breached Citadel*, rev. ed. (Toronto, ON: Canadian Scholars Press, 2004).

22 Chantalle F. Verna, *Haiti and the Uses of America: Post-U.S. Occupation Promises* (New Brunswick, NJ: Rutgers University Press, 2017); Millery Polyné, *From Douglass to Duvalier: U.S. African Americans, Haiti, and Pan Americanism, 1870–1964* (Gainesville: University Press of Florida, 2010); and Matthew J. Smith, *Red and Black in Haiti: Radicalism, Conflict, and Political Change, 1934–1957* (Chapel Hill: University of North Carolina Press, 2009).

23 Jacques Stephen Alexis, *In the Flicker of an Eyelid*, trans. Carrol F. Coates and Edwidge Danticat (Charlottesville: University of Virginia Press, 2002).

24 Edwidge Danticat, *Breath, Eyes, and Memory* (New York: Vintage, 1994), 102, 25.

25 Julia Alvarez, *In the Time of Butterflies* (New York: Plume, 1995), also recalls the story of Dominican guerrilla fighters, the *gavilleros*, who protested against the U.S. invasion.

26 Kenneth M. Bilby, *True-Born Maroons* (Gainesville: University Press of Florida, 2005), 24.

27 Chimamanda Ngozi Adichie, "The Danger of a Single Story," TEDGlobal, 2009, 18:49, https://www.ted.com/talks/chimamanda_ngozi_adichie_the_danger_of _a_single_story/transcript?language=en.

28 Ulysse, *Why Haiti Needs New Narratives.*

29 On a subsequent field trip to examine the centennial commemoration of the U.S. invasion in 2015, more women participated in this conversation. For my interviews from 2006 to 2008, I created a set of ten to twelve open-ended questions. I asked participants to choose the language of our interaction, Haitian Kreyòl or English. The interviews ranged from thirty to forty-five minutes. My open-question format encouraged a range of responses. My primary questions centered on the significance of Péralte to the nation's history and to the Haitian state in 2006 and 2008. All the interviewees consented to participating in the project. Everyone declined to sign a waiver form. While many of the respondents were surprised at my request to audiotape our interactions, seven consented to this option. The participants responded similarly when I invited them to ask any questions of me. Most inquired about the project's purpose, and they asked if I would return to Haiti to teach on this subject. These inquiries were enlightening. Their questions explained why they declined to sign a written consent. They knew their input was valuable to my research. Their requests were an invitation for reciprocity.

30 Thank you to Yolanda Martínez-San Miguel for providing me with this language.

31 In fact, Sandino's fight against the U.S. military from 1927–1934, his assassination, and his depiction in U.S. military records as a bandit bear many similarities to Péralte. Headquarters, Eastern Area, Nicaragua, Marine Barracks, Puerto Cabezas, Nicaragua, July 24, August 14, 1928 and October 24, 1932; Carlos Amador Fonseca, *Long Live Sandino* (Managua, Free Nicaragua: Department of Propaganda and Political Education of the FSLN, 1984). In Nicaragua, the U.S. Marines and their trained *Guardia Nacional* fixated on the anti-U.S. sentiments brewing amongst the population, the actions of Augusto Sandino and guerrilla bands that waged wars against the U.S. presence in the country.

32 Castor, *L'occupation américaine d'Haïti*, 157.

33 Fischer, *Modernity Disavowed*; Dayan, *Haiti, History and the Gods*; and Toni Pressley-Sanon, *Istwa across the Water: Haitian History, Memory, and the Cultural Imagination* (Gainesville: University Press of Florida, 2017).

34 As quoted in Bilby, *True-Born Maroons*, 56.

35 *Kote Famn Yo?* means "Where are the women?"

36 Renda, *Taking Haiti*, 165–166.

37 Marisa J. Fuentes, *Dispossessed Lives: Enslaved Women, Violence, and the Archive* (Philadelphia: University of Pennsylvania Press, 2016), 5–9, 146–148.

38 Nadève Ménard, "The Occupied Novel: The Representation of Foreigners in Haitian Novels Written during the United States Occupation, 1915–1934," PhD diss., University of Pennsylvania, 2002, and "Foreign Impulses in Annie Desroy's *Le Joug*," in *Haiti and the Americas*, ed. Carla Calargé, Raphael Dalleo, Luis Duno-Gottberg, and Clevis Headley (Jackson: University Press of Mississippi, 2013), 161–174.

39 Haitian feminist Paulette Poujol Oriol noted how Desroy finished her text between 1930 and 1931, but published the work when critique against the "Yankiez" was

permitted; Poujol Oriol, "La femme haïtienne dans la littérature: Problèmes de l'écrivain," *Journal of Haitian Studies* 3/4 (1997–1998), 80–86.

40 Madeleine Sylvain-Bouchereau, *Haïti et ses femmes: Une étude d'évolution culturelle* (Port-au-Prince: Fardin, 1957); my translation, 12.

41 Myriam J. A. Chancy, *Framing Silence: Revolutionary Novels by Haitian Women* (New Brunswick, NJ: Rutgers University Press, 1997), 6, 23, 167.

42 Chancy, *Framing Silence,* 20.

43 Sylvain-Bouchereau, *Haïti et ses femmes*; Carolyn E. Fick, *The Making of Haiti: The Saint Domingue Revolution from below* (Knoxville: University of Tennessee Press, 1990), 170–176.

44 Évelyne Trouillot, *The Infamous Rosalie*, trans. Marjorie Attignol Salvodon (Lincoln: University of Nebraska Press, 2013).

45 The state granted *Ayisienne* the right to vote in municipal elections in 1950 and national elections in 1957.

46 Bellegarde-Smith, *Haiti,* 41.

47 Patrick Bellegarde-Smith documents Haitian women's contributions in *Haiti*, 36–45.

48 Grace Louise Sanders, *"La Voix des Femmes*: Haitian Women's Rights, National Politics and Black Activism in Port-au-Prince and Montreal, 1934–1986," PhD diss., University of Michigan, 2013.

49 Gilbert M. Joseph, Catherine C. LeGrand, and Ricardo D. Salvatore, eds., *Close Encounters of Empire: Writing the Cultural History of U.S.–Latin American Relations* (Durham, NC: Duke University Press, 1998).

Chapter 1   Liberty, Equality, and Fraternity/Humanity

1 "Draft of a letter in Regard to Relations between the United States and the Republic of Haiti from 1914 to Ratification to be signed by Mr. Robert Lansing," Papers of John H. Russell Jr., Manuscript Box 2 Haiti, Folder 1, Background on Occupation of Haiti, undated typescript, Marine Corps Archives and Special Collections, Gray Research Center, Quantico, VA (hereafter Russell Papers).

2 Julia Gaffield, "I Have Avenged America," Haiti and the Atlantic World, August 2, 2013, https://haitidoi.com/2013/08/02/i-have-avenged-america/.

3 Jean McCarroll, ed., *The Negro in the Congressional Record: Eighteenth and Nineteenth Congress, 1824–1827* (New York: Bergman, 1971), 66.

4 Plummer, *Haiti and the Great Powers*, 42. The year of the United States' belated acknowledgment ranges from 1862, 1863, and 1865. The larger point is that it took decades to recognize one of their immediate neighbors.

5 Frederick Douglass, "Lecture on Haiti," Folder 8 of 14, Manuscript / Mixed material, Library of Congress, https://www.loc.gov/item/mfd.27013/.

6 Laurent Dubois, *Haiti: The Aftershocks of History* (New York: Metropolitan, 2012), 177.

7 Douglass, "Lecture on Haiti," Folder 1 of 14, Manuscript / Mixed Material, Library of Congress, https://www.loc.gov/item/mfd.27006/?sp=5.

8 Fischer, *Modernity Disavowed*, 3.

9 "Intervention in Hayti Imminent, Washington Fears," *New York Herald*, July 23, 1914.

10 United States Senate, *Inquiry into Occupation and Administration of Haiti and Santo Domingo: Hearings before a Select Committee on Haiti and Santo Domingo* (Washington, DC: Government Printing Office, 1922), 1:63 (hereafter referred to as *Senate Hearings*, 1922); Department of State, Division of Latin American Affairs, Memorandum to Mr. [Robert] Lansing, Department of State, August 5, 1915, p. 6, Record Group 59 M610, Haiti: Internal Affairs, 1910–1929, General Records of the

Department of State, College Park, MD; R. B. Coffey, "A Brief History of the
Intervention in Haiti," *U.S. Naval Institute Proceedings* 48, no. 234 (August 1922),
1325–1344; John J. Rogers, "The Haitianization of the Garde d'Haiti," *The Leather-neck* 16, no. 10 (October 1933), 3–6.

11 Plummer, *Haiti and the Great Powers.*

12 Verna, *Haiti and the Uses of America*, 31; Dubois, *Haiti*, 102.

13 "German Activity in Hayti Cause of Apprehension," *New York Herald*, May 25,
1914; "Europeans Seek Control of Hayti," *New York Herald*, May 8, 1914.

14 For more information on the Banque Nationale d'Haïti's history and operations in
France and Haiti, see Plummer, *Haiti and the Great Powers*, 106–107, 141, 144.

15 Lester D. Langley, *The Banana Wars: United States Intervention in the Caribbean,
1898–1934* (Lexington: University of Kentucky Press, 1985), 118–119.

16 Schmidt, *United States Occupation of Haiti*, 48 and 51–53.

17 For details about the J. P. MacDonald affair and the national and international
concerns it raised about Haiti's regional and economic affairs, see Plummer, *Haiti
and the Great Powers*, and Millet, *Les paysans haïtiens*, 29–30.

18 Verna, *Haiti and the Uses of America*; Geggus, *Impact of the Haitian Revolution*;
Fischer, *Modernity Disavowed.*

19 Fick, *Making of Haiti*, 207; Laurent Dubois, *Haiti*, 31

20 Fick, *Making of Haiti*, 170–174.

21 Plummer, *Haiti and the Great Powers*, 10.

22 Dubois, *Haiti*, 79.

23 David Nicholls, *Haiti in the Caribbean Context: Ethnicity, Economy, and Revolt*
(Houndsmills, Basingstoke: Palgrave Macmillian, 1985), 88, also discusses the brief
period where André Rigaud ruled La Grande'Anse, a department in the south.

24 Trouillot, *Silencing the Past*, 38–39.

25 Plummer, *Haiti and the United States*, 52–59.

26 I note the presence of the southern peasant movement mobilized as L'Armée de
Soufrrant (the army of sufferers) in 1843–1844. Because of their 8-foot pike
weapons, individuals have referred to L'Armée as the *piquets*. While the movement
also promoted some citizens' calls for Haiti's interests above foreigners and for
ending the 1825 French indemnity agreement, the bulk of the *piquets*' demands
advocated for internal changes, including: upholding the 1843 constitution, access
to public education, and land reform. For a history of one of these actions, that of
the *piquets*, see Mimi Sheller, *Democracy after Slavery: Black Publics and Peasant
Radicalism in Haiti and Jamaica* (Gainesville: University Press of Florida, 2001),
and "The Army of Sufferers: Peasant Democracy in the Early Republic of Haiti,"
New West Indian Guide / Nieuwe West-Indische Gids 74, no. 1/2 (2000), 33–55; and
Nicholls, *Haiti in the Caribbean Context*. For works that examine the *piquets* during
the late nineteenth century, see Alyssa Sepinwall's *Haitian History: New Perspec-tives* (New York: Routledge, 2013); Alex Dupuy's *Haiti in the World Economy: Class,
Race, and Underdevelopment since 1700* (Boulder, CO: Westview, 1989); and
Matthew Smith's *Liberty, Fraternity, Exile: Haiti and Jamaica after Emancipation*
(Chapel Hill: University of North Carolina Press, 2014).

27 It should be noted that women appear in Haiti's 1805 constitution exclusively in a
gendered manner (as wives and mothers).

28 The irony of this fort, however, was the Haitian state's alleged use of forced laborers
from the population of recently freed slaves.

29 Bellegarde-Smith, *Haiti*. Ironically, during the U.S. invasion, the *cacos* and U.S.
military used the various forts.

30 Fischer, *Modernity Disavowed*, 253.

31 Plummer, *Haiti and the Great Powers*, 42 and 63.

32 Anténor Firmin, *The Equality of the Human Races: Positivist Anthropology*, trans. Asselin Charles (New York: Garland, 2000), 295.

33 Ludwell Montague, *Haiti and the United States, 1714–1938* (Durham, NC: Duke University Press, 1940), 32; Walter LaFeber, *The New Empire: An Interpretation of American Expansion* (Ithaca, NY: Cornell University Press, 1963), 127–130.

34 Dubois, *Haiti*, 166, 180.

35 Maroonage communities, also spelled *mawonage* in Haitian Kreyòl and *cimmarones* in Spanish, were groups of runaway enslaved Africans. They were freedom fighters in a struggle to flee from slavery.

36 Gaillard, *Charlemagne Péralte*, and Michel, *Charlemagne Péralte*.

37 Interview with community activist, by the author, August, 18, 2007, Hinche, Haiti.

38 Interview with community activist.

39 Michel, *Charlemagne Péralte*.

40 For information about these 1911–1914 insurrections and Haitian *caudillismo*, see the works of Brenda Gayle Plummer and Patrick-Bellegarde Smith.

41 Saül Péralte, letter to the president, *Le Nouvelliste*, September 1, 1915.

42 Michel, *Charlemagne Péralte*, 8. Michel also provides a full description of the role of commander of the arrondissement (administrative district).

43 Plummer, *Haiti and the Great Powers*, 206.

44 Interview with community activist.

45 Charlemagne Péralte to General Aspelly Joseph, March 22, 1919. Translation of a letter found on the body of General Celisma Pierre, Marine Corps Archives and Special Collections, Gray Research Center, Quantico, VA.

Chapter 2   U.S. Invasion

1 "All Haiti's Affairs Now in Our Hands," *New York Times*, August 10, 1915, 4.

2 Acting secretary of the navy to Rear Admiral Caperton, August 7, 1915. The message instructed Caperton to "Conciliate Haitians to fullest extent consistent with maintaining order and firm control of the situation, and issue following proclamation"; Marine Archives Haiti, Operations, Other Reports, Report on Haiti, 1915–1920, Archives Branch, Marine Corps History Division, Quantico, VA (hereafter Marine Archives Haiti), p. 16; *Le Matin*, August 9, 1915.

3 *Le Matin*, August 9, 1915.

4 *Le Nouvelliste*, September 4, 1915.

5 Foreign Relations of the United States, Robert Lansing Papers, 1914–1920, vol. 2, 711.38/24a, Library of Congress, Manuscript Division.

6 Langley, *Banana Wars: United States*, 125.

7 Foreign Relations of the United States, Robert Lansing Papers, 1914–1920, vol. 2, 1914–1920, 711.38/24a, Library of Congress, Manuscript Division.

8 Langley, *Banana Wars: United States*, 131.

9 *Army and Navy Journal*, September 4, 1915, 9.

10 "Pending Ratification by the American Senate. A PROTECTORATE AT ONCE All Custom Houses to be Taken and Constabulary Under American Officers Established," special to *New York Times*, August 28, 1915, 2.

11 Department of State, Division of Latin American Affairs, Memorandum to Mr. [Robert] Lansing Department of State, August 5, 1915, 1, Record Group 59

M610, Haiti: Internal Affairs, 1910–1929, General Records of the Department of State, College Park, MD (hereafter Record Group 59).

12 Langley, *Banana Wars: United States*, 132.

13 Leon D. Pamphile, *Contrary Destinies: A Century of America's Occupation, Deoccupation, and Reoccupation of Haiti* (Gainesville: University Press of Florida, 2015), 16, 25.

14 Schmidt, *United States Occupation of Haiti*, 72.

15 Roger Gaillard, *Les cent-jours de Rosalvo Bobo; ou, Une mise à mort politique* (Port-au-Prince: Presses Nationales, 1973).

16 Concitoyen, *Le Nouvelliste*, July 30, 1915; Concitoyen, *Le Matin*, July 30, 1915; This use of revolutionary language is discussed at length in Euclides da Cunha's *Rebellion in the Backlands (Os sertões)*, trans. Samuel Putnam (Chicago: University of Chicago Press, 1944).

17 Edmond Polynice served as the chairman of the Committee of Public Welfare. Castor, *L'occupation américaine d'Haïti*, 127–128.

18 *Le Nouvelliste*, August 10, 1915; and Marine Archives Haiti, Operations, Other Reports, Report on Haiti, 1915–1920, p. 17.

19 *Le Nouvelliste*, July 30, 1915.

20 Marine Archives Haiti, Operations, Operations Reports, July 28 to August 4, 1915, Report of Ops.

21 *Le Matin*, August 2, 1915.

22 *Le Matin*, August 2, 1915.

23 Report of Operations from July 28 to August 10, 1915, Record Group 45, National Archives at College Park, MD (NACP) (hereafter Record Group 45). Note that the record includes a compilation of telegrams, dispatches, and other correspondence between commander cruiser squadron, acting secretary of the navy, and secretary of the navy and Rear Admiral Caperton among others during these dates.

24 *Le Matin*, August 4–6, 1915, and *Le Nouvelliste*, November 18, 1915.

25 *Le Matin*, August 3, 1915. Routine reporting included the following as an example: "American troops killed two people who did not provoke them. Today, the troops stopped a wedding ceremony to search the men, women, and young ladies" (*Le Nouvelliste*, August 7, 1915).

26 Marine Archives Haiti, Operations, Other Reports, Report on Haiti, 1915–1920, p. 13.

27 *Le Nouvelliste*, August 7, 1915.

28 "The Troubles in Hayti," *Army and Navy Journal*, August 14, 1915, 1595.

29 *Le Nouvelliste*, August 11, 1915.

30 *Le Nouvelliste*, August 11, 1915.

31 Dubois, *Avengers of the New World*, 42. Dubois quotes Dessalines, stating: "We have paid these true cannibals back crime for crime, war for war, outrage for outrage, I have saved my country. I have avenged America," 301.

32 Dantès Bellegarde, "President Alexandre Petion," *Phylon* 2, no. 3 (1941): 205–213.

33 *Le Nouvelliste*, August 11, 1915, and Michel, *Charlemagne Péralte*, 67.

34 *Le Matin*, August 12–13, 1915.

35 "The Troubles in Hayti," *Army and Navy Journal*, August 14, 1915, 1595.

36 Marine Archives Haiti, Report on the History of the Garde d'Haiti, History, 1915–1920, The Formative Period, p. 8 (hereafter Marine Archives Haiti, Garde d'Haiti).

37 Foreign Relations of the United States, Robert Lansing Papers, 1914–1920, vol. 2, 838.00/1275d, Library of Congress, Manuscript Division.

38 Renda, *Taking Haiti*, 116.
39 Foreign Relations of the United States, Robert Lansing Papers, 1914–1920, vol. 2, 838.00/12751/2a, Library of Congress, Manuscript Division.
40 Benjamin R. Beede, ed., *The War of 1898 and U.S. Interventions, 1898–1934: An Encyclopedia* (New York: Routledge, 1994), 157–158.
41 Schmidt, *United States Occupation of Haiti*, presents a Waller who publicly aired his racist views toward Haitians whom he labeled "niggers" and "coons," 79.
42 Office of the Provost Marshal, Alexander S. Williams, Captain, U.S. Marine Corps, Provost Marshal, Port-au-Prince, Haiti, September 3, 1915, Russell Papers, Manuscript Box 2 Haiti, Folder 2.
43 Renda, *Taking Haiti*, 31.
44 *Le Matin*, August 4, 1915.
45 Michel, *Charlemagne Péralte*, 66, and *Le Nouvelliste*, August 10, 1915.
46 Michel, *Charlemagne Péralte*, 64.
47 *Le Nouvelliste*, August 4, 1915.
48 *Le Nouvelliste*, August 2, 1915, and Michel, *Charlemagne Péralte*, 165.
49 Russell Papers, Manuscript Box 2 Haiti, Folder 8, Civilian and Caco Documents.
50 Millet, *Les paysans haïtiens*, 87.
51 Interview with community activist.
52 Michel, *Charlemagne Péralte*, 70.
53 Interview with community activist.
54 In *Les paysans haïtiens*, Kethly Millet describes Saül Péralte's appointment by Charles Zamor to describe his involvement in *cacos* activity between 1911 and 1915.
55 Interview with community activist.
56 Marine Archives Haiti, Treaties, 1916 Treaty with Haiti, Archives Branch, Marine Corps History Division, Quantico, VA (hereafter Marine Archives Haiti, 1916 Treaty).
57 Marine Archives Haiti, 1916 Treaty.
58 Marine Archives Haiti, 1916 Treaty.
59 Marine Archives Haiti, 1916 Treaty.
60 Louis A. Pérez Jr., *Cuba under the Platt Amendment, 1902–1934* (Pittsburgh, PA: University of Pittsburgh Press, 1991).
61 In a letter to Mr. Long of the Department of State, Office of the Solicitor, dated August 6, 1915, a U.S. American wrote, "an agreement for applying the principle of the 'Platt Amendment' to Haiti," Record Group 59, M610 #7 Haiti: Internal Affairs, 1910–1929.
62 Marine Archives Haiti, 1916 Treaty.
63 Marine Archives Haiti, 1916 Treaty.
64 Marine Archives Haiti, Garde d'Haiti, History 1915–1920, The Formative Period, pp. 8–14.
65 Marine Archives Haiti, Garde d'Haiti, History, 1915–1920, The Formative Period, p. 21.
66 Marine Archives Haiti, Garde d'Haiti, History, 1915–1920, The Formative Period, p. 24.
67 James McCrocklin offers a comprehensive guide in his compilation *Garde d'Haiti, 1915 to 1934: Twenty Years of Organization and Training by the United States Marine Corps* (Annapolis, MD: United States Naval Institute, 1956).
68 Marine Archives Haiti, Treaties, Gendarmerie Protocol, September 1916, pp. 1–10.

69 For further information on this 1864 legislation, specifically the roles of the state and chef section in instituting and supervising the *corvée*, see Millet, *Les paysans haïtien*, 20–24.

70 Marine Archives Haiti, Garde d'Haiti, History, 1915–1920, The Formative Period, p. 25.

71 Russell Papers, Manuscript Box 2 Haiti, Folder 3, The Occupying Force.

72 Marine Archives Haiti, Garde d'Haiti, History, 1915–1920, The Formative Period, p. 26.

73 Marine Archives Haiti, Garde d'Haiti, History, 1915–1920, The Formative Period, p. 26.

74 Marine Archives Haiti, Operations, Other Reports, Report on Haiti, 1915–1920, pp. 54–55.

75 Marine Archives Haiti, Garde d'Haiti, History, 1915–1920, The Formative Period, p. 26.

76 Millet, *Les paysans haïtiens*, 67–68; my translation.

77 Marine Archives Haiti, Garde d'Haiti, History, 1915–1920, The Formative Period, p. 27.

78 Marine Archives Haiti, Legal, Courts Martial, "Upon the Subject of corvée," pp. 1–10.

79 Marine Archives Haiti, Garde d'Haiti, History, 1915–1920, The Formative Period, p. 27; Millet, *Les paysans haïtiens*, 79.

80 *Le Nouvelliste*, October 16, 1919.

81 Millet, *Les paysans haïtiens*, 85, 105–106.

82 Kate Ramsey, *Vodou and Power in Haiti: The Spirits and the Law* (Chicago: University of Chicago Press, 2011), 120–128, 135.

83 Millet, *Les paysans haïtiens*, 85, 94.

84 *Le Nouvelliste*, August 7, 1915.

Chapter 3   Haitians—Rise and Defend!

1 H. Pauléus Sannon, *Histoire de Toussaint-Louverture* (Port-au-Prince: Augustin A. Héraux, 1920).

2 André-Georges Adam, *Une crise haïtienne, 1867–1869: Sylvain Salnave* (Port-au-Prince: Henri Deschamps, 1982); Roger Gaillard and Gusti-Klara Gaillard-Pourchet, *Le cacoïsme bourgeois contre Salnave, 1867–1870* (Port-au-Prince: Fondation Roger Gaillard, 2003); and Odette R. Fombrun, *Histoire d'Haïti: De l'indépendance à nos jours* (Port-au-Prince: Henri Deschamps).

3 "Development of the Republic of Haiti," John Houston Craige, Captain, U.S. Marine Corps. Two written notes indicate that Craige published this in the *Military Engineer*, June 1929.

4 Major General John H. Russell, "Why We Went to Haiti," Box 3:13, p. 9, Russell Papers, Box 3, Folder 5.

5 Commander C. S. Baker (SC), U.S. Navy, "Some Colorful Haitian History," *U.S. Naval Institute Proceedings* 50, no. 255 (May 1924), 723–743.

6 Dubois, *Haiti*, 257.

7 Castor, *L'occupation américaine d'Haïti*, 138.

8 The letter was already translated into English: "General Pierre Benoit Rameau, Counsellor to the Department of War and Marine on the march against the Capitol." It is signed P. B. Rameaux.

9 *Papers Relating to the Foreign Relations of the United States, with the Address of the President to Congress December 7, 1915*, ed. Joseph V. Fuller (Washington,

DC: Government Printing Office, 1924), File No. 838.00/1325. In "Brief History," Coffey wrote: "and the railroad from Gonaives to Ennery was opened, but not without resistance from the Cacos who opened fire on our troops and attempted to tear up the railroad" (1341).

10 Millet, *Les paysans haïtiens*, 45.

11 *Le Nouvelliste*, August 18, 1915.

12 Marine Archives Haiti, Operations, Other Reports, Report on Haiti, 1915–1920, p. 38.

13 Marine Archives Haiti, Operations, Other Reports, Report on Haiti, 1915–1920, p. 23.

14 Headquarters Naval Landing Force, Cape Haitien, Haiti, Order No 2, August 10, 1915.

15 Proclamation to the People of Port-au-Prince, Haiti, W. B. Caperton, Rear-Admiral, United States Navy, Commanding the Forces of the United States of America in Haiti and Haitian Waters, September 3, 1915.

16 Marines' translation of an article in *La Plume*, September 19, 1915.

17 Renda, *Taking Haiti*, 141.

18 Rear Admiral Caperton to the Secretary of the Navy, September 4, 1915, p. 43 of this compiled report and in Marine Archives Haiti, Operations, Historical Outline of Military Occupation of Haiti, p. 8.

19 Rear Admiral Caperton to the Secretary of the Navy, September 4, 1915, p. 47 of this compiled report and in Marine Archives Haiti, Operations, Historical Outline of Military Occupation of Haiti, p. 8.

20 Rear Admiral Caperton, September 18, 1915, p. 47, of this compiled report.

21 *Papers Relating to Foreign Relations*, 1915, File No. 838.00/1289.

22 On September 20, 1915, Rear Admiral Caperton proposed, p. 47 of this compiled report.

23 Marine Archives Haiti, Operations, Operation Reports, Cape Haitien, Haiti, September 29, 1915: agreement between Colonel L.W.T. Waller, USMC, Commanding U.S. Expeditionary Forces on Shore, representing the United States and Haitien Government and Generals Antoine Mor[e]ncy and Jn. Baptiste Petion, representing the Cacos of Haiti (hereafter Marine Archives Haiti, Waller agreement).

24 Marine Archives Haiti, Waller agreement.

25 Marine Archives Haiti, Waller agreement.

26 Marine Archives Haiti, Waller agreement.

27 Caperton's letter to Captain E. H. Durell, USN, Commanding USS Connecticut, Cape Haitien, August 29, 1915, https://www.globalsecurity.org/military/library /report/1995/BPL.htm.

28 *Army and Navy Journal*, October 9, 1915, 169. U.S. troops reported, "A detachment of U.S. Marines in Hayti found it necessary to attack on Oct. 7 some isolated bands of rebels who refused to lay down their arms and cooperate with rear Admiral Caperton to establish peace throughout the republic."

29 Major Butler's radiographic report to Col. Cole at Cape Haitien of this reconnaissance, p. 54 of untitled report and in Marine Archives Haiti, Operations, Historical Outline of Military Occupation of Haiti, p. 11.

30 Marine Archives Haiti, Commendations, Letter from The Major General Commandant to the Chief of the Bureau of Navigation, p. 4, May 14, 1917.

31 *Army and Navy Journal*, October 30, 1915, 265.

32 On October 29, 1915, Col. Waller informed Rear Admiral Caperton, p. 56, of untitled report and Marine Archives Haiti, Operations, Historical Outline of Military Occupation of Haiti, p. 12.

33 *Papers Relating to Foreign Relations*, 1915, File No. 838.00/1361.

34 Interview with community activist.

35 Marine Archives Haiti, Operations, Historical Outline of Military Occupation of Haiti, p. 13; *Papers Relating to Foreign Relations, 1915*, File No. 838.00/1370.

36 Marine Archives Haiti, Operations, Historical Outline of Military Occupation of Haiti, pp. 13–14; *Papers Relating to Foreign Relations, 1915*, File No. 838.00/1370.

37 Marine Archives Haiti, Commendations, Letter from The Major General Commandant to the Chief of the Bureau of Navigation, p. 4, May 14, 1917; Marine Archives Haiti, Commendations, General Order No. 319, August 25, 1917, "announces the award of medals of honor . . . in capturing Fort Riviere" in untitled report.

38 Marine Archives Haiti, Operations, Other Reports, Report on Haiti, 1915–1920, p. 39.

39 Marine Archives Haiti, Operations, Other Reports, Report on Haiti, 1915–1920, p. 43.

40 *Army and Navy Journal*, January 15, 1916, 627.

41 *Army and Navy Journal*, January 8, 1916, 593.

42 Caperton, in a communication with the number 22121 advised the secretary of the navy that "Misral Dodio had been tried by provost court charged with conspiracy against the Republic of Haiti and the United States forces, found guilty and sentenced to 15 years hard labor; and Exilaum Codion, tried by provost court for assisting Mizrael Codio to escape and conspiracy, found guilty and sentenced to 3 years hard labor" (22121 Caperton).

43 It is unclear if Dodio and Codio were kin. The military repeatedly listed their names with different spellings. If they were kin, it shows the family lineage of resistance like the Péralte brothers.

44 Marine Archives Haiti, Operations, Other Reports, Report on Haiti, 1915–1920, p. 42.

45 Marine Archives Haiti, Operations, Other Reports, Report on Haiti, 1915–1920, p. 42.

46 Marine Archives Haiti, Operations, Other Reports, Report on Haiti, 1915–1920, p. 43.

47 Marine Archives Haiti, Garde d'Haiti, History, 1915–1920 The Formative Period, p. 19.

48 *Le Nouvelliste*, May 6, 1916.

49 Renda, *Taking Haiti*, 135; Ramsey, *Vodou and Power in Haiti*, 75.

50 Renda, *Taking Haiti*, 78.

51 Rear Admiral Caperton's dispatch to the Secretary of the Navy, November 19, 1915, *Papers Relating to Foreign Relations, 1915*, File No. 838.00/1370.

52 Rear Admiral Caperton's dispatch to the Secretary of the Navy, November 19, 1915, *Papers Relating to Foreign Relations, 1915*, File No. 838.00/1370.

53 Marine Archives Haiti, Operations, Operation Reports, Expeditionary Commander to Commander Cruiser Squadron, Subject: Report of operations in North Haiti 1915 until arrival at Hinche, p. 30, January 10, 1916.

54 Arthur Chester Millspaugh, *Haiti under American Control, 1915–1930* (Boston, MA: World Peace Foundation, 1931), 89–90.

55 My translation as cited in Castor, *L'occupation américaine d'Haïti*, 133.

56 Jane Rausch, "Dartiguenave, Philippe Sudre," in *The War of 1898 and US Interventions, 1898–1934: An Encyclopedia*, ed. Benjamin R. Beede (New York: Routledge, 1994), 157–158.

57 Jan Lundius and Mats Lundhal, *Peasants and Religion: A Socioeconomic Study of Dios Olivorio and the Palma Sola Movement in the Dominican Republic* (New York: Routledge, 2000), 108.

58 Bruce J. Calder, *The Impact of Intervention: The Dominican Republic during the U.S. Occupation of 1916–1924* (Austin: University of Texas Press, 1984), 120; Michel, *Charlemagne Péralte*, 26.

59 Marine Archives Haiti, Garde d'Haiti, History, History of the Military Department of Port-au-Prince, p. 59.

60 Marine Archives Haiti, Garde d'Haiti, History, History of the Military Department of Port-au-Prince, p. 60.

61 Department of State, Division of Latin American Affairs, Telegram to Secretary of State from Mr. Blanchard, October 18, 1918. Close to a year later, on March 15, 1919, Blanchard reported to the Department of State that the "number of bandits have increased in the mountains, especially in the district of Hinche and vicinity of Dominican border," Department of State, Telegram to Secretary of State from Mr. Blanchard, March 15, 1919.The full telegrams between the two can be found at Papers Relating to the Foreign Relations of the United States, 1919, vol. II, 838.00/1563

62 Headquarters, First Provisional Brigade, United States Marine Corps, Daily Diary Report, A. W. Catlin, April 6–16, 1919.

63 Lundius and Lundhal, *Peasants and Religion*, 107, 376.

64 Interview with Charlemagne Péralte's stepson, August 18, 2007, Hinche, Haiti.

65 Calder, *Impact of Intervention*, 65.

66 Letter to Mr. McLean, November 11, 1915, Record Group 127, 1915–1920, Records of the United States Marines Corps, National Archives, Washington, DC (hereafter Record Group 127).

67 H. S. Knapp, Proclamation, November 1916, Russell Papers, Box 2 Haiti, Folder 4 Daily Diary Reports by Commander, 1st Provisional Brigade.

68 Renda, *Taking Haiti*, 143.

69 See Ramsey, *Vodou and Power in Haiti*.

70 Ramsey, *Vodou and Power in Haiti*, 131.

71 Letter to Rear-Admiral H. S. Knapp Headquarters First Provisional Brigade, U.S. Marines, Port-au-Prince, Haiti, April 13, 1917, Record Group 127.

72 Brigadier General Cole, May 27, 1917, Marine Archives Haiti, Operations, Other Reports, Report on Haiti, 1915–1920, p. 52.

73 Marine Archives Haiti, Operations, Other Reports, Report on Haiti, 1915–1920, p. 52.

74 Letter to Rear-Admiral H. S. Knapp Headquarters First Provisional Brigade, U.S. Marines, Port-au-Prince, Haiti, July 19, 1917, Record Collection 1911–1927 Box 747 of 1830, Record Group 127.

75 Chart attached to reports on political situations occurring between February 14–19, 1917.

76 Russell Papers, Manuscript Box 2 Haiti, Folder 8, Civilian and Caco Documents, "Translation of three letters from Widow Mass[é]na P[é]ralte," undated.

77 Russell Papers, Manuscript Box 2 Haiti, Folder 8 Civilian and Caco Documents, "Translation of three letters from Widow Massena P[é]ralte," undated.

78 Marine Archives Haiti, Garde d'Haiti, History, History of the Military Department of Port-au-Prince, p. 59.

79 *Le Nouvelliste*, August 8, 1915.

Chapter 4   Péralte Leads

1 David Ronfeldt, *U.S. Involvement in Central America: Three Views from Honduras* (Santa Monica, CA: Rand Corporation, 1989). In Honduras, U.S. Americans did the same in 1982.

2 Marine Archives Haiti, Treaties, Constitution of 12 June 1918.

3 Russell Papers, Manuscript Box 2 Haiti, Folder 3, The Occupying Force, report, 1917 to May 1921.

4 Russell Papers, Manuscript Box 2 Haiti, Folder 5 Special Correspondence with Higher Headquarters, "Adoption of the new constitution in Haiti."

5 The US military created the Garde, known in French as Gendarmerie d'Haïti, with the explicit purpose to monitor and curb Haitian resistance to the U.S. invasion. Castor, *Occupation américaine d'Haïti*, discusses how the Garde continued to be a tool of U.S. rule in the postoccupation period.

6 Russell Papers, Manuscript Box 2 Haiti, Folder 3 The Occupying Force, Circular Letter, Alex S. Williams, Chief of the Gendarmerie d'Haiti, May 20, 1918.

7 Russell Papers, Manuscript Box 2 Haiti, Folder 3 The Occupying Force, Circular Letter, Alex S. Williams, Chief of the Gendarmerie d'Haiti, May 20, 1918.

8 Russell Papers, Manuscript Box 2 Haiti, Folder 3 The Occupying Force, Voting Places, June 12, 1918.

9 Russell Papers, Manuscript Box 2 Haiti, Folder 3 The Occupying Force, Voting Places, June 12, 1918.

10 Brigade Commander to Chief of Naval Operations, "Anti-Government and Occupation activity in Haiti," June 9, 1918, pp. 1–2, Record Group 127.

11 Russell Papers, Manuscript Box 3 Writing for Publication, Folder 5 Typescript, "Why We Went to Haiti," by Major General Commandant John H. Russell, as told to Captain Charles P. Williamson, 1935.

12 Letter to British Consul Resident in Haiti from Charlemagne M. Péralte, Army Headquarters, June 3, 1919. A. W. Catlin [Brigade Commander] included a copy of the letter in the "Daily Diary Report" dated July 5, 1919, Record Group 127.

13 Untitled four-page report on activities between March 14, 1919, and summer of 1920, pp. 1–2, Record Group 127.

14 Castor, *L'occupation américaine d'Haïti*, 138.

15 Marine Archives Haiti, Garde d'Haiti, Military Department of the North, May 12, 1934, p. 20; Castor, *L'occupation américaine d'Haïti*, 138. Both Roger Gaillard, *Les blancs debarquent, 1919–1934: La guérilla de Batraville* (Port-au-Prince: Roger Gaillard, 1981), and Millet, *Les paysans haïtiens*, offer discussions on Batraville's practice of Vodou. Millet argues that Batraville's religious practice, among other attributes, encouraged Péralte's choice of his lieutenant due to the connections it facilitated among the mass of *cacos* followers (92).

16 Michel-Rolph Trouillot, *Silencing the Past: Power and the Production of History*, 20th ed. (Boston: Beacon, 2015).

17 Marine Archives Haiti, Garde d'Haiti, History, 1915–1920 The Formative Period, p. 31.

18 Marine Archives Haiti, Garde d'Haiti, History, 1915–1920 The Formative Period, p. 31.

19 Marine Archives Haiti, Garde d'Haiti, History, 1915–1920 The Formative Period, p. 32; Trouillot, *Silencing the Past*.

20 Brigade Commander report, October 17 and 19, 1918. Marine Archives Haiti, Operations, Other Reports, Report on Haiti, 1915–1920, p. 65.

21 Marine Archives Haiti, Garde d'Haiti, History, 1915–1920 The Formative Period, p. 50.

22 Untitled document that has an introductory message from Rear Admiral Knapp 10427. The two-page source discusses events in Haiti from September 16, 1918, to April 1920. It is a compilation of reports made by and to the secretary of the navy, Record Group 45.

23 Letter from Charlemagne M. Péralte to General Ripkin, Camp Général[e], April 18, 1919, Marine Corps Archives and Special Collections, Archives Branch, Marine Corps History Division, Gray Research Center, Quantico, VA.

24 Charlemagne Péralte to General Aspelly Joseph, March 22, 1919. Translation of a letter found on the body of General Celisma Pierre, Marine Corps Archives and Special Collections, Archives Branch, Marine Corps History Division, Gray Research Center, Quantico, VA.

25 Untitled four-page report on activities between March 14, 1919, and summer of 1920, p. 1, Record Group 127, Records of the United States Marines Corps, National Archives, Washington, DC.

26 Russell Papers, Manuscript Box 2 Haiti, Folder 8 Civilian and Caco Documents, "List by Charlemagne P[é]ralte of 18 officers and noncommissioned officers of the Gendarmerie whose heads he wants."

27 John H. Russell, Daily Diary Report, Headquarters, First Provisional Brigade, U.S. Marine Corps, Port-au-Prince, Republic of Haiti, November 24, 1918. Record Group 127.

28 "List of Active Bandits," April 18, 1919. Record Group 127.

29 A. W. Caitlin, Daily Diary Report, Headquarters, First Provisional Brigade, U.S. Marine Corps, Port-au-Prince, April 16, 1919, Record Group 45.

30 A. W. Caitlin, Daily Diary Report, Headquarters, First Provisional Brigade, U.S. Marine Corps, Port-au-Prince, April 21, 1919, Record Group 45.

31 A. W. Caitlin, Daily Diary Report, Headquarters, First Provisional Brigade, U.S. Marine Corps, Port-au-Prince, April 25, 1919, Record Group 45.

32 Russell Papers, Manuscript Box 2 Haiti, Folder 2 Proclamations, "Proclamation to the Haitian People in the Districts Where There Are Bandits," Colonel R. S. Hooker, U.S. Marine Corps [Chief of Gendarmerie d'Haiti]. The translation is by Mrs. Heinl. This is Nancy G. Heinl, wife of Robert D. Heinl (chief of U.S. Naval Mission to Haiti). Together they wrote *Written in Blood: The Story of the Haitian People, 1492–1995*. While the proclamation is undated, Hooker's mention of Charlemagne Péralte and the heightened efforts to kill him in 1919 date the proclamation to this year, despite its listing in the archival record as circa 1921.

33 *Senate Hearings*, 1922, 1659.

34 Russell Papers, Manuscript Box 2 Haiti, Folder 2 Proclamations, "Proclamation to the Haitian People in the Districts Where There Are Bandits."

35 Marine Archives Haiti, Legal, Court Martials, "Memorandum Re General Courts-Martial, July 28, 1915 to July, 1920 Inclusive." The U.S. troops associated with these offenses were: Private Charles D. Molson (May 3, 1918), Private Herman Heft (July 25, 1918), Private Arthur L. Favorite (September 3, 1919), Private Joseph R. Schram (May 20, 1919), and Private Charlie D. Sears (May 20, 1919).

36 Marine Archives Haiti, Legal, Court Martials, "1919–1920 Investigation into Unlawful Executions." Various testimonies are included.

37 Russell Papers, Manuscript Box 2 Haiti, Folder 3 The Occupying Force, "Memo: Hooker to Little, concerning a report of interrogation," pp. 17–18. For fuller testimonies see *Senate Hearings*, vol. 1.

38 Russell Papers, Manuscript Box 2 Haiti, Folder 2 Proclamations, "Proclamation to the Haitian People in the Districts Where There Are Bandits."

39 Garrigus, *Le Code Noir*.

40 Russell Papers, Manuscript Box 2 Haiti, Folder 2 Proclamations, "Proclamation to the Haitian People in the Districts Where There Are Bandits."

41 Russell Papers, Manuscript Box 2 Haiti, Folder 8 Civilian and Caco Documents, "Le départ du Colonel Hooker," by J. F. [Jolibois Fils]. Russell notes that Mrs. Heinl translated the original.

42 *Senate Hearings*, 1922, 81.

43 *Senate Hearings*, 1922, 823.

44 Marine Archives Haiti, Legal, Court Martials, "1919–1920 Investigation into Unlawful Executions."

45 Russell Papers, Manuscript Box 2 Haiti, Folder 3 The Occupying Force, "Interrogation report: A caco from Jaco."

46 Russell Papers, Manuscript Box 2 Haiti, Folder 3 The Occupying Force, "Interrogation report: A caco from Jaco."

47 Henry Montas to General Catlin, Chief of the American Occupation in Haiti, May 2, 1919, Record Group 45.

48 Letter to British consul resident in Haiti from Charlemagne M. Péralte, Army Headquarters, June 3, 1919. A. W. Catlin [brigade commander] included a copy of the letter in the Daily Diary Report dated July 5, 1919. Record Group 127.

49 A. W. Caitlin, Daily Diary Report, Headquarters, First Provisional Brigade, U.S. Marine Corps, Port-au-Prince, July 5, 1919, Record Group 45.

50 Charlemagne Masséna Péralte, Supreme Chief of Haitian Revolution to French Resident Minister in Port-au-Prince, July 27, 1919, Record Group 127.

51 Russell Papers, Manuscript Box 2 Haiti, Folder 9 Investigating The Occupation, "Statement of Colonel John H. Russell, U.S. Marine Corps, Commanding 1st Brigade, U.S. Marines, Port-au-Prince, Haiti," pp. 16–17.

52 Russell Papers, Manuscript Box 2 Haiti, Folder 9 Investigating The Occupation, "Statement of Colonel John H. Russell, U.S. Marine Corps, Commanding 1st Brigade, U.S. Marines, Port-au-Prince, Haiti," pp. 16–18.

53 Major J. L Doxey to the Department Commander, Dept. of Port-au-Prince, October 7, 1919, Report of disorder which occurred in Port au Prince on October 7, 1919, p. 2, Record Group 127.

54 Department Commander to Chief of the Gendarmerie d'Haiti, October 11, 1919, Record Group 127.

55 "Memorandum Order #2 Hinche, Republic of Haiti, Oct 28, 1919," L. McCarthy Little, Lt. Col. U.S.M.C, Record Group 127.

56 *Le Nouvelliste*, October 13, 1919.

57 Russell Papers, Manuscript Box 2 Haiti, Folder 2 Proclamations, "Nouvelle Adresse a la Population," John H. Russell, Colonel du Corps d'Infanterie de Marines.

58 Marine Archives Haiti, Garde d'Haiti, History, 1915–1920 The Formative Period, p. 52.

59 Marine Archives Haiti, Garde d'Haiti, History, 1915–1920 The Formative Period, p. 34.

60 Marine Archives Haiti, Garde d'Haiti, History, 1915–1920 The Formative Period, p. 34.

61 Russell Papers, Manuscript Box 2 Haiti, Folder 9 Investigating The Occupation, "Statement of Colonel John H. Russell, U.S. Marine Corps, Commanding 1st Brigade, U.S. Marines, Port-au-Prince, Haiti," pp. 16–18.

62 "Memorandum Order #2 Hinche, Republic of Haiti, Oct 28, 1919," L. McCarthy Little, Lt. Col. U.S.M.C, Record Group 127.

63 From District Commander, Grande Rivi[è]re to Chief of the Gendarmerie d'Haiti via Department Commander, Dept. of the Cape, Charlemagne P[é]ralte, death of., November 1, 1919, Record Group 127.

64 Russell Papers, Manuscript Box 2 Haiti, Folder 3 The Occupying Force, "Second Regiment message 1 November 1919 1255 P.M., to Brigade Port-au-Prince."

65 Smedley D. Butler Collection, Series 8. Photographs, negatives, drawings, and postcards, 1900–1940, COLL/3124, Archives Branch, Marine Corps History Division, Gray Research Center, Quantico, VA.

66 Headquarters Gendarmerie d'Haiti, Report from Chief of the Gendarmerie d'Haiti to All Gendarmerie Officers, signed by John H. Russell, November 6, 1919, p. 2, Record Group 127.

67 Medical Inspector to Department Commander, "Identification of the body of Charlemagne P[é]ralte." November 1st, 1919, Record Group 127.

68 Toussaint L'Ouverture, as quoted in Thomas S. Malcolm, "The Republic of Hayti," *Pacific Appeal*, May 31, 1873, 1.

69 District Commander, Grande Rivière to Chief of the Gendarmerie d'Haiti, Report of Conditions, October 1919 to October 31, 1919, Record Group 127.

Chapter 5   Violence

1 Alexis Clark, "How the History of Blackface Is Rooted in Racism," History website, February 15, 2019, https://www.history.com/news/ blackface-history-racism-origins.

2 Papers of Smedley D. Butler, Series 8, Photographs, negatives, drawings, and postcards, 1900–1940, COLL/3124, Archives Branch, Reference Collection, Marine Corps History Division, Quantico, VA.

3 Renda, *Taking Haiti*, 343.

4 *Le Nouvelliste*, November 10, 1919.

5 Marine Archives Haiti, Operations, Other Reports, Report on Haiti, 1915–1920, p. 79.

6 Marine Archives Haiti, Operations, Other Reports, Report on Haiti, 1915–1920, p. 80.

7 In fact, Trujillo's record of brutalizing an underage Dominican girl was buried. Only a few years later, he seized the presidency and became the longest-ruling dictator in the Dominican Republic, his rule replete with the most racist policies despite his own Black body and heritage.

8 The soldiers included Captain Hanneken, Colonel James Jose Maude, Lieutenant Harold Ray Wood, William Robert Button, Gendarme Jean Edmond François, Sergeant Démétrius Mompremier, Corporal Kernizan Raymond, and Gendarme Fable Célestin, among others.

9 Brigade Commander to Major General Commandment Headquarters and U.S. Marine Corps, Washington, DC, November 17, 1919, Record Group 127.

10 For an audio and visual representation of the term Strange Fruit, please consult Billie Holiday's song with the same name and this PBS film that documents her song as well as the origin of this terminology for lynching: https://www.pbs.org /independentlens/strangefruit/film.html.

11 Untitled four-page report on activities between March 14, 1919, and Summer of 1920, p. 2, Record Group 127; Marine Archives Haiti, Garde d'Haiti, History, 1915–1920 The Formative Period, p. 85. For a fuller account on Batraville's and Péralte's relationship, consult Gaillard, *Charlemagne Péralte le Caco*.

12 Gaillard documents four possible birth years for Batraville (1875, 1879, 1881, and 1885) in *La guérilla de Batraville* (Port-au-Prince: Le Natal, 1983), 54.

13 Gaillard, *La guérilla de Batraville*, 52.

14 Gaillard, *La guérilla de Batraville*, 51–66, and Millet, *Les paysans haïtiens*, 92–94.

15 Marine Archives Haiti, Garde d'Haiti, History, 1915–1920 The Formative Period, p. 43, 46–47; Marine Archives Haiti, Operations, Other Reports, Report on Haiti, 1915–1920, p. 79; and a six-page missive on Batraville and the *cacos* were found in Colonel John H. Russell, Summary of Military Situation, January–July 1920, 2, Marine Archives Haiti, Operations, Other Reports, Report on Haiti, 1915–1920.

16 Marine Archives Haiti, Garde d'Haiti, Military Department of the North, May 12, 1934, pp. 58–59 (hereafter Marine Archives Haiti, Garde d'Haiti, North).

17 Marine Archives Haiti, Garde d'Haiti, History, 1915–1920 The Formative Period, pp. 35–36.

18 Marine Archives Haiti, Garde d'Haiti, Military Department of the North, May 12, 1934, p. 59, and Marine Archives Haiti, Garde d'Haiti, History, 1915–1920 The Formative Period, pp. 35–36.

19 Russell Papers, Manuscript Box 2 Haiti, Folder 8 Civilian and Caco Documents, "1920 Proclamation issued by Papillion Fils, January 8, 1920."

20 Russell Papers, Manuscript Box 1 General Career Documents, Folder 5 The Butler Problem, "Transcript of General Butler's speech of 1 November 1935 made by James H. Fowler, reported for Passaic Herald News."

21 Renda, *Taking Haiti*, 104 and 138.

22 Russell Papers, Manuscript Box 1 General Career Documents, Folder 5 The Butler Problem, "Transcript of General Butler's speech of 1 November 1935 made by James H. Fowler, reported for Passaic Herald News."

23 Ramsey, *Vodou and Power in Haiti*, 143, and Renda, *Taking Haiti*, 122.

24 Marine Archives Haiti, Garde d'Haiti, History, 1915–1920 The Formative Period, p. 47.

25 Marine Archives Haiti, Garde d'Haiti, History, 1915–1920 The Formative Period, pp. 43–44, 46; Colonel John H. Russell, Summary of Military Situation, January–July 1920, pp. 1–2.

26 Marine Archives Haiti, Garde d'Haiti, History, 1915–1920 The Formative Period, p. 88–89.

27 *Senate Hearings*, 588–589. For more on Spear's discussion about the "unlawful executions of Haitiens called Cacos," see Marine Archives Haiti, Operations, Other Reports, Report on Haiti, 1915–1920, p. 99.

28 Undated report from John H. Russell that references the period from January 15, 1920, to April 20, 1920, p. 1, Record Group 127.

29 "Proclamation issued by John H. Russell, Colonel U.S. Marine Corps, First Provisional Headquarters, Port-au-Prince, January 19, 1920," Record Group 127.

30 Russell Papers, Manuscript Box 2 Haiti, Folder 11, Relations with The Nation, "27 Jul 1920 Captain J. L. Perkins, U.S. Marine Corps, to Brigade Commander: "Account of patrol made in company with Mr. Herbert J. Seligman, 3–7 April 1920.""

31 Russell Papers, Manuscript Box 2 Haiti, Folder 11, Relations with The Nation, "27 Jul 1920 Captain J. L. Perkins, U.S. Marine Corps, to Brigade Commander: "Account of patrol made in company with Mr. Herbert J. Seligman, 3–7 April 1920." Marine Corps Archives and Special Collections, Gray Research Center, Quantico, VA.

32 Russell Papers, Manuscript Box 2 Haiti, Folder 11, Relations with The Nation, "24 Apr 1920 Josephus Daniel, Secretary of the Navy to Russell: forwarding The Nation article 'The Conquest of Haiti' and requesting a statement."

33 Herbert Seligmann, "The Conquest of Haiti," *The Nation*, July 10, 1920, 35.

34 Russell Papers, Manuscript Box 2 Haiti, Folder 11, Relations with The Nation, "13 Dec 1921 Captain Jesse L. Perkins to Commander, Department of the South: sworn statement concerning The Nation representative Seligman on 3–7 April 1920 patrol." Marine Corps Archives and Special Collections, Gray Research Center, Quantico, VA.

35 Gaillard, *Charlemagne Péralte*, 35–38.

36 I am referring to the high number of lynching during this period in the United States. Further, the surveillance of the Garvey and Dubois families are but two examples of the U.S. government monitoring Black leadership.

37 Sanders, "*La Voix des Femmes.*"

38 Marine Archives Haiti, Garde d'Haiti, History, 1915–1920 The Formative Period, p. 89.

39 *Le Nouvelliste*, December 11 and 15, 1919.

40 Memorandum for Rear Admiral Snowden, Military Representative of the United States in Haiti, Concerning the Work Accomplished in Haiti by the Military Invasion During the Period from October 1, 1919 to July 20, 1920, 1. Record Group 45.

41 Report from Major General Commandant to the Secretary of the Navy, "Report of the military situation in Haiti during the period, July 1, 1920, to date, and a report of my inspection of the First Brigade, U.S. Marines, stationed in the Republic of Haiti," October 4, 1920, Record Group 45. He documented the arrests of three Germans, Otto Scott, Walter Schmidt, and Herbert Tischer, in addition to Charles Zamor.

42 Russell Papers, Manuscript Box 2 Haiti, Folder 5 Special Correspondence with Higher Headquarters, "High Commissioner to Secretary of State: report on use and need for martial law and provost courts to impose stability in Haiti," September 6, 1922.

43 Russell Papers, Manuscript Box 2 Haiti, Folder 5, Special Correspondence with Higher Headquarters, "Brigade Commander to Chief of Naval Operations, Report on the political situation in Haiti in its relation to the military, November 1920," Confidential report dated December 4, 1920.

44 J. Finlay Wilson to Honorable Warren G. Harding, February 9, 1922; Norman Thomas, also wrote the following letter to President Warren Harding on March 7, 1922: "May I urge that you have now an opportunity to re-establish the faith and confidence not only of Americans in our own traditions but also of the weaker peoples in us? Few deeds would, I think, speak more clearly of peace and justice then restoration of full sovereignty to Haiti as a precedent to whatever further negotiations may seem desirable. Surely American help to the weak ought not to mean American coercion of them." Norman Thomas from *The Nation* to President Warren G. Harding, March 7, 1922 (author's personal collection).

45 Russell Papers, Manuscript Box 2 Haiti, Folder 5 Special Correspondence with Higher Headquarters, "Brigade Commander to Chief of Naval Operations, Report on the political situation in Haiti in its relation to the military, November 1920," Confidential report dated December 4, 1920; Russell Papers, Manuscript Box 2 Haiti, Folder 3 The Occupying Force, "List: "Haitian Newspapers of Recent Publication," Tabulates name, address, editor's name, political/financial backing, political stance," September 20, 1921.

46 From Brigade Commander to the Major General Commandant, Headquarters, USMC, Washington, DC, December 11, 1919, pp. 1–3, Record Group 127.

47 Russell Papers, Manuscript Box 2 Haiti, Folder 6 Russell Describes the Occupation, "Penciled draft, incomplete, on the challenge of the occupation, 1919." In a report, Rear Admiral H. S. Knapp wrote, "The mulattoes are, generally speaking, to be found in the ascendant class, which the ignorant black peasant distrusts and fears. The population as a whole is densely ignorant. An educator from the United States who has recently spent several years in Haiti estimates the percentage of illiteracy as high as 97. In addition, the general mentality is of a low type." Report of Rear Admiral H. S. Knapp, U.S.S. "Minnesota," Flagship, Port-au-Prince, Haiti, October 14, 1920, to the Secretary of the Navy, Record Group 45. H. P. Davis,

"Haiti after 1936: So Far Intervention Has Failed," *Outlook and Independent*, March 19, 1930, 443–446, 475.

48 Russell Papers, Manuscript Box 2 Haiti, Folder 5 Special Correspondence with Higher Headquarters, "Brigade Commander to Chief of Naval Operations, Report on the political situation in Haiti in its relation to the military, November 1920," Confidential report dated December 4, 1920. In 1930 the Forbes Commission enunciated similar thoughts, writing, "The masses of Haiti are poor and ignorant. Generally speaking, they are of pure African descent," in "Report of the President's Commission for the Study and Review of Conditions in the Republic of Haiti, March 26, 1930," Record Group 127.

49 In this typical doublespeak manner, the invaders claimed *cacos* resistance ended in 1917, and then in 1919, disregarding the consistent *cacos*' presence from 1915 to 1922.

50 Many Americans made note of the protest activities occurring in Haiti and urged the U.S. government to cease its imperialist actions on the island. Ernest Gruening and Herbert Seligmann were among many who used *The Nation* as a forum against the invasion. In one article published in July 10, 1920, Seligmann boldly wrote, "To Belgium's Congo, to Germany's Belgium, to England's India and Egypt, the United States has added a perfect miniature in Haiti." For more on the black press protest against the invasion, see Polyné, *From Douglass to Duvalier*.

51 Members of the Society for the Independence of Haiti and the Dominican Republic included Moorefield Storey (president), Mrs. Weed (secretary general), Ernest Gruening, Robert Herrick (treasurer), and Mr. Angell (counsel to the society and the NAACP during the 1921–1922 Senate hearings on the occupation).

52 Furthermore, the UNIA, founded by Marcus Garvey, Amy Ashwood, Amy Jacques Garvey, and others, also found a nationalist home in Haiti. For more information about the UNIA presence and the sale of Black Star line stock in the nation, see Plummer, *Haiti and the United States*, 121–122.

53 In response to requests by Americans to end the U.S. invasion, Rear Admiral Henry S. Knapp reasoned that "all good accomplished in Haiti as a result of American intervention will be lost if the US withdraws its military forces for a great many years to come," *New York Times*, October 21, 1920.

54 Report from Major General Commandant to the Secretary of the Navy, "Report of the military situation in Haiti during the period, July 1, 1920, to date, and a report of my inspection of the First Brigade, U.S. Marines, stationed in the Republic of Haiti," October 4, 1920, Record Group 45.

55 John H. Russell's Summary of Intelligence for the period from April 1, 1921, to April 30, 1921, inclusive. Headquarters First Provisional Brigade, U.S. Marine Corps, Port-au-Prince, Republic of Haiti, April 30, 1921, Record Group 45.

56 John H. Russell's Summary of Intelligence for the period from April 1, 1921, to April 30, 1921, inclusive. Headquarters First Provisional Brigade, U.S. Marine Corps, Port-au-Prince, Republic of Haiti, April 30, 1921, Record Group 45; Intelligence Report, U.S. Marine Corps, by R. L. Shepard of Haiti, Hinche, May 21, 1921, Record Group 45. The marines surveyed the towns of Aux Cayes, Bahon, and Port-de-Paix in June 1921.

57 Intelligence Report, U.S. Marine Corps, by R. L. Shepard of Haiti, Hinche, May 21, 1921, Record Group 45.

58 Intelligence Report, U.S. Marine Corps, by R. L. Shepard of Haiti, Hinche, May 21, 1921, Record Group 45. Reference is also found in a separate four-page document with the title "Detailed Description" [of Hinche], author unknown, Record Group 45.

59 Four-page document with the title "Detailed Description" [of Hinche], author unknown, Record Group 45.

60 Interview with community activist.

61 James Scott, "Resistance without Protest and without Organization: Peasant Opposition to the Islamic Zakat and the Christian Tithe," *Comparative Studies in Society and History* 29, no. 3 (1987), 421.

62 John H. Russell's Summary of Intelligence for the period from May 1, 1921, to May 31, 1921, inclusive, Headquarters First Provisional Brigade, U.S. Marine Corps, Port-au-Prince, Republic of Haiti, June 3, 1921, Record Group 45.

63 John H. Russell's Summary of Intelligence for the period from August 1, 1921, to August 31, 1921, inclusive, Headquarters First Provisional Brigade, U.S. Marine Corps, Port-au-Prince, Republic of Haiti, September 1, 1921, Record Group 45; *Le Nouvelliste*, August 12, 1921.

64 Russell Papers, Manuscript Box 2 Haiti, Folder 5 Special Correspondence with Higher Headquarters, "High Commissioner to Secretary of State: Report on use and need for martial law and provost courts to impose stability in Haiti," September 6, 1922.

65 First Sergeant Newcomb Smith, "Watching Bandits in Haiti from the Air," *Recruiters' Bulletin*.

66 Lieut. Wm Morrison Barr, "Tells How Marine Fliers Hunt down Bandits," Marines Flying Force, Haiti, *Recruiters' Bulletin*, p. 5; Marine Archives Haiti, Operations, Other Reports, The Annual Reports of General George Barnett, Commandant of the United States Marines Corps, to the Secretary of the Navy, for the fiscal years 1914 to 1919 inclusive, contain the following reports on the work done by the Marines in Haiti during these years.

Chapter 6   We're Still Fighting

1 Allan R. Millett, *Semper Fidelis: The History of the United States Marine Corps* (New York: Macmillan, 1980), 196–199.

2 Renda, *Taking Haiti*, 165–166.

3 Renda, *Taking Haiti*, 163.

4 Marine Archives Haiti, Casualties, "Haitian Casualties Since the Occupation of Haiti By the U.S. Marines." List covers from August 1, 1915, to January 15, 1920. For example, on December 7, 1919, the troops noted that Private R. S. Grenfeldt killed "native woman, Zuli Petit Joison, through criminal negligence."

5 Schmidt, *United States Occupation of Haiti*, 106, 120–122; Renda, *Taking Haiti*, 191; Dubois, *Haiti*, 250–252.

6 *Senate Hearings*, 1922, 909–911.

7 *Senate Hearings*, 1922, 909–911.

8 *Senate Hearings*, 1922, 911.

9 *Senate Hearings*, 1922, 903–904.

10 *Senate Hearings*, 1922, 903–904.

11 *Senate Hearings*, 1922, 903–904.

12 *Senate Hearings*, 1922, 900–902.

13 *Senate Hearings*, 1922, 902.

14 *Senate Hearings*, 1922, 891–893.

15 *Senate Hearings*, 1922, 926–928.

16 *Senate Hearings*, 1922, 928–929.

17 Schmidt, *United States Occupation of Haiti*, 123.

18 Marine Archives Haiti, Garde d'Haiti, History, 1921–1925 The Training Period, p. 11.

19 Schmidt, *United States Occupation of Haiti*, 120–123.

20 Russell Papers, Manuscript Box 1 General Career Documents, Folder 1 Career Milestones, "Brigadier General John H. Russell appointed as the High Commissioner and Ambassador Extraordinary, by President Harding February 11, 1922.

21 Schmidt, *United States Occupation of Haiti*, 164.

22 In the following telegram sent to the State Department about President Dartiguenave on January 25, 1922, marines noted: "I am reliably informed that the President of Haiti is pursuing a policy of dismissing pro-American officials and appointing in their places men who are admittedly anti-American. A notable instance is the recent dismissal from the Council of State of Dr. D. Garo, he who is strongly pro-American. Alfred N. Auguste also is in danger of dismissal from the Council of State. These acts of the President have had a serious and damaging effect upon the American influence here and upon the pro American element, many of whose members have either been silenced or have ostensibly changed their attitude." Other documents about this matter include *Papers Relating to the Foreign Relations of the United States, 1922*, ed. Joseph V. Fuller (Washington, DC: Government Printing Office, 1938), vol. 2, 711.38/156a, President Harding to President Dartiguenave, February 13, 1922.

23 Russell Papers, Manuscript Box 3 Writing for Publication, Folder 2 Binder, "Address by General Russell on Haiti," February 2, 1923.

24 Paul H. Douglas, "The American Occupation of Haiti I," *Political Science Quarterly* 42, no. 2 (June 1927), 228–258.

25 Schmidt, *United States Occupation of Haiti*, 128.

26 Millett, *Semper Fidelis*, 196.

27 My translation, Castor's *L'occupation américaine d'Haïti*, 163–166.

28 *Le Matin*, May 17, 1921.

29 "Marines Raise Flag in Haiti," Archives and Special Collections, Archives Branch, Marine Corps History Division, Gray Research Center, Quantico, VA.

30 *Le Matin*, May 19, 1921.

31 *Le Matin*, May 28, 1921. By 1928, one soldier noted that twenty-seven Haitian journalists were in jail during his residence in Port-au-Prince, which revealed how the United States attempted to contain critics and the people who launched them.

32 *Le Nouvelliste*, November 10, 1919, to August 20, 1921.

33 *Le Matin*, July 4, 1921.

34 Millet, *Les paysans haïtiens*, 58.

35 *Le Nouvelliste*, January 22 and February 22, 1923. Four years later, the dismal compensation of Haitians working on U.S. American plantations and part of Haitian American Sugar Company (HASCO) remained. Millet, *Les paysans haïtiens*, 116–118.

36 *Le Nouvelliste*, January 8, 1923.

37 Haitians were used to facing racism when traveling or moving abroad. In the 1920s, it is unclear if Haitians were aware of the racial tensions in Cuba at this time as outlined in Marc C. McLeod, "Undesirable Aliens: Race, Ethnicity, and Nationalism in the Comparison of Haitian and British West Indian Immigrant Workers in Cuba, 1912–1939," *Journal of Social History* 31, no. 3 (spring 1998), 599–623. Previously, in 1912, thousands of Afro-Cubans were massacred for their articulation of basic civil rights, such as free speech, participation in the army, and equitable wages. The Moret Law placed a ban on forming political parties along racial lines, which describes the legislative restrictions on Afro-Cubans' rights. It dismissed the

history of Africans, free and enslaved, who contributed to building the Cuban republic during colonial and imperial times. Additionally, the U.S. sugar companies that dominated Cuba's economy enforced a Jim and Jane Crow structure, keeping White and Black Cuban workers apart. What is more, this type of resistance—a physical departure from oppression—was really only partial in that the United States had a military presence in Cuba. The options for true physical escape were few.

38 From Grand Lodges, Cap Haïtien to all the Grant Oriente, Grand Lodges and Masonic Powers, June 14, 1923.

39 George Sylvain and others had previously formed L'Union Patriotique in August 1915, calling for the invasion's end. Millet, *Les paysans haïtiens*, 88–9, 112; Renda, *Taking Haiti*, 191.

40 Note about "Ligue Patriotique," Record Group 127. The United States kept a sharp eye and ear out for the *cacos* and other Haitian agitators. This type of surveillance was reminiscent of the U.S. stakeout of the promoters of Black nationalism, Marcus and Amy Jacques Garvey. When Hoover worked for the intelligence department, the agency planted informants at halls where Garvey spoke on issues for Black liberation in the 1920s. Thus, U.S. surveillance in the occupied states was not surprising. In fact, there is a burgeoning body of work about Haitians' membership of the UNIA that will complement the existing scholarship on the role of the NAACP during the invasion.

41 Russell Papers, Manuscript Box 2 Haiti, Folder 4, Daily Diary Reports by Commander, 1st Provisional Brigade, Daily Diary Report, Port-au-Prince, Haiti, April 4, 1921; *Le Nouvelliste*, May 17–18, 1921; and Leon D. Pamphile, "The NAACP and the American Occupation of Haiti," *Phylon* 47, no. 1 (1986), 91–100.

42 Sylvain-Bouchereau, *Haïti et ses femmes*, 86. Referring to her mother by her married name, Sylvain-Bouchereau notes that Mrs. Georges Sylvain helped guide members of the 1926 Women's International League for Peace and Liberty during their travel to Haiti.

43 Millet, *Les paysans haïtiens*, 119.

44 Herbert J. Seligmann, Lewis Gannett, James Weldon Johnson, and Ernest Gruening were all members of the Haiti-Santo Domingo Independence Society.

45 Second Lieutenant Ernest E. Linsert, Marine Barracks San Michel, Haiti, November 21, 1923, and December 21, 1923, Record Group 127.

46 Second Lieutenant Roland E. Simpson, Patrol Report, San Michel, Haiti, March 24, 1933. Other patrol reports can be found in Marine Archives Haiti, Garde d'Haiti, History, History of the Military Department of Port-au-Prince

47 Marine Archives Haiti, Annual Reports, 1923 Annual Report.

48 Annie Desroy, *Le Joug* (Port-au-Prince: Imprimerie Modelé, 1934); Virgile Valcin, *La blanche négresse* (Port-au-Prince: Presses Nationales d'Haiti, 1934); Price-Mars, *Ainsi parla l'oncle*; Alexis, *In the Flicker of an Eyelid*; and David Nicholls, *From Dessalines to Duvalier: Race, Colour, and National Independence in Haiti* (New Brunswick, NJ: Rutgers University Press, 1996), 152–164.

49 Jacques Roumain, *L'Action: Journal de La Masse, Organe de la Ligue de la Jeunesse Patriote Haïtienne*, June 1, 1929. Roumain was also affiliated with founding the Haitian Communist Party in 1934; Castor, *L'occupation américaine d'Haiti*, 199.

50 *L'Action*, June 15 and September 26, 1929.

51 Ménard, "The Occupied Novel."

52 Russell Papers, Manuscript Box 2 Haiti, Folder 14 Binder of Items Compiled December 1928–December 1929, Letter from F. H. Cooke, Public Works Officer, Philadelphia Navy Yard to Russell: forwarding derogatory article from New York

World, 10 February; six-page typed copy of article by Napoleon Bonaparte Marshall, former clerk in U.S. Consulate, Port-au-Prince, denouncing the occupation in general, February 15, 1929.

53 Office of The American High Commissioner. American Legation, Port-au-Prince, Haiti to the Honorable, The Chairman of the President's Commission for the Study and Review of Conditions in the Republic of Haiti, March 13, 1930, Russell Papers, Manuscript Box 2 Haiti, Folder 5 Special Correspondence with Higher Headquarters.

54 Millet, *Les paysans haïtiens*, 120.

55 Marine Archives Haiti, Operations, Intelligence Reports, Various Intelligence Reports. In one intelligence report from the district commander of Port-de-Paix, dated about December 1929, the district commander noted agitation among schoolchildren who staged a three-day demonstration; Millet, *Les paysans haïtiens*, 121.

56 Marine Archives Haiti, Operations, Historical Outline of Military Occupation of Haiti. The inserted written date is October 11, 1920 but the typed report covers the years 1915–1929.

57 Annual Report of The Major General Commandant of the Marine Corps for the fiscal year, 1930, p. 17. Source found in various places including Marine Archives Haiti, Operations, Historical Outline of Military Occupation of Haiti.

58 Marine Archives Haiti, Commendations, "Letter of Commendation from The Major General Commandant to First Sergeant John F. Fitzgerald-Brown, U.S.M.C, June 19, 1930."

59 "Report of the President's Commission for the Study and Review of Conditions in the Republic of Haiti," March 26, 1930. Record Group 127.

60 Sylvain-Bouchereau, *Haïti et ses femmes*, 86. The Forbes Commission made casual reference to the women's protest, writing, "Women, singing the same songs, thronged the rural highways," in "Report of the President's Commission for the Study and Review of Conditions in the Republic of Haiti," March 26, 1930. Record Group 127.

61 "Report of the President's Commission for the Study and Review of Conditions in the Republic of Haiti, March 26, 1930. Record Group 127; Schmidt, *United States Occupation of Haiti*, 214.

62 Marine Archives Haiti, Garde d'Haiti, History, 1930–1934 The Haitianization Period p. 121; "Report of the President's Commission for the Study and Review of Conditions in the Republic of Haiti, March 26, 1930. Record Group 127.

63 Davis, "Haiti after 1936," 443–446, 475.

64 Russell Papers, Manuscript Box 2 Haiti, Folder 5 Special Correspondence with Higher Headquarters, "Russell tendering resignation to the Secretary of State," October 6, 1930.

65 Russell Papers, Manuscript Box 2 Haiti, Folder 16 The Forbes Commission, "22-page refutation of testimony of 11 Haitian political figures who had presented complaints to the Commission," March 13, 1930.

66 "La Garde," May 31, 1931, Record Group 127. On December 26, 1931, the Garde officers noted that the play was shown by Louis Theard and that the production critiqued President Louis Borno, Record Group 127.

67 Louis Diaquor, "Tombes de Cacos," *L'Action*, June 3, 1930.

68 Monthly Intelligence Report, January–May, 1931, Record Group 45.

69 Schmidt, *United States Occupation*, 219.

70 Marine Archives Haiti, Garde d'Haiti, History, 1930–1934 The Haitianization Period p. 132. U.S. troops noted that Vincent had a "strongly nationalist government" and an "administration avowedly anti Occupation."

71 January 30, 1932, Record Group 127; Record Books, Port-au-Prince, Haiti, December 24, 1932 and February 17, 1933, Record Group 84, Records of the Foreign Service Posts of the Department of State, National Archives Records Administration, Washington, DC (hereafter Record Group 84).

72 Record Books, Port-au-Prince, Haiti, and August 7, 1933, Record Group 84; "Marines in Haiti," *Army and Navy Register*, August 12, 1933.

73 Sylvain-Bouchereau, *Haïti et ses femmes*, 87.

74 Castor, *L'occupation américaine d'Haïti*, 200.

75 Address of the President at Cape Haitien, Haiti, July 5, 1934, Collection FDR-PPF, President's Personal File, 1933–1945, Franklin D. Roosevelt, Papers as President, Franklin D. Roosevelt Presidential Library and Museum, Hyde Park, New York; "Final Ceremonies in Haiti," *Marine Corps Gazette*, November 19, 1934. For additional information on how the Garde continued to foster Haiti's dependence on the U.S, see Castor's section "The New Militarianism," in *L'occupation américaine d'Haïti*.

76 "7 Important Events in the District, con't" [documents events from May 14, 1934 through February 22, 1935. Record Group 127.

77 US Consular Records, July 5 and August 1, 1934; "Haiti-Evacuation of Marine Forces of Occupation," Record Group 127.

78 "Haiti-Evacuation of Marine Forces of Occupation," Record Group 127. The source notes the departure of "79 officers and 747 enlisted men . . . [who] returned to the U.S. on board the U.S.S. WOODCOCK, BRIDGE, ARGONNE, and U.S.A.T. CHATEAU THIERRY."

Chapter 7   Second Revolution

1 Selden Rodman, *Renaissance in Haiti: Popular Painters in the Black Republic* (New York: Pellegrini and Cudahy, 1948), 27.

2 In a telegram to President Roosevelt, President Vincent expressed: "I am happy at the moment when the last Marines are embarking to renew to you the assurance of my gratitude, that of the Government, and of the Haitian people for your generous and intelligent policy of the good neighbor which has effectively aided me in accomplishing national liberation and which assures the continuation of the cordial relations now existing between our two countries." August 15, 1934, Record Group 127.

3 Reciprocal Trade Agreement between the United States of America and Haiti, Executive Agreement Series, No. 78, March 28, 1935, Record Group 127.

4 Smith, *Red and Black in Haiti*, 29.

5 For additional information and examples on some of these loans and policies, see Castor, *L'occupation américaine d'Haïti*, 220–225.

6 Smith, *Red and Black in Haiti*, 188.

7 Record Book, December 8 and 12, 1941, Department of State General Records, 1933–1957, Port-au-Prince, Haiti, Record Group 84; *Le Nouvelliste*, January 4, 1945.

8 Castor, *L'occupation américaine d'Haïti*, 220–225.

9 For additional information on Lescot's and Estimé's rule, see Castor's section "Black Oligarchy" in *L'occupation Américaine d'Haïti*.

10 Castor, *L'occupation Américaine d'Haïti*, 220–223.

11 *Le Nouvelliste*, April 18, 1945; May 27, 1945; and December 25, 1945.

12 Smith, *Red and Black in Haiti*, 133.

13 Marine Archives Haiti, Annual Reports, Annual Report Gendarmerie d'Haiti, 1923, p. 3.

14 Rodman, *Renaissance in Haiti*, 35.

15 Millet also describes how Péralte's tomb became a pilgrimage site in *Les paysans haïtiens*, 87.

16 The painting can be found at http://collection.mam.org/details.php?id=4141.

17 Rodman, *Renaissance in Haiti*, 28.

18 Smith, *Red and Black in Haiti*, 72–76.

19 Sylvain-Bouchereau, *Haïti et ses femmes*, 96.

20 Smith, *Red and Black in Haiti*, 93.

21 Cary Hector, Claude Moise, and Émile Olivier, *1946–1976: Trente ans de Pouvoir Noir en Haïti*, vol. 1, *L'explosion de 1946: Bilan et Perspectives* (LaSalle, QC: Collectif Paroles, 1976), 22.

22 Sylvain-Bouchereau, *Haïti et ses femmes*, 97.

23 Sylvain-Bouchereau, *Haïti et ses femmes*, 100.

24 Sylvain-Bouchereau, *Haïti et ses femmes*, 101.

Chapter 8   Péralte Resurrected

1 Note about Legislation Passed Giving Suffrage to the Women of Haiti, February 1, 1957, Record Group 59; Sylvain-Bouchereau, *Haïti et ses femmes*, 95; Nicholls notes the presence of Lydia Jeanty as the first female cabinet minister that year in *Haiti in Caribbean Context*, 128.

2 Bureau of Inter-American Affairs/Office, September 22, 1957, Record Group 59; "Memoire Relative to the Situation in Haiti," Parti National of Haiti, August 15, 1960, p. 1, Record Group 59.

3 Interview with observer, Brooklyn, NY, March 29, 2010.

4 "Memorandum of Conversation, Subject: Harassment of the Catholic Church, American Embassy, Port-au-Prince, December 12, 1960," Record Group 59.

5 Note of how President Duvalier issued a warning that he would deal severely with any further student dissidence at the reopening of schools and University on January 9th and January 16th, Record Group 59.

6 Alice Dunnigan, Educational Consultant to Robert A. Stevenson, Deputy Director Office of Caribbean and Mexican Affairs, Department of State, Washington, DC, July 6, 1961, Record Group 59.

7 Michel-Rolph Trouillot, *Haiti: State against Nation: Origins and Legacy of Duvalierism* (New York: Monthly Review,1990), 161.

8 "[Memoire Relati]ve to the Situation in Haiti, Gaston Jumelle, President of the Parti National Haitien, August 11, 1960," p. 6, Record Group 59.

9 Carolle Charles, "Gender and Politics in Contemporary Haiti: The Duvalierist State, Transnationalism, and the Emergence of a New Feminism (1980–1990)," *Feminist Studies* 21, no. 1 (1995), 135–164.

10 Interview with observer.

11 Trouillot, *Haiti: State against Nation*, 178–179.

12 "[Memoire Relati]ve to the Situation in Haiti, Gaston Jumelle, President of the Parti National Haitien," August 11, 1960, p. 12, Record Group 59.

13 Patrick Lemoine, *Fort Dimanche, Fort-La-Mort* (Port-au-Prince: Editions Regain, 1996).

14 Mr. Alex Moore, Jr. Program Officer, Mr. David J. Keogh, Deputy Director, Bernard Immerdauer, Assistant Program Economist, "Conversation with Mr. Sansaricq, Part Owner of Blanchet & Fils," February 12, 1962, Record Group 59.

15 Col. Robert D. Heinl's arrival, January 20, 1959, Record Group 59.

16 Military Assistance Program, From William A. Wieland to Mr. Rubottom, Subject: MAP Support for Haitian Army, March 18, 1960, Record Group 59.

17 Letters from President of Republic, François Duvalier at the National Palace, Port-au-Prince to President Dwight Eisenhower, July 12, 1960, Record Group 59.

18 "[Memoire Relati]ve to the Situation in Haiti, Gaston Jumelle, President of the Parti National Haitien, August 11, 1960," p. 11, Record Group 59.

19 "Letter from Louis G. Hatten to Robert Newbegin, American Embassy, Port au Prince, Haiti," October 10, 1960," Record Group 59. Duvalier released Kouri on February 10, 1961, in same record collection.

20 Letter from Robert Newbegin to Norman Warner, Officer in Charge of Haitian Affairs, November 28, 1960. Record Group 59.

21 "Memorandum of Conversation. Subject Political Developments and Views, Mexican Embassy, Port-au-Prince. Mr. Francisco Vazquez Treserra, Mexican Ambassador to Haiti and Mr. Philip P. Williams, Counselor of Embassy, February 2, 1961." Record Group 59.

22 "Memorandum of Conversation. Subject Political Developments and Views, Mexican Embassy, Port-au-Prince. Mr. Francisco Vazquez Treserra, Mexican Ambassador to Haiti and Mr. Philip P. Williams, Counselor of Embassy, February 2, 1961." Record Group 59.

23 Letter from Mrs. William F. Frome, Jr. Cataño, Puerto Rico to President Kennedy, March 20, 1963. Record Group 59.

24 Secret List of Haitian Opposition Personalities, pp. 1–3, Container 4, 1962, Record Group 59.

25 National Security Action Memorandum NO. 246, McGeorge Bundy to The Secretary of State, The Secretary of Defense, and The Director of Central Intelligence, May 23, 1963, Record Group 59.

26 Note on Tomb of Duval Duvalier in Port-au-Prince, May 29, 1959, Record Group 59.

27 "[Memoire Relati]ve to the Situation in Haiti, Gaston Jumelle, President of the Parti National Haitien, August 11, 1960," Record Group 59.

28 "[Memoire Relati]ve to the Situation in Haiti, Gaston Jumelle, President of the Parti National Haitien, August 11, 1960," Record Group 59.

29 Alexis, *In the Flicker of an Eyelid*.

30 Note: "5 Haitian-an alleged Cuban inspired revolt. Group were captured in Northern Haiti," April 28, 1961, Record Group 59.

31 In Intelligence Note 334 from INR-Thomas L. Hughes to the Secretary Through, Subject: Haiti: Duvalier Cracks Down on Communist, the writer noted, "Duvalier has mounted a campaign apparently aimed at crushing the small communist movement in Haiti. More than 100 suspected communists, including known leaders of the movement, have been arrested . . . , and a number have probably been executed," May 1, 1969, Central Files 1967–69, POL 23–7 HAI, Record Group 59; Edwidge Danticat, *Create Dangerously: The Immigrant Artist at Work* (New York: Vintage, 2011).

32 Dom Bonafede, "10,000 Haitian Exiles Want Refuge Here, Say Benoit," *Miami Herald*, September 13, 1963.

33 Carlos Martinez, "Men Behind Invasion Plot Are Contrast in Ideologies," *Miami Herald*, January 4, 1967.

34 Carlos Martinez, "Story of an Invasion that Never Happened," *Miami Herald*, November 24, 1966. A follow-up article noted the sentence given to these men, with Masferrer receiving four years, an American Martin Francis Xavier Casey given nine months, and Reverend Georges sixty days; Margaret Carroll, "Five Haitians Invaders Dealt Prison Terms," *Miami Herald*, February 29, 1968.

35 Martha Weirman Lear, *New York's Haitians: Working, Waiting, Watching BéBé Doc, New York Times,* October 10, 1971.

36 Weirman Lear, *New York's Haitians,* and Joe Crankshaw, "Alleged Secret Policeman Tells of Arrests, Torture," *Miami Herald,* November 24, 1979.

37 An article in *Le Nouvelliste* noted that the Planning Commission in New York estimated that the number of Haitian residents in the city's five boroughs was 200,000. *Le Nouvelliste,* September 25, 1972; *Le Matin,* November 4, 1976. Additionally, in 1984, *Le Nouvelliste* reported on the presence of 200,000 undocumented Haitians and 34,000 legal migrants in the Dominican Republic.

38 *Le Nouvelliste,* June 8, 1984.

39 Jonathan D. Salant, "Dade Oaks Relocation Aid Pact," November 5, 1980; Gene Miller and Guillermo Martinez, "102 Marooned, Then Ignored," November 8, 1980; and Brenda Ealy, "Kentucky Lawyers not Ready for Haitian Hearings," August 21, 1981; articles courtesy of the Cuban Heritage Collection, University of Miami Libraries, Coral Gables, Florida (hereafter Cuban Heritage Collection).

40 Brenda Ealy, "Detention Camps Add to Illegal-Alien Fiasco," June 7, 1981; Brenda Ealy, "Haitian Killing Said to Prove Repression," November 1, 1980; [List of names and birthdates from] DETAINED EXCLUSION KROME, April 7, 1981; Cuban Heritage Collection.

41 "The Other Refugees," *Wall Street Journal,* April 22, 1980; Cuban Heritage Collection.

42 Jack Anderson, "Immigration Applies Political Catch 22 to Haiti's Refugees," *Miami Herald,* March 25, 1979..

43 Brenda Ealy, "Haitian Killing Said to Prove Repression," November 1, 1980; Cuban Heritage Collection.

44 "Journey's End is Death for Some," October 28, 1979; Richard Moran, "Haitians Prefer Death to Trip Back," *Miami Herald,* November 12, 1980; Cuban Heritage Collection.

45 Francis Ward, "Deported Refugees Wind up in Haitian Prisons," September 11, 1979; Cuban Heritage Collection.

46 On October 2, 1984, and December 5, 1984, articles in *Le Nouvelliste* mentioned the repatriation of Haitian boat people. On January 15, 1986, there is also mention of Haitian repatriation.

47 François Pierre-Louis Jr., *Haitians in New York City: Transnationalism and Hometown Associations* (Gainesville: University Press of Florida, 2006), and Michel S. Laguerre, *Diasporic Citizenship: Haitian Americans in Transnational America* (New York: St. Martin's, 1998).

48 Marvine Howe, "Haitians Quietly Find Better Life in the City, Despite Their Fears," *New York Times,* May 22, 1984, B1.

49 Elizabeth Mary McCormick, "HIV-Infected Haitian Refugees: An Argument against Exclusion," *Georgetown Immigrant Law Journal* 7, no. 1 (March 1993), 149–171.

50 Yvon "Kapi" André, *Mizik Sou Brooklyn Bridge,* Afro-Caribbean Project, 2014, compact disc.

51 Cuban Heritage Collection, Box 20: Haitian Refugee Center. These folders contain materials on the 1974 formation of the Haitian American Community of Dade County (HACAD), the Haitian Refugee Center in Miami, Florida, under the Reverend Jean Juste, Cuban Heritage Collection. Thanks to François Pierre-Louis Jr. for clarifying who started the organization.

52 Pierre-Louis, *Haitians in New York City,* 36; and Kathleen Teltsch, "Haitians in City to Study Creole as Literacy Aid," *New York Times,* October 24, 1983.

53 Pierre-Louis, *Haitians in New York City*, 43.

54 Marlene Laurent, a Haitian woman exiled to the United States in 1980, led the Charlemagne Péralte Center in the Crown Heights section of Brooklyn. While her insights as the executive director of this center and from her identities as a Black immigrant female would have been enlightening, I have not yet located Laurent for an interview. The Péralte Center no longer exists as its own entity but is still part of the Haitian Centers Council. Marvin Howe, "Haitians Quietly Find Better Life in the City, Despite Their Fears," *New York Times*, May 22, 1984, B1.

55 *Le Nouvelliste*, January 18 and 27, April 7, June 6, September 1, November 21, 1972; *Le Nouvelliste*, January 15 and 24, 1976, and *Le Matin*, May 11, July 16, 1976.

56 Trouillot, *Haiti: State against Nation*, 220.

57 Trouillot, *Haiti: State against Nation*, 217.

58 "Visite d'Une Commission Militaire d'Enquête au Cap Haitien," *Le Nouvelliste*, January 29, 1986 and Trouillot, *Haiti: State against Nation*, 226.

59 *Le Nouvelliste*, February 11, 1986.

60 *Le Nouvelliste*, April 16, 1986. The writer declared that Christopher Columbus did not discover America.

61 Trouillot, *Silencing the Past*, 155.

62 *Le Nouvelliste*, April 16, 1986.

63 Gérald Brisson's argument about Haiti under Duvalier rule as a "parasitic and wasteful state" is found in his text, Brisson, *Les relations agraires dans Haïti contemporaine* (Mexico City: Mimeo, 1968).

64 Manifeste et Programme Politique du Front Charlemagne P[é]ralte de Liberation Nationale (Manifesto and Political Program of the Charlemagne P[é]ralte National Liberation Front), 29. University of Florida, Gainesville, Latin American and Caribbean Collection.

65 Manifeste et Programme Politique, 29.

66 Trouillot, *Haiti State against Nation*, chapters 7 and 8.

67 Manifeste et Programme Politique, 29–30.

68 Manifeste et Programme Politique, 40.

69 Manifeste et Programme Politique, 38.

70 Manifeste et Programme Politique, 48–49.

71 Manifeste et Programme Politique, 39.

72 Manifeste et Programme Politique, 49.

73 Manifeste et Programme Politique, 49.

74 Manifeste et Programme Politique, 49.

75 Manifeste et Programme Politique, 31.

76 *Le Nouvelliste*, June 12, 1986.

77 *Le Nouvelliste*, April 4, April 16, May 19, June 30, July 18, July 28, and November 13, 1986.

78 Trouillot, *Haiti: State against Nation*, 225.

79 Trouillot, *Haiti: State against Nation*, 226.

80 Trouillot, *Haiti: State against Nation*, 227.

81 "Open Letter to the Director of Schools in Port-au-Prince, National Minister of Education," *Le Nouvelliste*, December 1986.

82 "The Debate of the Day Surrounding the Constitutional Project," *Le Nouvelliste*, December 18, 1986.

83 Trouillot, *Haiti: State against Nation*, 224 and 227.

Chapter 9 Liberation with Péralte

1 Robert Fatton Jr. *Haiti's Predatory Republic: The Unending Transition to Democracy* (Boulder, CO: Lynne Reiner, 2002), 59–60; Alex Dupuy, *Haiti in the New World Order: The Limits of the Democratic Revolution* (Boulder, CO: Westview, 1997), 49–50; and Trouillot, *Haiti: State against Nation*, 218.

2 "Les protestations contre tout départ du Père Aristide," *Le Nouvelliste*, May 19, 1986.

3 Raymond A. Joseph, *Haiti Observateur* 30, no. 50 (December 8–15, 2004), 15.

4 Jean-Bertrand Aristide and Christopher Wargny. *Aristide: An Autobiography* (Ossing, NY: Orbis, 1993), 191.

5 Aristide and Wargny, *Aristide*, 203.

6 Sound recording, author's personal collection.

7 Nicholas Rossier, dir., *Aristide and the Endless Revolution*, Baraka Productions, 2005.

8 Audio Recording, "Lavalas and Charlemagne Péralte," 2:08 minutes (author's personal file).

9 Dupuy's *Haiti in the New World Order* has a riveting analysis of Aristide's critique of the Church on pages 74–79.

10 *L'Union*, November 26 and 27, 1991.

11 *Le Nouvelliste*, October 18, November 13, November 20, and December 6, 1990.

12 Dupuy, *Haiti in the New World Order*, 81.

13 Dupuy, *Haiti in the New World Order*, 89.

14 Haitian scholars Alex Dupuy and Robert Fatton, and Aristide himself—have scrutinized his politics and administration of Haiti from 1990 and 2004.

15 *L'Union*, November 26 and 27, 1991.

16 *L'Union*, November 26 and 27, 1991.

17 Howard French, "Aristide Seeks More than Moral Support," *New York Times*, September 27, 1992; French argues: "His salutations have long invoked the name of Charlemagne Péralte, a leader of the Haitian resistance to the United States' occupation early in the century, so he himself recognizes the trickiness of calling for stronger American measures."

18 Interview with drummer, August 4, 2007, Port-au-Prince, Haiti.

19 Fatton, *Haiti's Predatory Republic*, chapter 4.

20 Elaine Sciolino, "The Last Time the Marines Landed, They Stayed for 19 Years," *New York Times*, May 22, 1994, E5. The author noted: "When he ran for president, he regularly saluted the crowds with the name of Charlemagne P[é]ralte, an army officer who resigned to lead the guerrilla fight against the first occupation. . . . It makes some officials in Washington wonder whether Father Aristide would turn on his own liberators after riding back into power on their wings."

21 "New Protectorate Won't Do in Haiti," *Haiti Observateur*, , April 23, 2003.

22 Interview with drummer.

Chapter 10 Péralte Will Never Die; He Remains Alive in Popular Memory

1 Jacqueline Charles, "Aristide Pushes for Restitution from France," *Miami Herald*, December 18, 2003. A video of President Aristide delivering this speech is available at https://www.youtube.com/watch?v=S8ywg8YOJhE.

2 These momentous occasions inspired *Haiti Fights Back* and its examination of the use of collective national memory for resistance.

3 Wyclef Jean, *Welcome to Haiti Creole 101*, Sak Pasé Records, KOC-CD-5783, 2004. LP.

4 Interview with professor, July 27, 2007, Port-au-Prince, Haiti.
5 Interview with professor, July 27, 2007, Port-au-Prince, Haiti.
6 Interview with Péralte's granddaughter, August 18, 2007, Hinche, Haiti.
7 Lila Abu-Lughod, "The Romance of Resistance: Tracing Transformations of Power through Bedouin Women," *American Ethnologist* 17, no. 1 (February 1990), 41–55.

Bibliography

Primary Sources

ARCHIVES AND MANUSCRIPT COLLECTIONS

Haiti
Bibliothèque Nationale, Port-au-Prince
Saint-Louis Gonzague, Port-au-Prince

United States
Beinecke Rare Book and Manuscript Library, Yale University
Cuban Heritage Collection, University of Miami Libraries, Coral Gables, Florida
Franklin D. Roosevelt, Papers as President, Franklin D. Roosevelt Presidential Library
    and Museum, Hyde Park, New York
Latin American Collection, University of Florida, Gainesville, Florida
Papers of Frederick Douglass, Library of Congress, Manuscript Division
Foreign Relations of the United States, Robert Lansing Papers, 1914–1920, Library
    of Congress, Manuscript Division
Marine Corps Archives and Special Collections, Archives Branch, Marine Corps
    History Division, Gray Research Center, Quantico, VA

Personal Papers Collections
Papers of John H. Russell Jr., Marine Corps Archives and Special Collections, Gray
    Research Center, Quantico, VA
Papers of Smedley D. Butler, Reference Collection, Marine Corps History Division,
    Quantico, VA

United States National Archives Records Administration I, Washington, DC
Record Group 38, Records of the Office of the Chief of Naval Operations
Record Group 45, Naval Records Collection
Record Group 84, Records of the Foreign Service Posts of the Department of State
Record Group 127, Records of the United States Marine Corps

United States National Archives Records Administration II, College Park, MD
Record Group 59, General Records of the Department of State
Record Group 80, General Records of the Department of the Navy

Interviews with the Author
Anonymous, Port-au-Prince, Haiti, July 17, 2007
Author, New York, October 24, 2010
Charlemagne Péralte's granddaughter, Hinche, Haiti, August 18, 2007
Charlemagne Péralte's son, Port-au-Prince, Haiti, August 2007
Charlemagne Péralte's stepson, Hinche, Haiti, August 18, 2007
Community activist, Hinche, Haiti, August, 18, 2007
Drummer, Port-au-Prince, Haiti, August 4, 2007
Madame A, Brooklyn, NY, March 28, 2010
Observer, Brooklyn, NY, March 29, 2010
Professor, Port-au-Prince, Haiti, July 27, 2007
Radio personality, Miami, FL., August 29, 2008

Journals, Newspapers, and Periodicals

L'Action (Haiti)
Army and Navy Journal
Bleu et Rouge
Daily Financial America
Haïti Observateur
The Leatherneck
Marine Corps Gazette
Le Matin (Haiti)
Miami Herald
Le Moniteur (Haiti)

Nation
Negro World
New York Herald
New York Times
Le Nouvelliste (Haiti)
Pacific Appeal
La Plume (Haiti)
Recruiter's Bulletin
L'Union (Haiti)

PUBLISHED PRIMARY SOURCES

Baker, C. S. "Some Colorful Haitian History." *U.S. Naval Institute Proceedings* 50, no. 255 (May 1924): 723–743.

Boyer, Jean-Pierre. *Correspondence Relative to the Emigration to Hayti, of the Free People of Colour in the United States Together with the Instructions to the Agent.* New York: Mahlon Day, 1824.

Coffey, R. B. "A Brief History of the Intervention in Haiti." *U.S. Naval Institute Proceedings* 48, no. 234 (August 1922): 1325–1344.

Davis, H. P. *Black Democracy: The Story of Haiti.* New York: Biblo and Tannen, 1967.

———. "Haiti after 1936: So Far Intervention Has Failed." *Outlook and Independent,* March 19, 1930.

Desroy, Annie. *Le Joug.* Port-au-Prince: Imprimerie Modelé, 1934.

Douglas, Paul H. "The American Occupation of Haiti I." *Political Science Quarterly* 42, no. 2 (June 1927): 228–258.

Garrigus, John, trans. *Le Code Noir ou recueil des reglements rendus jusqu'à present.* Paris: Prault, 1767. Reprinted by Société d'Histoire de la Guadeloupe, 1980.

Jefferson, Thomas. *Notes on the State of Virginia.* Baltimore, MD: W. Pechin, 1800.

"Journey's End is Death for Some," *Miami Herald,* October 28, 1978.

Malcom, Thomas S. "The Republic of Hayti." *Pacific Appeal,* May 31, 1873.

Manifeste et programme politique du Front Charlemagne P[é]ralte de Liberation Nationale (Manifesto and Political Program of the Charlemagne P[é]ralte National

Liberation Front). University of Florida, Gainesville, Latin American and Caribbean Collection, [ca. 1986].

Papers Relating to the Foreign Relations of the United States, with the Address of the President to Congress, December 7, 1915. Washington, DC: US Government Printing Office, 1924.

Price-Mars, Jean. *Ainsi parla l'oncle.* Port-au-Prince: Bibliothèque Haitienne, 1928.

Redpath, James. *A Guide to Hayti.* Boston, MA: Haytian Bureau of Emigration, 1861.

Rogers, John J. "The Haitianization of the Garde d'Haiti." *The Leatherneck* 16, no. 10 (October 1933): 3–6.

Roosevelt, Theodore. *Presidential Addresses and State Papers of Theodore Roosevelt.* New York: P. F. Collier and Son, 1905.

Sannon, H. Pauléus. *Histoire de Toussaint-Louverture.* Port-au-Prince: Augustin A. Héraux, 1920.

St. John, Spencer. *Hayti, or the Black Republic.* New York: Scribner and Welford, 1889.

Sylvain-Bouchereau, Madeleine. *Haïti et ses femmes: Une étude d'évolution culturelle.* Port-au-Prince: Fardin, 1957.

"Tureene St. Juste and Louis Poux, arrest of," memo from District Commander, District of Port de Paix to Chief of the Gendarmerie, Port au Prince, April 26, 1919 (author's personal collection).

United States Senate. *Inquiry into Occupation and Administration of Haiti and Santo Domingo: Hearings before a Select Committee on Haiti and Santo Domingo.* 67th Cong., 1st and 2nd sess., 1921–1922. 2 vols. Washington, DC: Government Printing Office, 1922.

Valcin, Cléanthe (Virgile). *La blanche négresse.* Port-au-Prince: Presses Nationales d'Haiti, 1934.

Woodson, Carter G. *A Century of Negro Migration.* Washington, DC: Association for the Study of Negro Life and History, 1918.

Secondary Sources

Abu-Lughod, Lila. "The Romance of Resistance: Tracing Transformations of Power through Bedouin Women." *American Ethnologist* 17, no. 1 (February 1990): 41–55.

Adam, André-Georges. *Une crise haïtienne, 1867–1869: Sylvain Salnave.* Port-au-Prince: Henri Deschamps, 1982.

Alexis, Jacques Stephen. *In the Flicker of an Eyelid.* Translated by Carrol F. Coates and Edwidge Danticat. Charlottesville: University of Virginia Press, 2002.

Allewaert, Monique. "Superfly: François Makandal's Colonial Semiotics." *American Literature* 91, no. 3 (2019): 459–490.

Alvarez, Julia. *In the Time of Butterflies.* New York: Plume, 1995.

Aristide, Jean-Bertrand, and Christopher Wargny. *Aristide: An Autobiography.* Ossing, NY: Orbis, 1993.

Aya, Rod. "Theories of Revolution Reconsidered: Contrasting Models of Collective Violence." *Theory and Society* 8, no. 1 (1979): 39–99.

Beede, Benjamin R., ed. *The War of 1898 and U.S. Interventions, 1898–1934: An Encyclopedia.* New York: Routledge, 1994.

Bellegarde, Dantès. "President Alexandre Petion." *Phylon* 2, no. 3 (1941): 205–213.

Bellegarde-Smith, Patrick. *Haiti: The Breached Citadel.* Revised edition. Toronto, ON: Canadian Scholars Press, 2004.

Bickel, Keith B. *Mars Learning: The Marine Corps Development of Small Wars Doctrine, 1915–1940.* Boulder, CO: Westview, 2001.

Bilby, Kenneth M. *True-Born Maroons*. Gainesville: University Press of Florida, 2005.

Black, George. *The Good Neighbor: How the United States Wrote the History of Central America and the Caribbean*. New York: Pantheon, 1988.

Blok, Anton. *Honour and Violence*. Malden, MA, and Cambridge: Polity, 2001.

Bonilla, Yarimar. *Non-Sovereign Futures: French Caribbean Politics in the Wake of Disenchantment*. Chicago: University of Chicago Press, 2015.

Brisson, Gérald. *Les relations agraires dans Haïti contemporaine*. Mexico City: Mimeo, 1968.

Brunk, Samuel, and Ben Fallaw, eds. *Heroes and Cults in Latin America*. Austin: University of Texas Press, 2006.

Bulmer-Thomas, Victor. *The Economic History of Latin America Since Independence*. Cambridge: Cambridge University Press, 2003.

Calargé, Carla, Raphael Dalleo, Luis Duno-Gottberg, and Clevis Headley, eds. *Haiti and the Americas*. Jackson: University Press of Mississippi, 2013.

Calder, Bruce J. "Caudillos and *Gavilleros* versus the United States Marines: Guerrilla Insurgency during the Dominican Intervention, 1916–1924." *Hispanic American Historical Review* 58, no. 4 (1978): 649–675.

———. *The Impact of Intervention: The Dominican Republic during the U.S. Occupation of 1916–1924*. Austin: University of Texas Press, 1984.

Castor, Suzy. *La ocupación Norte Americana de Haití sus consecuencias, 1915–1934*. Mexico City: Siglo Veintiuno Editores, 1971.

———. *L'occupation américaine d'Haïti*. Port-au-Prince: Société Haïtienne d'Histoire, 1988.

Césaire, Aimé. *Discourse on Colonialism*. New York: Monthly Review, 1972.

Chancy, Myriam J. A. *Framing Silence: Revolutionary Novels by Haitian Women*. New Brunswick, NJ: Rutgers University Press, 1997.

Charles, Carolle. "Gender and Politics in Contemporary Haiti: The Duvalierist State, Transnationalism, and the Emergence of a New Feminism (1980–1990)." *Feminist Studies* 21, no. 1 (1995): 134–164.

Chomsky, Aviva, and Aldo Lauria-Santiago, eds. *Identity and Struggle at the Margins of the Nation State: The Laboring Peoples of Central America and the Hispanic Caribbean*. Durham, NC: Duke University Press, 1998.

Clark, Alexis. "How the History of Blackface Is Rooted in Racism." History website, February 15, 2019. http://www.history.com/news/blackface-history-racism-origins.

Courlander, Harold. *Haiti Singing*. Chapel Hill: University of North Carolina Press, 1939.

Da Cunha, Euclides. *Rebellion in the Backlands*. Translated by Samuel Putnam. Chicago: University of Chicago Press, 1944.

Danticat, Edwidge. *Breath, Eyes, and Memory*. New York: Vintage, 1994.

———. *Create Dangerously: The Immigrant Artist at Work*. New York: Vintage, 2011.

Dayan, Joan (Colin). *Haiti, History and the Gods*. Berkeley: University of California Press, 1995.

Dent, David W. *The Legacy of the Monroe Doctrine: A Reference Guide to U.S. Involvement in Latin America and the Caribbean*. Westport, CT: Greenwood, 1999

Dubois, Laurent. *Avengers of the New World: The Story of the Haitian Revolution*. Cambridge, MA: Harvard University Press, 2004.

———. *Haiti: The Aftershocks of History*. New York: Metropolitan, 2012.

Dubois, Laurent, and John D. Garrigus. *Slave Revolution in the Caribbean, 1789–1804: A Brief History with Documents*. New York: Bedford / St. Martins, 2016.

Dupuy, Alex. *Haiti in the New World Order: The Limits of the Democratic Revolution*. Boulder, CO: Westview, 1997.

———. *Haiti in the World Economy: Class, Race, and Underdevelopment since 1700.* Boulder, CO: Westview, 1989.

———. *The Prophet and Power: Jean Bertrand Aristide and the International Community.* Lanham, MD: Rowman and Littlefield Publishers, 2006.

Edwards, Brent Hayes. "The Uses of Diaspora." *Social Text* 19, no. 1 (2001): 45–73.

Fanon, Frantz. *Black Skin, White Masks.* Translated by Charles Lam Markmann. New York: Grove, 1967.

Fatton, Robert, Jr. *Haiti's Predatory Republic: The Unending Transition to Democracy.* Boulder, CO: Lynne Reiner, 2002.

Ferguson, James. *Papa Doc, Baby Doc: Haiti and the Duvaliers.* New York: Blackwell, 1987.

Fick, Carolyn E. *The Making of Haiti: The Saint Domingue Revolution from below.* Knoxville: University of Tennessee Press, 1990.

Firmin, Anténor. *The Equality of the Human Races: Positivist Anthropology.* Translated by Asselin Charles. New York: Garland, 2000.

Fischer, Sibylle. *Modernity Disavowed: Haiti and the Cultures of Slavery in the Age of Revolution.* Durham, NC: Duke University Press, 2004.

Fombrun, Odette R. *Histoire d'Haïti: De l'indépendence à nos jours.* Port-au-Prince: Henri Deschamps, 1990.

Fonseca Amador, Carlos. *Long Live Sandino.* Managua, Free Nicaragua: Department of Propaganda and Political Education of the FSLN, 1984.

Fuentes, Marisa J. *Dispossessed Lives: Enslaved Women, Violence, and the Archive.* Philadelphia: University of Pennsylvania Press, 2016.

Gaffield, Julia. "I Have Avenged America." Haiti and the Atlantic World, August 2, 2013. https://haitidoi.com/2013/08/02/i-have-avenged-america/.

Gaillard, Roger. *Les blancs débarquent, 1919–1934: La guérilla de Batraville.* Port-au-Prince: Roger Gaillard, 1981.

———. *Les cent-jours de Rosalvo Bobo; ou, Une mise à mort politique.* Port-au-Prince: Presses Nationales, 1973.

———. *Charlemagne Péralte: Le Caco.* Port-au-Prince: Roger Gaillard, 1982.

———. *La guérilla de Batraville.* Port-au-Prince: Le Natal, 1983

———. *Premier écrasement du cacoïsme.* Port-au-Prince: Roger Gaillard, 1981.

Gaillard, Roger, and Gusti-Klara Gaillard-Pourchet. *Le cacoïsme bourgeois contre Salnave, 1867–1870.* Port-au-Prince: Fondation Roger Gaillard, 2003.

Geggus, David P., ed. *The Impact of the Haitian Revolution on the Atlantic World.* Columbia: University of South Carolina Press, 2001.

———. *Haitian Revolutionary Studies.* Bloomington: Indiana University Press, 2002.

Gilroy, Paul. *The Black Atlantic: Modernity and Double Consciousness.* Cambridge, MA: Harvard University Press, 1993.

Hector, Cary, Claude Moise, and Émile Ollivier. *1946–1976: Trente ans de Pouvoir Noir en Haïti.* Vol. 1, *L'explosion de 1946: Bilan et Perspectives.* LaSalle, QC: Collectif Paroles, 1976.

Hobsbawm, Eric J. *Bandits.* London: Weidenfeld and Nicolson, 1969.

Higginson, John E. *A Working Class in the Making: Belgian Colonial Labor Policy, Private Enterprise, and the African Mineworker, 1907–1951.* Madison: University of Wisconsin Press, 1989.

Hopkirk, J. G. *An Account of the Insurrection in St. Domingo, begun in August 1791 taken from authentic sources.* Edinburgh: William Blackwood, 1833. http://digitalcollections.nypl.org/items/510d47e3-feec-a3d9-e040-e00a18064a99.

Hunt, Alfred N. *Haiti's Influence on Antebellum America: Slumbering Volcano in the Caribbean.* Baton Rouge: Louisiana State University Press, 1988.

Immerman, Richard. *The CIA in Guatemala: The Foreign Policy of Intervention.* Austin: University of Texas Press, 1982.

James, C. L. R. *The Black Jacobins: Toussaint L'Ouverture and the San Domingo Revolution.* New York: Vintage, 1963.

Jordan, Winthrop D. *The White Man's Burden: Historical Origins of Racism in the United States.* New York: Oxford University Press, 1974.

Joseph, Gilbert M., Catherine C. LeGrand, and Ricardo D. Salvatore, eds. *Close Encounters of Empire: Writing the Cultural History of U.S.–Latin American Relations.* Durham, NC: Duke University Press, 1998.

Katz, Friedrich. *The Life and Times of Pancho Villa.* Stanford, CA: Stanford University Press, 1998.

Kelley, Robin D. G. "'We Are Not What We Seem': Rethinking Black Working-Class Opposition in the Jim Crow South." *Journal of American History* 80, no. 1 (1993): 75–112.

LaFeber, Walter. *The New Empire: An Interpretation of American Expansion.* Ithaca, NY: Cornell University Press, 1963.

Laguerre, Michel S. *Diasporic Citizenship: Haitian Americans in Transnational America.* New York: St. Martin's, 1998.

Langley, Lester D. *The Banana Wars: An Inner History of American Empire, 1900–1934.* Lexington: University of Kentucky Press, 1983.

———. *The Banana Wars: United States Intervention in the Caribbean, 1898–1934.* Lexington: University of Kentucky Press, 1985.

LeBlanc, Maude. "Haiti Is No Stranger to War Crimes of the Former Colonial Powers which Now Make up NATO." *Haiti Progrès*, November 2, 2005.

Lemoine, Patrick. *Fort Dimanche, Fort-La-Mort.* Port-au-Prince: Editions Regain, 1996.

Lundius, Jan, and Mats Lundhal. *Peasants and Religion: A Socioeconomic Study of Dios Olivorio and the Palma Sola Movement in the Dominican Republic.* New York: Routledge, 2000.

Maguire, Robert, and Scott Freeman, eds. *Who Owns Haiti? People, Power, and Sovereignty.* Gainesville: University Press of Florida, 2017.

Mallon, Florencia E. *Peasant and Nation: The Making of Postcolonial Mexico and Peru.* Berkeley: University of California Press, 1995.

Mayes, April J. *The Mulatto Republic: Class, Race, and Dominican National Identity.* Gainesville: University Press of Florida, 2015.

McCarroll, Jean, ed. *The Negro in the Congressional Record: Eighteenth and Nineteen Congress, 1824–1827.* New York: Bergman, 1971.

McCormick, Elizabeth Mary. "HIV-Infected Haitian Refugees: An Argument against Exclusion." *Georgetown Immigrant Law Journal* 7, no. 1 (March 1993): 149–171.

McCrocklin, James H. *Garde d'Haiti, 1915 to 1934: Twenty Years of Organization and Training by the United States Marine Corps.* Annapolis, MD: United States Naval Institute, 1956.

McLeod, Marc C. "Undesirable Aliens: Race, Ethnicity, and Nationalism in the Comparison of Haitian and British West Indian Immigrant Workers in Cuba, 1912–1939." *Journal of Social History* 31, no. 3 (spring 1998): 599–623.

Ménard, Nadève. "Foreign Impulses in Annie Desroy's *Le Joug.*" In *Haiti and the Americas,* edited by Carla Calargé, Raphael Dalleo, Luis Duno-Gottberg, and Clevis Headley, 161–174. Jackson: University Press of Mississippi, 2013.

———. "The Occupied Novel: The Representation of Foreigners in Haitian Novels Written during the United States Occupation, 1915–1934." PhD diss., University of Pennsylvania, 2002.

Michel, Claudine, and Patrick Bellegarde-Smith, eds. *Vodou in Haitian Life and Culture: Invisible Powers*. New York: Palgrave Macmillan, 2007.

Michel, Georges. *Charlemagne Péralte and the First American Occupation of Haiti: UN Centenaire, 1885–1985*. Translated by Douglas Henry Daniels. Dubuque, IA: Kendall Hunt, 1995.

Miller, Jake C. *The Plight of Haitian Refugees*. New York: Praeger, 1984.

Millet, Kethly. *Les paysans haïtiens et l'occupation américaine d'Haïti, 1915–1930*. LaSalle, QC: Collectif Paroles, 1978.

Millett, Allan R. *Semper Fidelis: The History of the United States Marine Corps*. New York: Macmillan, 1980.

Millspaugh, Arthur Chester. *Haiti under American Control, 1915–1930*. Boston, MA: World Peace Foundation, 1931.

Mitchell, Nancy. *The Danger of Dreams: German and American Imperialism in Latin America*. Chapel Hill: University of North Carolina Press, 1999.

Montague, Ludwell. *Haiti and the United States, 1714–1938*. Durham, NC: Duke University Press, 1940.

Moore, Barrington, Jr. *Injustice: The Social Bases of Obedience and Revolt*. White Plains, NY: M. E. Sharpe, 1978.

Nelson, William Javier. *Almost a Territory: America's Attempt to Annex the Dominican Republic*. Newark: University of Delaware Press, 1991.

Neptune, Harvey R. *Caliban and the Yankees: Trinidad and the United States Occupation*. Chapel Hill: University of North Carolina Press, 2009.

Nicholls, David. *From Dessalines to Duvalier: Race, Colour, and National Independence in Haiti*. New Brunswick, NJ: Rutgers University Press, 1996.

———. *Haiti in Caribbean Context: Ethnicity, Economy, and Revolt*. Houndsmills, Basingstoke: Palgrave Macmillian, 1985.

Ott, Thomas. *The Haitian Revolution, 1789–1804*. Knoxville: University of Tennessee Press, 1973.

Pamphile, Leon D. *Contrary Destinies: A Century of America's Occupation, Deoccupation, and Reoccupation of Haiti*. Gainesville: University Press of Florida, 2015.

———. "The NAACP and the American Occupation of Haiti." *Phylon* 47, no. 1 (1986): 91–100.

Paquin, Lyonel. *The Haitians: Class and Color Politics*. New York: Multitype, 1983.

Pérez, Louis A. Jr., *Cuba under the Platt Amendment, 1902–1934*. Pittsburgh, PA: University of Pittsburgh Press, 1991.

———. *Cuba between Empires, 1878–1902*. Pittsburgh, PA: University of Pittsburgh Press 1998.

Pierre-Charles, Gérard. *L'Économie Haitienne et Sa Voie de la Développement*. Paris: Maisonneuve et Larose, 1967.

Pierre-Louis, François, Jr., *Haitians in New York City: Transnationalism and Hometown Associations*. Gainesville: University Press of Florida, 2006.

Plummer, Brenda Gayle. "The Afro-American Response to the Occupation of Haiti, 1915–1934." *Phylon* 43, no. 2 (1982): 125–143.

———. *Haiti and the Great Powers, 1902–1915*. Baton Rouge: Louisiana State University Press, 1988.

———. *Haiti and the United States: The Psychological Moment*. Athens: University of Georgia Press, 2003.

———. *Rising Wind: Black Americans and U.S. Foreign Affairs, 1935–1960*. Durham: University of North Carolina Press, 1996.

Polyné, Millery. *From Douglass to Duvalier: U.S. African Americans, Haiti, and Pan Americanism, 1870–1964*. Gainesville: University Press of Florida, 2011.

———. *The Idea of Haiti: Rethinking Crisis and Development*. Minneapolis: University of Minnesota Press, 2013.

Poujol Oriol, Paulette. "La femme haïtienne dans la littérature: Problèmes de l'écrivain." *Journal of Haitian Studies* 3/4 (1997–1998): 80–86.

Pressley-Sanon, Toni. *Istwa across the Water: Haitian History, Memory, and the Cultural Imagination*. Gainesville: University Press of Florida, 2017.

Price-Mars, Jean. *So Spoke the Uncle / Ainsi parla l'oncle*. Translated by Magdaline W. Shannon. Washington, DC: Three Continents, 1983.

Ramsey, Kate. *Vodou and Power in Haiti: The Spirits and the Law*. Chicago: University of Chicago Press, 2011.

———. "Without One Ritual Note: Folklore Performance and the Haitian State, 1935–1946." *Radical History Review* 84 (2002): 7–42.

Rausch, Jane. "Dartiguenave, Philippe Sudre." In *The War of 1898 and U.S. Interventions, 1898–1934: An Encyclopedia*, edited by Benjamin R. Beede, 157–158. New York: Routledge, 1994.

Renda, Mary A. *Taking Haiti: Military Occupation and the Culture of U.S. Imperialism 1915–1940*. Chapel Hill: University of North Carolina, 2001.

Rodman, Selden. *Renaissance in Haiti: Popular Painters in the Black Republic*. New York: Pellegrini and Cudahy, 1948.

Ronfeldt, David. *U.S. Involvement in Central America: Three Views from Honduras*. Santa Monica, CA: Rand Corporation, 1989.

Sanders, Grace Louise. "*La Voix des Femmes*: Haitian Women's Rights, National Politics and Black Activism in Port-au-Prince and Montreal, 1934–1986." PhD diss., University of Michigan, 2013.

Schmidt, Hans. *Maverick Marine: General Smedley D. Butler and the Contradictions of American Military History*. Lexington: University Press of Kentucky, 1987.

———. *The United States Occupation of Haiti, 1915–1934*. New Brunswick, NJ: Rutgers University Press, 1971.

Scott, James. "Resistance without Protest and without Organization: Peasant Opposition to the Islamic Zakat and the Christian Tithe." *Comparative Studies in Society and History* 29, no. 3 (1987): 417–452.

Scott, Julius S. *The Common Wind: Afro-American Currents in the Age of the Haitian Revolution*. New York: Verso, 2018.

Seabrook, William. *The Magic Island*. New York: Harcourt, Brace, and Co., 1929.

Sepinwall, Alyssa. *Haitian History: New Perspectives*. New York: Routledge, 2013.

Shannon, Magdaline W. *Jean Price-Mars, the Haitian Elite, and the American Occupation, 1915–1935*. New York: St. Martin's, 1996.

Sheller, Mimi. "The Army of Sufferers: Peasant Democracy in the Early Republic of Haiti." *New West Indian Guide / Nieuwe West-Indische Gids* 74, no. 1/2 (2000): 33–55.

———. *Democracy after Slavery: Black Publics and Peasant Radicalism in Haiti and Jamaica*. Gainesville: University Press of Florida, 2001.

Smith, Matthew J. *Liberty, Fraternity, Exile: Haiti and Jamaica after Emancipation*. Chapel Hill: University of North Carolina Press, 2014.

———. *Red and Black in Haiti: Radicalism, Conflict, and Political Change, 1934–1957*. Chapel Hill: University of North Carolina Press, 2009.

Suggs, Henry Lewis. "The Response of the African American Press to the United States Occupation of Haiti, 1915–1934." *Journal of Negro History* 73, no. 1/4 (1988): 33–45.

Tenenbaum, Barbara A., ed. *Encyclopedia of Latin American History and Culture.* Volume 4. New York: Simon and Schuster, 1999.

Trouillot, Évelyne. *The Infamous Rosalie.* Translated by Marjorie Attignol Salvodon. Lincoln: University of Nebraska Press, 2013

Trouillot, Michel-Rolph. *Haiti: State against Nation: Origins and Legacy of Duvalierism.* New York: Monthly Review, 1990.

———. *Silencing the Past: Power and the Production of History.* 20th ed. Boston, MA: Beacon, 2015.

Turits, Richard. *Foundations of Despotism: Peasants, the Trujillo Regime, and Modernity in Dominican History.* Stanford, CA: Stanford University Press, 2002.

Ulysse, Gina A. *Why Haiti Needs New Narratives: A Post-Quake Chronicle.* Middleton, CT: Wesleyan University Press, 2015.

United Nations Security Council (UNSC). "Security Council Establishes UN Stabilization Mission in Haiti for Initial Six-Month Period." United Nations, April 30, 2004. https://www.un.org/press/en/2004/sc8083.doc.htm.

Verna, Chantalle F. *Haiti and the Uses of America: Post-U.S. Occupation Promises.* New Brunswick, NJ: Rutgers University Press, 2017.

Womack, John, Jr. *Zapata and the Mexican Revolution.* New York: Vintage, 1968.

Wucker, Michelle. *Why the Cocks Fight: Dominicans, Haitians and the Struggle for Hispaniola.* New York: Hill and Wang, 1999.

Audio and Visual Sources

André, Yvon "Kapi." *Mizik Sou Brooklyn Bridge.* Afro-Caribbean Project, 2014, compact disc.

Jean, Wyclef. *Welcome to Haiti Creole 101.* Sak Pasé Records, KOC-CD-5783, 2004. LP.

Lavalas and Charlemagne Péralte recording, compact disc, 2:08 minutes.

Ngozi Adichie, Chimamanda. "The Danger of a Single Story." TEDGlobal, 2009. http://www.ted.com/talks/chimamanda_ngozi_adichie_the_danger_of_a_single _story/transcript?language=en.

Rossier, Nicholas, dir. *Aristide and the Endless Revolution.* Baraka Productions, 2005.

Unnamed Mural of Charlemagne Péralte and Jean-Jacques Dessalines, Port-au-Prince, Haiti

Unnamed Mural of Haiti's Tug of War, Port-au-Prince

Wyclef Jean, *Welcome to Haiti Creole 101*, Sak Pasé Records, KOC-CD-5783, 2004. LP.

Index

Affiba, Geneviève, 19

Alexis, Jacques Stephen, 13, 139, 164

Aristide, Jean-Bertrand, 1, 9, 20, 182–187, 189, 190, 229n2, 229nn4–5, 229n7, 229n9, 229n14, 229n17, 229n20, 229n1; critical of U.S. imperialism, 185; defeat of Bazin, Marc, 185; image and political rhetoric, 183–184; implicating U.S. and France in Haiti's underdevelopment, 184, 190; involuntary departure from Haiti (2004), 1; letter to Woodrow Wilson, 185; submitted reparations bill to France, 190–91; U.S. assisted return to Haiti, 186–88; use of Péralte's speech against foreign powers, 183

Ayisienne (Haitian women), 17–19, 54, 87, 105, 130, 138, 140, 143, 147, 154, 155–56, 194, 195; granted local suffrage (1950), 204n45; granted national suffrage (1957), 158; historical silence on, 17; rape by U.S. soldiers, 123; struggle for suffrage and equity, 155

Batraville, Benoît, 8, 57, 59, 72, 75, 84, 85, 90, 92, 93, 98, 112–116, 120, 121, 122, 148, 195, 213n15, 216nn11–15; reported as Voduizan, 75; school teacher and *houngan* (Vodou male priest), 57

Bélair, Sanité (Suzanne), 19

Bobo, Rosalvo (M.D.), 37–38, 39–40, 42, 72, 83, 90, 120, 195, 207n15; backed by Revolutionary Committee for president, 39; desire for presidency, 37; founding member of the Revolutionary Committee, 38; framing of U.S. imperialism with the image of the U.S. eagle's wings, 40; opposed by U.S., 37–38, 42; Vodou practitioner, 57. *See also* Revolutionary Committee

Borno, Louis (Secretary of State, President), 47, 49, 135, 137, 141–142, 143, 144, 145, 151, 223n66; illusion of Haitian control, 135; "joint dictatorship" with U.S., 135; made President by U.S., 135. *See also* Russell H., Jr., John

Bwa Kayiman (21 August 1791), 16–17

Birth of a Nation, The, 110; showing at the White House (1914), 110

cacos, 2, 3, 4, 5, 6, 7, 8, 9, 10–12, 13, 14, 15, 16, 17, 19, 20, 21, 33, 34, 38, 39, 40, 43, 44, 47, 53–79, 80–99, 101–9, 111–16, 118–24, 125–28, 129, 131–34, 135–37, 138, 139–41, 142, 145, 147, 148, 149, 150, 152, 153, 156, 163, 165, 171, 174, 175, 176, 177, 178, 182, 183, 185, 186, 188, 190, 191, 192, 194, 195, 201n12, 202n21, 205n29, 208n49, 208n54, 209n2, 209–10n9, 210n23, 212nn76–77, 213n15, 214n26, 214n41, 215nn45–46, 216n11, 216n15, 217n19, 217n27, 219n49, 222n40, 223n67; assessment of movement's success, 11; as "bandits," 72; *cacoïsme,* 202n21; central to abolition movement, 55; class diversity of, 58; considered freedom fighters, peasants,

cacos (continued)
bandits, *mawons*, and guerilla fighters, 55; as defenders of Haiti, 58; First Cacos War, 73, 74; infiltration of *gendarmerie*, *corvée* system, and prisons, 60; as laborers for Haiti, 58; map of resistance zones, 100; as political movement, 10, 11, 19, 38, 72, 77, 86, 101, 103, 105, 148, 153; recruitment of men and women, 60; some acted for Haiti's good and others for personal gain, 57; war against U.S. military, 20; women members/fighters and leaders, 17, 98, 109, 120, 121. *See also* Péralte, Charlemagne; Pétion, Jean Baptiste; *taccos*;

Castro, Fidel (President), 157, 176

Chancy, Myriam J.A., 18, 204nn41–42

Christophe, Henri (King), 16, 28, 29, 67; built the Citadel, 29

Citadelle, the (Citadel Laferrière), 16, 29, 31, 33, 202n21

Codio, Misael (General), 68, 211nn42–43

Codio Affair, 144

corvée labor, 6, 11, 50–53, 57, 58, 60, 70, 72, 82, 86, 95, 103, 104, 112, 119, 148, 152, 209n69, 209n78; banned three times, 82; "camps" for, 50–51; "*corvée* killings," 52; in lieu of taxes, 50; likened to slavery, 6; purchase of exemption to, 51; torturing and killing of *corvée* labor escapees (corvées), 6; U.S. imposition of unpaid labor, 6; U.S. kidnapping of *corvées*, 57; U.S. view as tool of modernization, 50

Cuba/Cubans, 15, 20, 35, 36, 37, 48–49, 57, 65, 72, 89, 137, 143, 157, 158, 159, 160, 161, 162, 164, 167, 168, 175, 177, 186; used as pawn by Duvalier, 159;

Dartiguenave, Philippe Sudré (President), 37–38, 40, 42–43, 46, 49, 51, 52–53, 59, 63, 72, 101, 111–12, 120, 122, 123–24, 131, 134–35, 211n56, 221n22; acquiesced to U.S. financial control, 37; blamed Haitians for the destruction and chaos of the U.S. invasion, 123; decoration of U.S. soldier who killed Péralte, 111; support for U.S. military presence, 122

Dayan, Joan (Colin), equitable land distribution as cause for assassination of Dessalines, 28

dechoukaj (uprooting of Duvaliers), 170–71. *See also* Duvalier, Jean-Claude

Dessalines, Jean-Jacques (Emperor), 1, 2, 4–5, 9, 19, 20, 23, 24, 28, 29, 31, 34, 41, 55, 59, 60, 67, 91, 108, 113, 138, 152, 168, 177, 178, 183, 184, 187, 188, 189, 190, 191, 195, 207n31, 222n48; L'Acte de l'Indépendance, 4; considered a Black *nasyonalis*, 41; considered a hero in the Haitian Revolution, 1; formerly enslaved, 24; Haitian Empire, 5; and Haitian independence (1 January 1804), 4; led Battle of Vertières (1 January 1803), 4; mural with Péralte, Charlemagne, 2. *See also* Haitian Independence; Péralte, Charlemagne;

Desgraves, Cléante (Virgile Valcin), 18, 140

désoccupation (1930–1934), 8, 20, 148, 150, 153, 154, 155, 156, 165, 171, 179; as second independence, 150. *See also* political moments in Haiti

Desroy, Annie, 18, 140, 203nn38–39, 222n48

Dodio, Missal. *See* Codio, Misael

Dominican Republic, 11, 15, 20, 28, 30, 32, 51, 56, 57, 61, 66, 69, 72, 73–75, 84, 87, 89, 106, 110, 126, 128, 136, 137, 151, 157, 175, 194, 203n25, 211nn57–58, 212n61, 216n7, 219n51, 227n37. See also *gavilleros*;

Douglass, Frederick, 24, 202n22, 204n5, 204n7, 219n50; appointed to Haiti, 24. *See also* Hyppolite, Florvil

Duvalier, François (Papa Doc), 8–9, 157–70; brutal dictatorship, 8; created Volontaires de la Sécurité Nationale (1962, VSN); expelling of clergy (1958–1959), 158; letter to Eisenhower, 160–61; supported by U.S. presidents, 157; surveillance of Haitian communities in the U.S., 167; terrorist state, 158; three-tier laws enforcement structure, 159; Unity Party, 158. *See also* Tonton Macoutes; Volontaires de la Sécurité Nationale

Duvalier, Jean-Claude (Baby Doc), 158, 170–72; emergence of the idea of *dechoukaj* (uprooting) of, 170; exodus from Haiti (1986), 171; named President for life by his father, 166–67; Radio Soleil, 170. *See also* Duvalier, François

Estimé, Dumarsais (President), 151, 156, 157, 224n9; charged with practicing "Yankee imperialism," 151

Fatiman, Cécile, 16, 19, 194

Firmin, Anténor, 24–25, 28, 30–31, 139, 206n32; asserted Black people are equal to Whites, 30

Fiyet Lalo, 159, 180; as terrorist women, 159; supported François Duvalier, 159

Forbes Commission (Hoover Commission), 143, 219n48, 223n60, 223n65; acknowledged failures of U.S. occupation, 143; chaired by W. Cameron Forbes (Governor, Occupied Philippines), 143

Front Charlemagne Péralte de Liberation Nationale (FCPLN), 9, 172–79, 183, 184, 188, 228nn64–65, 228nn67–75; political party founded in 1986, 8–9

Flon, Catherine, 19

Fortuné, Lilli, 154

Gaillard, Roger, 11, 12, 32, 54, 201n12, 202n21, 206n36, 207n15, 209n2, 213n15, 216nn11–14, 217n35

gavilleros, 57, 72, 73–74, 194, 203n25; defined, 73. See also Dominican Republic

Guittone, (Madame), 19, 27

Haiti: a republic and monarchy, 28; L'Acte de l'Indépendance (1804), 4; banned slavery (1805), 23; bicentennial celebration of Independence (2004), 1, 57, 189, 190, 191, 193; financial strangulation, 26; first Constitution (1805), 4; first independent Black republic, 22; Haitian American Treaty (1915), 36, 47–53; Haitian Armed Forces for Revolution (FARH), 164; Haitian Empire, 5; Haitian Revolution (1791–1804), 1, 4, 8, 9, 10, 11, 23, 58, 85, 108, 171, 192, 202n16, 205n18, 215n50; Haitian Revolution for independence not viewed as a revolution for human rights, global emancipation, nor as example of Western Civilization, 10; indemnity agreement with France (1825), 27; internal divisions related to political control, land, and power, 26–28; independence from France (1804), 4; irony in U.S. invasion of Haiti, 22; struggle to define itself politically, 27; U.S. military withdrawal (1934), 8

Haitians: activism and art, 1–3; diasporic communities, 13, 14, 163, 167, 169, 190, 193, 194; double standard applied to

Haitian refugees (in contrast to Cuba and Vietnam), 168; fleeing the repressive Duvalier state, 168; image of Péralte as alive, not as a victim of assassination, 12; protest against U.S. invasion not spontaneous, 31; protest murals in Cité Soleil, 2–3; refugees imprisonment in the Krome detention center, 167; relocation of refugees from the Krome center to prisons in Puerto Rico, New York, and Texas, 167; Tonton Macoutes refugees in Florida, 167; uprooting of Columbus statute in Port-au-Prince, 172; U.S. classification of refugees as economic migrants, 167;

Heureuse, Claire, 19

historical nationalism, 8, 19, 192; deployed by Péralte, 19; Péralte, as central to Haitians, 8. See also nasyonalisme

Hooker, Richard S. (Marine Captain/Colonel), 73, 78, 93–98, 214n32, 214n37, 214n41

Hoover, Herbert (President), 143, 144, 222n40; creation of Forbes/Hoover Commission, 143. See also Forbes Commission

Hyppolite, Florvil (President), 24, 28; offered Haiti as a protectorate of the U.S., 28

Kreyòl (Haitian Creole), 3, 11, 17, 119, 125, 175, 194, 202n18, 203n29, 206n35; challenge in translation into English, 14–15; dismissed by U.S. military, 81; Kouto 2 bò (a double-edged knife), 11; lakou (Haitian diaspora community), 169; pas conné, 94; presence in Haitian diasporic communities in the U.S., 169; U.S. invention of terms in, 94; Voye wòch, kache men (one who throws rocks and hides their hands), 11

Lamartinière, Marie-Jeanne, 19

Lansing, Robert (Secretary of State), 25, 36, 42, 110, 204n1, 204n10, 206n5, 206n7, 206n11, 207n37, 208n39

Lescot, Élie (President), 151, 153, 154–55, 156, 224n9; assistance to WWII effort hurt Haitians, 151; opened Haiti to rubber and sisal cultivation, 151; opposed Jewish genocide in Germany, 151;

Lescot, Élie (continued)
    as pawn to U.S. economic imperialism,
    151; as postoccupation president, 151;
    support for the U.S. during WWII, 151.
    See also *désoccupation*
Ligue Féminine d'Action Sociale (1934), 147,
    155; *Ayisienne* founders, 147
L'Ouverture, Toussaint, 8, 19, 27, 29, 30, 59,
    61, 108, 138, 170, 187–88, 190, 201n5,
    216n68; and Haitian Revolution, 108;
    death in French prison, 8; never knew of
    Haiti's independence, 8

Madiou, Léonie, 154
Magdelon, (Madame), 19
massacres of Haitians: Aux Cayes Massacre
    (6 December 1929), 142; of prisoners
    ordered by President Sam (27 July 1915),
    44; River Massacre by President Trujillo
    (2 October 1937), 74
mawon/mawonage, 31, 55, 61, 85, 87, 93, 95,
    96, 194; defined, 206n35. See also *cacos*;
memory, historical/social: assemblages
    contribute to historiography, 17; collective
    remembrance, 9, 21; collective remem-
    brance of Péralte as a story about the power
    to resist and be named, 193; effort to
    explore memory of Péralte, 9; and the
    eruption of history in physical landmarks
    and people, 16; Haitians paradoxical use of
    Péralte's memory, 9; Haitian view that the
    past is not the past, 13; historical nostalgia,
    9; history as a living, tangible, accessible,
    material good, 16; Péralte's assassination
    in public forms of remembrance, 12;
    performances of history, 17. *See also* silence
Misaelcodio. *See* Codio, Misael
Morency, Antoine (General), 63, 78

nasyonalis, 3, 7, 8, 32, 33, 45–46, 47, 58, 64,
    86, 88, 125, 129, 147, 157, 192; cacos as, 136;
    contrast to nationalist, 3; defined in
    Haitian context, 3; Jean-Bertrand
    Aristide, as, 184; Kreyòl origins of term,
    3; movement, 64; Philomé Obin, as, 149.
    See also Dessalines, Jean-Jacques; Péralte,
    Charlemagne; *nasyonalisme*
nasyonalisme, 3, 4, 5, 6, 87, 90, 139, 152, 172,
    178; two-part foundation of, 5. See also
    nasyonalis

National Association for the Advancement
    of Colored People (NAACP), 70, 126, 138,
    219n51, 222nn40–41
Nicolas, Louise, 19

Obin, Philomé, 8, 127, 149, 150, 152–55, 156,
    157, 165, 166, 173, 188; artistic protest
    against Duvalier, 8; artistic protest
    against U.S. invasion, 8; *Crucifixion de
    Charlemagne Péralte pour la Liberté*, 166;
    *Les Funeralles de Héros Charlemagne
    Péralte*, 149 inclusion of Madame
    Masséna in paintings of Charlemagne
    Péralte, 149, 165; *as nasyonalis*, 149

patriotic kinship/kin, 7, 20, 38, 41, 87, 88, 89,
    90, 93, 96, 97, 103, 104, 105, 107, 108, 109,
    113, 119, 123, 140, 148, 152, 154, 165, 166,
    170, 174, 177, 183, 184, 188, 193; Aristide
    sought to incite, 183–184; as resistance
    activity, 7; link to artwork, 166; used by
    Charlemagne Péralte, as political
    strategy, 7
Péralte, Charlemagne (1885–1919), 1, 2–9,
    11–12, 13, 14, 15, 17, 18, 19, 20, 31–34, 38, 39,
    40, 41, 44–47, 53, 57, 58, 59, 60, 61, 64, 71,
    72, 74, 75, 77, 78–79, 80, 83–94, 97,
    98–99, 101, 103–9, 111–116, 120, 122, 124,
    126–27, 129, 135, 136, 137, 138, 139, 141, 143,
    147, 148, 155, 156, 182, 183, 184, 185, 186,
    187, 188, 201n3, 215n50, 201n12, 202n21,
    203n29, 203n31, 206n36, 206n39, 206n42,
    206n45, 207n33, 208nn45–46, 208n48,
    208n52, 211n58, 212n64, 213n12, 213n15,
    213n23, 214n24, 214n32, 215n48, 215n50,
    216n11, 217n35, 225n15, 228n54, 229n8,
    229n17; assassinated by U.S. (31 October
    1919), 3, 106–107; barber shop in
    Brooklyn, 14; birth (10 October 1885), 4;
    as a Black Jesus, 165; boy's school in
    Hinche, 193; *cacos* fighters of, 2;
    Charlemagne Péralte Park in Hinche, 14;
    competing historical narratives about, 3;
    continued legacy to the present, 189–95;
    deployed patriotic kinship as political
    strategy, 7; did not witness the end of
    U.S. invasion, 8; escape from prison (3
    September 1918), 83, 126; on Haitian
    stamp, 13; historical memory of in the
    U.S., 190; imprisoned at Cap Haïtien

(1918); as intellectual and guerrilla fighter, 3; as *nasyonalis*, 4, 7, 47, 129, 147; as *nasyonalis* martyr, 3, 7, 150, 157; park named after him in Montreal, Canada, 9; as patriot, savior, and *nasyonalis*, 170; posthumous impact on Haitian struggle for sovereignty and resistance to foreign occupation, 148–155, 156; public spectacle of death, 111; relative killed at prison massacre (1915), 44; reported as *Voduizan*, 75; resurrected in struggle against Duvalier regimes, 157–181; sided with Sam in opposition to Théodore, 33; as useful commentary and example of anti-U.S. imperialist ideology and action, 7; U.S. symbolic violence against, 108. *See also* cacos; Dessalines, Jean-Jacques

Péralte, Madame Masséna, 31, 45, 77–78, 98, 112, 212n77; as a Black Mary, 165; buried three of her sons, 112; Charlemagne's mother, 31; included by Philomé Obin in painting of Charlemagne Péralte, 149

Pétion, Alexandre (President), 2, 19, 28, 29, 41, 91, 152, 207n32; Pétionville, 40

Pétion, Jean Baptiste (General), 63, 78, 210n23

piquets (L'Armée de Souffrant), 19, 205n26; explained, 29

Platt Amendment (1901), 20, 48, 49, 208nn60–61; similarities to Haitian American Treaty (1915), 49

political moments in Haiti: authoritarian dynasty (1957–1986), 8; *désoccupation* (1930–1934), 8; fleeting democracy (1986–1991), 8; foreign intervention (2004–present), 8; Haitian Revolutionary Era (1791–1804), 4; populism (1946–1948), 8. *See also désoccupation*

postoccupation, 8, 151, 155, 156, 158, 179; postoccupation presidents, 156, 175

Price-Mars, Jean, 138, 139, 222n48

Puerto Rico, 15, 37, 65, 89, 143, 162, 164, 167, 194, 226n23; Lolita Lebrón, 194

Rameaux, Pierre Benoît (P. B.), 58–60, 62, 98, 120, 209n8; *cacos* leader, 58; viewed forced *corvée* labor as a form of slavery, 58

Revolutionary Committee, 38–40, 42, 43, 44, 64, 72, 78–79; advocated Haitian sovereignty, 39; attacks against U.S. military, 38; Benoît Batraville, member of

and *caco*, 72; composed of all-male Haitian politicians, 38; infiltration of U.S. military, 38; initially considered supportive of U.S. troops, 38–39; overlap with cacos, 39, 40; as passive beings in U.S. Marine Archives, 38; peaceful and military resistance to U.S. presence, 38; Péralte's participation in, 38, 39; supported Rosalvo Bobo, 39; U.S. use of Haitian journals against, 43; Zamor, member of and *caco*, 64. *See also* Bobo, Rosalvo

Roosevelt, Franklin D. (President), 28, 80, 147, 152, 153, 154, 155, 156, 224n75, 224n2; earlier role in the invasion (1918), 147; visit to Haiti to end invasion (1934), 147

Roy, Eugene (Provisional President), 143, 144, 145; U.S. and Haitian selection as President, 143. *See also* Borno, Louis; Russell, John H. Jr.

Russell, John H. Jr., 25, 52, 102, 111, 112, 115, 122, 123–125, 126, 127, 128, 130, 134, 135, 137, 140, 141, 142, 143, 145, 204n1, 208n42, 208n49, 209n71, 209n4, 212n67, 212nn76–77, 213nn3–4, 213nn6–9, 213n11, 214nn26–27, 214n32, 214n34, 214nn37–39, 214n40–41, 215nn45–46, 215n51–52, 215n57, 215n61, 215n64, 216n66, 216n15, 217nn19–20, 217n22, 217n25, 217n28, 217nn30–32, 217n34, 218n42, 218n45, 218n47, 219n48, 219nn55–56, 220nn62–64, 221n20, 221n23, 222n41, 222n52, 223n53, 223nn64–65; accused *cacos* of forcefully recruiting poor Haitians in their resistance to U.S., 56; arrived in Haiti on October 1, 1919, 101; description of Charlemagne Péralte and resistance, 102; "joint dictatorship" with Louis Borno, 135; resignation after eleven-year presence in Haiti, 144; statement on fourth abolition of *corvée*, 103. *See also* Borno, Louis

Ryswick, Treaty of (1697), 28; partitioning of Española/Hispaniola, 28

Saint-Domingue (colonial Haiti), 4, 5, 10, 27, 28, 54, 194, 201n5s

Salnave, Sylvain (President), 19, 28, 55, 209n2

Sam, Vilbrun Guillaume (President), 32, 33, 38, 39, 190; massacre of prisoners (27 July 1915), 44; political appointment of Charlemagne and Saül Péralte, 33

Sanders Johnson, Grace (Louise), 19, 120, 198, 204n48, 218n37

silences: an active strategy to maintain power, 10; of *cacos* as political actors pursuing a political end, 10; Haitians speaking through, 20; historical silence on *Ayisienne*, 17–19; intentional silences on the part of a subject, 17; removes attention from the injustice of slavery, 10; in repression, 12; scholars role in silencing Haiti's location in the Age of Revolutions, 9; and tandem support for *cacos'* struggles, 94; U.S. silencing of *cacos* as patriotic actions, 11; U.S. silencing of *cacos* movement through public diatribes, 10; U.S. silencing of Péralte's story, 9. *See also* memory

St. Marc, Henriette, 19

Sylvain, George, 138, 222n39, 222n42; founded Ligue Patriotique (1915; L'Union Patriotique). *See also* L'Union Patriotique

Sylvain-Bouchereau, Madeleine, 18, 20, 138, 143, 147, 155, 156, 204n40, 204n43, 222n42, 223n60, 224n73, 225n19, 225nn22–24, 225n1; and founding of Ligue Féminine d'Action Sociale, 147

taccos, 55, 58; preceded *cacos*, 55. *See also cacos*

Théodore, Davilmar (President), 32, 33; ousted President Zamor, Oreste, 33

Tonton Macoutes, 159, 167, 180, 184; Haitian elites and army seen as, 184; refugees in Florida, 167. *See also* Duvalier, François

Trouillot, Évelyne, 204n44

Trouillot, Michel-Rolph, 9, 85, 159, 172, 174, 180, 202nn15–16, 205n24, 213n16, 213n19, 225n7, 225n11, 228nn56–58, 228n61, 228n66, 228nn78–80, 228n83, 229n1; Duvalier's autocratic neutralization, 159; Haitian Revolution as unthinkable history, 85

Trujillo, Rafael Leonidas (President), 74, 151, 157, 159, 216n7; genocide of Haitians and darker-skinned Dominicans (1937), 74, 151

L'Union Patriotique (Ligue Patriotique), 136, 138, 144, 145, 148, 150, 185, 222nn39–40, 229n10, 229nn15–16; collaboration with the NAACP, 138; invoked images of

Dessalines and L'Ouverture, 138; trip to Washington, D.C., 138. *See also* Sylvain, George; Price-Mars, Jean; Vincent, Sténio

United States: assassination of Péralte, 3; assertion of white masculinist and racialist rhetoric actions, 4; awarded Navy Cross to marines who killed Péralte, 143; "bandits" label, 57 ; doublespeak of fighting resistance, but acting as if resistance did not exist, 11; forced unpaid *corvée* work, 6; invasion of Haiti (1915), 1, 58; Thomas Jefferson, Mayo Court of Inquiry, 95; military policy emerged from invasion of Haiti, 15; occupation of Cuba, Puerto Rico, Guam, Philippines, Haiti, Dominican Republic, Panama, Nicaragua, and Mexico, 15; patrolled Haiti as a colony, 25; soldiers rape Haitian women, 123; spying on National Association for the Advancement of Colored People (NAACP) and Universal Negro Improvement Association (UNIA), 70; stabilization rationale, 6; torture and murder of corvée workers, 6; used Haitian revolt to argue against abolition, 24; view of Péralte as lawless bandit,

United Nations Stabilization Mission in Haiti (MINUSTAH), 1–3, 20, 189, 190, 191, 192, 194, 201n2; as arm of the United State, 1; Haitian confront the Mission, 2; occupation under (2004), 1

Universal Negro Improvement Association (UNIA), 70, 219n52, 222n40

Vincent, Sténio (President), 8, 138, 145, 148, 149–51, 154, 155, 156, 173, 183, 188, 223n70, 224n2; agreement with U.S. businesses, 150; conceded U.S. monopoly on Haiti's agricultural products, 151; deployment of Péralte's memory for political gain, 150; mock funeral for Péralte, Charlemagne, 8; revival of L'Union Patriotique, *138;* symbolic opposition to U.S. imperialism, 150. *See also* Sylvain, Georges; Price-Mars, Jean

Volontaires de la Sécurité Nationale (VSN), 159; civil militia created by Duvalier, 159; functioned as private militia for Duvalier, 159. *See also* Duvalier, François

Wiener, Jacqueline, 154
Wilson, Woodrow (President), 4, 10, 20, 35, 36, 42, 43, 61, 91, 99, 110, 185, 201n12; view of U.S. invasion, 4

Zamor, Charles, 38, 57, 64, 72, 78, 83, 90, 208n54, 218n41; brother of Oreste Zamor (President), 38; intermediary between Haitians and U.S. military, 64; member of the Revolutionary Committee and *cacos* movement, 38, 64. *See also* Revolutionary Committee

Zamor, Oreste (President), 32, 38; brother of Charles Zamor, 38; overthrown by Davilmar Théodore, 33

About the Author

YVELINE ALEXIS is an associate professor of history in the Africana and Comparative American Studies departments at Oberlin College. Her scholarly and creative works have appeared in the *Journal of Haitian Studies, Transatlantic Feminisms*, and *So Spoke the Earth / Tè-a Pale*.